MISSIONARY DIPLOMACY

MISSIONARY DIPLOMACY

RELIGION AND NINETEENTH-CENTURY AMERICAN FOREIGN RELATIONS

EMILY CONROY-KRUTZ

CORNELL UNIVERSITY PRESS

Ithaca and London

First published 2024 by Cornell University Press

Library of Congress Cataloging-in-Publication Data

Names: Conroy-Krutz, Emily, author.
Title: Missionary diplomacy : religion and nineteenth-
    century American foreign relations / Emily
    Conroy-Krutz.
Description: Ithaca [New York] : Cornell University
    Press, 2024. | Includes bibliographical references and
    index.
Identifiers: LCCN 2023022411 (print) |
    LCCN 2023022412 (ebook) | ISBN 9781501773983
    (hardcover) | ISBN 9781501774003 (epub) |
    ISBN 9781501773990 (pdf)
Subjects: LCSH: Christianity and international
    relations—United States—History—19th century. |
    Missionaries—Political activity—History—
    19th century. | Protestantism—Influence. |
    United States—Foreign relations.
Classification: LCC BR115.I7 C65 2024 (print) |
    LCC BR115.I7 (ebook) | DDC 261.8/7—dc23/eng/
    20230907
LC record available at https://lccn.loc.gov/2023022411
LC ebook record available at https://lccn.loc.gov/
    2023022412

Contents

ACKNOWLEDGMENTS

It can be hard to tell how long you've been working on a book sometimes, but one way I've been able to track the years of research and writing is by looking at a drawing that has hung over the desk in my office since my daughter was young. I had just started figuring out what the book would be about when she offered to help me come up with the title and the cover. Her suggestion, *The Long Time Ago World Adventures*, features an illustration of a missionary standing atop a globe that resembles a chocolate-chip cookie, shouting out an invitation "Do You Wot TO Be A CiGih?" The artist is now old enough that she can't tell what that is supposed to mean (for those readers not used to translating the handwriting of first graders, it says: "Do you want to be a Christian?"). Measuring the development of a book alongside the growth of your child is one very clear way to realize just how long a project can take. There are so very many people to thank along the way.

First I must thank the wonderful people at Cornell University Press. This book was shaped by conversations with Michael McGandy over many years, and I am so grateful for his guidance, gentle prodding, and keen questions. I am especially grateful for his continued interest in this book after he moved to South Carolina (and I hope he will forgive the use of adverbs as I try to express how very much this means to me). Mahinder Kingra and Sarah Grossman have both been wonderful to work with, and I appreciate the work that they, along with the copy editors and designers, have done to bring this book to life. I want to give special thanks to Jacqulyn Teoh for going above and beyond in her help with map formatting.

I am grateful for the generous support of the Humanities and Arts Research Program at Michigan State University and from the Charles Warren Center for Studies in American History at Harvard University. Both gave me the gift of time at key moments in the research and writing of this book without which I would not have been able to complete the work. The Warren Center Fellowship also gave me the gift of community—a particular treat coming as it did during a year when the COVID-19 pandemic kept so many of us isolated. Thank you to Catherine Brekus, David Holland, and James Kloppenberg for convening our seminar on Religion and American Public Life.

The archival research for this book took me to the Presbyterian Historical Society in Philadelphia; Houghton Library at Harvard University; the National Archives in College Park, Maryland; Burke Library at Union Theological Seminary; the Yale Divinity School Library; and the Library of Congress. Thank you to the archivists and librarians who helped me in my work. Thank you, too, to the editorial teams of the John Quincy Adams Digital Diary, the Theodore Roosevelt Papers, the Papers of Woodrow Wilson, the Foreign Relations of the United States, and Hathi Trust whose digitization projects made it possible to continue my research during the pandemic. A special thanks to Sara Georgini at the Massachusetts Historical Society for her help with John Quincy Adams.

My research sits at the intersections of diplomatic history, religious history, and nineteenth-century studies, and there are a great many readers and conversation partners across these groups who have helped to shape my thinking about this book. A huge thank you to Kristen Beales, Michael Blaakman, Melissa Borja, Cara Burnidge, Kate Carté, Heath Carter, Carol Chin, Heather Curtis, Kon Dierks, Jon Ebel, Curtis Evans, Brian Franklin, Jen Graber, Nick Guyatt, Christine Heyrman, Kristin Hoganson, Daniel Immerwahr, Julia Irwin, Ryan Irwin, Kathryn Gin Lum, Melani McAlister, Max Meuller, David Milne, Kate Moran, Chris Nichols, Dael Norwood, Eva Payne, Seth Perry, William Schultz, Jay Sexton, David Sim, Lauren Turek, Daniel Vaca, Mike Verney, Karine Walther, and Tisa Wenger. Enormous thanks to Nicole Phelps for answering all my questions about consuls and sharing sources. I am especially grateful to Amy Greenberg, Andrew Preston, and Matt Sutton, who each read a full draft of the manuscript and helped me hone my argument and narrative.

The history department at Michigan State University has been a wonderful home. I am grateful to the members of the long-nineteenth-century workshop for their helpful comments and camaraderie over the years: Michael Albani, Jen Andrella, Peter Berg, Sharon Leon, Anthony Padovano, Nikki Parker, Justin Simard, Steve Stowe, Tom Summerhill, Ramya Swayamprakash, Helen Veit, Brooks Winfree, and Laura Yares. Thank you to Sidney Lu, Michelle Moyd, Mindy Smith, and Yulian Wu for helping me with the Asian and African historiography I needed for portions of this book. Especially big thanks to Michelle for providing feedback on a chapter before she had even officially joined the department. Walter Hawthorne, Lisa Fine, and Mickey Stamm have provided wonderful support as department chairs while I worked on the book. Elyse Hansen has made sure everything ran smoothly. In another part of campus, Stephanie Nawyn has been my writing accountability buddy. I am so grateful for her friendship and for her making sure that I (mostly) stayed off Twitter and got words down on the page.

During the summer of 2016, I had the tremendous good fortune of meeting Jessica Lepler at back-to-back conferences when we were both debating between possible topics for our second books. Those conversations eventually turned into the SHEAR Second-Book Writers' Workshop and gave me a dear friend. Thank you, Jess, for the collaborations, strategizing, and always-astute feedback. And thank you, SHEAR, for letting us set up a workshop where we could get the support and community we knew we needed (as it turns out, we were not alone). I am so grateful to the members, mentors, and panelists who took part in 2BWW over the years and helped shape my thinking about this book, especially Joseph Adelman, Tom Balcerski, Lindsay Chervinsky, Rachel Hope Cleves, Seth Cotlar, Kathleen DuVal, Paul Erickson, Cassie Good, Ronald Angelo Johnson, Cathy Kelly, Ben Park, Honor Sachs, Rachel Shelden, Tamara Thornton, Serena Zabin, and Rosemarie Zagarri.

Gale Kenny and Ben Wright might have read some of these chapters as many times as I have. I do not have the words to express how much I appreciate our writing group. For the good cheer, the feedback, the arguments, the joint archive trips, the happy hours, and for generally keeping me from looking like an idiot in public (most of the time): thank you.

My biggest thanks go to my family: to Lizzie, who drew me a cover for this book when it was just barely starting to be an idea in my head, and to Jeff, who has listened to me rant and rave about the research and the writing, and has even listened to me read portions of the book aloud. Jeff also helped to make the beautiful maps and put up with my watching over his shoulder as he worked his GIS magic. He deserves a medal, or at the very least a margarita. Mom, Dad, and Julie helped me celebrate every step along the way. Thank you all for supporting me always and for being my family. I love you.

A Note on Terminology and Place Names

This is a book about, among other things, American missionaries who traveled around the world and positioned themselves as experts, even though they quite often did not understand what they were seeing. They made their homes abroad, but their vision was shaped by their place of origin: the nineteenth-century United States. Their assumptions about race and gender were powerful lenses that could distort the accuracy of missionary reporting, even as they claimed to be uniquely able to see the world as it really was. The power of expertise rests in the perception, not always the reality, of legitimacy and factuality on the part of the purported experts. When I discuss missionary intelligence and missionary expertise throughout the book, it is with the full understanding that missionary intelligence included many errors. How those errors came to be regarded as true—and the effects of those mistakes—is one of the subjects of my inquiry.

Since the nineteenth-century period in which the events in this book took place, many place names have changed—due to political developments as well as shifts in the Anglicization of non-English place names. Throughout the text, I use the place names as they appeared in the contemporary US sources, with the modern name in parentheses at the first appearance.

MISSIONARY DIPLOMACY

Prologue
A Missionary-Diplomatic Family

As one civil war threatened to explode in the United States, Divie Bethune McCartee watched with anxiety as another civil war approached his new home in China. McCartee had been in Ningpo (Ningbo) for more than a decade, ever since a treaty between the United States and China had opened up the port city to US residents in 1844. Now, the uprising against the Qing Empire known as the Taiping Rebellion threatened his ability—and that of all other Americans in the region—to live and work in safety. Just a few years earlier, McCartee had been able to assure his friends at home that even as fighting broke out elsewhere in China, he was still able to work in "peace and quietness all the time."[1] By 1860, he reported that the fighting was closing in on Ningpo. As the interpreter for the US consul, McCartee's role was an important one. His duty, as he understood it, was "to act as mediator and prevent slaughter of innocent blood."[2]

The Taiping Rebellion was a crisis point in Chinese history, much as the US Civil War was in US history. The Chinese war arose out of long-festering anxieties and resentments within the Qing Empire and ultimately claimed between twenty and thirty million lives. American observers were not quite sure what to make of these events. Some were excited by what they saw as a Christian undercurrent in the philosophy of its leader.[3] Yet the violence, on the other hand, was overwhelming.

It threatened the Western trade and Christian missionaries who had only recently gained access to more of China. Americans like McCartee watched the spreading violence and puzzled over how to protect American lives and US interests. In 1861, the US government sent a small delegation of naval officers aboard the US flagship *Hartford* to negotiate with the Taiping rebels. McCartee was among them.

Divie Bethune McCartee was not a naval officer, and he was not an ambassador. He was a missionary, sent to China by the Presbyterian Church to evangelize the people of Ningpo. Like many other US Protestant missionaries in the nineteenth century, he found that his evangelistic work was deeply entwined with diplomatic work. In order to serve his God, he would also have to serve his nation; if he was able to advance the interests of the United States, he believed he would also be advancing the interests of Protestantism. Good diplomatic relations, he hoped, would open the door for the spread of Christianity. When he was asked to join the *Hartford* delegation, McCartee asked himself "whether my duties as a missionary or as a citizen of the USA were most urgent."[4] Should he board the *Hartford* and help negotiate with the Taiping rebels, or should he remain at his mission? Ultimately, as with many mid-nineteenth-century missionary diplomats faced with times of crisis, he found that serving the mission and serving the state were inextricable.

Though the *Hartford* delegation intended to project US power, there was in truth very little that they could hope to accomplish. The diplomats hoped to gain assurances that if the Americans remained neutral in the conflict, the Taiping rebels would protect US residents and trade from attack. Such a guarantee was nearly impossible in the face of so much turmoil. While the promise of safety was minimal, McCartee managed to include a clause extending protection specifically to American "teachers of religion," as well as their students and converts.[5] When negotiating protection for US citizens, McCartee wanted to be sure that missionaries would be included.

For much of the nineteenth century, US diplomatic officials supported such cooperation between Protestant missionaries and US diplomacy. Ansom Burlingame, the US minister to China, was delighted by McCartee's work during the Taiping Rebellion and offered him additional work for the US delegation throughout the 1860s. In a letter to Secretary of State William Seward, Burlingame praised McCartee as a man of "rare qualities as a Christian, a patriot, and a scholar."[6] Missionaries like these were just the sort of men the State Department needed in the nineteenth century.

Throughout his five-decade career in China and Japan, McCartee served his country and his God through work as a medical missionary, consul, translator, professor of international law, and more. He was far from alone. Over the course of the nineteenth century, the state regularly turned to missionaries to assist in US foreign relations. Missionaries served as consuls and translators. They corresponded with and advised US diplomats, sometimes even testifying before Congress about international affairs. They were trusted experts who wrote for US domestic audiences about the world and its people. This perceived expertise had its benefits. Their mission boards regularly corresponded with the State Department, and they advocated for the appointment of their favored officials in international posts. At moments of crisis, they called for political and even military support for their missionaries around the world. Missionaries found that expanding the reach of the US state would result in the expansion of Protestant missions—and vice versa. Christian foreign missions, in turn, were an essential part of the toolkit for US diplomacy.

Over the course of McCartee's life, the United States went through profound changes on the world stage. At the time McCartee was born in 1820, US politicians struggled to articulate a foreign policy position for the United States that could simultaneously encourage global commerce while avoiding the kinds of political entanglements that the relatively weak state could not sustain. By the time of McCartee's death in 1900, the United States had claimed its position as an imperial power. In the decades in between, there was one constant in America's role overseas: Protestant missionaries and their supporters played a key role in projecting US power and defining US interests.

The story of missionary diplomacy is one of overlapping political and religious narratives that are far too often told separately. Over the course of the nineteenth century, the United States and its State Department expanded in geographic reach and political power. At the century's beginning, the country occupied the eastern portions of North America and held colonizing ambitions to claim the entire continent. By the century's end, the United States not only claimed territory from the Atlantic to Pacific coasts, but also colonies overseas, all of which served to provide markets and raw materials for an industrial and commercial economy with global reach.

At the same time, the nineteenth century saw profound changes in American religious life. Christian benevolent societies, animated by the conviction that Christianity was the path toward progress and modernization in all parts of life, sought to spread the blessings of so-called civilization throughout the country and the world. As the decades passed, new denominations formed and old denominations split. Protestants argued bitterly about theological questions as well as hot-button political issues, including slavery, race, empire, and the proper relationship between church and state. They argued, too, over whether missionaries ought to prioritize evangelization or broader cultural changes—and whether one might even be a necessary prerequisite of the other. Foreign missionary organizations took part in all of these developments, from the departure of the first US missionaries overseas in 1812 through the proliferation of missionary organizations in the decades following the Civil War. In South and East Asia, Africa, the Middle East, and the Pacific Islands, Protestant foreign missionaries brought America to the world and the world to America.

Generations

Four generations of the McCartee family can help us to survey these intertwining global histories of church and diplomacy over the course of the century. McCartee's family had been connected to US foreign missions since the very beginning of the movement. His grandfather, Divie Bethune, had been a founding member of the New York Missionary Society in the late eighteenth century. In those early years, Americans Protestants focused their attention on evangelizing Native American nations in North America. Yet from the beginning, the ambition to take part in a global mission movement was evident. Bethune hosted British missionaries who visited New York on their way to China and India. He decorated his home with artwork celebrating British missionaries in Tahiti and India. He filled his library with missionary periodicals and memoirs. Bethune remained in New York, but his financial contributions and his vision helped pave the way for a US foreign missionary movement with global reach.

By the time that Bethune's daughter was coming of age, US Protestants were venturing overseas as missionaries. Growing up immersed in her father's New York missionary world, Jessie Graham Bethune had always wanted to be a missionary herself. Like hundreds of other American Protestant girls in the era of the early republic, she was inspired by the stories of missionary men and women who made great personal sacrifices to spread Christianity around the world. She had burned to go to China after meeting the British missionary Robert Morrison.

Instead, she stayed at home, married the minister Robert McCartee, and never did get to China. Settled in New York, she spent her life engaged in benevolent causes, continuing to be an active part of US missionary culture that her parents had helped create. She read missionary memoirs and reports to her son Divie, the oldest of her ten children. She was an eager consumer of missionary intelligence: information about the world shared by missionaries with the intention to increase knowledge and encourage support for mission work.

Divie grew up reading the memoirs of US missionaries in addition to the British texts his mother had loved. In the 1820s and 1830s of his youth, US Protestants were establishing missions in India, Burma (Myanmar), Liberia, the Sandwich Islands (Hawaii), and across the North American continent. American missionaries explored the Levant and sent gripping narratives to readers at home. Divie Bethune McCartee read them all and would later recall that missionary names were "household words" in their home.[7]

When Divie McCartee finished his medical training in the early 1840s, the opportunities for mission work had expanded even further. Euro-American imperialism and international commerce had made new regions increasingly accessible to missionaries, who in turn were expected to provide a "civilizing" and "benevolent" influence on a capitalist empire. Shortly after he felt called to combine his work as a doctor with evangelism, new treaties between the United States and China allowed Protestant denominations to begin planning new missions to fulfill their long-held dreams of evangelizing China. Within months of the Sino-American treaty's ratification in 1844, McCartee was on his way to Ningpo, where he eventually married his wife Juana Knight. There, they served alongside Juana's sister and brother-in-law, Mary Knight and Henry Rankin.

The Rankin's son, Henry William Rankin, would continue the family tradition of enthusiastic domestic support of missions into the twentieth century. Like many missionary children of his generation, Rankin had returned to the United States for his education as an adolescent but would be forever shaped by his early childhood experience in China. In the United States, the young Rankin followed the missionary careers of his family in East Asia (his parents remained in China, while his aunt and uncle spent over a decade in Japan as well) while also noting tremendous transformations in US religious and political life. In many ways, the United States where Rankin came of age was foreign to the country his uncle had known. The post–Civil War United States created a far more powerful and centralized federal government. An important point of continuity was the missionary culture that the whole family took part in. If anything, the missionary movement that had nurtured McCartee had only grown by the time that Rankin was an adult, with more and more missionaries leaving the United States for an increasing number of locations. American missionaries established schools, hospitals, and churches in Asia, Africa, the Middle East, the Pacific Islands, and Latin America. By the second half of the century, women outnumbered men in these endeavors, as women's missionary societies sent more and more single women to work as teachers, nurses, and doctors alongside ordained male missionaries to spread the gospel and to transform the world.

Rankin spent his adult life reading, thinking, and writing about this mission movement and its political consequences. He was particularly fascinated by China and its relationship to the United States. Through his studies, he was struck by a truth that has escaped many scholars of US foreign relations. Like his uncle and so many other American Protestants, he saw the foreign mission movement as the key to the relationship of the United States with China and, indeed, the rest of the world. He celebrated his uncle as a missionary diplomat and a model for US foreign relations.

When Divie McCartee died in 1900, Rankin was convinced that Americans needed to carry on his uncle's work into the twentieth century. It was a new era in US foreign relations, marked most dramatically by the Spanish-American War and domestic debates about imperialism. International crises increasingly demanded the attention of US humanitarians, and missionaries joined other Americans in debating how the United States ought to respond. "The evangelization of the world in this generation" had become the watchword for the missionaries whom Rankin worked with. Shaped by a confidence in their country's power and in technological developments in transportation and communications, this rising generation of US Protestants expected to be able to transform the world. But for all the new opportunities they embraced in the world, they also found that they faced new constraints from a more centralized and powerful State Department.

This book tells the story of the men and women like McCartee and his family who saw foreign missions as an essential part of nineteenth-century US foreign relations. Some were Americans at home, consuming missionary intelligence, donating funds, and trusting in missionary expertise to explain the world, its peoples, and their needs to the United

States. Some were missionaries in the field, balancing their roles as missionaries and as Americans in diverse places and contexts. Some were diplomats and statesmen, whose religious identities could lead them to identify missionary priorities and interests with those of their country. And some were diplomats who, despite some reservations, believed that Protestant missionary work would advance US interests. Over the course of the century, these missionary-diplomats and their supporters revealed the deep connections between an evangelical Protestant mission and US foreign relations. These connections were particularly significant during a century marked by the slow growth and professionalization of the apparatus of the US state. Foreign missionaries played a key role in nineteenth-century US diplomacy.

The Career of a Missionary-Diplomat

Divie McCartee's story is but one example of how this worked. In China, McCartee began a truly remarkable career. Over his years in China and Japan, he bridged the fields of mission work, educational reform, and diplomacy with an ease that marked him as exemplary of the mid-century missionary diplomats. He served wherever he felt his skills would be of use. And his skills were of a diverse sort indeed.

It was his medical credentials that brought McCartee to China in 1844. Missionary societies had come to understand that institutions like medical dispensaries and schools could draw people into the missionary orbit. Doctors like McCartee hoped their healing ministry would facilitate evangelization. By his own estimates, he saw between 150 and 200 patients a day in this early period.[8] When he wasn't at the dispensary, he was studying. Other Americans in East Asia—consuls, sailors, and naval officers—tended to remain only for short periods and to restrict their visits to ports. Missionaries' long residence in the area and frequent interactions with local people meant that their language skills regularly outpaced those of their American peers. McCartee, though, proved unusually adept at picking up on multiple dialects, and he soon distinguished himself as the lone Anglophone person in the area who could understand Mandarin. He traveled throughout the region, providing medical care and learning about the culture and natural surroundings he passed.

The rich ethnographic, ecological, and political detail of McCartee's journals are typical of his missionary peers. Missionaries were often men and women with wide interests who recognized their unique opportunity to contribute to American understandings of both the wider world and scientific knowledge as they went about their prose-lytizing. McCartee, for example, sent reptile and insect specimens for the collection of the Academy of Natural Sciences of Philadelphia.[9] He shared research on thumb printing in China with Americans who were developing it as a means of identification in the United States.[10] He cor-responded with the American Geographical Society of New York and the American Oriental Society, sharing copies of his own publications, for-warding maps, answering questions about China, and providing speci-mens of Chinese calligraphy and lithography. McCartee both respected and was fascinated with the country he had taken for his new home. While he had no doubt of the superiority of Christianity to all other reli-gions, he found China to be a civilized country with a rich history and present. McCartee and the other missionary-diplomats eagerly shared this vision with their correspondents back at home.[11]

It was not only science that interested McCartee. Politics, too, drew his attention and consumed much of his efforts. His experience dur-ing the Taiping Rebellion was far from his only political or diplomatic work. McCartee took the scriptural command to "go into all nations" to preach God's word "literally," as he explained to a friend. He saw it as his duty to serve not only as a missionary, but to "apply to go as an interpreter, naval agent, or anything" that would allow him to reach new lands and new people.[12] McCartee understood that missions and the US government alike would benefit from general good relations among Asian and Western powers. Accordingly, he worked alternatively for the American, Chinese, and Japanese governments in a range of capacities: as a translator and interpreter for all three governments, as an asses-sor on the Mixed Court in China that oversaw criminal and civil cases involving Americans and other foreigners, and as a professor of Interna-tional Law at Tokyo University.[13] He traveled to Japan as a translator for Vice Consul George W. Fish in 1858. When a Portuguese trading ship trafficking Chinese laborers grounded in Japan, McCartee made use of his Chinese and Japanese language skills to help resolve the immediate crisis. He saw the political role of the missionary as based not in nation-alism, but in a sort of humanitarianism, advancing peaceful relations between countries and promoting "civilization" alongside Christianity. This, McCartee and other missionaries believed, was what the United States ought to stand for on the world stage.

During the McCartees' extended furlough in the United States, Divie continued to act as a missionary diplomat. Like so many other missionaries on furlough, he educated his fellow Americans about the faraway lands where he had spent so many decades of his life. As he toured, he explained the culture, history, and crucially, the contemporary politics of these countries to US audiences. When he was in New York, he spent his days working as a translator for the Chinese Consulate.[14] In Washington, he served as the temporary English secretary of the Japanese minister.[15] And all the while, he sought information to bring back to Asia about US educational institutions that might provide models for mission schools in China, Japan, and Korea.[16] As he returned to the United States for what would be the last time, he was just beginning to hear news of the unrest in China that the world would come to know as the Boxer Uprising. The missionary diplomacy that had guided his career would prove key to the American understanding of that crisis and the way forward.[17]

What a Missionary Is Good For

McCartee's stories of diplomatic work inspired his nephew, who had left Ningpo as a boy and grew up idolizing his uncle. As an adult, the two were close; Rankin clearly saw McCartee as something of a father figure after the death of his own father. They shared a great many interests, none as deeply held as their passion for Asia and Christian missions. Working as a librarian at a mission-oriented school, Rankin was able to spend much of his time reading, writing, and compiling scrapbooks. As the century came to its close, US relations with Asia and the position of the foreign mission movement in US diplomacy had become Rankin's major theme.

McCartee's last letter to Rankin was written in San Francisco on January 19, 1900, just after his eightieth birthday. He had come to California for his health, hoping that the milder climate would ameliorate the vague illness that seemed to be wearing him down. He had what "for want of a better name, people called 'heart failure,'" he explained to his nephew. His handwriting was shaky. He was working on his reminiscences, intended for publication someday. A recent improvement in his health left him hopeful. If he continued to feel better, he might return to Japan. Within seven months, he had died.[18]

By the time that McCartee died in San Francisco in the fall of 1900, much had changed in both missionary and diplomatic circles. Observers, as Rankin noted with concern, were looking askance at missionaries, not sure of their value to America's work in the world. For Rankin, missionaries like McCartee—and there were quite a number of missionaries who had been like his uncle—had played an essential role in US diplomacy. Missionaries, he was sure, were the key. To turn away from missionaries was, for US foreign policy, perilous.

Rankin dedicated himself to the project of memorializing his uncle. Between 1900 and 1907, Rankin worked on multiple versions of obituaries and articles for different venues. His major goal was to publish McCartee's own reminiscences, which he eventually did with the help and editorship of Presbyterian missionary leader Robert Speer. As he worked, he took copious notes, corresponded with anyone he could think of who might have new information about McCartee's activities, and critiqued other people's writings on McCartee.

Rankin did not approve of the obituary by David Murray in the *New-York Observer*. Murray's obituary, which identified McCartee as a "pioneer missionary to China and Japan," seemed to divide McCartee's missionary work from his other accomplishments. This, Rankin argued, would not do. The problem was that Murray misunderstood McCartee's work as a missionary: "All of his literary, educational, scientific and political work was merely incidental to his life as a missionary," Rankin explained. McCartee was "always a missionary *de facto*," even when other responsibilities took him away from official missionary service. McCartee had enjoyed a long and varied career, but he was a missionary first and always. And his missionary outlook could not be separated from what had come to seem, by the early twentieth century, as more secular pursuits.

That was not the only problem Rankin had with the obituary. Murray didn't only misunderstand McCartee as a missionary. He also did not understand the degree of McCartee's significance as a diplomat.[19] McCartee, he insisted, deserved the credit for all of the "good relations" between China and Japan during his tenure, and also, "in some measure, the very founding of the modern diplomatic relations that exist." That was all due to his missionary character. "When this missionary had anything to do with politics it was wholly in the interest of international comity and mutual understanding on all sides," Rankin wrote. This was the central idea that he gained from his years of correspondence with his uncle.

As Rankin reflected on his uncle's life, he found an ideal example of how the role of missionary and diplomat ought to be fused in the interest of international connections.[20] The stakes seemed high: the turn of the century was a moment of potential transition for US diplomacy. To forget about the stories of the missionary-diplomats, Rankin argued, was not only to forget about a part of history. It was also, far more dangerously, to choose a wrong path for US foreign relations in the new century. As Rankin looked at the story of the mid-century missionary diplomats, he saw the best bet for mutually beneficial relations between the United States and Asia. In other words, the life of Divie Bethune McCartee could provide "the best possible answer to the question now so widely raised—what is a missionary good for anyway?"[21]

This, at least, was the way that the Bethune, McCartee, and Rankin families answered that question. As we shall see, they were not alone. If we want to understand the development of US diplomacy across the nineteenth century and into the twentieth, it is essential that we uncover the significant role of Protestant foreign missions in shaping the project of US foreign relations.

Protestant Missions and the State Department

This book examines the connections between the State Department and the Protestant mission movement over the nineteenth century through the lives and work of missionary diplomats like the McCartee family. At the start of the century, both the State Department and the mission movement were small and weak, with outsized ambitions for eventual influence over the whole world. Examining the evolution of both the state and missions together reveals how entangled their roots were and the ways that they would shape each other's growth over the century and into the next.

Part I opens with an examination of the creation and consumption of missionary intelligence. In the first decades of the century, when the United States diplomatic corps was small, weak, and focused on European and Latin American affairs, missionary intelligence brought information about new and different parts of the world to American audiences. These missionary authors presented American readers with a world that needed their help, and they called on the religious community of US Protestants to help the suffering, feed the hungry, and clothe the naked. As they did so, they urged American international action—and not always in ways that the US government supported. But politicians, too, read missionary intelligence. The missionary vision of the United States was quite influential.

After all, missionaries and diplomats operated in different geographies for much of the century. The places that mattered most to missions tended to matter less to the State Department, allowing missionaries to emerge as key experts and influences when the state began to pay more attention to places outside of Europe and Latin America. The chapters in the book's second section follow the missionaries around the globe, where they served as key figures in the development of US relations in Asia, the Pacific, and the Middle East. Missionaries served as consuls, translators, and occasional troublemakers who forced the State Department to take actions it otherwise would have avoided.

Once they were in the field, missionary diplomats made demands on their government. They insisted that officials send consuls, defend missionaries' rights, and enable missionaries to travel where they wanted to go in pursuit of their evangelistic work. Because the State Department throughout the nineteenth century largely agreed with missionaries and their supporters that missionaries were key partners in advancing US interests abroad, these missionaries and their priorities created many elements of US policy.

But as the century went on and the State Department grew, these missionary "troubles" (as the diplomats called them) came to seem more problematic. In some regions, missionaries faced physical violence. Foreign governments seized Bibles and other missionary publications. Missionaries claimed their rights were violated. They used creative interpretations of treaties to locate missions in places where they were not welcome and then demanded US protection. Missionaries, in short, drew US diplomats into places and questions that they had not expected and did not want. As the decades passed, more Americans began to question the propriety of missionaries' power. Were missionaries serving the interests of US diplomacy? Or were they creating unnecessary problems? Were they, perhaps, doing both?

The book's third part focuses on case studies in the Philippines, China, Congo, and Turkey to explore how these arguments played out in the changing political context of the turn of the century. By the 1890s, the State Department was larger, stronger, and more professionalized than it had been in the 1820s and 1830s. The US government was far better placed to enact any grand ambitions for the country on the world stage. Missionaries could be a major asset to this work—or a major hindrance.

Across the century, missionaries forced the government to articulate new conceptions of the rights of US citizens abroad and of the role of the United States as an engine of humanitarianism and religious freedom. This is where many historians begin the story of religion and US foreign relations.[22] But it has far deeper roots that stretch back into the nineteenth century. By the time the United States entered the First World War, missionary diplomacy had for nearly a century created the conditions for some Americans to embrace a vision of their country as an internationally engaged world power. Missionaries introduced Americans to new places, people, and problems, and in so doing, their missionary diplomacy shaped America's strategic interests around the globe.

PART I

Missionary Intelligence, 1810s–1840s

As the story goes, it was a gathering during a rainstorm that set in motion the beginnings of American foreign missionary work. A group of students huddled under a haystack for protection from the weather and began to pray. As the rain fell, they experienced a calling to answer the scriptural commission to spread the gospel and "teach all nations."[1] There were millions of souls around the world, they believed, who were suffering for want of the gospel. Without it, they could not be saved. In this life, they could expect oppression or depravity. In the life to come, they could only expect damnation. If Christians could reach them and evangelize to them, they would be able to offer them salvation and, at the same time, would fulfill Jesus's Great Commission. It was a challenging calling, but one that offered the potential for glory.

The immediate result of this Haystack Meeting, as the gathering has been remembered, was the creation of the American Board of Commissioners for Foreign Missions (ABCFM) by American Congregationalists in 1810. Over the next several years, they were joined by missionary organizations from all of the major US Protestant denominations. These missionaries generally carried with them a commitment not only to their faith, but to the particular form that it took in the United States. They were invested in both Christianizing and "civilizing" the globe, and their work encompassed preaching, teaching, translation, medicine, and more.

When the first eight missionaries left the United States for India in 1812, the State Department staff consisted of the secretary of state, a chief clerk, and ministers to the United Kingdom, France, Russia, and Portugal. By 1848, when US Protestants supported missionaries in Asia, Africa, the Mediterranean, the Americas, and the islands of the Pacific, the State Department had similarly grown, particularly in its representation in Latin America. But there remained large swathes of the globe without a US diplomatic presence. Missionaries looked to the non-Christian "heathen world" as the space of highest priority. The State Department's primary interest, however, was in supporting US commerce, and its focus continued to be on Europe and Latin America even as Turkey and China recently joined the list of places that housed official representatives of the United States.

If the late eighteenth century had seen the United States fight for its independence from the British Empire, the first decades of the nineteenth saw the government work to fully realize that independence. Weakness is a key theme in the diplomatic history of the early American republic. So, too, is the ambition for greatness and power. The United States was interested in demonstrating its membership in the community of nations and its equality with European states. The foreign missionary movement was just one embodiment of these ambitions. The early years of US Protestant missions developed in the midst of political discussions about the rights of neutral nations in the face of ongoing war between Britain and France, the creation of the Monroe Doctrine, and the relentless expansion of settler colonialism across the North American continent. Over the course of these decades, the US military fought England, Mexico, and Indigenous American nations in various efforts to claim new territory and assert American independence, honor, and power.

The history of the mission movement in these same years was, in many ways, quite similar. Missionaries, like politicians, claimed more strength for their country than was merited. That first group of US missionaries who left the United States in 1812 were shortly arrested by British officials after their arrival in India. They did not, in fact, have the right to be there, not as Americans who were currently at war with Great Britain, and not as missionaries who were currently barred from evangelizing in the East India Company's territories. Yet these missionaries and their supporters at home remained undeterred. Their movement

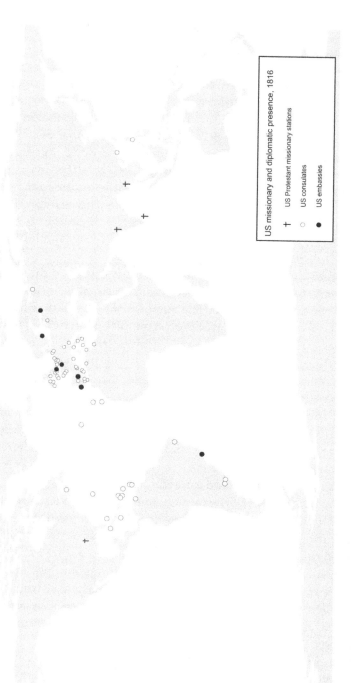

Figure I.1. World map of US missionary and diplomatic presence, 1816. In 1816, John Quincy Adams was serving as the US minister to England and both the Protestant foreign mission movement and the US State Department were beginning to expand their respective reach. Only two foreign missionary societies were in operation this early in the century: the American Board of Commissioners for Foreign Missions and the Baptist Board of Foreign Missions.

Sources: Department of State, *A Register of Officers and Agents*; American Board of Commissioners for Foreign Missions, *Report of the American Board of Commissioners for Foreign Missions* (Boston: Samuel T. Armstrong, 1816); Baptist Board of Foreign Missions, *The Second Annual Report*.

was both optimistic and urgent. Trusting in God's Providence to direct them, US Protestant missionaries went out into the world confident of their right to work wherever they could gain access.

This confidence served them well, in some ways. Seeking passage on the ships of US merchants who were similarly interested in expanding their reach to new markets and sources of raw materials, missionaries set down roots all over the world. Because American missionaries and the US government emphasized different regions of the world, missionaries emerged as the American experts on the places where they lived and worked. They were trusted by home audiences for the information they shared about the peoples they interacted with. As they shared missionary intelligence about the non-Christian world and urged Americans to support their efforts, missionaries presented Americans with an alternate vision for the role of the United States in the world.

Religious revivals in the early nineteenth century expanded the numbers of Americans who were concerned about spiritual salvation and the spread of the kingdom of God. The numbers of missionary societies grew, as did the geographic spread of Protestant missionaries. They went into what they called the "heathen world," driven by a calling to evangelize and civilize all peoples. This focus on the non-Christian world brought missionaries into a different geography than their diplomatic peers. Though limited in their choice of locations by the commercial and political connections that could provide missionaries transportation and relative safety where they worked, missionaries wanted to work in spaces beyond the diplomatic priorities of Europe and Latin America. This gave missionaries the opportunity to become the American experts on the spaces where they lived and worked.

From the very beginning of the century, missionaries told Americans that they had a duty to be active in the world and to care about the lives and needs of people who lived far away. And missionaries were prolific as they spread this message. Missionary texts hoped to inspire a domestic American enthusiasm for supporting a foreign mission movement, but they were not solely concerned with cosmic questions about the kingdom of God. They were, at times, quite earthbound and concerned with practical and political questions about peoples, governments, and civilization. The work of evangelization combined the earthly and the spiritual every day. Missionary magazines and published sermons and tracts were an obvious place to receive this sort of information about the world, but missionary intelligence was much more broadly available. Even Americans who might not have shared the evangelical

Figure I.2. World map of US missionary and diplomatic presence, c. 1830. By 1830, missionaries from the American Board for Commissioners for Foreign Missions, the Baptist Board of Foreign Missions, and the Domestic and Foreign Missionary Society of the Protestant Episcopal Church were all active in foreign mission work.

Sources: Smith, *America's Diplomats and Consuls of 1776–1865*, 56–127; "Brief View of the American Board of Commissioners for Foreign Missions and Its Operations," *Missionary Herald* (January 1831), 3–4; Baptist Board of Foreign Missions, "Report of the Board of Managers, for the Year ending April 29, 1831," *American Baptist Missionary Magazine* 11 (June 1831): 167–182; Domestic and Foreign Missionary Society of the Protestant Episcopal Church in the United States of America, "Missionary Societies Throughout Christendom and Their Missions," 33–35.

goal of world conversion consumed missionary writing in geographic, scientific, historical, and travel sources.

As missionaries asserted their positions as experts on the world stage, they spoke to a wide range of American readers—the missionary public. As the century progressed, that expertise would allow missionaries access to influence American diplomacy in unexpected ways. But first, they had to build an audience.

CHAPTER 1

Politicians

It was a Sunday morning, so President John Quincy Adams went to church. On this particular week, the president gathered with the congregation to listen to Charles Stewart, a former missionary to the Sandwich Islands (Hawai'i). Stewart had chosen Acts 26:18 for his text: "To open their eyes, and to turn them from darkness to light, and from the power of Satan unto God, that they may receive forgiveness of sins, and inheritance among them which are sanctified, by faith that is in me."

Charles and Harriet Stewart had been part of the ABCFM mission at Lahaina from 1822 to 1825, when illness brought the couple back to the United States. Compared to their missionary brethren, it was a short stay. But even in those few years, Stewart learned enough about the Sandwich Islands to become a trusted expert for a US audience. When competing accounts of the Sandwich Islands threatened to create "erroneous impressions" on the minds of those at home, the *North American Review* assured its readers that Stewart could be relied on to provide "correct information" that would help Americans "discriminate between undoubted facts and heedless conjecture." Earlier in the week, Stewart had visited President Adams at the White House, introducing himself as an expert who could share information about the islands that had captured the imaginations of American Christians and merchants alike.[1]

When the president met the missionary, Stewart's journals and letters could be found in missionary and other periodicals. His book, *Residence at the Sandwich Islands*, would be published the following year and would go through several editions in the United States and England.[2] Like many other returned missionaries, Stewart also preached at various churches and shared his experiences with those gathered in the pews. These sermons were intended to edify, entertain, and exhort listeners to take action in the work of world evangelization. In this, they were part of a broader literature known as "missionary intelligence."

And so, on a Sunday in March 1827, Stewart preached in Washington, DC. In his diary, Adams described the sermon as "a very particular and minute account" of the success of the mission in transforming Hawaiians from "the primitive barbarism of the savage state." The president found the missionary's tales of Hawaiian culture to be "horrible and disgusting—Treachery and Cruelty; Parricide and Infanticide were among their most ordinary practices." But Adams noted, too, the signs of improvement that Stewart claimed. The islanders, according to the missionary, were now "more than half civilized."[3] Remarkable progress, it seemed, in such a short time.

This was not the only missionary sermon that Adams would attend. On a snowy Easter morning the following year, Adams listened to a sermon from Jonas King, then a missionary in Palestine. King had been introduced to the president in March, and apparently made enough of an impression to gain an invitation to dinner the following week, though he did not attend.[4] On Easter Sunday, April 6, King preached in the US Capitol on "the goodness and severity of God." Adams described the sermon as having "the tone and Style of conversation," though he did not intend that as a compliment. King's main purpose was to discuss the duty of American Christians to support his mission in Palestine due to "the severity of God to the inhabitants of Asia Minor" and "the goodness of God to ourselves" in the United States. King's description of Constantinople around this time was bleak. It was, he wrote, a place "full of oppression, deceit and false religion, of confusion, plague, and death."[5] Adams was not much impressed. The missionary, Adams concluded, was "grave and earnest, but not eloquent."[6]

A decade later, Adams, now in the middle of his postpresidential career as a congressional representative for Massachusetts, heard an "urgently mendicant" sermon on the "melancholy picture" of the Ottoman

Empire preached by missionary Harrison Otis Dwight. Dwight was home from his mission in Constantinople (Istanbul) and had taken the Gospel of Matthew verse "the field is the world" as his sermon theme.[7] Adams, at least, was not moved by what he heard as Dwight described the limited success of Protestant missions in the region. In a field of Turks, Greeks, Armenians, and Jews, the missionaries had converted almost no Muslims or Jews to Christianity. Instead, the "sum total of accomplishment," as Adams put it, was "the conversion of a small number of Armenian Christians of the Greek Church into Christians of the Presbyterian Church." What was the point? To Adams, this seemed like misdirected effort. After all, he had recently read an article in the *Emancipator* about two men, formerly enslaved on a plantation in Virginia, who were escaping to Canada. One of them, at thirty-five years old, had never heard of Jesus Christ, nor been in a house of worship. "This is the fate of millions of natives of our own country," Adams concluded, "and we are spunged [*sic*] for contributions to teach Armenian Christians evangelical Presbyterianism."[8] There was greater need, he felt, far closer to home.

Perhaps more than any other single figure, John Quincy Adams shaped nineteenth-century US foreign relations.[9] We do not expect him to have needed the mission movement to tell him about the world. By the time he listened to Stewart and King, he had already enjoyed a remarkable diplomatic career, with positions in Paris, Leiden, St. Petersburg, the Hague, London, and Berlin. He had served as a member of the Massachusetts legislature, the United States Senate, secretary of state, and president. By the time he grumbled about Dwight's misguided efforts, he was a congressman serving on the House Foreign Affairs Committee. Yet even with all of this international experience, Adams consumed—and could even be transformed by—missionary intelligence. In certain regions of the world, it turned out, the missionaries knew more than the US statesman. Much more. For these regions, missionary intelligence could influence American ideas about what the world was like and how Americans ought to interact with it.

Adams was not a part of the evangelical denominations that made up the mission movement's most passionate supporters. He was, however, a man of faith. Born into a Congregational-Unitarian family, Adams spent his adulthood visiting different types of churches at home and abroad, reflecting on the role of faith in public life. During the years when his political career introduced him to various missionaries, Adams maintained pews at Presbyterian and Episcopal churches in Washington in addition to Unitarian and Episcopal churches in Quincy,

Massachusetts.[10] Attending the churches and reading the publications that circulated missionary intelligence, he was part of a larger missionary public. And missionary intelligence, it turned out, focused its attention on a different geography than what consumed Adams during his tenures as a diplomat, secretary of state, president, and then member of congress. Europe and Latin America loomed largest for Adams and the US government in the first half of the century; Asia and the Middle East captivated the missionaries.

These sermons were not Adams's first nor his only direct experiences with missionaries sharing news and urging action. During his tenure as secretary of state, he had a number of encounters with missionaries traveling through Washington. Jeremiah Evarts, one of the leaders of the ABCFM, visited on several occasions to pass along requests, official statements, and updates on behalf of his organization.[11] Missionaries Levi Parsons and Pliny Fisk visited before they traveled to Palestine. They needed passports and learned that there were no US consuls in the regions they planned to travel. Adams could offer them passports and letters, but little else.[12] Missionaries to the Sandwich Islands came to request money to bring as gifts from the US president to the chiefs in Hawai'i.[13] British missionaries, too, visited and provided Adams with samples of the printing that they were able to do in Calcutta.[14] When missionaries in the Sandwich Islands came into conflict with a naval officer, one of them was introduced to Adams by General Van Rensselaer, a congressional representative who just happened to be serving as president of the ABCFM at the time.[15]

Throughout the diplomatic crises of the first half of the nineteenth century, missionaries could play an important role behind the scenes, shaping public interest and priorities. The places where they did, and did not, influence American thinking reveals as much about US diplomacy as it does about the foreign mission movement.

There was one region in particular where Adams's ideas were shaped by missionary intelligence: China. At other key moments of diplomatic crisis—the framing of the Monroe Doctrine, the controversy over Indian removal, the Mexican War—Adams also received and considered missionary intelligence and appeals. At times he rejected it, finding the interests of the federal government and the missionary movement to be at odds. At other times, Adams accepted a key tenet of missionary diplomacy: missionary intelligence and action enabled US state action. Adams's missionary contacts knew that the reverse could be true, too. Sometimes, US state action enabled missionary entry. Each of these dynamics described the relationship between the government and the mission movement in the middle of the nineteenth century.

When it came to determining which type of relationship would emerge, geographical context was the key. Missionaries and government officials had distinct, if often overlapping, ideas about which places mattered to US interests and how Americans ought to intervene in foreign affairs.

Adams Meets Parker, 1841

From 1841 to 1843, as the US government and missionaries alike attempted to imagine what the results of the Opium War between Great Britain and China might be, Adams served as chair of the House Foreign Affairs Committee. The Treaty of Nanking that ended the war would transform Chinese relations with the West. President John Tyler asked Adams's committee to report on possible measures that might improve US opportunities in the region as well. Adams, like many Americans, seemed to be of two minds about what had just happened and what the United States should do next. Western nations, Adams reported, now enjoyed access to more of China as a result of a "conquest" of "questionable morality." Yet he hoped that the war's effects would be "auspicious" for the United States, opening up new possibilities for improved relations.[16]

During the years of Adams's terms as secretary of state and president, China had been by far a more powerful country than the United States. While Western powers were eager to possess the tea, porcelain, silks, and other goods that China brought to market, there was comparatively little that Europeans and Americans could offer in exchange. Much of America's early Pacific explorations were focused on the China trade: the sandalwood and bêche-de-mer that Americans could find in the Sandwich Islands and Fiji were the keys to securing US trade in China, as the fur trade had been in earlier years.[17] Far more troubling than an unbalanced trade relationship, though, was the control that China maintained over the foreign visitors who came to its shores. Americans, like Europeans, were restricted to the foreign district in Canton (Guangzhou), forced into what Adams called the "humiliating" position of being considered "outside barbarians" by the Chinese. Writing for the Foreign Affairs Committee, Adams explained that this dynamic was the "root and substance" of the conflict that led to the Opium War. The war, he insisted, had been about "equal rights of independent nations, against the insolent and absurd assumption of despotic supremacy." Here, the independent nations he worried about were Britain and the United States; the insolent despot was China. The war's end promised a new era. For merchants, China represented a great potential trading partner and market. For missionaries, it represented a great field of souls in need of conversion. For all, China was an important key to their vision for the future.

Adams's explanation of the conflict at the root of the Opium War was a willful misreading of Chinese diplomacy. In the 1830s, Chinese relations with the various Western powers were severely tested by the opium trade. The sale of opium was illegal in China, yet smuggling flourished. Missionaries were early opposed to the trade for humanitarian reasons, but often kept quiet about their concerns. They saw it as a harmful drug and were troubled to see Western merchants enriching themselves through it. Further, for practical reasons they hoped the illegal trade would cease. Smuggling set the Chinese authorities against all outsiders, and so complicated the ability of all Westerners to gain a foothold in China and challenged missionaries' understanding of the linked goals of the two groups. But some of the major donors to the China mission and its philanthropic institutions were smugglers, so missionaries kept their mouths shut.

Eventually, missionaries like Elijah Bridgman began voicing their concerns in print. Writing for US audiences, they tended to emphasize that the majority of the illicit trade was done by British, not US, ships. But they called attention to American participation as well. In 1839, Bridgman was able to push American merchants to agree to Chinese demands to give up the trade. Few kept to their word.[18] In the next year, opium joined a list of trade goods including liquor and tobacco that received the ABCFM's opprobrium.[19] This was not just a question of the morality of drug use or even of public health. The illegality of the trade and the flagrant disregard of the laws brought the missionary response to the opium question into the realm of foreign relations.

In 1839, the Chinese government stepped up its efforts to halt the opium trade. The emperor wrote to Queen Victoria, urging her to take action to stop British smuggling. In China, officials tightened restrictions against the trade yet again. Eventually, the Chinese seized supplies of English opium and blockaded European shipping coming into Canton. The aggression of the British in response would become a major problem for American merchants and missionaries alike. Unwilling to accept Chinese efforts to curtail the trade, the British insisted on the right to free commerce and backed up their demands

free trade
sovereignty

with naval force. The Opium War, which lasted from 1839 to 1842, would lead to a profound shift in Chinese relations with the Western nations by forcing the Chinese to grant more concessions to foreign powers who were anxious to trade.

In the United States, the Opium War led to confusion and anxiety. Within the government, some worried that the British would try to gain exclusive trading rights and usurp any US position in China. The House Committee on Foreign Affairs received a petition from a group of merchants in January 1840 who were very concerned about the potential blockade of Chinese ports and sought protection from the government.[20] It was not entirely clear how the United States ought to respond to these events.[21]

John Quincy Adams, like many American observers, agreed with the central premise of the British position: that free trade was not just an economic issue, but an ethical one as well. "Commerce," Adams had written, was "among the natural rights and duties of men," but in China "everyone has a right to buy, but no one is obliged to sell." Calling the Chinese attempt to control its foreign trade "churlish and unsocial," Adams echoed the British critique of China as setting itself apart and above other countries.[22] Whatever they did, Americans wanted to protect their trading interests and their equality with other nations.

The wartime years coincided with missionary Peter Parker's visit to the United States, which allowed missionaries to become both informants to the American public and advisors to the US government. Parker had been a medical missionary in Canton since 1834, where he worked alongside Elijah Bridgman, Samuel Wells Williams, and Edwin Stevens. His duties included caring for the health of his missionary brethren as well as establishing a dispensary and hospital in Canton. Parker's hospital saw long lines of Chinese patients. The mission provided treatment for free, for which the missionaries received patients' gratitude, if not their presence at worship. Though Parker employed a local Christian to evangelize at the hospital, he had little time for evangelism himself. His work at the hospital and at the Medical Missionary Society, an international organization of medical missionaries serving in China, consumed the majority of his time.[23] By the late 1830s, Parker began to add government work to his list of tasks.

It was the Chinese, not the US, government that Parker assisted first. Commissioner Lin, appointed by the Chinese emperor to suppress the opium trade as the customs inspector in Canton, had asked Parker to help him in his negotiations with the British by translating several passages from Vattel's *Law of Nations* on war, blockades, embargoes, and the right of a state to exclude foreign merchandise and confiscate smuggled goods. Lin wanted to come to the table prepared to argue with the British in terms that they would understand and accept. He trusted Parker to prepare him for such a debate. After the Vattel translations, Lin had Parker translate into English his official communication with Queen Victoria about opium. Parker did not expect this to be effective, as indeed it was not. In theory, Vattel may have been on China's side, but the British would not accept the right of an Asian power to define what sort of trade was or was not permissible. In the summer of 1840, war officially began with the arrival of British forces and the blockade of Canton. The fighting effectively closed the hospital for a time, and Parker returned to the United States in July for a brief visit.[24]

The timing of Parker's arrival was ideal for opening the door for conversations with the powerful figures who could shape the United States' China policy. At the time, the US consulate in Canton was staffed by a single consul, and direct information from China was highly valuable. Parker's friends in New Haven urged him to Washington, where they thought he might be of some use in sharing his knowledge of recent events and Chinese society and culture with politicians. There, he met with the ambassadors of Spain, France, Austria, and Russia, in addition to President Martin Van Buren, Secretary of State John Forsyth, President-Elect William Henry Harrison, and Daniel Webster, who would be Harrison's secretary of state. He preached a missionary sermon in Washington in January and was then invited to preach again in the chambers of Congress on the following Sunday. John Quincy Adams attended both events.

For Parker, this was an incredible honor. He was preaching in front of what he described as "one of the most enlightened audiences of any age or nation, the Senate and House of Representatives." It was also an excellent opportunity to share his views about what the United States needed in China.

Parker found an interested audience in Daniel Webster. Their meeting concluded with a request from the incoming secretary of state to the missionary to bring written suggestions for the United States' future China policy. Parker was happy to comply. At the top of his list was the need for a US minister plenipotentiary to be appointed. This diplomat, he hoped, might help lead peace talks between England and China, end the opium traffic, and restore trade. Parker's initial hope was that John Quincy Adams might serve in that role.[25]

Parker had visited Adams to discuss the proposals he would make to Webster. In a forty-five-minute interview, Parker explained that he was urging the United States to appoint a minister of the United States to China, and he thought that Adams was the man for the job. Adams, though, was not sure. "The time has not yet come," Adams wrote in his diary, "for a diplomatic mission from the United States to the Celestial Empire." In 1841, the conflict between China and England was too significant, and US relations with Great Britain were not strong enough to allow the United States to serve in a mediating role. Adams advised waiting.[26]

A year later, as Parker prepared to return to China, the government appeared to have abandoned plans for an embassy in China. Parker met with President John Tyler, who had come to the White House after the death of Harrison, and again urged Webster to send someone to China.[27] Adams now supported this project. It seemed important, Adams reflected, for some "intelligent and discreet and spirited informal commissioner" of the United States to take residence in China, empowered "to take advantage of any incident which might occur to open a communication with the Chinese Government, to sustain and promote the interests, political and commercial, of our country." Parker agreed. The president, too, had assured Parker that "he had his eyes fixed upon China."[28]

Tyler's first move was to send Commodore Lawrence Kearny and the East India Squadron to China in 1842. Kearny's instructions urged him to maintain strict neutrality between the Chinese and the British while protecting American shipping and taking steps to punish American participation in the opium trade or any smuggling that was being perpetrated under the American flag. In this work, he, too, received missionary assistance. Elijah Bridgman, one of Parker's missionary brethren in Canton, served as Kerny's translator and advisor. What was supposed to be a few days' work for the missionary ended up lasting two months as Bridgman helped Kearny to resolve a dispute over property losses and the death of an American sailor during the previous year. Following Bridgman's advice, Kearny welcomed Chinese officials onboard the American ships, in hopes of fostering better relations between the countries.[29]

As Bridgman and Kearny laid the groundwork for better relations between the United States and China, Parker returned to China with his new wife Harriet Webster. The couple had met in Washington. Their marriage, uniting a cousin of Daniel Webster with the missionary, further enmeshed missionary and diplomatic circles. They arrived in Canton in July 1842, just before the negotiations between the British and the Chinese began. The resulting Treaty of Nanking would transform Western relations with China. Most important, the treaty opened up new ports to Western residents and Western trade. Outsiders would no longer be restricted to Canton.

This new state of affairs provided a new urgency to Parker's recommendation of a US mission to China. If European powers were taking on a more extensive presence in China, the United States wanted to be there as well. In short order, Caleb Cushing, the congressman from Massachusetts who followed Adams as chair of the House Foreign Affairs Committee, was appointed to the role. His first priority was to negotiate with the government the terms of a new treaty between China and the United States.

As he prepared for his new diplomatic mission, Cushing reviewed Parker's writings on China. He accepted the ABCFM's offer of help, and asked Parker and Bridgman to serve as assistants throughout the treaty process.[30] They complied. Parker secured a student to cover his hospital duties during his absence and joined Cushing in Macao to begin the negotiations.[31] Bridgman was less enthusiastic about this work, and not at all initially convinced that Cushing's diplomatic mission would have much benefit to the evangelical mission. Yet within the United States, Rufus Anderson of ABCFM was convinced that the two missions shared many goals. While the political project "could not be the same," as the religious one, the ABCFM trusted that a favorable treaty would "facilitate the measures for the religious improvement of the Chinese empire" by opening the door to more evangelism.[32]

The negotiations that led to the 1844 Treaty of Wanghia reveal the fruits of missionary influence. The treaty extended many of the recent British gains to the United States, most importantly the opening of five new ports to foreign residence. Parker was a helpful presence in the US delegation; through his medical practice, he had treated the parents of two of the Chinese delegates and counted another as a close friend. The two missionaries assisted in a line-by-line scrutiny of the proposed text. Bridgman and Parker were particularly attentive to articles that would protect missionary efforts in these new treaty ports. They made sure that hospitals and houses of worship were included on the list of types of property foreigners were allowed to own in the treaty ports. They also secured the right of US citizens to employ Chinese language teachers and assistants in literary labors, such as translating and publishing religious tracts and scripture. This had previously been banned, which created obvious obstacles for missionaries interested in learning the language, translating scripture, and distributing religious print widely.

The Treaty of Wanghia, in short, gave missionaries their long-sought ability to evangelize more openly in China and initiated a new era in the complex relations between missionaries and merchants.[33] Caleb Cushing returned to the United States in 1844 with the treaty, leaving behind Parker as the official secretary to the US Mission in China, complete with a salary paid by the US government.[34]

As soon as news of the treaty circulated in the United States, missionary societies prepared to send missionaries out to new stations in China. The _Missionary Herald_ celebrated the ways that China's new treaties had begun the work of "breaking down the walls of seclusion with which that country has been so long encircled."[35] The numbers of missionaries in China would soon balloon, ushering in a new era of US-China relations. In many ways, these treaties and the provisions for missionary activity were the results of missionaries' longstanding efforts to distribute missionary intelligence among Americans at home.

Cushing returned to Washington in 1845 and met with Adams. The two men discussed the history of the Opium War and the present state of US-China relations. Adams wanted to know about religion and morality in China, reflecting that "there were differences of international law between nations, modified by their systems of religion." Christian nations related to each other on the basis of "the fundamental moral principle of Christianity—brotherly love among men," while China relied on another system entirely. Cushing described it as "the relation of authority and obedience between parent and child."[36]

Adams's logic—that religion was the basis for a country's approach to international relations—illuminates the reason why missionaries and diplomats could see eye to eye in China and other missionary lands. On some level, missions that sought to convert communities and cultures to Christianity would serve the interests of the US government. But Adams was not always persuaded that missionary and government interests aligned.

Adams Meets King and Robertson, 1828 and 1830

Adams's embrace of missionary intelligence in China stands out because earlier in his career, he had bristled when missionary writings and priorities threatened to create diplomatic challenges for the United States.

In 1823, as secretary of state, Adams made what might have been his longest-lasting influence in US foreign relations when he helped draft President James Monroe's address that would be remembered as the Monroe Doctrine. The doctrine set out some of the basic principles of US foreign policy at the time: nonengagement in European political conflict and opposition to European colonizing efforts in the Americas. As Adams had explained in an earlier address, the United States would not go out into the world "in search of monsters to destroy."[37] One of the main priorities of US international relations was commerce, and the government sought to support whatever policies would create the best possibilities for Americans to trade. Yet some Americans could imagine very different priorities for US foreign relations. Missionaries and their supporters at home, for example, not only saw monsters around the world, but wondered if perhaps the United States ought to try to destroy them after all.

It was in the midst of debate over precisely this tension that Adams wrote the Monroe Doctrine. In the early 1820s, revolutions in Latin America captured American enthusiasm while prompting some anxiety about the future of independent republics throughout the Americas.[38] At the same time that Adams considered these events in Latin America, his attention was also drawn to the unfurling controversy surrounding the Greek Revolution and the American response to it. Many Americans saw this revolution across the Atlantic, as they had the French Revolution before it, as an inheritor of the principles of the American Revolution. Unlike the French Revolution, however, the Greek Revolution set off a proto-humanitarian interest as well, with distinctly religious and racialized dynamics. This was, American observers understood, more than just a war for independence; it was a battle between persecuted Christian Greeks and oppressive Muslim Turks.[39]

American coverage of the war was marked by anti-Muslim fervor. Muslims, according to these stories, were inherently cruel and violent; Greek Christians, accordingly, were the victims of horrific persecution. As Americans read reports of what was happening in Greece from Philhellenic writers like Lord Byron, they were struck by the injustice and depravity of the treatment of Greeks. Sympathetic observers reacted with particular horror to stories of violent attacks against women, who were shown bare-chested and brutalized in the illustrations accompanying some of the reporting. Modest Christian women, they understood, needed to be protected from violent and lascivious Muslim men. American Protestants called for government action in response.

The United States, they argued, was a Christian nation. As such, they ought to come to the aid of persecuted Christians across the ocean.[40]

This was not an argument that convinced the US government. Pragmatic commercial concerns outweighed humanitarian appeals. The Ottoman Empire, of which Greece was then a part, was a powerful force and important to US trading interests. American diplomats found themselves in the uncomfortable position of having to explain to Ottoman officials why Americans were actively organizing on behalf of the Greeks. The public enthusiasm for Greece, and the religious tone that it took, raised doubts about the assertion in the 1796 Treaty of Tripoli between the United States and representatives of the Ottoman Empire that the United States was "not in any sense founded on the Christian religion."[41]

Adams, as secretary of state, was quite concerned that the public uproar on behalf of the Greeks would create a crisis in US-Ottoman relations.[42] It was this thought that animated Adams's statements about monsters across the globe. Regardless of what Philhellenes urged, Adams insisted that the US government would not get involved in humanitarian crises. Yet the US public was another thing altogether. If the government would not provide aid, American missionary and benevolent societies could. Missionaries had not been active in Greece before, but they had been working with Orthodox Christians elsewhere in the Ottoman Empire.[43] The war changed this. Jonas King, one of the ABCFM's early missionaries to Palestine, was one of the American Philhellenes who helped to draw American attention to the plight of Greece. King had long relied on violent stereotypes of Muslims in his writings about the Ottoman Empire. He had described Constantinople as "full of oppression, deceit and false religion, plague, and death."[44] It was unsurprising, then, that on a tour of the United States in 1827 he became a prominent proponent of the Greek cause against the Turks.

King visited Washington, DC, while serving as an agent of the ABCFM, traveling through the country and fundraising for foreign missions. There, he met with Daniel Webster, Henry Clay, and others. It was on this trip that King preached before an unimpressed Adams. It was not the politicians but the groups of benevolent-minded Americans with whom he had the greatest impact. The Ladies' Greek Committee of New York, one of many Philhellenic organizations created in the United States to organize support for the Greek cause, soon hired him as their missionary to Greece. Despite his title as "missionary," it was not an evangelistic position. He was to travel to Greece, establish schools, distribute Bibles and religious tracts, and see how US donations might be best put to use. But more evangelical organizations supported King's work as well. Both the American Bible Society and the American Tract Society supported King's mission to Greece and provided religious materials for distribution.[45]

Once he was in Greece, King began to use American money to build schoolhouses. King worked with the Greek government in going about this project, and his American supporters were delighted to learn that the new Greek president, Ioannis Kapodistrias, shared their sense that education was the key to transformation in the country.[46] Schools, indeed, were a major emphasis of US missionaries around the world. Here, though, they took on a particular poignancy. American missionaries believed schools to be transformative cultural institutions. The United States, too, had seen major reforms in its educational system in the decades since the American Revolution. Academies, women's seminaries, and public schools had all expanded in order to provide what reformers believed was a republican education. They understood that the civic and political life of a republic demanded an educated populace. Now that Greece had gained its independence from the Ottoman Empire and become a republic as well, it only stood to reason that they, too, needed schools to train new republican citizens.

The humanitarian aid of the war years thus expanded to include educational institution building. King's schools grew alongside other American-sponsored schools, and soon he was joined by American missionaries sponsored by other denominational groups.[47] The Episcopal Church sent reverends John Robertson and John Hill to Athens. Within two years of their departure, Robertson and Hill reported great success in their work. They found large numbers of students interested in attending their schools and public officials ready to support them.[48] They continued to urge multiple types of US intervention, including Protestant evangelization. Robertson echoed King's evaluation of Greece, writing to his American supporters that the country was in "a most wretched state." Ongoing violence created ongoing dangers. Yet their work was promising. By 1832, the missionaries had published religious tracts and textbooks (in arithmetic and modern Greek grammar and reading) and were busy with their schools. Only want of funds kept them from immediately building more.[49] As with all such appeals, Robertson hoped that his US audience would donate the additional gifts that would allow him to enhance his missionary work.

By the 1830s, Adams found such missionary appeals less threatening than he had in 1823. When he heard Robertson preach about his work

Greek Rev.
JQA: commerce > humanitarianism

in Greece, the now former secretary of state described his message as "affecting." "It would seem as if within the last seven years one-half the population had perished," Adams reflected. Those who survived were left in conditions "wretched beyond description," but the missionary inspired Adams with his stories of their "passion to obtain education and to seek after wisdom."[50]

The difference, of course, had a great deal to do with the context of who was taking action and how. It would have been untenable for the United States to intervene in a foreign war over humanitarian and religious concerns in 1823. The United States was far too weak and could not afford to anger the much more powerful Ottoman Empire. Further, other diplomatic crises closer to home demanded attention. As secretary of state, Adams had been unmoved. Now that Greek independence had been secured, and now that the actors in question were missionaries, and not the government, Adams was able to react differently. Missionaries, after all, were not the state. They could respond to humanitarian concerns in a different way than the US government could at this early moment in the century.

Adams Meets Worcester and McCoy, 1819 and 1828

In the same year that Adams listened to Robertson preach about Greece, President Andrew Jackson signed the Indian Removal Act. Here, too, missionary intelligence sought to influence US political action. For decades, the missionaries and the federal government shared a perspective of their goals and interests in relation to the various Indigenous nations of North America. "Indian Missions" fell under the umbrella of foreign missions in the early nineteenth century, directed as they were to non-US populations who had sovereign power over their own territory. Accordingly, Adams had met with missionaries to Native Americans during his earlier tenure as secretary of state.

Samuel Worcester called on Adams in late February 1819, long before Worcester would give his name to one of the most significant Supreme Court cases dealing with US-Indian relations. Worcester was in Washington with a group of Cherokees who were then negotiating a treaty with the US government involving land cessions and the migration of some of the tribe west of the Mississippi. He came to Adams for help in securing guarantees for government support "of schooling and religious instruction for these unfortunate Indians," and Adams promised to aid him. But Adams was busy with other matters and admitted in his diary that "I have not even had time to acquire an exact knowledge of what this is."[51]

It would not be long before Adams and the rest of the American public had a far better understanding of the issues at stake in the missionary role in government relations with American Indians. Missionaries came to the debates over removal with a long history of understanding their work to be connected with government Indian policy. Since their beginnings in the 1810s, American missionary organizations had enjoyed federal support of their Indian missions through the financial distributions of the Civilization Fund, a portion of the federal budget that was intended to support educational and "civilizing" efforts among Native Americans. Receipt of these funds required the missionaries send an annual report to the Department of War, which oversaw Indian relations. Both the Department of War and the missionary organizations wanted the same information to judge the missions' progress.[52] While the federal money was technically allocated to nonreligious purposes (the purchase of farming equipment or other materials for schools), these missions combined religious and secular work seamlessly in a way that did not create any problems for either the government or the mission boards. When various Native nations had attempted to negotiate with the federal government about land and removal, missionaries could accordingly serve as helpful allies and advocates.[53] It was in this capacity that Adams first met Samuel Worcester.

Nearly a decade later, another missionary, Isaac McCoy, visited Adams in his new role as president. McCoy was a Baptist missionary who came seeking government protection for American Indians through removal. He and Worcester represented, in many ways, the two sides of the coin in missionary responses to the government policy of Indian removal. Where Worcester insisted that the Cherokee had the right to their ancestral lands as a sovereign people who had become civilized and Christianized, McCoy argued that white civilization posed, on the contrary, a danger to Indians. Their only hope of survival, McCoy felt, was to migrate to protected reservations where they might preserve traditional ways of life and remain safe from the violent and dangerous incursions of white American settlers.[54] Each was convinced that his own approach was benevolent toward Indian nations, and each believed that his experience working at government-sponsored missions gave him the expertise to understand the situation and provide advice to policymakers.

Adams and McCoy talked at some length about the issue in 1828, and Adams reflected that the United States had not been consistent in its actions. "We have talked of benevolence and humanity, and preached them into civilization," he recorded in his diary, "but none of this benevolence is felt where the right of the Indian comes in collision with the interest of the white man." Adams thought the "most benevolent course" of action would be to make the Indians into US citizens, but he also believed that this was not a practical solution.[55] The issue was at the heart of the 1828 presidential election, which Adams lost to Andrew Jackson. Jackson had gained national fame through his military exploits against Indigenous Americans. As president, he would usher in a far more aggressive phase of Indian removal in the federal government, signing the Indian Removal Act into law in 1830.

The US government's Indian policy was a form of foreign relations. But unlike other foreign affairs officials, the personnel for Indian Affairs were part of the Department of War, not the Department of State, and it was Indian agents, not ambassadors or consuls, who represented the US government. But as the early emphasis on treaties suggests, US government officials well understood themselves to be dealing with sovereign foreign powers. These negotiations were some of the most significant moments of American state-building over the first half of the century. Missionaries, too, categorized American Indians as "foreign" in the early decades of the century (though they would migrate to the lists of "domestic" or "home" missions as the century progressed). As the competing perspectives of McCoy and Worcester suggest, missionaries were deeply enmeshed in the political conflicts over removal and were far from united in their approach.

Given the long history of missionary and government cooperation in Indian affairs, it should come as little surprise that some of the most prominent antiremoval voices among white Americans came from missionaries and their supporters. When Georgia passed state laws asserting the sovereignty of the Georgia government over Cherokee land in 1825, the missionary political response was decisive. Jeremiah Evarts, corresponding secretary of the ABCFM, authored the William Penn Essays, a series of anonymous appeals that sought to gather US support for the right of Native Americans to remain on their ancestral lands. This had been a cause close to Evarts's heart for years. In 1827, Evarts had the Sandwich Islands missionary Charles Stewart introduce him to the president, taking the occasion to discuss the situation in Georgia.[56] He had hoped that Adams was inclined to take action on behalf of the Cherokee, but in this he was disappointed. Two years after the men met, Jackson was in the White House and Evarts began writing his anonymous essays.

Evarts

At the heart of Evarts's argument was the idea that Indians from the so-called Civilized Tribes (including the Cherokee and Choctaw, both beneficiaries of ABCFM missions) had adopted the habits and culture of Protestant America and thus deserved to keep their land. But this was not all. Evarts included a lengthy history lesson to argue that native nations were sovereign and had always been treated as such by the federal government. It was a political as well as a moral critique of removal efforts. In addition to this published (if anonymous) activity, Evarts also encouraged family friend Catharine Beecher to appeal to American women using the same arguments. Her "Circular Addressed to Benevolent Ladies of the United States" inspired a widespread petition movement among white women to attempt to stop removal and similarly blended moral, political, and Christian arguments. These petitions, however, were unsuccessful.[57]

Members of the ABCFM also worked with Cherokee leaders to directly challenge the laws. It was on the advice of these missionaries that the Cherokee brought suit against Georgia. And it was with the ABCFM's full support that missionaries Samuel Worcester and Elizur Butler refused to follow the new laws, resulting in their arrest, imprisonment, and eventual Supreme Court case. Among those who influenced these developments behind the scenes was Senator Theodore Frelinghuysen, a vigorous opponent of the Indian Removal Act and a member of the ABCFM who advised the board about lawyers and legal strategy in these cases.

Missionaries did not determine the government response to removal. Those who opposed it, after all, failed. For all that missionaries had presented Indians as sovereign foreign nations, the Supreme Court rejected this logic in the 1831 case *Cherokee Nation v. Georgia*, creating instead the new legal category of domestic dependent nations. When missionaries challenged their arrest under the new Georgia laws, it seemed momentarily possible that the US government would recognize Cherokee sovereignty more fully. In 1832, the court deemed the state laws that claimed the right to govern Indian lands and imprison missionaries to be unconstitutional in the decision for *Worcester v. Georgia*.[58]

After church on a Sunday in March 1832, John Quincy Adams, now a congressman representing Massachusetts, returned home to read "attentively" Justice Marshall's opinion in the case involving that missionary he had met so long before. He understood immediately what the true outcome of *Worcester v. Georgia* would be. With Jackson supporting the Georgia government and Congress divided, the court was powerless to enforce its ruling. Bleakly, Adams predicted that "the Constitution and law of the Union and its judicial authority will be prostrated before the despotic power of the State." While the missionaries remained in prison and their supporters in Boston debated further government action, Adams concluded that as he could "effect nothing," he would "withhold [him]self from all action concerning it."[59] As a member of Congress, he was probably correct that there was not much he could have accomplished to change matters, though this sort of uphill battle never stopped him from speaking out against the evils of slavery.

Adams's bleak predictions were accurate. The inability of the Supreme Court to enforce its decision meant that, eventually, the missionaries gave in. Though the ABCFM considered bringing further suit, Worcester and Butler eventually capitulated. After an apology to the Georgia governor, they were released and eventually joined the Cherokee on the long and deathly march west of the Mississippi known as the Trail of Tears. Once in Indian Territory, the relationship between missions and the government returned to its previous status. Within these new territories, missionaries again served as "civilizing" elements who worked alongside the government. They had proven that they could influence public discussion of Indian rights, but they had also demonstrated how difficult it would be to make any real difference in treating Indians as anything but domestic dependent nations. Over time, missionary societies shifted their interpretation of Indian missions from the category of "foreign" missions to that of "home" missions. From within this framework, they would continue to influence the government development of a new generation of "civilizing" work and boarding schools.

Adams had been largely optimistic about the imperial ambitions that brought the British to fight China in the Opium War. He was far more outspoken in his criticism of the imperialism that undergirded the United States' war with Mexico. Adams's commitment to the antislavery cause had been at the root of his critiques of the efforts for expansion into the Southwest that took up so much of US political debate in the 1840s.[60] John Quincy Adams had long opposed the annexation of Texas, for example, seeing it as an attempt to expand slavery in the United States. But in July 1845, news reached the US Congress that Texas had accepted the terms of annexation to the United States. "If the voice of the people is the voice of God," Adams drily reflected in his diary, "this measure has now the sanction of Almighty God." In this dark mood, Adams could find only the slightest hint of hope, and that was in his trust that the future was "in the hands of Providence." Perhaps it was still possible that the "ultimate result" of the annexation of Texas would disappoint those who had advocated for it.[61]

When Congress voted to declare war on Mexico a year later, Adams was one of only fourteen members who voted against it. The war would ultimately lead to the expansion of the territory of the United States, giving the continental United States its current shape. It would also, as Adams well understood, lead to the expansion of the territorial and governmental power of slaveholding in the United States.

In short, it was a war that seemed to have little to do with the goals or interests of the foreign mission movement. Yet, in a pattern that would continue for decades, missionary supporters saw the hand of God in these militaristic developments. In particular, Protestant supporters saw the war as being a potential avenue for defeating Catholicism in the region. The Southern Baptist Convention's Committee on Foreign Missions, for example, saw the war as a way to save Mexico "from the withering reign of the Man of Sin."[62] While many may have opposed the war itself, they found that its effects presented opportunities. Like Adams, they trusted God to direct human events. American missionaries had long understood empire to create a path for mission work; the Mexican War represented simply another step in this process.

But because this would be a case of missions following the flag, Protestant missionaries did not have the sort of influence in these matters that they had found in other foreign relations events of the first half of the century. They did not shape events; instead, they shaped the interpretations of events. Missionaries provided a logic for some observers to make sense of the presence of God in violent political events. In 1841, *The Missionary Herald* had noted that the new Republic of Texas had prepared the way for more than Catholic missionary efforts there.[63] By 1845, the Baptist Home Missionary Society and the Methodist Episcopal Missionary Society had stations in Texas.[64] Over the next few years, the Bible Society and Tract Society designated funds for the distribution of Protestant texts in Mexico. Soon after the war, home missionary societies turned their attention to Indian groups within the new territories of Texas and New Mexico. What had once been challenging potential sites for foreign missions had become domesticated.[65] In a pattern that would be followed in later American imperialistic ventures, the cross followed the flag and provided the justification for violence and colonialism.

By the time of Adams's death in 1848, missionaries were accepted as experts on their fields of action who could reach a wide audience about the issues that mattered the most to them. For decades, they had traveled the globe in the interests of evangelism. Along the way, they had developed a reputation for more than just piety. They wrote for US audiences as historians, scientists, and explorers, all attempting to tell Americans about what issues, places, and peoples they should care about. And their audiences were wide. As John Quincy Adams's interactions with missionaries and the mission movement over the course of his career in Washington reveal, missionaries could even reach the ears of the political elite.

Adams, like many American Protestants in the mission movement, found that a faith in Providence and the providential role of the United States could explain all sorts of things. The United States might not go out looking for monsters to destroy, but perhaps they came to believe, God might place Americans in positions where they could be prepared to fight monsters regardless. Missionary intelligence and missionary diplomacy prepared them to do just that.

1) China / Opium War / Treaty of Wanghia
   affinity: free trade
            religious liberty

2) Greek Rev: tension
   commerce
   weak state   >   humanitarianism

3) Georgia + Cherokee
   State > missionaries

CHAPTER 2

[Experts]

Two hundred people crowded into the assembly hall, eager to hear Samuel Wells Williams's lecture about China. It had been twelve years since Williams had left the United States for Canton and Macao in 1833, and much had changed in the meantime. Then, the Chinese government limited Western access to the country and restricted visitors to Canton, the single port that housed all of China's commercial exchange with Europe and America. Williams had joined a small American community of merchants who lived side by side with their peers from other foreign countries and strained against the limitations placed on them by the Chinese government. Non-Chinese residents were not even supposed to be able to learn the language. Merchants and missionaries alike wanted access to more of China—to markets and souls, respectively—and they prickled at the perceived self-importance of the Chinese who wished to contain them. But by the time Williams mounted the lectern in 1845, new treaties had opened up new ports to US diplomats, merchants, and missionaries. In the wake of the Opium Wars between Britain and China, the possibilities for Sino-American relations seemed to be entering a new era.

Americans, Williams found, were hungry for information. They wanted to learn about economic opportunities and about the spread of Christianity in this part of the world that had long seemed mysterious and distant. And so Williams embarked on a speaking tour. He found that audiences trusted him to explain Chinese "polity and character" as a true expert. He could, after all, claim to have lived for years in China among the Chinese, "speaking their language and studying their books," as he put it. Williams lectured to audiences in cities like Utica, Cleveland, Buffalo, and New York, teaching them about China and its geography, population, arts, customs, and science. To bring this information to a still wider audience, Williams expanded his lectures and published his work as *The Middle Kingdom* in 1848.[1]

It was a large book, aiming to be a "survey of the geography, government, education, social life, arts, religion, &c" of China. Its twelve hundred pages were originally bound into two volumes with bright yellow covers, richly illustrated by a scene at a Chinese gate. A group of men are pictured walking through the portal, dressed in what Americans would recognize as Chinese garb. In the foreground, a young Chinese woman sits, her parasol resting at her feet. Dragons top the structure, which is engraved with Chinese characters. Inside the book, Williams provided a translation for his US readers: "He who is benevolent loves those near, and then those who are remote."[2] This definition of benevolence, he hoped, might prick the attention of US readers and cause them to take to heart his lessons about a group of people who lived so far away.

The Middle Kingdom granted US readers a window into the Chinese Empire that had only recently been opened for US diplomats, merchants, and missionaries. The title page lists Williams's credentials as a linguistic expert: he is author of *Easy Lessons in Chinese* and *English and Chinese Vocabulary*. What he is not identified as is a missionary. But that is precisely what he was.

Williams had been sent to China by the American Board of Commissioners for Foreign Missions (ABCFM) as a printer, tasked with running a press in both the Chinese and English languages. In China, he was among the first of the missionary diplomats, finding ways to link his evangelistic work with efforts to secure US political and commercial presence in the country. Over the course of his career, he served both the ABCFM and the US Department of State. As an author, he brought his missionary and diplomatic worlds into harmony between two yellow covers. Though he elides his missionary identity in some places in the book, it is evident in others: the lectures in upstate New York and Ohio were fundraisers for a Chinese type for the missionary press. Those who encouraged him to publish the book had done so in the hopes that the information he shared could raise American enthusiasm for the

Figure 2.1. Title page, Samuel Wells Williams, *The Middle Kingdom*. The title page illustration is from the 1848 original edition.

evangelization of China. At times, his analysis of China revealed his commitment to transforming it through Christianity, as when he discussed the legal system in the country. If the laws were well and fairly administered, Williams reflected, "it would be incomparably the best governed country out of Christendom," but the corruption and "wicked rulers" got in the way. As Williams explained, this went to prove "the utter impossibility of securing the due administration of justice without higher moral principles than heathenism can teach." Christian evangelism was needed to ensure good order.[3]

Reviews of the book reflected this dance between emphasis and elision of Williams's missionary identity. In the religious and the mainstream press, readers celebrated the book for its comprehensive view of China and recognized the author as an expert, by virtue of his long residence and diverse knowledge. That it was missionary work that brought him to China, and that his missionary background might have shaped the picture of China he provided, was not always as carefully noted.

Williams was hardly the only missionary who wrote about his field for US audiences. In the first decades of the century, missionary intelligence could be found in published letters and journals that appeared in magazines and newspapers, as well as a few early books. By the mid-nineteenth century, the genre became prolific. Missionary-authored historical works and travel narratives ran a wide range. Pious memoirs of missionaries and converts, such as those of Harriet Newell or Catherine Brown, found wide audiences eager to emulate the lives of these Christian exemplars.[4] Other readers flocked to missionary histories, such as Rufus Anderson's multiple histories of the ABCFM, the missions to India, and the missions to the Sandwich Islands (Hawai'i).

Still others, including many who might not have even cared about missionary work itself, would sit down to read the general histories and travel narratives that came from missionary pens. On India, they might pick up David Allen's *India, Ancient and Modern* (1856), or Hollis Read's *India and its People, Ancient and Modern* (1859). If they wanted to learn about Hawai'i, they might turn to Hiram Bingham's *The Civil, Religious, and Political History of the Sandwich Islands* (1847). Cyrus Hamlin's *Among the Turks* (1878) or *Bible Work in Bible Lands*, by Isaac Bird (1872), might teach them about the Ottoman Empire. John Leighton Wilson's *Western Africa: Its History, Condition, and Prospects* (1856) was the first American history of that region. The missionary identity of these authors shaped the histories that they told but did not limit their readership. For the most popular titles, missionary authors were able to claim expertise from their experiences without implying that only religious readers would profit from the information that they shared.

The full range of missionary intelligence revealed strikingly broad claims of expertise. An 1881 tabulation of missionary literature coming out of the ABCFM alone counted thirty-two missionary authors who appeared in the *Journal of the American Oriental Society* at least once, thirty-four in *Bibliotheca Sacra*, and twenty in the *New Englander*. By that time, forty-five memoirs of ABCFM missionaries had been published, alongside nine of prominent converts, twenty-seven works of history, and fifty-five books on travel and miscellaneous subjects.[5] These works collectively served to argue that missionaries were figures who could explain the world to America and America to the world. By the middle of the century, leading geographers admitted their reliance on missionary sources, praising missionary periodicals like the *Missionary Herald* as "a rich store of scientific, historical, and antiquarian details" that could not be found elsewhere.[6]

Some Protestant critics worried that this emphasis on missionary intelligence was too worldly, drawing the focus too far away from evangelism. But missionary leaders such as David Greene of the ABCFM well understood that "there is no method more effectual in awakening a missionary spirit" than missionary intelligence. Not only did the ABCFM want to educate Americans about "the superstitions and idolatry, the vice and the wretchedness of the people, together with their customs and manner of life," they also found that geographical information could help to "bring the heathen distinctly before the mind, to give a knowledge of their condition and wants and awaken and keep up a lively interest in them." This wide-ranging missionary intelligence would inform the community of the importance of missionary work.[7]

Power is at the heart of discussions of expertise. In claiming to be experts, missionaries were participating in the sort of knowledge production about the colonized world for Western audiences that marked many imperial projects of the nineteenth century. Experts knew the world, and as they translated and packaged that knowledge for Western consumption, they asserted a power over the people they described. They claimed to create order out of disorder and to reveal what had previously been mysterious, often positioning themselves as rational and enlightened observers. Missionary claims of expertise helped to enforce an American (and European) worldview that justified and accepted as natural the dominance of the West over the East. The power relations of missionary expertise could have important real-world effects.[8]

Missionary leaders in the 1820s and 1830s understood that ignorance was a problem. When they tried to understand the reasons why more US Christians did not eagerly fund the work of foreign missions, they continually returned to the theme of ignorance. The problem, they were sure, was that not nearly enough Americans knew about the world, its people, or their needs. The solution was to simple: teach them.[9]

Missionary authors like Samuel Wells Williams returned to similar themes over and over again across multiple genres and for multiple audiences. These texts revealed an ongoing cycle of information that operated between the United States and the foreign world, with missionaries acting as the embodiment of the transfer of knowledge. Shaped by the US context in which they grew up, they went out into the field with expectations about what they would find and what they should do once they were there. These expectations shaped their perceptions and writing, even as their real-world experiences could challenge and alter their preconceptions. When they created texts for American audiences to read, they shared both what they thought was important and what they thought would be of interest: geography and climate, commerce and trade, politics and history, and the role of women. And so these missionary writings would, in turn, shape the perceptions and expectations of a new group of readers who were thinking about the world beyond the borders of the United States. The themes that they returned to again and again reflected a body of implicit assumptions shared by missionaries and many other Americans about the world and its people.

Their work and its reception demonstrate that there was no clear division between "religious" and "secular" texts in this mid-century moment. Efforts to demarcate a secular outside of religion would emerge later, but for many of these mid-nineteenth-century US audiences, a Protestant outlook suffused their understandings of civilization, good government, culture, and society. Neither missionaries nor their US audiences could imagine a world that clearly segmented religious and nonreligious categories. They divided the world in two—the Christian world and the heathen world—and they suffused religious meaning into descriptions of racial, gendered, and political groups. As they shared missionary intelligence with their readers at home, mid-nineteenth-century missionaries claimed the ability to shape American ideas about their country's place in the world.[10]

Williams on China

Samuel Wells Williams was born in Utica, New York, in 1812, the same year that the first ABCFM missionaries left the United States for Asia. After he graduated from the Rensselaer Institute, his father volunteered him as a printer for the ABCFM's China mission. Though he had struggled with his faith as a young man, his mother's piety swayed him to his future career. In 1831, she had placed a slip of paper into her church's offering plate that read "I give two of my sons." She died shortly after, and Williams would find himself in Canton fulfilling her promise two years later.

In China, Williams's work focused on the publication of missionary texts and the *Chinese Repository*, an English-language periodical designed for the foreign population in China (though it had some readers in the

United States and England as well). It was a missionary project, published on the mission press, but it was not solely evangelical in its goals. Rather, like so much else at mid-nineteenth-century missions, it understood religious change to be part and parcel of a larger cultural and political project. The *Repository* was designed to introduce the West to China and the Chinese to the West. Funded by the evangelical merchant D.W.C. Olyphant, the *Repository's* articles were designed to appeal to the merchants and traders who needed to understand China in order to do business there. It provided Western readers with a window into Chinese history, culture, and politics. While it would have been clear to readers that the writers and editors of the *Repository* believed that China desperately needed Western influence and intervention, that influence was not solely about Christianity.[11]

This genre-blurring was typical of missionary writers, who saw little distinction between their interests in evangelism and the spread of Western influence more generally. In China as elsewhere, the missionary project was closely linked to other branches of US cultural influence. Even if missionaries could often find themselves disagreeing with other Americans abroad about how to behave (sailors were a frequent sore spot for missionaries), they by no means disapproved of commercial and political influence as such.[12] Rather, missionaries worried that the wrong sort of Westerner would give a poor impression of Christianity. The solution was not to separate missionaries from other Americans abroad. Instead, they sought to center missionary interests within US foreign relations.

Williams was one of the more prominent missionaries to embrace this project. Over the two decades between the 1830s and 1850s, as he joined his fellow missionaries in learning the language, he wrote more than a hundred articles for the *Repository* on a wide range of subjects: trading rights, the limited spread of Christianity in China, geography, natural history, Chinese daily life, and major political events. It was these articles that would later form the core of *The Middle Kingdom*. Altogether, this allowed Williams to attract a reputation as an American expert on China.[13]

In *The Middle Kingdom*, Williams explained that his audience was "the general reader." This audience needed information that was, above all else, reliable and accurate. After all, most Americans shared misconceptions about China. They looked to China with a "peculiar and almost undefinable impression of ridicule," Williams reflected. Westerners looked at Chinese dress, culture, and physiognomy and laughed. They called the Chinese an "uncivilized 'pig-eyed' people," and described them as "at once conceited, ignorant, and almost unimprovable." Williams set out to vigorously counter all such assumptions and stereotypes. He wanted Americans to understand the Chinese correctly and to approach the people and the country with respect.[14]

This did not mean he was not interested in transforming China—far from it. His title *The Middle Kingdom* had a useful double meaning for Williams: it was both the name that the Chinese used themselves for their country, and a way to mark China's halfway status between barbarism and civilization. Like so many other missionary writers of the era, Williams walked a line of respect and blistering critique, rejecting one set of stereotypes only to bolster another.[15]

The book itself had chapters on geography, political history, natural history, government, the educational system, the written language, literature, the arts and sciences, architecture, dress, diet, social life, commerce, agriculture, the mechanical and industrial arts, and religion. Over the coming years, there was a steady stream of demand for the book. The book had a second edition in 1849, a third in 1851, and was in its fourth edition a decade later.[16] A revised edition appeared in 1883 and was continually in print into the early twentieth century. In addition, an excerpt of just the historical chapters were published separately as *History of China* in 1897.[17] By 1872, sales had been sufficient to sponsor the building of a new hospital in Shandong, named in Williams's honor.[18]

Williams found the wide audience he was looking for, and his influence went beyond his book sales. The book was not only reviewed, but summarized and discussed (sometimes at length) in a wide range of periodicals. It was not only the missionary public that took an interest in Williams's work. Within months of the book's original 1848 publication, the *United States Magazine and Democratic Review* argued that readers needed Williams's work in order to "cure" themselves of their mistaken understanding of the Chinese. For readers who might not have the time or inclination to peruse Williams's two-volume work, the magazine provided a sixteen-page summary.[19] Readers of *New Englander*, too, received a full-length article on Williams's work, complete with lengthy excerpts and discussions of the importance of China as a trade partner and "the oldest existing repository of civilization."[20] Shorter reviews in *Holden's Dollar Magazine* and *The Friend* echoed this sense of confidence in Williams.[21] In recognition of his work on *The Middle Kingdom*, Williams was elected to the American Ethnological Society.[22]

The Middle Kingdom was hardly the first source of American information about China. After all, China had long figured as a space of interest and excitement for Americans anxious to open trade relations. But earlier discussions tended to be brief and marked by offensive stereotypes. The middle of the century and increased contact with China brought with it a new wave of sources that claimed to be more knowledgeable about what China was really like. Williams's publication emerged as one of the most influential works in this shift.[23]

If you were lucky enough to live in a place like Salem, Massachusetts, with its long history of East Asian trade and local associations like the East India Marine Society, you might have been able to access even more sources of information. The Essex Library holdings on China are a good measure of what those with the most access to books on Asia could find. In the library catalog's "General Information" category, only three titles with US imprints predate Williams's first edition of *The Middle Kingdom*. These are all limited in their scope: a 1796 reprint of Lord Macartney's embassy to China, an 1836 sketch of Portuguese settlements and Catholic missions in China, and an 1846 discussion of the tea and opium trades. The other thirty-two general works on China published before Williams in this collection were European imports.

Readers who were more interested in travel narratives had slimmer options in these early decades. While the second half of the century would see an impressive number of US accounts of China from the pens of travelers, the first half of the century was much more limited. The Essex Library held two different 1830s editions of the China journals of David Abeel, a missionary of the American Reformed Church, alongside those of S. Shaw, the first US consul at Canton, and a few other titles: C. T. Downing's *Stranger in China*, H. Malcolm's *Travels in South-eastern Asia*, and J. N. Reynold's *Voyage of the U.S. Frigate Potomac*.[24]

Such a range of options was a best-case scenario available to those readers who could access such an impressive library. For readers in Boston, being able to access such an array of works could depend on which libraries you had access to. The private Boston Athenaeum, like the Essex Institute, had a good collection of China titles. The Boston Public Library, however, was not founded until 1850 and held only six titles on China in its collections by 1872. Williams was the earliest of these. In other cities and towns, options would have been even more limited.[25]

Before Williams, then, other books were available to American readers, but none took on the encyclopedic scope that he attempted, and few even attempted to present an evenhanded account of the Chinese people that did not rely on stereotypes and ridicule. His book was popular because readers accepted him as an expert. His long missionary residence seemed to make him so. While not all of his readers were motivated by missionary interests, Williams knew that their acceptance of his understanding of China in America was essential if the work of missions was going to have any kind of long-term success.

Perkins on Persia

Williams was not alone in commanding this authorial expertise, nor was he the first missionary to do so. Justin Perkins, the author of *Residence of Eight Years in Persia*, was similarly understood to be uniquely situated, because of his missionary work, to describe and explain Persia (Iran) to American readers. As one reviewer explained, Perkins had "rare advantages of becoming acquainted with their manners, customs, habits, character, and peculiarity" that allowed him to write on topics beyond his "strictly missionary" labors. Multiple reviewers emphasized Perkins's value to readers who did not particularly care about missions: they judged the information the book contained to be honest, interesting, and enlightening. One did not need to care about evangelism to be taken with Perkins's descriptions of people, places, and adventures—nor did one need to support mission work to be shaped by his worldview. Reviewers expected the book to command a wide audience.[26]

If Americans' knowledge of China had been limited and one-sided, the same could be said for their knowledge of Persia. The US presence in the region was limited at this time. From the mission's establishment in the early 1830s, US missionaries had to rely on British and Russian diplomats for protection; there were no consular or ambassadorial representatives of the United States in the region. Protestant missionaries hoped this would change: the mission was still petitioning the government for a consul in the 1860s. In the first half of the century, then, missionaries could claim a monopoly on American knowledge.[27]

Justin Perkins had established the mission in Oroomiah (Urmia) in 1834, and his book about the Nestorian Christians and Muslims he met there was published in 1843. He, like Williams, introduced non-missionary topics to his readers. Though the goals of this work had been "strictly missionary," Perkins wrote, his "observations have been general." His aim in the book was to entertain and edify a general audience through an engaging combination of "miscellany and incident with accurate, missionary and general information." He was blunt in claiming his expert status: "No American was ever a resident in that ancient and celebrated country before me," he wrote. He had taken great care to rely not only on his own personal observation, but "the facts." Illustrated with a map and colored plates that featured both people and landscape, the book took the form of a journal of his travels through the region, complete with discussions of geography, gender relations, dress, politics, and religion. It was less encyclopedic than Williams's book and far more driven by anecdote and personal experience. Chapters were not organized by theme, but by the chronology of when Perkins encountered them. Yet even within a diary framework, Perkins was able to cover a wide range of topics and gave readers a similar sense that they were seeing Persia accurately and fully.[28]

A graduate of Amherst College and Andover Theological Seminary, Perkins was typical of the ABCFM missionaries in these decades. He came from a farming family in New England but would, alongside his wife Charlotte, make his life far from home. In Persia, Perkins focused his attention on the Nestorian Christian population, though his work was not limited to evangelism. Instead, he worked to commit the vernacular language to writing and it was this, as much as anything else he accomplished, that would make his reputation.

As elsewhere, the mission establishment included a mission press and schools: a seminary for the higher education of both boys and girls in addition to local free schools for younger children. In its first year, the press printed 1,600 volumes and 3,600 tracts. Quite quickly, the schools claimed to educate nearly five hundred students.[29] Perkins also worked as a linguist and biblical scholar. Like other missionaries with academic interests, Perkins made use of his local contacts to obtain materials for collections in the United States and Europe. Like Williams, then, he served not only as a missionary but also as a scholar, and used that reputation to position himself as an expert on his region of the world for a US audience.[30]

A Residence of Eight Years in Persia was reviewed in general periodicals, including the *North American Review*, which considered Perkins's book to be "of great importance and utility," even as the reviewer had some complaints about its organization and style.[31] The reviewer described the Nestorian Christians of northern Kurdistan as a long-inaccessible community only recently reached by Western travelers, thanks to the interest and enterprise of US missionaries who had been inspired by a single paragraph on the region in a British missionary report. It was this religious effort, the review claimed, that "first enabled the eye of science to penetrate" the region.[32] The review claimed there was a symbiotic relationship between scientific and missionary exploration. In 1830, the ABCFM had sent its first missionary explorers to the region, whose book on their travels had already become "well known to be one of the most accurate and trustworthy books of travels which have appeared in modern times."[33]

In the interest of space, the *North American Review* chose not to include the many anecdotes in Perkins's five hundred-page book about the mission or the Nestorian people themselves. Instead, the scientific interests of the reviewer were reflected in his emphasis on details about the lake in Oroomiah (its depth, length, and elevation; the presence of islands; its salinity and wildlife) and the surrounding mountains and plains. But some of Perkins's ethnographic descriptions made it into the review as well. Readers learned that the Muslims and Christians who inhabited the region were both "a fine-looking race, of good stature, fair complexion, and with features regular, manly, intelligent, and often handsome." They were patriarchal and have a custom of "blood-revenge," both qualities that the Protestant missions would presumably seek to change, though this was not a subject of interest for the review.[34]

For a review of a missionary text, there is a notable absence of any discussion of Perkins's purpose in coming to Persia: evangelization. While the missionaries were recognized here for their work in spreading the gospel, they are more vocally celebrated for the intellectual cultivation they brought to the region and for their ability to tell the rest of the world about the Nestorians and their land. As with Williams, Perkins's topic was understood to be broader than simply evangelism. Perkins was, as reviewers at the *North American Review* assessed, "particularly adapted to win his way, and be the pioneer of literature and science to a people whose vernacular language was not yet to be written down; and the herald of Gospel light and truth to a nation which had long sat in darkness and the shadow of death."[35] Literature, science, and Christianity—in that order.[36]

Missionary Intelligence in the American Press

The Middle Kingdom and *Eight Years Residence* were part of a broader group of "contribution[s] to the progress of literature and science from the pen of a missionary," as the *North American Review* put it. These missionary-authored texts had become "at once standard and indispensable works" that would edify both "the devout and benevolent" reader and "the merely curious inquirer."[37] They were written by missionaries but, as reviewers took care to note, should be of interest to a much broader audience. Over the middle decades of the nineteenth century, missionary writings appeared regularly in the pages of this influential US periodical, spreading missionary intelligence to new audiences.

What made missionary literature stand out? Reviewers of prominent titles agreed that missionaries had unique access and a unique perspective. Missionaries could reach people and places that other travelers missed. As the *North American Review* explained, "Where commercial enterprise has furnished charts of a coast, religious zeal has penetrated the remotest interior. Where scientific research has offered us a few salient features of outward nature, the servant of the cross has gauged society in every dimension and painted it in every respect. Where the philologist has half gleaned and half imagined a scanty vocabulary to sustain a preconceived theory, the missionary has mastered the most intractable dialects, codified their laws and idioms, constructed alphabets, and created a written literature."[38]

While such enthusiasm for missionary expertise might be expected in the pages of the religious press, the *North American Review* was a literary journal with a different profile. Launched in 1815, the magazine covered a wide range of subject matter, including science, politics, and literature in addition to some religious topics. Its publishers intended that the *North American Review* would be something new: "pure literature" that was "distinctively American in character." There were few literary and political topics that they did not cover, and missionary intelligence fit in easily with this wide-ranging scope. It was a powerful magazine, widely available and read by people of intelligence and influence—or those who wanted to be seen as such.[39]

Starting around 1830 and continuing throughout the century, missionary topics and authors regularly appeared in the magazine. After all, as Williams's reviewer expressed it, without such missionary writers, Americans would know little about the South Sea islands, Asia, Africa, and even much of North America. Missionary literature allowed Americans to become "intimately conversant" about all of these regions about which they had previously been "in utter ignorance."[40] Within the pages of the journal, the missionaries existed alongside other travelers and experts in science and learning who could share information of interest to a general US public. Religion may not have been major topic for the *Review* in the antebellum years, but travel was.[41]

Writers at the *North American Review* valued missionary contributions to knowledge, encouraging readers to see missionaries not only as spiritual figures, but as "men of liberal culture" who possessed "a native breadth of vision and grasp of intellect."[42] In comparing the work of Rev. William Ellis, a British missionary in the Sandwich Islands, with Edmund Goodenough's *Voyage of His Majesty's Ship Blonde*, the reviewers were quite clear that Ellis was both more trustworthy and more entertaining. All of the best material in the other book had been taken from missionary sources, they reported. Given that, the reviewer took offense at Goodenough's critical descriptions of missionaries. The *North American Review* dismissed *Voyage* as "nearly worthless," and would not have bothered to mention it all, except for the "highly pernicious" tendency of it and similar titles to shape opinions and worldviews. Readers needed to understand that missionary intelligence could be trusted. The journal urged readers to rely on missionaries for their moralizing and civilizing power that was the necessary partner of commercial interests.[43]

This emphasis on nonmissionary topics within discussions of missionary writings could be found also in the coverage of writings by Hawaiian missionaries. In 1826, the *North American Review* ran a thirty-one-page review of *Journal of a Tour Around Hawaii*, a volume published the previous year by ABCFM missionaries. Though the purpose of the missionaries' tour (and of their report) was to select new locations for mission stations, the review made it clear that this information could be put to far wider uses. In this review, nine pages of which were direct quotations (of a book that was itself only 264 pages), readers learned about the history of the region, its government, religious culture, architectural styles, volcanoes, and linguistics. In addition to the book being reviewed, the article quoted from the *Missionary Herald* and the mission-authored *Memoir of Keopuolani, Late Queen of the Sandwich Islands*.[44]

Throughout, the *North American Review* argued that missionaries were the authorities who could accurately inform Americans about Hawai'i. Missionary population estimates corrected those previously circulated by Captain Cook (who had vastly overestimated the population). Missionary research similarly corrected previous philological theories about the links between Polynesian and Malaysian languages. Missionary travel provided accurate information about the size of the volcanoes. Though other Americans were present on the islands, their influence was understood to be negative (these merchants brought the "vices" of civilization).[45]

The *Review*'s appreciation for missionary writing resulted in short notices of some titles as well as long-form articles (some even reaching forty pages) based on the contents of missionary publications covering a wide range of political and cultural themes. Readers of the *Review* would have learned about the Sandwich Islands from C. S. Stewart, about Greece from Rufus Anderson, about India from David Allen, South Africa from Lewis Grout, and Damascus from Josias Leslie Porter, in addition to coverage of China from Williams and Persia from Perkins.[46] Missionary memoirs, too, were occasionally mentioned, with articles celebrating the careers of G. D. Boardman, David Tappan Stoddard, Adoniram Judson, and Emily C. Judson, remembered here not so much as a literary figure in her own right than as a missionary wife.[47]

Missionaries were not the only experts to whom US audiences could turn. These same middle decades of the century saw the publication of Orientalist scholarship that exhibited a similar fascination with exotic foreignness while claiming authority and power. In the pages of the *North American Review*, these multiple voices could exist side by side. Missionary writings on Islam or Islamic regions, for example, could be reviewed alongside those of Orientalists with both sets of writers presented as equally learned. An 1846 article on George Sale's translation of the Koran prompted Christian readers to think about Mohammed's place in world history. The article critiqued the "tone of the Crusaders" that many Western writers on Islam had taken up and instead embraced a more scholarly approach. Despite their religious identities, missionaries were not generally read as modern-day Crusaders, but as experts.[48]

Reviewers at the *North American Review* described missionary David Allen and his writings about India in these terms. In a forty-page review of *India, Ancient and Modern* (1856), the review concluded that the book would become "a standard work of history,—a book of permanent value and of frequent reference." The article emphasized Allen's mastery of Indian history, particularly the history of the East India Company. In multipage excerpts, Allen describes the wars between France and England, the relations between the British government and its colonial subjects, the company's effects on manufacturing and commerce, the extent to which the British government supported education and public works, and the important political question of how long the British could be expected to maintain their power in India and throughout Asia. Allen's discussion of Christian evangelism and missionary work is only mentioned at the end of the article.[49]

Allen's subtitle suggests the wide range of subjects that he considered in the full six-hundred-page volume: *Geographical, Historical, Political, Social, and Religious; with a Particular Account of the State and Prospects of Christianity.* Like Williams and Perkins, he had written a large and broad book that used a missionary perspective to frame a wide range of subjects. Allen had written for an explicitly American audience. Too much of what was available seemed to be aimed at British readers focused on learning about their imperial possessions. Allen hoped instead to inform his readers about "the state and character of the people of India," and the political and cultural changes that missionaries and colonial officials had brought about.

The spread of Protestantism in India was deeply important to this missionary who had spent more than twenty years away from the United States. He understood that it was missions that made many Americans interested in India. For Allen, the story of US engagement with India began in the 1790s, when Americans could first read about British missions to the country. He understood the progress of his missionary goals to be deeply connected to all of these other aspects of Indian life and history.[50] And based on the reviews that his work garnered, this sense of connection was shared. The *Review* emphasized the schools that missionaries established (126 of them, serving 14,562 students). These taught the English language which, though it would soon become controversial in some missionary discussions, was here seen as essential. Only English, the *Review* agreed with Allen, could teach Indian students the literature, science, and theology that would prepare them to become Christian and civilized.

The acceptance of missionaries as experts did not mean that readers or reviewers embraced the missionary cause. Alongside celebrations of missionary intelligence, magazines like the *North American Review* included criticism of missionary methods and focus. A discussion of Egyptian politics in the 1847 *North American Review*, for example, argued that "steam and commerce" would be more potent missionaries than either "Jesuit or Protestant."[51] And by 1868, a short review of Rev. C. H. Wheeler's *Ten Years on the Euphrates* contained a biting critique of the "primitive missionary policy" that embraced evangelism without a focus on civilization. This sort of work, the reviewer seemed quite sure, "does not seem to be of that large and practical kind which gives any promise of permanent results." Missionary intelligence was most useful, for this reviewer, when it was paired with attention to cultural change.[52]

Despite their claims of expertise, cultural biases and stereotypes were evident in missionary writing. Over the course of the century, missionary writings reflected their complex understandings of empire and race. Many missionaries did go out into the field interested to explore and to learn about foreign peoples. Many of them were transformed by the experience. Many more of them remained convinced of the religious and cultural superiority of American Christianity, whatever they had experienced abroad.

The result was that missionary publications were often selective in the versions of non-Christian religions and cultures that they depicted. Often, these writings were decidedly negative in their outlook, emphasizing the superiority of Christianity and Western culture in part out of an interest in fundraising and supporting the future of the missionary movement. Yet because missionaries could claim a more authentic knowledge than other Americans, their depictions could be read as accurate and valuable depictions of the foreign world.[53] Missionary biases, then, could be extremely influential.

As a writer for the *North American Review* put it, the "great diversity" of travel writing was obvious: while some works could "excite attention and reward a careful perusal," however remote the subject of the work, others could be "nothing but tedious specimens of barrenness and stupidity," even if they were describing places of tremendous interest. So many of these titles, in fact, were put together "without the slightest sense of responsibility" to the facts, the people, or the places being described. The result was troubling. "Erroneous impressions are made upon the minds of multitudes of all parts of the civilized world; and not a few individuals, who would otherwise have been impartial, form and cherish antipathies which will never be eradicated."[54] Missionaries entered this packed field committed to countering such a trend.

As Samuel Wells Williams's reviewer in *New Englander* mused, it may not have been the intention of the earliest organizers of US foreign missions that missionaries would become prominent authors, but this was indeed what had happened. Missionary authors like Williams and Perkins were trusted because readers "know that the authors have had better opportunities than any other foreigners—diplomatic functionaries not excepted—for learning the real condition of the people whom they describe." American readers needed "just such information as none but missionaries can give or acquire," not because of their evangelistic value, but because of the expertise they possessed.[55] In contrast, the *North American Review* argued, diplomatic writers were content to focus only on politics and the court, and commercial writers only cared to discuss trade and harbors. To really learn about a place and its people, to get the most "thorough, symmetrical, and trustworthy" information, you had to look to missionary intelligence.[56]

After the publication of *The Middle Kingdom*, Samuel Wells Williams returned to China, where he would spend the next several decades as one of America's foremost experts on the country. He continued to write for US audiences, with publications in the 1870s that took on an increasingly direct political focus. In an article on "Our Relations with the Chinese Empire," he criticized the United States for failing to treat the Chinese with "the commonest rights of humanity." Despite a history of good relations between the United States and China, he feared that the United States was increasingly failing to uphold its treaties. Instead, the United States treated the Chinese as "weak, ignorant, poor, and unprotected." Perhaps most disturbingly for Williams, Americans were working to limit Chinese immigration. He, like many missionaries who had worked in China, argued against these efforts forcefully. "Is not our Christian civilization strong enough to do right by them?" he asked his readers.[57]

Williams's history of US treaties with China was written with the perspective of an insider. After all, by this point he was not only a China expert by virtue of his missionary position, but also because of his later career within the US Legation to China in the 1850s and 1860s. He had served as an interpreter for Commodore Perry's expedition to China and Japan and was then, in 1855, appointed as US secretary and interpreter in China. When he wrote to Secretary of State William Marcy to request a raise, he could trust that Marcy and the members of the House who determined the budget would be "aware of his experience, reputation, and merits, in regard to Chinese dialects, customs, and affairs." As Marcy put it: "There is cause, indeed, to believe that, in those respects at least, he surpasses any individual in the service of any other government."[58] This trust in his expertise allowed him—like other missionaries of his time—to serve as missionary diplomats.

Williams ended his career as the Yale professor of Chinese and the president of the American Oriental Society. Like many other missionaries of the mid-nineteenth century, he would split his work between evangelism and assisting the American state. By virtue of their perceived expertise on international matters, these missionary diplomats were able to rise to positions of influence and put their expertise in the service of US foreign relations. As they did so, their missionary priorities became enmeshed in their government's diplomacy.

PART II

Missionary Troubles, 1840s–1880s

The front page of the *New York Times* on July 4, 1862, was full of news of war. Surrounding a map of recent battles, the paper informed readers of the immense losses on both sides of the ongoing Civil War, with a list of the recently killed and wounded carrying on for multiple columns into the interior of the paper. The long and bloody war would continue for several more years, but in Canton, US missionaries anticipated other news.[1]

On that day, the missionaries in China gathered to celebrate US independence. By 1862, the US presence in China had grown far beyond what Samuel Wells Williams had experienced. New treaties had opened up more and more of China to US trade and evangelization, and missionary organizations had taken full advantage of the opportunity. Canton alone was home to missionaries of multiple denominations from Pennsylvania, Ohio, Mississippi, New York, Connecticut, South Carolina, Maryland, West Virginia, and Tennessee—an interesting mix of Americans from northern and southern states. On the Fourth of July, this group gathered to reflect on the civil war that had been tearing their country apart on the other side of the world. The missionaries were hopeful. The last they heard, New Orleans had fallen to Union forces. They had every expectation that soon the Civil War would be over, the

Union would be restored, and even the southern missionaries found this to be good news.

In a collective letter, they thanked President Abraham Lincoln for the "great service he has rendered to our native land." They understood the war to be a "national calamity." The United States had to trust in God for deliverance. But the missionaries also trusted in the earthly power of the United States. As they wrote to the secretary of state, they insisted that they had "every confidence in the wisdom and integrity" of the government. They felt so strongly about it that they wrote these thoughts down, signing their names alongside their home states, and sent them directly to the government in Washington, all the way from China.[2]

Three years later, with the war finally over, the Americans in Bangkok gathered to celebrate the Fourth of July. The sermon at that gathering, delivered by missionary and former consul Stephen Mattoon, described the Union's victory as his country's "resurrection" now that the "curse of slavery" had finally been ended in the United States. Similar sermons could be heard from pulpits throughout the United States on that day, but Mattoon was in Siam (Thailand), and he took the opportunity to muse on the international implications of America's status as the home of liberty in the world.

The US flag, Mattoon reflected, was the symbol of liberty throughout the world. American missionaries, as citizens of the United States with unique opportunities to transform foreign cultures, had a role to play in spreading not only the gospel, but what he called "the principles of liberty" abroad. It would be hard work; the missionary described Bangkok as "heavy laden with oppression." But in time, liberty would reign even there, through the grace of God and the "moral means" of the American missionaries.[3]

These missionary expressions of patriotism—and of the importance of their US citizenship—were not new in the Civil War era, and they were not limited to Independence Day. Decades earlier, Rev. Eli Smith had preached to an audience of "weather-beaten sailors" and curious onlookers from a pulpit fashioned out of a flag-covered capstan on the *Delaware*, then visiting the missionary's city of Beirut. As he preached behind the stars and stripes, Smith took his theme as "the unequalled privileges" of the United States, especially in comparison to the "land of darkness" where the Americans now found themselves. As he prayed for the "light from heaven" to descend on Beirut, Smith was overtaken by emotion and wept. It had been years since Smith had been in the United

States, and the distance only served to make him more convinced of the superiority of his home country.[4]

Through the middle decades of the century, missionaries continued to provide US audiences with intelligence about the world at large. These were years of profound transformation. Within the United States, they were years of social and political upheaval, civil war, and its aftermath. Divisions touched nearly every part of American life. These years saw the fracturing of the Union, followed by the rebuilding of a new and much more centralized federal state. Within the churches, passionate debates over slavery divided denominations along sectional lines and raised challenging new questions about religion and politics. The war ended slavery but was soon followed by racial segregation and violence that was paired with new theories about race and racial difference rooted in white supremacy. Through all of this turmoil, US Christians continued sending missionaries out into the world.

These missionaries found a world in similar turmoil. Asian nations faced increasing aggression from European empires and internal rebellions. In Africa and the Pacific Islands, European empires sought new colonies. Nationalist and republican movements remade the landscape of Europe, Latin America, and the Middle East, creating new nation-states and challenging the ability of large empires to maintain rule over vast holdings. The decades from the 1840s through the 1880s were years of profound transition in global politics and the world economy.

At the center of much of this turmoil were questions about power, justice, and civilization that had long animated the missionary movement. Nationalist movements and wars for empire challenged Americans to consider the logic behind the division of humanity into distinct communities. What unites a group of people? Who or what creates the hierarchies that determine their relative power? Missionaries approached these political questions with a commitment to the ultimate sovereignty of God. But that commitment was shaped by a conviction that God favored the sort of republican government, capitalist economy, and liberal educational institutions that they knew in the United States. For mid-century missionaries, this faith emerged as a particular kind of missionary patriotism.

Missionaries did not only think about these things on the Fourth of July, or when a naval ship happened to pass through. Throughout the middle of the nineteenth century, their relationship to the United States mattered. Citizenship was both a practical issue of protection and a profound matter of identity. Missionaries continued their earlier role

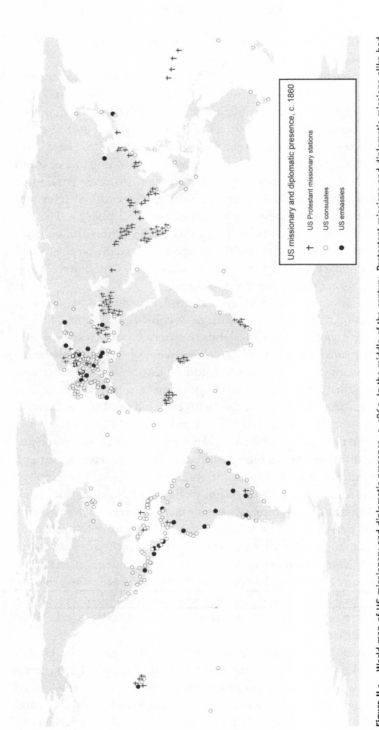

Figure II.1. World map of US missionary and diplomatic presence, c. 1860. In the middle of the century, Protestant missions and diplomatic missions alike had expanded across the globe, though the two continued to focus on slightly different geographies. In the decades after the Civil War, the number of Americans abroad from both groups would grow immensely.

Sources: Department of State, *List of Ministers, Consuls, and Other Diplomatic and Commercial Agents of the United States, in Foreign Countries* (Washington: Department of State, 1859); Methodist Episcopal Church, *Fortieth Annual Report of the Society of the Methodist Episcopal Church* (New York: Printed for the Society, 1859); Rev. J. Logan Aikman, *Cyclopedia of Christian Missions: Their Rise, Progress, and Present Position* (London: Richard Griffin and Company, 1860); Presbyterian Church in the USA, *The Twenty-Second Annual Report of the Board of Foreign Missions of the Presbyterian Church in the United States of America* (New York: Published for the Board at the Mission House, 1859); William Gammell, *A History of American Baptist Missions in Asia, Africa, Europe, and North America, Under the Care of the American Baptist Missionary Union* (Boston: Gould and Lincoln, 1854); ABCFM, *Report of the American Board of Commissioners for Foreign Mis-*

Within figure legend:

US missionary and diplomatic presence, c. 1860

+ US Protestant missionary stations
○ US consulates
● US embassies

as unofficial ambassadors. Through missionary intelligence, they represented the world to the United States and the United States to the world. But as the missionary movement grew, it demanded that the US government grow along with it. Through years of turmoil at home and abroad, American missionaries wanted and needed connections to their home government.

In these decades, missionaries appealed for an increased consular footprint for the United States. Consuls, whose official duties focused on the protection of US trade, could also be key to the success of missionary work. As representatives of the US state, their support could protect and even enable missionary endeavors. In the 1840s and 1850s, missionaries found that the US government, while not always present in the regions where missionaries were most active, was generally sympathetic with the goals and work of the Protestant missionaries.

Missionaries, after all, were citizens of the United States. As such, they had the right to the protection of their government when they were abroad. Occasionally, missionaries found themselves in great need of that protection. Their increasing demands on the government gave rise to new questions about what rights, exactly, missionaries had that the government needed to protect. US citizens had the right to government protection when they were going about legitimate business overseas. But what, exactly, *was* missionary business? And to the extent that missionary business was evangelism, when and how should the US government protect it?

The answer to this question had important implications for the legal interpretation of missionaries' relationship to the US government. The twin commitments of the United States to religious liberty and the separation of church and state made this a tricky question to answer. Missionary methods had, by the Civil War era, become quite diverse. Missionaries evangelized, of course, and they continued to write about the world for US audiences. They also translated scripture and published books and periodicals of multiple genres into foreign languages. They founded schools, colleges, medical dispensaries, and hospitals. After the Civil War, the creation of women's mission boards further diversified missionary methods and personnel. Missionaries could be ordained male ministers, or they could be men with certain types of professional training (doctors, printers, and the like). They could be wives or unmarried women who were more likely to serve as teachers, nurses, or doctors than as evangelists. All of this was missionary work. For the missionaries, all of it was religious. For the US government, however, some practices were more obviously religious than others.

By the 1880s, this question of what counted as religious began to create more and more challenges for missionaries in their interactions with foreign governments. "Missionary troubles," as the State Department termed these issues, appeared with growing frequency in the correspondence between the mission boards and the State Department. In the post–Civil War era of increased power in the central government, politicians in Washington began to notice the ways that missionaries seemed to be driving US interests in key regions of the globe, including Asia and the Middle East.

Missionary troubles—and the State Department's response to them—took many forms in the years between 1840 and 1890. Foreign missionaries claimed the rights of citizenship. Missionaries worked for the government as consuls and interpreters. When they faced violent opposition, they demanded their government intervene to protect them. Sometimes, however, the troubles that they got into seemed self-inflicted. By the last decades of the century, as the State Department grew in its size, professional organization, and knowledge about missionary regions, diplomats and others began to wonder if missionaries might be less victims and more troublemakers. They debated the meaning of missionary labor and its status as religious or secular. Throughout these complex discussions, however, missionaries and diplomats alike recognized that the mission movement and the United States were connected by similar goals and a similar vision of the United States as a force for good in the world.

CHAPTER 3

Citizens

In 1839, the French frigate *L'Artémise* arrived in Hawai'i with an ultimatum. French merchants had been increasingly incensed by their treatment on the islands over the past two decades. The wine and brandy they hoped to trade were not permitted on the islands; Catholic worship, too, was not freely permitted. If the Hawaiian kingdom did not agree to a new treaty and a significant payment, the frigate would blockade the harbor and attack.[1] The goals could be summarized briefly: commercial access, religious freedom, and extraterritoriality. In many ways, these demands would be echoed in other ports by representatives of the United States in the decades to come.

The French captain Cyrille Pierre Laplace did not communicate only with the Hawaiian government. He also brought a message for the US consul. He promised safety for all US residents on the islands—except for the missionaries. France, he explained, considered the American missionaries to be "a part of the native population." The French blamed the missionaries for many of the difficulties they faced on the islands. Missionaries "direct [the king's] counsels, influence his conduct, and are the true authors of the insults given by him to France," Laplace claimed. If war came between France and Hawai'i, the missionaries would have to suffer alongside their flock.[2] Remembering these events later, the missionaries recalled feeling both shocked and frightened. They gathered together and united in a hymn, seeking safety under God at a time when "their own government afforded none."[3] The French refused to recognize their rights as US citizens, and it was unclear what their country would or could do to protect them.

Within the United States, Protestant observers were shocked by France's behavior in Hawai'i. The kingdom, these Americans argued, had every right to prefer Protestantism to Catholicism. The *North American Review*, for example, summed up the root of the conflict: France was willing to go to war to "compel" another country to welcome Catholic worship.[4] The Hawaiian government was entirely in its right, the *Review* insisted. Prohibiting native access to Catholic worship may have been "indiscreet and unjust," but the government was not acting inappropriately.[5] The Hawaiian government had as much right to their course of action as Massachusetts might have "to prevent a half dozen Hindoo widows burning themselves alive any Sunday evening on Boston Common."[6] Sovereignty, the US missionaries and their supporters believed, entitled a state to exclude or welcome religious groups as it saw fit.

This, at least, was what they said when the group being excluded was Catholic. American Protestant missionaries often found themselves excluded by local governments who did not grant them the full scope of religious freedom that missionaries demanded. While government-established religions could (and did) shape missionary methods around the world, they rarely deterred missionaries from any and all attempts to evangelize. In the Ottoman Empire, China, Greece, and elsewhere, American missionaries did what they could to circumvent restrictions and assert their right to live and work freely where they chose. In such cases, US missionaries might, like the French priests in Hawai'i, turn to their government to protect their right to evangelize. Hawai'i was unique in the extent to which US Protestant missionaries found encouragement from the local government. Yet even here, as the crisis with *L'Artemise* revealed, it was far from clear how much protection they could expect from their own government when troubles arose. Throughout the mid-nineteenth century, missionaries and diplomats alike raised new questions about what citizenship rights missionaries had that the US government might have to protect.

The meaning of religious liberty was central to these discussions, as was the legal principle of extraterritoriality. In the Hawaiian case, American observers were shocked that the French wanted to violate "that universal principle of international jurisprudence, that every state shall try offenses committed within its jurisdiction." By allowing a Frenchman in Hawai'i to be tried not by the Hawaiian legal system, but by a special system in which he would be judged by his own countrymen, they argued, extraterritoriality would allow foreigners to entirely evade the law.[7] Yet at other times and places—such as when US missionaries were found in violation of local laws and facing unsympathetic legal systems—the United States would find itself sounding much like France as it demanded redress.

This was not mere hypocrisy; rather, it reflects how Protestant missionary goals could influence US foreign policy goals. In Hawai'i, Americans found French extraterritoriality inappropriate because it attempted to supersede laws that supported contemporary Protestant worship and values. A few years later, US diplomats come to a very different conclusion in Greece when US missionary Jonas King was brought to trial for violating laws that protected the Greek Orthodox Church. In China, extraterritoriality would be a longstanding goal of US and European diplomacy.

The Hawaiians signed the treaty with the French and paid the money. War did not come. But the questions raised by this incident are important for understanding the place of missionaries in the US diplomatic landscape. After all, the French had named them as outside of the proper circle of American protection: in moving to Hawai'i and working closely with the Hawaiian government, they had become, according to the French, Hawaiian themselves. But the missionaries, and many American supporters both inside and outside the government, continued to see Protestant missionaries as US citizens who went into the world to represent, if not their country, then their countrymen. As such, they demanded respect and protection.

Often, they got it. Lobbying efforts from missionary organizations in the United States and the often quite close relationships between missionaries and diplomats abroad meant that the US government could not ignore missionaries, even if it had wanted to. Defining the rights of missionaries became a vexing task for the US government. As Americans worked out the meaning of citizenship at home, missionary claims became a key venue for determining the full extent of citizenship rights in the mid-nineteenth century.

The Rights of Missionary Citizenship

Over the course of the antebellum decades, Americans were determining the meaning of citizenship in part through the experiences—and particularly the challenges—of Americans abroad. Sailors and missionaries forced the US government to consider what rights citizens had when they left the shores of the United States and what, if any, limits there were to which types of people could claim the protection of their government. There were no obvious answers. Citizenship was not defined in the US Constitution. Did moving to another country for the rest of your life involve revoking your citizenship? Did marriage to a non-American affect one's citizenship? What about the citizenship of children born abroad? Missionaries confronted all of these questions and more in the 1830s and 1840s. None of them had clear answers in the decades before Reconstruction.[8]

With the meaning of citizenship in flux, it is little wonder that Laplace's claim that missionaries had forfeited their right to be considered US citizens struck a nerve. As much as the missionaries bristled at Laplace's disrespect for Hawaiian sovereignty, they were far more upset by his suggestion that they had been involved in—had, in fact, orchestrated—the persecution of Catholics in Hawai'i and had thus forfeited their claims to protection as US citizens.[9] As they sought to defend themselves, the missionaries had to address questions about their relationship with the government, the appropriate limits of missionary intervention, and the implications that missionary work had on their identity as US citizens.

Laplace based his claims on stories about the arrival of two Catholic priests, one French and one Irish, in 1827, seven years after the US missionaries began their work in the Sandwich Islands. These were years of turmoil and change within Hawaiian politics and culture. Two leaders claimed the power of the regency: Boki, the governor of Oahu, and Kaahumanu, the mother of the king and a devoted Protestant convert. It was Boki who had invited the priests, only to have them denied the right to preach to any but foreigners. Kaahumanu ordered them off the islands and provided a boat to carry the priests to California. Meanwhile, the Hawaiian government began a to arrest Catholic converts, considering some Catholic practices to be a violation of anti-idolatry laws. Some of these Catholics were sentenced to hard labor.[10] Laplace asserted that this persecution was the work, not of the Hawaiian government, but of the US Protestant missionaries. They had insinuated themselves into the government, he claimed, and advanced their own goals at the expense of religious liberty. The Protestant missionaries were certainly anti-Catholic. However, it was not immediately clear if they had actually been a force behind the laws against Catholicism in the Sandwich Islands. It was also not clear whether doing so would have involved relinquishing their US citizenship.

American Protestant missionaries did have a close relationship with the Hawaiian chiefs, many of whom were Protestant converts. In the same year as Laplace's arrival, the missionaries would even open a new boarding school especially for the children of chiefs to train them for future leadership.[11] It was understandable, then, that the French would have assumed missionary involvement in anti-Catholic persecution. Proof, however, was hard to demonstrate. In official correspondence, the king asserted all of the laws originated with himself and the chiefs. The missionaries, he insisted, played no part.[12]

Critics, however, found many hints of missionary malfeasance. It was hard for them to imagine that the kingdom had acted without outside influence. Critics and missionaries alike understood the Hawaiians to be childlike and in need of guidance.[13] In this context, foreign observers easily assumed that missionary influence was pervasive. American merchants, too, complained about missionary influence on the islands. An anonymous report of the event spent seventy-two pages countering missionary claims of innocence. Missionaries believed it was written by J. C. Jones, a former US consul with whom they had frequently been in conflict. The missionaries had not kept out of politics, Jones claimed, and they drastically understated the reality of Catholic persecution. At the very least, missionaries were aware of atrocities and responded without compassion. But Jones suggested that the missionaries' actions were far more nefarious.[14]

Jones's main focus was on the brutal treatment of Hawaiian Catholics. The pamphlet's illustrations depict bare-chested women tied to trees and lashed, only for the "unpardonable crime of believing in the church of Rome." He tells of mothers with babies slung on their backs being forced to bear heavy stones to build a wall in Honolulu. Damningly, he claims that Hiram Bingham, one of the founding ABCFM missionaries on the islands, witnessed this but still described Catholic Hawaiians to US audiences as "deluded pagans" who had not yet learned of the truth of the Christian God.[15]

Bingham appears at several points in the pamphlet as a shadowy figure behind the Hawaiian government's anti-Catholicism. While Jones had little direct proof of missionary interference, he provides plenty of suggestive moments. He includes, for example, blistering anti-Catholic extracts from the geography textbook that missionaries printed on their press and used in their classrooms. He tells of Protestant missionaries who would "thunder from the pulpit" against the priests.[16] Again and again, Jones asserts that Kaahumanu was acting under *the advice and counsel of the American missionaries whose influence with that chiefess* [sic] *had more force, than any he had at that period been able to call into requisition.*"[17] Jones's most suggestive charges, however, come when he describes the role of Bingham as a translator in key moments of negotiation about the treatment of Catholics in Hawai'i.

One particularly tense moment arose in a meeting between Commodore John Downes of the US frigate *Potomac* and Kaahumanu. Downes had been horrified to find Catholics forced into hard labor and, like Laplace, urged the Hawaiian regent to adopt a policy of tolerance. Downes couched his suggestion in the language of religious liberty and civilization, insisting that in civilized countries, people were not punished for their religious beliefs. Catholic countries, he warned, *"might not view with indifference, such cruel treatment of Catholics."* This call for tolerance was, Jones argued, "liberal and truly Christian advice," but the Protestant missionaries did not see it this way. Bingham was present at this meeting, acting as translator. The missionary inserted himself into the conversation, insisting that the Hawaiian authorities were justified in their actions since not all civilized countries, and certainly not Spain, practiced religious toleration. Few present, Jones reflected, would "soon forget" Bingham's intervention.[18]

Bingham and the other missionaries taught that Catholicism was idolatry, a claim that was particularly loaded given its association for Christians with the traditional religion of the Sandwich Islands. They also taught that Catholicism had a history of inspiring its adherents to "wield the civil power and become the rulers of the country." They fully supported, even encouraged, the interpretation of Catholic worship as an antigovernment practice.[19]

In 1837, when the Catholic priests had been forced on board a ship and ordered to leave the island, Bingham again served as Kaahumanu's translator in her discussions with the visiting captains of British and French ships. The captains demanded the priests' immediate release. Bingham, far from simply translating what was being said, worked together with Kaahumanu to argue with what Jones described as "obstinacy and boldness." When the king arrived ten days later to continue negotiations, the captains refused to allow Bingham to continue as interpreter, removing the missionary from the conversation.[20]

Though the missionaries generally denied Jones's charges of government interference, there was some truth to his claims. While missionaries were not the authors of the laws against Catholics, they had indeed influenced the culture that led to the laws' adoption. The missionaries had debated whether they should, as a body, intervene to protect Catholics against persecution. The missionaries were of two minds. In the first place, they agreed that the Hawaiian government had the right to send the priests away and was under no obligation to welcome them into the kingdom. They agreed, too, that it was for the best that Catholic worship be banned, lest the Hawaiians be led astray. Yet they also understood that religious toleration was, as missionary Sheldon Dibble put it, "a principle of freedom which was of immense value to the world." As they could not decide between these competing perspectives, the Sandwich Islands missionaries decided that, as a group, they would do nothing. As individuals, however, they could answer questions truthfully if they were asked.[21]

Did any of this suggest that the missionaries had somehow forfeited their right to be respected as US citizens? The *l'Artemise* incident had left missionaries shaken. If foreign nations could deny their rights to be considered US citizens, what protections did they have? Missionaries eagerly queried representatives of the US government. Shortly after the departure of *l'Artemise*, the US frigate *Columbia* arrived in harbor. The missionaries asked Commodore George C. Read to launch an investigation into the question of their rights. Read demurred. Though polite in his response to the missionaries, he was not inclined to be drawn into this matter. The time for action had passed. With the French gone, there was no longer a direct threat. Any broader discussion about how to respond to the events should happen in Washington. Missionaries were US citizens, Read understood. They should trust their government to act appropriately.[22] But they did not yet have this claim positively affirmed by the government.

The ABCFM addressed this question of missionary citizenship at their 1841 Annual Meeting. Rufus Anderson, corresponding secretary of the ABCFM and the driving force behind its vision, assured the crowd that missionaries "retain their citizenship wherever they may be sent." This citizenship was never renounced. Rather, like merchants and other Americans whose work might take them to live abroad for some period of time, their core identity as Americans continued. They went out in service of organizations, like the ABCFM, that had been incorporated by state governments (in the case of the ABCFM, by Massachusetts in 1810) and thus, in at least this small way, had their work legitimized by state governments. And the federal government, well aware of their missionary identities, had issued them passports, essential documents of citizenship, signifying the government's own legitimation of missionary work. Just like merchants, Anderson and others argued, missionaries were fully within their rights to go about their legitimate business abroad.[23]

Both the State Department and missionaries made this comparison of missionaries to merchants as they discussed missionary rights of citizenship. The government protected merchants and their interests; so, too, it should protect missionaries and *their* interests.[24] Secretary of State Daniel Webster assured Hawaiian missionaries that they were "as much entitled to protection as merchants or sailors."[25] In a "commercial nation," as Thomas Scott Williams, a chief justice of the Connecticut Supreme Court and member of the ABCFM argued, it would be "most alarming" to deprive citizenship rights from those who had to reside abroad.[26] But the long experience of merchants revealed that Americans did not give up their rights on leaving their home country. Missionary supporters' belabored explanations of this logic suggest the potential difficulties that they faced. Missionaries, after all, were not really like merchants.

Justice Williams, in fact, argued that missionaries were better than merchants, going out into the world "not for his own good, but the good of others." For his part, Anderson highlighted the unique role of missionary work and other aspects of the ministry as fulfilling a "divine appointment." For both men, and for the audience of missionary supporters they were addressing, these divine and benevolent roles did not remove missionaries from the body politic. Far from it. Anderson was quick to note that missionaries served as "the agents, in this business, of a very numerous and respectable body of citizens." Acting on behalf of "many hundred thousands" in the United States, their rights were inextricably connected with those of their supporters at home. Williams went a step further. A missionary was "an ambassador," not of his government, but "the representative of a great number of his fellow citizens, to communicate knowledge to the ignorant and happiness to the miserable."[27]

The type of official statement that Sandwich Island missionaries had been seeking from the US government finally came in 1842. In that year, Secretary of State Daniel Webster instructed Commodore David Porter, the US ambassador to the Ottoman Empire, to extend protection to missionaries "in the same manner that you would to other citizens of the United States."[28] As in the Sandwich Islands case, there was considerable pressure from missionary supporters in the United States on the federal government to take such a stand in Ottoman territory. Missionary supporters celebrated Webster for this statement.[29] For his help to the cause of foreign missions, he was given an honorary membership in the ABCFM.[30]

Citizenship and Rights

The situation in the Middle East was different than that in the Sandwich Islands. Here it was not a fellow Western power that was refusing to recognize the citizenship rights of US missionaries, but a host government. Missionaries of the ABCFM had come into conflict with the Maronite Church in 1841 and were ordered to leave the region. When the missionaries asked for Ambassador Porter's assistance, he refused. In Porter's reading, the existing treaty between the United States and the Ottoman Empire were purely commercial in nature. Nothing in it allowed for the protection of American evangelism, and so he told the missionaries that he could not be of any help to them. If they were told to leave, they should go. In their capacity as missionaries, they were outside of his—and by extension the US government's—protection.[31] The missionaries, unsatisfied with this response, appealed again for help to the US consul in Beirut and then to supporters in the United States who could reach out to the secretary of state.

In the missionaries' telling, they had broken no laws. Their work did not disturb the peace, and the complaint from the Maronite Patriarch seemed unfounded. The missionaries had no relationship with the Maronite Church. They did not open any schools for Maronite students, did not operate in Maronite regions, and had not admitted any members of the Maronite Church to communion. For fifteen years they had operated in Syria without complaint, focusing their Beirut school on the Druze population. As they described their work, these missionaries positioned themselves as the victims of religious persecution. The Maronite Patriarch had "an inveterate enmity against Protestant Christianity." As evidence of this claim, they explained that the Bibles that were published by the Protestant press were collected and burnt; one convert had died in jail as a martyr. The laws of the Ottoman Empire, as the missionaries understood them, ought to protect their work. Christians were granted "liberty of Conscience." They were supposed to have the freedom to change sects if they so desired. Yet these rights were ignored; Protestant missionaries and converts alike were ill-treated.[32]

Unlike the converts, however, missionaries carried US passports. They understood these documents to guarantee them "the rights common to all American Citizens within the Dominions of the Sultan." Those rights, they claimed, included the right to remain where they were and to go about their business as missionaries. As they appealed to the US government for help, missionaries insisted that they fully understood the relevant local laws—wherever they served, they claimed to study the laws that they would need to obey. Now that they felt themselves to persecuted by this foreign power, they demanded their government to take action to defend them.[33]

Importantly, missionaries had powerful allies in the United States as they made this request. Samuel Turell Armstrong, a member of the ABCFM and the former governor of Massachusetts, agreed with their interpretation of things, and he said as much in his letter to Daniel Webster. Porter had effectively "denationalized" the missionaries, he argued, by refusing to protect them from removal. But much of Armstrong's argument was based in European practice, not Ottoman law. American missionaries should have the right to evangelize and to demand US government protection because British missionaries enjoyed this protection from *their* government. In the absence of a strong US diplomatic response, the American missionaries would need to turn to British officials for protection. What was at stake, Armstrong implied, was not just religious freedom, but America's international standing. Americans needed more consuls in the region who were willing to support missionaries' presence, in Armstrong's eyes. This would help to resolve what he found to be a "very embarrassing" situation for US missionaries.[34]

While Webster and President John Tyler agreed that the government should defend Protestant missionaries' right to remain and go about their work, it was not clear to all US diplomats that these were rights that missionaries actually possessed. Porter, for one, remained resistant. He explained to Webster that the existing treaty governing relations between the United States and the Ottoman Empire did not give US citizens "any right to interfere with the subjects of the Sublime Porte." Missionaries, he insisted, simply did not have the right to go wherever they wanted to go. And the US government did not have the right to force other governments to accept missionaries where they weren't wanted.[35]

The official policy that Webster put forward required diplomats to extend missionaries the same defense they would give to any US citizens, but what this actually meant going forward could be hard to define. US citizens had the right to reside in foreign countries as they went about their lawful business. But not everyone agreed about how "lawful" the business of evangelism was.

Questions about the "rights of missionaries" arose in West Africa, too. In Gabon, the French accused missionary John Leighton Wilson of being "the instigator" behind anticolonial resistance. As in Hawai'i, Westerners seemed to have a hard time attributing resistance to any indigenous sources and looked for outside influences. The missionaries became the ones to blame. When the French began shooting cannons at the coast and threatening the mission house, Wilson flew the US flag in an effort to assert his neutrality in the struggle with the French. This was not effective. Instead of being taken as a sign of neutrality, the French ship took it as a sign of aggression and began firing at the flag and the mission house.[36]

Was this the right move? Wilson would later ask visiting US vessels if it was appropriate for him as a "private citizen" to claim the protection of the US flag. All agreed that this was, indeed, a proper signal of his neutrality. But Wilson still wanted to know: What could he expect from his government in the face of such "outrages" against his person and his property? It was "a matter of some importance to American missionaries," he wrote in an 1845 letter that would later be published in the *Missionary Herald*, the ABCFM's periodical. Missionaries, he granted, were "not the political representatives of [their] country," but did it follow that they had "no political character distinct from the savage tribes among whom they may be found?" Did becoming a missionary, in other words, require a renunciation of the right to be respected as a US citizen? This could not be the case. But, he worried, this seemed to be how the French were looking at it. And missionaries around the world needed answers.[37]

The government, however, made no further response. In 1848, writers at the *New York Evangelist* asked again if the US government had a duty to protect the citizenship rights of missionaries. Again drawing on comparisons to merchants and sailors who could depend on the protection of the US government when they went out into the world for self-interest and trade, the article asked if "the benevolent considerations that move [missionaries] to their work make them aliens or outlaws, and involve a forfeiture of the rights of citizenship and protection?" The stakes were high. The answer to this question would reveal, the article concluded, "whether the government is made for the people, or the people for the government."[38]

The Trials of Jonas King

Mission supporters would get their answer when the government came to the defense of missionary Jonas King, on trial in Greece. King's incendiary writings against Islam in the 1820s had gained him an enthusiastic following among some US missionary supporters who appreciated his reputation as a particular kind of rugged and chauvinistic missionary.[39] King's early missionary career in Palestine had been spent in the Islamic world navigating how to work under a government that did not welcome Christians or Protestant missions, and the beginning of his time in Greece seemed to promise new opportunities. He arrived ready to help the country rebuild itself after the Greek War of Independence, excited to be in a Christian country that he had spent years depicting as the helpless victim of Islamic brutality. King sought first to distribute humanitarian relief from his fellow citizens, but his attention soon shifted to the sorts of long-term aid that missionaries across the globe understood to be essential to building Christian civilization: schools. In this effort, King initially received the approval and even the gratitude of the Greek government. But quite quickly, he would find himself in conflict with his hosts.[40]

If being in a Christian country created missionary opportunities, it also brought new challenges. The Greek Church was not Protestant. Greece was, for King and for many Protestants, missionary ground. King's mission was sponsored by the ABCFM, but he had American colleagues from other missionary societies as well: the Episcopal and Baptist denominations both supported Greek missions in these years. All focused on schools, scriptural translation into modern Greek, and the distribution of the Bible and other religious texts. This work would later be described by a US diplomat as the spread of "general knowledge," rather than sectarian evangelism. King insisted that he was not proselytizing.[41]

That claim was important, for proselytizing on behalf of Protestant churches was against Greek law. Greek officials did not share King's interpretation of his work. On no less than three occasions, Jonas King was charged with violating Greek laws about religion. In response, King aggressively asserted his right to religious liberty, also guaranteed in the Greek

Constitution, and argued with the government and his Greek detractors over doctrinal issues and the meaning of religious freedom.

King was not just a missionary. In spite of his frequent run-ins with the Greek government, he had been appointed to consular office. When Greece sentenced him to banishment in 1853, King called on the US State Department to intervene and protect his right to remain in Greece while working as a missionary. Like missionary diplomats elsewhere, King advocated for a US foreign policy that supported Protestant missionaries' freedom to evangelize. The State Department, under Daniel Webster and Edward Everett, supported this endeavor.

King's troubles began in 1845. In that year, the ABCFM's missionary manual included passports on their list of necessary items that missionaries would need to obtain before they traveled, alongside collared shirts with strong seams (to stand up to laundering on stones) and a select private library. These passports were "essential" for those missionaries who settled in "eastern countries," and King would soon discover why.[42]

King first came into trouble when he was charged with "impious language" about Mary, the Mother of God. Protestants like King found Greek Orthodox veneration of Mary to be idolatrous, and King openly disagreed with the Orthodox contention that Mary had remained a virgin throughout her life. In his defense, King assembled (and later published) writings from Orthodox Fathers that supported his interpretation of Christian doctrine. For this, he was charged with "falsifying the testimony of the fathers." The charges, and King's characteristically bombastic response to them, led to repeated threats. In 1847, King briefly left Greece for fear of his safety, only to return in 1848. Briefly chastened, King waited a few years before preaching again, but he continued distributing Protestant texts.

In 1851, King again found himself at the center of controversy in Greece. By this time, he had resumed preaching at the chapel in his home, and both the content of his preaching and his goals came under question. Chaos broke out one afternoon in March when a student asked to address the worshipers at the conclusion of the service. To the gathered crowd, which may have included members of the Greek House of Representatives, the student criticized King for many past sermons that had gone against various dogmas of the Greek Orthodox Church. When King tried to quiet him, the crowd insisted that the student be allowed to speak. The mood soon became tense, the crowd excitable. They refused to leave, even after King's wife asserted that this was a private home and they should go. They only did so after King brought out a United States flag and announced that they were not only gathered in his private home, but also in the US Consulate.[43]

King was indeed serving as consul at the time. While missionaries elsewhere served in similar capacities, King was an interesting choice for this role, considering his history of conflict with the Greek government. He would later tell this story in front of the US Senate, creating a "thrill" through those gathered there at this "glowing description of the power of the 'Stars and Stripes' to protect an American citizen."[44] Yet the flag itself was not enough to protect King from his troubles in Greece. Within months, he would face another criminal prosecution, this time for proselytizing and for malevolent speech against the Greek Orthodox Church. According to the charges, King's public discussions of doctrinal differences between the churches on such topics as Mary, the Mother of God, and the meaning of the eucharist amounted to attacks on the Greek Church, and thus, the Greek state.

Americans understood this case to be about religious freedom. Rufus Anderson would say the conflict was over the "freedom to worship God and preach the Gospel in Greece." Comparing King to Martin Luther, Anderson argued that this was a story about a much-needed and heroic reformer to a corrupt church.[45] This grandiose claim ignored the complex political factors at play, both within Greece itself and in Greco-US relations. It ignored, too, the different definitions of religious freedom that were at work in Greece and the United States at the time. During the trial and the international crisis that followed, Americans and Greeks debated the nature of religious tolerance, the importance of matters of doctrinal difference between different branches of Christianity, and the ability of foreign states to answer those questions for each other. For Americans, these questions again forced the issue of how much protection missionaries deserved or could expect from the federal government when they were overseas.

King had claimed that he did not proselytize or speak malevolently against the Greek Church, but his decades of history as an aggressive evangelist give credence to the claims of those who testified against him. Years earlier, King had been warned against similarly agitating a foreign government while traveling in France. There, he had been evangelizing among members of the French nobility and was warned by French Protestants that his "irrepressible" efforts could lead to trouble. In response, he asked his detractors if they would prefer that he "should be silent, and not speak the truths of the gospels" whenever and wherever the opportunity arose. Of course, he argued, he could not keep silent.[46] Similarly, King maintained that his speech against the Greek Church was unavoidable. As a Protestant, he must speak his beliefs. This would require him to speak against those of Orthodox Christians.

Just as he had been warned in France and, later, in Palestine, King had been warned in Greece to take care in how he talked about non-Protestant religions, lest he come into conflict with his host government. The schools in Greece had long been hot spots, largely due to the religious materials included in the curriculum. King refused to include the Greek catechism in his classrooms, while insisting on keeping the translated scriptures. In 1835, one supporter in Greece warned King that his schools were causing enough unrest that some worried that a "civil war on the subject of religion" might break out as a result of Greek audiences being unprepared "for such a change as those [Protestant] doctrines would bring in."[47] Yet King did not heed this warning. In his journals and published writings, King was scathing in his description of Greece and Greek Christianity. Greek Christians "profane the temple of the Lord," he wrote, "and seem to know but little of the nature of Christianity."[48] His role, as he understood it, was to correct their error.

King's students and others described him as eager to discuss religious topics, including controversial ones, in an attempt to convince others of the wrongness of Greek doctrine. Converts praised King for this practice. One reflected on how King was relentless in the face of the convert's early "obstinacy." He recalled King's efforts to explain the ways that Greek doctrines ("all essentially Roman-catholic") were in fact "in direct opposition to the gospel." He remained grateful that King "would not leave me to my blindness."[49] These same personality traits and actions would appear much less positive to Orthodox observers and the Greek government. Greek newspapers, for example, covered his attacks on Orthodoxy, and King did little to hide his actions.[50]

Accordingly, King was found guilty and sentenced to fifteen days in prison, followed by banishment from Greece. It was only at this point that King and his missionary brethren called on the US government to defend their rights as US citizens to peacefully reside in Greece as active Protestant missionaries. In 1852, King's missionary peers from the American Baptist Missionary Union and the Protestant Episcopal Church wrote to Abbot Lawrence, at the US Embassy in London, with a difficult request. They well understood that the US government would be reluctant to interfere in the workings of a foreign court system, especially one of a "friendly government." But they were quite sure that intervention was exactly what King needed. Their government needed to investigate "whether his *rights also* as a Citizen of the US residing here under the protection of the Laws of this Country have not been infringed, and his *religious liberty assailed*, by the proceedings in his case."[51]

King's case initially found a reluctant audience in President Millard Fillmore, who found US action to be unjustified. The two countries, he believed, were operating with different definitions of religious freedom and the missionaries' attempts to assert an American meaning to Greek laws were inappropriate. As more and more letters came to the State Department in support of King and protesting his treatment by the Greek government, however, Fillmore changed his mind. Secretary of State Daniel Webster had no such reservations. Webster, who had previously been celebrated by missionary supporters for his firm affirmation of missionary citizenship rights during his first term as secretary of state in 1842, was happy to restate this earlier policy in defense of missionaries.[52]

President Fillmore was correct, though, that the meaning of religious freedom under Greek law was different from its meaning in the United States. The Greek Constitution guaranteed toleration of other religious groups. For some groups, such as Catholics, these rights were further buttressed by treaties with European powers. There was, however, no statement of "universal religious liberty and equality" under Greek law, however much missionaries hoped to stretch the meaning of existing statutes. But the laws' emphasis on toleration created real constraints for missionary evangelism.

It all came down to the meaning of toleration. The Greek Penal Code of 1853 criminalized "reviling and malevolently assailing the doctrines, rites, or customs of *any* religious sect." Under this definition, proselytizing was criticism of other religions and thus illicit. American Protestant missionaries did not have the right to freely evangelize as they believed they did. But Americans like King insisted that it was impossible to explain evangelical Protestantism without, at least at times, speaking against those parts of the Orthodox Church that they disagreed with. Logically, they argued, if Protestant missionaries were to be tolerated, they needed to be able to vocally disagree with the Greek Orthodox Church. The Greek government disagreed.[53]

Webster's instructions to George Perkins Marsh, the US minister at Constantinople who was charged with assisting King, were quite clear. Marsh should conduct a thorough investigation into the relevant

Greek laws in order to determine if King's treatment had been fair or just. The US government, Webster explained, was unsure "precisely to what extent [religious] toleration is allowed in Greece," but had "good reason to believe" that Catholics, Jews, Muslims, and some Protestants had been allowed to expound on their views. In light of that, Webster was inclined to view King's treatment as "persecution" that required a robust response from the US government. The government would not protect citizens who violated local laws, but it would hold the Greek government to its treaty obligations to treat US citizens justly. Missionaries, Webster insisted, deserved protection on the same grounds as merchants, sailors, and soldiers.[54]

Quoting Thomas Scott Williams's statements from the 1841 discussion of missionary rights in Hawai'i, Webster informed Marsh that a missionary was "indeed, ambassador, not sent out by the government as their representative, but as the representative for great number of his fellow-citizens." As such, a missionary should expect full support from her government.[55] Webster ordered Marsh to travel from Constantinople to Athens aboard a US warship and called on the US Navy to keep part of its Mediterranean Squadron patrolling the area so long as Marsh remained in Greece.

Within weeks of his arrival in Athens, Marsh concluded his investigation. It was "past all doubt, that the government of Greece has treated Dr. King with flagrant injustice and bad faith," he found. The Greeks were guilty of an abuse of the legal principles of justice, and a perversion of the rules of law, as "flagitious as any that every disgraced the records of the Star Chamber." While he admitted that the forms of the law had not been violated, the "plain intent and meaning of the law" had.[56] Marsh found King to have been the victim of bad actors in the Greek government and deserving of US protection.

As a result, Marsh negotiated to have King's sentence revoked. King's banishment was reversed; he would remain in Greece until his death in 1869. It is easy to imagine a US government response that was much less supportive of King in his time of difficulty. After all, in only a few decades, diplomats would regularly refer to the "missionary troubles" that came about when US evangelists clashed with foreign laws. Yet King instead found enthusiastic support. The case was a landmark moment in the mid-century discussion of the rights of Americans abroad, and the duties of the US government to protect them.[57] Politicians and diplomats, in addition to missionaries, followed the case and boiled with indignation at King's treatment. Rejecting the Greek government's interpretation of the Greek constitution, they insisted that King's civil rights had been trampled and that his religious liberty had been denied.

The first decades of US missionary activity had brought challenges, certainly. What was new by the 1830s, 1840s, and 1850s was the response of the missionaries to those challenges. Now, they increasingly turned to their government for aid. This was a considerable shift. King and the Syria missionaries were not the first US missionaries who were told to leave their stations, after all. When the first group of US missionaries reached India in 1812, they were initially refused the right to remain. As they tried to fight back against their deportation, they never reached out to representatives of the US government for help. The idea did not occur to them. After all, there were none in Calcutta in 1812. Instead, the missionaries worked with British agents, missionaries, and eventually sympathetic officers of the East India Company to secure their right to work in Bombay. By the time that the missionaries in the Sandwich Islands, Syria, and Greece were facing challenges in the late-1830s and early 1840s, the opportunities for government aid had begun to grow.[58]

The twin goals of religious freedom and extraterritoriality were what had brought Laplace to the Sandwich Islands, and they would animate US missionaries at their various stations around the world. Defining both of these concepts, however, would remain contested for missionaries and diplomats alike. Throughout these many discussions, religious liberty remained a murky concept. In some ways, missionaries recognized that it was a deeply important right, but its application to their work was not always clear. The Americans ridiculed French claims in 1839 that religious toleration was "the established usage . . . of all civilized countries" and effectively a part of the law of nations.[59] Yet they simultaneously based their own claims to a freedom to evangelize in a broad understanding of both religious freedom and divine law. It was this reliance on divine law that ultimately undercut missionary claims that they should be treated like any other US citizens when they were abroad. Missionaries, after all, were not just like merchants.

CHAPTER 4

Consuls

In the summer of 1861, William Thayer was the new consul general for the United States in Egypt. He had hardly been in Alexandria a month when he met with the viceroy for the first time. The Egyptian leader peppered him for the latest news about the American Civil War as Thayer tried to change the subject to what he thought was a pressing matter: the protection of Faris-el-Hakim, a Syrian physician who had been working for American Presbyterian missionaries when he was attacked in a courtroom in Osiut (Asyut). The circumstances that brought Thayer to Faris's defense were somewhat unusual. Faris was neither a US citizen nor an American protégé with official connection to the United States. His employment by American Protestant missionaries, though, seemed enough to justify Thayer's attention and care. For Thayer—as for Secretary of State William Seward and President Abraham Lincoln—Faris's case would become an important test of both religious liberty around the world, and of the ability of the United States to lead, even in a time of national crisis.[1]

The story, which had only the most minor of connections to US diplomatic priorities, drew American attention with its combination of persecution and chivalry. Presbyterian missionaries Gulian Lansing, Samuel Ewing, and John Hogg hired Faris to travel about six hundred miles from Alexandria to Osiut, where he would distribute Bibles and other religious publications. The circulation of sacred texts was essential to their evangelism, and missionaries found that it could be more effective to have local Christians, rather than US missionaries, do this work. While there, Faris met a woman who needed his help. Though born a Christian, she had at some point become Muslim and now wished to renounce Islam and return to the church. Egypt had recently enacted new laws of religious toleration, which she hoped would allow her conversion to be recognized and accepted. In order to benefit from the legal protection of religious toleration, she would need to go in front of a court to formally declare this desire. She asked Faris to act as her attorney, and he agreed.

Once they arrived at the court, however, Faris found a large crowd of prominent citizens and "rabble" alike. Tensions were high. The government's promise of religious toleration meant little this far away from the reach of Alexandria. To the crowd at Osiut, Christianity was an "odious heresy," and Faris had placed himself in a difficult and dangerous position. He was forced to sit on the ground and was then bastinadoed, beaten, spat on, kicked, and maimed. He was imprisoned and only released when the jailor feared that he was dying. He survived, but he was left with permanent health complications.[2]

Faris's connection to the United States was slim. He was employed by the missionaries, but they never filled out the requisite paperwork for the local government that would have categorized Faris as an American protégé, under the protection of the US government. Yet after Faris was attacked, the missionaries immediately turned to the consular agent at Osiut, and then to Consul General Thayer. For Thayer, the missing paperwork was unimportant. He determined that Faris had been acting as the "agent and representative of two US citizens, engaged in a lawful missionary enterprise." Regardless of whether or not Faris met the formal definition of an American protégé, Thayer insisted that any attack on Faris was an attack on the missionaries. Accordingly, Thayer demanded that the Egyptian government respond quickly and decisively, just as he would have if the victim had been a US citizen. He demanded the imprisonment of the attackers, some of whom were officials in Osiut, and a hefty indemnity payment. In the end, thirteen men were sentenced to a year in prison (though pardoned after a bit more than a month) and Faris was granted 100,000 piastres (five thousand dollars) for his injuries.[3]

News of the case traveled to Washington, and President Lincoln expressed his gratitude to the viceroy for his "speedy" punishment of the Egyptian subjects who had been guilty of what the president called the "cruel persecution" of Faris. These events, Lincoln wrote, would be proof not only of the viceroy's friendship to the United States, but to the "firmness, integrity, and wisdom" of his government. The Christian world, Lincoln and Thayer alike claimed, would take notice.[4]

In his letter to the missionaries informing them of his success, Thayer expanded on this point. Clearly this was a victory for Faris and the missionaries, but it was more than this. It was, Thayer reflected, a victory for "the great multitude of Christians of all denominations—whether native or of foreign birth—throughout Egypt." And it was a victory for the United States. Thayer rejoiced that the US flag remained "as it always has been, the potent symbol alike of civil and religious liberty." The missionaries agreed. "As missionaries," they explained, they were glad that this particular decision advanced their work. But "as Americans," they took pride in this evidence of US influence toward "tolerance and right" in Egypt.

Thayer and the missionaries all agreed that Faris's case was about more than just this one particular story. It spoke to much larger issues: the influence of the United States in the world, US responsibility to stand for religious toleration and liberty around the globe, and the relationship between the American state and the missionary movement. The missionaries were grateful to Thayer for taking action as a consul and seeing the links between US and missionary goals. Not all consuls did so, but missionaries consistently believed that they should and complained when they didn't.

The consular system was an important arm of the Department of State in the nineteenth century. Its primary responsibility was to assist US commercial interests around the world. Accordingly, the consular system might seem at first glance to have little to do with missionary work. However, consuls could be extremely important missionary allies. Sympathetic consuls could help advance the missionary cause. They, like missionaries, at times assumed that commercial relations could only improve if non-Christian countries became Christianized.

"Civilization," many missionaries believed, was an essential byproduct of and companion to their evangelism. This realization was at the heart of much of the cooperation between the missionaries and the US government: both missionaries and consular officers often understood their goals to be linked. In spite of this, America's commercial and missionary interests could also clash. Not all consuls or all missionaries understood their work to be compatible. Conflicts overseas between US missionary and commercial representatives signaled important debates about the role of the United States in the world.

In Asia and the Middle East, US consuls took on particularly significant roles that went beyond commercial assistance. Here, missionaries and consuls were partners in shaping the American experience abroad. In these relationships, for good and ill, missionaries most directly faced the questions of how and when their religious and their political identities mattered.

The Consular System

In an era when the US diplomatic footprint was minimal, consuls were the main boots on the ground. American consuls could be found in international ports from the very beginning of the United States. Global commerce was a central goal of early US foreign relations, and so the consular system was an important component of US engagement with the world. By the middle of the century, the consular system had grown at an impressive rate, with more and more consuls appointed overseas to assist the flow of international commerce. In major port cities, US consuls served alongside the consular officers of other foreign nations maintaining the paperwork that allowed ships to carry goods to and from the United States.

The US consular presence in missionary lands expanded at mid-century. On an 1828 list of diplomatic and commercial officers of the United States, none were listed in East or Southeast Asia, the Pacific, or the Middle East—all regions that already had a US missionary presence. Two years later, the Sandwich Islands had a commercial agent, China had a consul, and the Ottoman dominions had a chargé d'affaires, a dragoman, and a consul, all of whom were based in Constantinople. These numbers would climb over the coming decades, with consuls soon being placed in Bombay, Singapore, and more locations in Turkey and Egypt. It was only in the 1840s that China welcomed a US ambassador and additional consuls, and in the 1850s the US presence in the Ottoman Empire extended to seven consuls in addition to the resident minister.[5] As consuls appeared in missionary territory, the missionary relationship to the US government—and individual missionaries' understandings of their rights as US citizens abroad—would evolve.

In its 1855 instructions to consular officers, the US State Department explained that the general role of a consul was "to discharge administrative and sometimes judicial functions in regard to their fellow-citizens, merchants, marines, travelers, and others who dwell or happen to be in such places." Missionaries fell under the category of "others," though depending on where the consuls were based, missionaries could occupy a fair amount of their time or energy. After all, consuls were tasked with promoting "the interests of the citizens of the United States who may require the exercise of consular functions."[6] These broad instructions saw consuls doing a wide range of things to assist missionaries. In Athens, Greece, the consul helped missionaries locate a teacher for a mission school in 1839.[7] In Fouchow (Fuzhou), China, the consul assisted missionaries in renting property and then held copies of the lease during a period of unrest and opposition to the missionary presence in 1856.[8] In Jerusalem, the consul helped missionary J. T. Barclay find a home to rent and negotiated a lower rent in 1872.

Wherever they served, missionaries understood that a friendly consul could make all the difference in the world to the missionary project. In Jerusalem, for example, the consul not only found Barclay a home—he helped him find a community. Shortly after Barclay's arrival, he was visited by a range of authorities and leaders in the city, all of whom had been informed of his presence by the consul.[9] Barclay soon hired the consul's brother, a member of the Presbyterian Church born in Bethlehem who had previously worked for the missionaries of the ABCFM, as a teacher and dragoman, further solidifying the positive relationship between the mission and the consulate.[10]

Considering their importance for America's international presence, consuls were very poorly paid. A consular office could be lucrative for those who could use their posts as a supplement to other commercial endeavors, but not all were successful. As a result, it could be difficult, particularly in less desirable locations, to attract skillful and responsible consuls to fill the available positions. To make things easier, regulations did not require US consuls or consular agents to be US citizens or even to speak English. The consul Barclay was so fond of, Jacob Serapion Murad, was one such example. When a disappointed US citizen who had hoped for the appointment to the post had complained to the president about being passed over by a non-American, the missionaries rose to Murad's defense. "Though an Armenian by nation," Barclay explained, Murad was "thoroughly an American in principle."[11] What mattered most, Barclay insisted, was that a consul possessed an understanding of local conditions and a willingness to pursue US interests, including those of the missionaries.[12]

Though the consular system had not been designed to protect or assist missionary endeavors, missionaries did their best to make the consular system work for them. For most of the parts of the world where missionaries worked, consuls were the only representatives of the American state to whom missionaries might look for assistance.

The frequent comparisons that missionaries had made between themselves and merchants suggested both that they understood themselves to be equally deserving of the protection of the US government overseas and that they feared that the government did not prioritize their protection as much as they did that of merchants. These could become arguments not only about the specific issues at hand, but about the broader questions of America's international standing and which groups of Americans were empowered to represent their country.

When missionaries came into conflict with merchants and sailors, as they did with some regularity in port cities in the Pacific and East Asia, the consuls well might side with the sailors in finding missionaries to be more meddlesome than benevolent. Such clashes were easy enough to explain. Missionaries came to these regions burning with religious fervor. They had a particular vision of what the US position in the world ought to look like. The United States, they argued, was a Christian nation and should be recognized as a leader in morality and civilized behavior. As they put forward these claims to those that they hoped to convert, missionaries could be incensed to see US sailors drinking, carousing, and generally behaving in ways that did not live up to their high moral standard. For their part, sailors and merchants could find missionaries to be sanctimonious and moralistic, which they undoubtedly were. Consuls and diplomats could find missionary priorities at odds with national policy. Conflict was inevitable. And consuls, with their primary allegiances to the commercial interests of the country, very well might agree with the more negative portrayals of missionaries and their impact on local culture and customs.[13]

But consuls could also be incredibly important allies to the mission movement. This had a great deal to do with the distinct roles of consuls who served in the non-Christian world. In Asia, the Middle East, and Africa, consuls took on judicial and diplomatic roles in addition to their commercial responsibilities. Ambassador Caleb Cushing explained the reasons for this in 1844 as he worked to negotiate the new treaty with China. This legal and diplomatic mindset saw the world divided in two parts: Christendom on the one side, and pagan and Muslim states on the other. The "law of nations," Cushing determined, only governed the relations between Christian powers. In "the greater part of Asia and Africa," on the other hand, "individual Christians" were at risk. They could not trust local governments to protect them from "the sanguinary barbarism of the inhabitants, or by their frenzied bigotry." And so, to protect the rights of US citizens who might be traveling or residing in such regions, extra protection was necessary.

This protection came in the form of extraterritoriality, a legal concept that allows foreigners to be subject to the laws and judgment of their own country, rather than those of the country where they are visiting. Treaty provisions for extraterritoriality required foreign consulates to create judicial systems and even prisons to handle any criminal behavior of their own citizens. And it allowed those citizens certain freedoms from local laws and regulations.

By the time Cushing worked to guarantee Americans extraterritoriality in China in 1844, the practice was already standard in Western treaties with the Barbary States, Turkey, and Muskat. In China, Britain and Portugal had taken similar measures. America, Cushing concluded, should do so as well.[14] Extraterritorial provisions, however, required a different organization of America's consular presence. In China and in the Ottoman Empire, these responsibilities developed gradually over the century as new treaties expanded US extraterritoriality and more consuls were placed in these regions.

Even as the numbers of consuls increased, they were expected to cover wide ranges of territory. The seven consuls in the Ottoman Empire in 1859, for example, were based in Constantinople, Smyrna, Beirut, Jerusalem, the Isle of Candia, the Isle of Cyprus, and Trebisond. These consulates did not exactly overlap with the locations of missionary stations.

In places where there were no US consuls, missionaries might turn for assistance to the consuls of other nations. English consuls could often be depended on to support US missionaries in the absence of a formal US presence. In 1849, for example, it was the English consul at Salonica who forced local leaders to reverse course in their attempts to bar a Jewish teacher from visiting with the US missionaries and instructing them in Hebrew. Under threat of the removal of English protection, the policy was immediately reversed. American audiences saw this as a victory for "the cause of religious liberty."[15]

Foreign consuls could assist when missionaries were physically attacked as well. In 1856, the missionaries in Persia suspected that one of their teachers and his family had been poisoned after two of his children and his wife became extremely sick after eating from a pot of soup

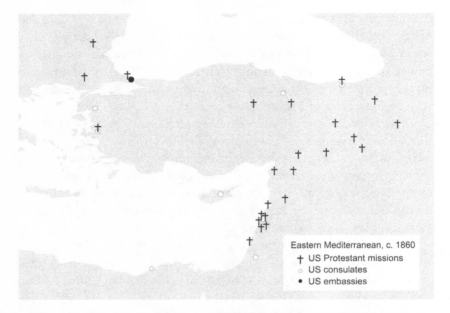

FIGURE 4.1. Circa 1860 both missionaries and the US government expanded their reach in the eastern Mediterranean. Outside of common centers like Constantinople, however, missionaries and consuls continued to settle in different locations.

Sources: Department of State, *List of Ministers, Consuls, and Other Diplomatic and Commercial Agents of the United States, in Foreign Countries* (Washington: Department of State, 1859); Methodist Episcopal Church, *Fortieth Annual Report of the Society of the Methodist Episcopal Church* (New York: Printed for the Society, 1859); Rev. J. Logan Aikman, *Cyclopedia of Christian Missions: Their Rise, Progress, and Present Position* (London: Richard Griffin and Company, 1860); Presbyterian Church in the USA, *The Twenty-Second Annual Report of the Board of Foreign Missions of the Presbyterian Church in the United States of America* (New York: Published for the Board at the Mission House, 1859); William Gammell, *A History of American Baptist Missions in Asia, Africa, Europe, and North America, Under the Care of the American Baptist Missionary Union* (Boston: Gould and Lincoln, 1854); ABCFM, *Report of the American Board of Commissioners for Foreign Missions, Presented at the Meeting Held at Philadelphia, PA, October 4–7, 1859* (Boston: Press of T.R. Marvin and Son, 1859).

that had been heated in a neighbor's home. They suspected arsenic poisoning and tested the soup on a cat to confirm their suspicions. The cat died instantly. Assuming this to be an attack on the mission, the Americans looked for help in pressuring the government to take the matter seriously. There was no US or British diplomatic or consular figure in the area, so the Americans turned to the Russian consul general, who had been an enthusiastic supporter of their work. The Russians acted in an unofficial capacity, which perhaps explains the reluctance of the government to conduct a thorough investigation. Suspects were called in for questions, but ultimately released.[16]

An efficient and effective consular service was a symbol of national pride. Inefficiency and ineffectiveness, on the other hand, could be a national embarrassment. Consuls and missionaries alike wanted the United States to be respected abroad. They wanted the United States to have the same level of protection and power that European nations enjoyed. Many of them sought a special role for the United States abroad. George Frederick Seward, the consul general to China, bemoaned the ways that European powers outstripped the United States in their influence over Chinese markets and media. But it was not US interest alone that motivated him; he felt sure that a stronger US presence would help protect China from being overpowered by European ambitions.[17] In the Levant, too, when diplomats considered closing some consular agencies it was ultimately the sense of competition with European powers that kept them open. If European countries had vice consuls and consular agents present, it simply would not do for the United States to close theirs. National pride was at stake.[18]

Asian Consuls

The right consul could mean the difference between protection and abandonment, between expanding access to new communities and being blocked. When new treaties opened up much of Asia to trade with the United States and other Western powers in the middle of the century, missionaries and their supporters were anxious to be sure that their own access to these countries would be similarly increased. Missionaries followed treaty developments closely, requesting their own copies from the State Department after ratification and publishing them in missionary periodicals and annual reports to make it clear to readers what the possibilities were for missionary activity.[19] When missionaries had the chance to advance missionary interests by serving the consulates directly, they tended to do so.

Missionaries in China often had close relationships with the consuls there. They regularly participated in the discussions surrounding treaties, serving as translators, consuls, and advisors throughout the process. Peter Parker was not the only American missionary who combined his missionary work with service to the State Department. Most of the early Canton missionaries did in some capacity or other. Elijah Bridgman had served alongside Parker as joint Chinese secretary to the US Legation and chaplain during Caleb Cushing's negotiation of the 1844 treaty. Samuel Wells Williams, in addition to his extensive publications, served as an official interpreter to the US delegation in Canton. In Ningpo (Ningbo), Divie Bethune McCartee served as acting consul for eleven years and was a frequent interpreter for the Americans in the decades that followed. Missionaries and consuls traveled together as well, such as when the Macao consul joined missionaries on a river journey to distribute copies of religious books and tracts.[20]

As US diplomats continued to "open" additional Asian countries to Western trade, they continued to follow the model of using missionaries as translators, interpreters, and consuls. Siam (Thailand) was another important site of American missionary activity, though one that generated much less commercial interest than China. High tariffs in the first half of the century had kept US merchants largely away, but missionaries remained interested in the region. When the United States sent Townsend Harris to Bangkok to negotiate a new treaty in 1856 that would guarantee a lower tariff rate, he found a community of US missionaries who had been in the country for decades. The missionaries had found a welcoming audience in King Mongkut, who appreciated the medical and scientific learning that these Westerners brought with their Bibles. It was a missionary, John Chandler, who had urged President Filmore and Secretary of State Webster in 1851 to send a diplomat to Siam to push for a revision to the existing treaty that governed trade between the countries.[21] Five years later, the United States sent Townsend Harris to Bangkok to negotiate a new treaty. Because the missionaries had fluency in the language and good relations with the Siamese government, Mongkut as well as Harris turned to them as advisors and translators during their negotiations.

Like the treaty with China, the US treaty with Siam was modeled on an earlier British treaty that had established an unequal relationship between the Asian and Western nations. The similarities between treaties were not accidental. Both England and the United States used some of the same diplomats to negotiate multiple Asian treaties, and the same motivations animated them all. The British treaty with Siam that Harris used as a model had been negotiated by the men who had earlier negotiated the British treaty with China. After Siam, Harris would go on to negotiate the US treaty with Japan, applying similar principles.[22] The main priority of all these Western treaties was trade, but commerce was not the only thing that these treaties affected. Americans were granted extraterritoriality, allowed to purchase land and settle in Bangkok, and to travel freely throughout the country. Most important, like the other treaties, this one granted the United States most-favored-nation status, meaning that any further privileges granted to other nations in future treaties would apply to the United States as well. Harris secured the rights that the British had negotiated in 1855, and nothing more.

Chandler, like some other optimistic observers, was disappointed. Writing to the secretary of state about the negotiations, Chandler complained that Harris had been "in too great a hurry" and "lost his patience and self command, and failed to secure any advantages over treaties up to that date."[23] The Americans, he believed, might have gotten much more out of the treaty. In practice, because of his good relationship with the missionaries, Mongkut allowed the missionaries even more freedoms than the treaty required. American missionaries settled throughout the country, not just in Bangkok, establishing missions where they went.[24]

When Harris left Bangkok, he named Stephen Mattoon, a Presbyterian missionary who had been living in Bangkok since 1847, as the first US consul to Siam. Harris had met Mattoon while negotiating the treaty, but Mattoon's appointment was first suggested by the Siamese. As Harris later explained, an official had "strongly recommended" Mattoon on the basis of his long residence and linguistic skills. More than this, he argued that Mattoon "was a discreet good man; that they had full confidence in him; that *he never lied*; and that he never got angry." Harris agreed with this assessment, and Mattoon would serve in this role for three years.[25] When Mattoon stepped down from the role due to financial concerns (the consulate, at this time, was an unpaid position), he was replaced with John Hassett Chandler, previously associated with the Baptist mission in Bangkok. Missionary wife Margaret Landon would later refer to Mattoon's departure from the consulate as a "calamity" for both US diplomatic and missionary relations with Siam. Those who followed were, in her opinion, "a series of consummate rascals."[26] Chandler served as vice consul and consul, even as he polarized much of the American community in the city. In the years after the Civil War, the position was usually filled by political appointees from Washington, though Presbyterian missionary Noah McDonald served as acting consul three different times between 1868 and 1886. Other missionaries, including Samuel Reynolds House and William Dean, served the consular system in other roles, including as judges in the extraterritorial court.[27]

American missionaries enjoyed good relations with the Siamese government, making the intervention of the United States on their behalf largely unnecessary before the 1870s. Once consuls began arriving in Siam as political appointments from the United States, however, conflicts followed. Missionaries and consuls soon found themselves at odds.

The conflicts between consul George Frederick Partridge and the missionaries, for example, were many. Some seem to have been personal (as when Partridge reportedly unsuccessfully tried to "bribe" women "of bad character" to discredit missionary Samuel House), but others spoke to broader concerns about the position of the United States. As part of Partridge's efforts to encourage US trade, he sold licenses that permitted the buyer to sell low-duty alcohol in Bangkok. Liquor shops that possessed the license took to displaying the American flag as a sign of their immunity from Siamese taxes. The result, soon enough, was that missionaries were afraid to fly American flags over their own buildings because, as they explained "the natives thought it was the sign of a liquor store."[28]

This was precisely the type of incident that was designed to frustrate American missionaries and make them question the relationship of their work to the US diplomatic project. For all that they needed a consul in place, particularly as missionaries and converts began to face persecution from local governments in the 1870s, missionaries were concerned that the behavior of this undisciplined and unrespectable man would harm their own cause by associating the United States, not with a superior religion and moral system, but with drinking and all the bad behavior that followed from it.

As in China and Siam, Japan was the site of new treaties that allowed missionaries and consuls to both work together and argue over the proper role of the United States. Commodore Matthew Perry first opened trade between Japan and the United States in 1854, accompanied by missionary translators. Two years later, Townsend Harris arrived as the first US consul general to Japan. Missionaries celebrated Harris's new treaty with Japan, which not only expanded trade, but included provisions about religious freedom. Americans living in Japan were granted free exercise of religion and the right to build churches. These provisions for religious freedom were essential prerequisites to mission work and were obtained at the explicit direction of Secretary of State Marcy, who had urged Harris to do whatever could be done for future missionary efforts.[29]

Though this religious freedom was not extended to any potential Japanese converts, missionary supporters assumed that this would eventually follow, as it had done in China. After all, the Japanese knew enough about Christianity, they believed, to understand that evangelism would follow the recognition of Christian practice. The right to religious freedom "must be followed by its propagation," one article in a missionary magazine explained. The Japanese were shrewd enough to understand "that the exercise of our religion involves making converts and planting churches." Harris was not a missionary, but he had worked alongside them before and now brought a major victory for the cause. Missionary supporters accordingly celebrated Harris and the United States alike, noting with pleasure that "we have, as a nation, opened a way through their wall of exclusion, and this without bloodshed." God's hands, they could see, were at work in opening Japan for the United States.[30]

But Harris's treaty actually did not secure missionaries the right to evangelize. They were explicitly warned, in fact, not to do anything "calculated to excite religious animosity." The Japanese commissioners in the treaty negotiations had resisted all the religious concessions. While they backed down on some points, on this they remained firm.[31]

The *Missionary Herald* nonetheless celebrated Harris's treaty as "The Good News from Japan." Henry Blodgett, a missionary in Shanghai, argued that Japan "ought to be occupied today."[32] This militaristic language of occupation echoed the strong arm that Commodore Perry had used to open Japan for trade. As the century progressed, the United States' sense of its right to be active in whatever countries it wanted to be was more fully developed than it had been earlier in the century. Missionaries were not immune to this, either.

The Episcopal, Presbyterian, and Dutch Reformed churches all sent out missionaries to Japan in the 1850s; the ABCFM followed shortly thereafter. They found, however, that in spite of their optimistic predictions after the new treaties with Japan, missionary work was still quite difficult. An 1864 article in the *Missionary Herald* summarized the challenges as "the known aversion to intercourse with foreigners, the bitter, long-continued hostility to Christianity, or the peculiar and not well understood character of the Government."[33] As they had earlier done in China, missionaries remained convinced that they might do useful preparatory work for the time when they would have more freedom to evangelize. In the meantime, they worked on language acquisition, translation, and text distribution. With the help of the US consul, one missionary found work as an English language teacher to Japanese government interpreters.[34]

There was little else that missionaries could do, given that the Japanese government turned to the death penalty to punish any Japanese who became Christian. Harris had suggested that missionaries confine themselves to the sale of books, as "the only safe ground" for them to stand on under existing law.[35] Over the course of the 1860s, missionaries reported government officials breaking up any religious classes that they tried to organize. Very few, they explained, were willing to even step inside of a church building. The solution was not to back away. Rather, missionaries urged the US government to take action.

In 1867, missionary Paul Bagley wrote to President Andrew Johnson directly to request a US response to a Japanese edict that made it a capital offense to become Christian. The law did not concern the religious freedom of Americans, but of the potential converts of the missionaries, and Bagley was concerned.[36] By 1871, the American Board missionaries took this case public in the pages of the *Missionary Herald*. The time was rapidly approaching for a revision of the treaty between the United States and Japan, and missionaries urged the government to insist on the adoption of religious toleration "for humanity's sake, if not on religious grounds." This was, they wrote, supported by the US minister in Japan. "Some may say foreign powers have no right to interfere," the missionaries acknowledged, but they strongly disagreed. While force might not be justified from outside powers, Christian countries like the United States "certainly may and ought to remonstrate, and do all they possibly can to show the Japanese the folly and the wickedness of their course."[37]

In the meantime, missionaries did what they could, often with the effect of blending their religious work with politics. As had been the case earlier and elsewhere, they well understood that their ability to evangelize was tied to the government's ability to secure further American access to Japan. Commerce and missions again seemed to go hand in hand. Missionaries like Divie Bethune McCartee helped to establish the new university at Tokyo, hoping that encouraging educational systems that resembled Western institutions would lead to a greater welcome for the Westerners. McCartee, with only his background in medical missions and consular work in Ningpo, became a professor of International Law.

Middle Eastern Consuls

Like Asia, the Middle East was an important exception to the usual functioning of the US consular system. Here, too, consuls took on judicial roles to enable the extraterritorial system of the United States to function in the region. From 1830, US treaties with the Ottoman Empire required that if any US citizen was charged with a crime, they must be tried before a US consul or minister. In this, the Americans were again following European example.[38] The United States accordingly appointed consuls in Constantinople and Beirut in addition to consular agencies in Ramle (Ramla), Acre (Akko), and Jaffa.[39] Yet for the missionaries who were spread throughout Ottoman territories, this did not seem to be nearly enough. Missionaries in Asia tended to find the consular support that they needed, given US commercial interests in the region. In the Middle East, however, missionaries regularly requested more US representation.

Missionaries in the Ottoman Empire were working under governments that did not support their presence, and they often delighted in shows of US power. Beirut missionaries celebrated in 1834, for example, when US warships arrived in Syria. Writing about the visit later, the missionaries reflected on both the pleasure they took in "the sight of our flag, and the presence of so many of our countrymen," as well as the ability of the ships to "give the people an idea of our distinct national existence." The visit, they hoped, would give people pause if they ever thought of threatening the missionaries. It should be clear to all who observed them that the missionaries "expected to derive important protection in times of danger." At the time, there was no consul in the immediate region, so the missionaries had good reason to worry. They were relieved to find the commodore interested in their welfare and willing to patrol the coast in the summer. In their letters, later published in the *Missionary Herald*, they hoped that US merchants might take notice as well and begin to trade there.[40]

Consuls were essential for missionaries to feel secure in territory that did not always welcome evangelism. In their basic capacity as defenders of US citizens' rights to property and safety abroad, consuls could be key allies of the missionaries. For example, hostilities in the Mount Lebanon region of Syria resulted in government orders forcing all foreigners, including the American missionaries, into Beirut. With only ten days' notice, missionaries were forced to abandon much of their property just as they were beginning to rebuild the mission structure after an earlier wave of violence had forced their departure. It was the consul who could do the necessary work to ensure the safety of missionary property left on the mountain. When the minister of foreign affairs sought to limit any guarantee to those damages that might occur "in case of insurrection or revolution," the consul, at the missionaries' urging, protested and insisted that the Turkish government protect the property from any damages whatsoever.[41] Missionaries had good reason to worry that without a consul present to serve as an advocate, they might face considerable difficulties.

One solution to this problem might have been for the missionaries simply to abandon plans to evangelize in regions where they could not expect the welcome of the local government. But missionaries seem not to have ever taken such an option seriously. Although missionaries did consider practical issues about their safety and about their likelihood to be effective in any given area before opening missions, their faith in the ultimate importance of their work overtook all other concerns. And in this region in particular, they balanced several competing concerns. If the Ottoman government was not particularly welcoming, this did not mean that individual communities would not be. American missionaries generally did not expect to work among Muslims in Ottoman territory, well understanding the risks of such an approach. They focused, instead, on bringing Orthodox Christians (whom they often referred to as "nominal" Christians) into the Protestant fold. This was, they understood, entirely legal.

By 1856, the Ottoman government granted equal rights to Christians and other non-Muslims to protection of their persons and property, freedom of worship, education of children of all religions, and permission for foreigners to acquire land. Under these laws, Orthodox Christians had the right to become Protestant, a freedom that did not extend to Muslims. Yet the missionaries still faced considerable opposition in many locations. A nearby consul, they hoped, could provide protection from attacks on their person or property, or from overzealous local officials who might seek to hinder their work.

Occasionally, missionaries themselves could serve as consuls in Ottoman territories, just as they did in Asia. Missionary James Barclay was regularly considered for consular roles (though he refused the positions). Charles Saunders, a Seventh Day Baptist missionary, served as the consular agent in Jaffa. John Baldwin Hay, who later held the Jaffa consular agency, was the son and brother of Episcopal missionaries. He used his position to help them establish a mission school.

Whenever possible, missionaries and their supporters reminded the US government that more consuls were needed. Rufus Anderson, secretary of the ABCFM, took Secretary of State Edward Everett's request for information about Americans living in Jerusalem in 1852 as an opportunity to make this point. In addition to the resident missionaries, Anderson described a rising group of US tourists coming through the region. Anderson expected missionary writings to only increase the numbers of travelers in the region. In the absence of nearby consuls, missionaries were finding themselves increasingly taxed by requests to accommodate these travelers. Missionaries, he went on to explain, were reliant on consuls far from their own places of residence. For US missionaries in Upper Mesopotamia and on the Tigris River, Beirut—more than five hundred miles away—was the closest consulate. This was far from ideal.[42]

Missionaries needed consuls for more than just the protection of their property. They also feared for their physical safety. In 1859, missionaries in Constantinople sent the US government a memorial asking for more aid.[43] When a group of Christians in Lebanon were killed by Muslims in the 1860s, the American Board again reached out for protection. The State Department promised protection to the American missionaries and sent a warship to the Mediterranean.[44] In the coming years, mission boards would continue to keep in touch with Washington and comment on the effectiveness of the consular system in protecting their missionaries. By the 1870s, the US government increased the numbers of consuls so that consular agencies were responsible for areas within a nine-hour journey. But even so, confusion remained about who had oversight of which area. Americans in Washington and the Levant disagreed over the strategic importance of the region.[45]

The missionary connections to consuls in this region could lead potential converts to confuse the roles of consuls and missionaries and, relatedly, the political effects of conversion. In 1844, for example, missionaries in Syria were approached by a group who wanted to join the Protestant church. In their interviews with the missionaries, it became clear that their primary motivations were political, not religious. They expected that affiliation with Protestantism, rather than Greek Orthodoxy, would provide them with protection against the oppression they faced as Orthodox Christians. As the missionaries reported, these potential converts had hoped they might be protected against Turkish law, excused from paying their taxes, and benefit from the intervention of US consuls. None of these, the missionaries were quick to explain, were benefits of membership in the Protestant church. The missionaries were, accordingly, doubtful that their desire to convert was in earnest.

Ultimately, it was to the consul, not the missionaries, that the converts proved their sincerity. During Lent, they staged their break with Orthodoxy in front of the consul's door. Traditionally, they would have refused to eat meat during this season of repentance. Instead, they gathered to share a dish of leben and announced their conversion to Protestantism, saying: "In this religion I will live, and in this religion I will die." This, the missionaries understood, was "most solemn in itself, and most momentous in its consequences." As notable as it is that the converts chose the consul's home as the place to perform this sign of their departure from the Greek church, it is equally notable that their choice worked. No missionaries were present, yet missionaries were told about what happened, presumably by the consul, and quickly understood its significance. The converts had not been sure at first whom they should address about securing a Protestant minister and teacher: the consul or the missionaries. They saw the two roles as somehow connected. And as much as the missionaries were insistent that they were distinct, and that no secular benefits would follow from conversion, they could not deny the reality that there was indeed some sort of link between consul and missionary.[46]

"Missionary Patriotism"

Most of the time, missionaries never had to do much to explain the relative importance of their allegiances to their country or their faith. They emphasized their Americanness or their transnational Christian identity how and when it suited any particular situation. But when missionaries served as consuls and consular agents, they had to directly confront a question that otherwise could simmer under the surface: What was their relationship to their country when they were evangelizing overseas?

Working directly for the US government required a different form of missionary patriotism. It made it quite clear that missionaries served two masters: God and state. Sometimes, missionaries were able to do both at once: serving their mission boards while also taking on some government responsibilities. But at other times, the work for the consulate was too demanding, and they had to step away from missionary work, at least for a time. Doing so was worth it if their diplomatic efforts could open the door to more evangelism. Some government work, like translation, involved travel that took missionaries away from their stations. The judicial responsibilities that could come with US consulates, too, could put missionaries in uncomfortable situations. At the very least, it contributed to the sense among some observers that missionaries were united with foreign governments in colonizing efforts.

The various missionary organizations had different responses to this problem. As the largest of the mission boards, the ABCFM's evolving policies on missionary service to government is instructive. Initially, the ABCFM had been enthusiastic about missionary government work. Rufus Anderson, one of the American Board's corresponding secretaries and its leading strategist in the mid-nineteenth century, had volunteered missionary support of the US government in China.[47] Anderson's experience of watching Peter Parker's work for the government, however, led to a shift in attitude. In 1847, Parker officially and permanently parted ways with the ABCFM, ostensibly because his government work, now on a permanent and salaried basis, would prevent him from fulfilling his missionary obligations. In that year, the ABCFM included a statement in its annual report that it would now be a "settled principle" that "a missionary, going into civil or political life, ceases de facto, from his connection with the Board."[48] Yet even after his departure from the mission, Parker would continue much of the same medical work that he had done as a missionary. The problem was not that his government work consumed all of his time and kept him from his missionary responsibilities. It was not so simple, then, as the official language of the ABCFM statement had made it seem.

Instead, we might look at Parker's departure from the ABCFM as emblematic of several ongoing debates about missionary methods. The reason that Anderson had at first supported Parker's work for the government was that he understood that there was a significant overlap between the goals of the US government and the missionary movement. But Anderson was also at the center of debates about the appropriateness of medical missions and other expensive missionary efforts that focused on institution-building and gradual, long-term efforts over an evangelization that emphasized preaching alone. This debate was theological, but it was also about money and method. Anderson favored missions that were modeled on building churches that were self-supporting, self-governing, and self-propagating. Medical missions presented challenges to this model. While medical missionaries like Parker trained local doctors, nurses, and assistants, and while some funding support could be supplied locally, it remained the case that medical missions required significant financial obligations on the missionary societies. Anderson and other skeptics did not feel that these costs were outweighed by the benefits that medical establishments could supply by bringing people into the mission's orbit. When schools and hospitals did not result in large numbers of baptisms, these critics wondered if they were worth the money. The institutions seemed more focused on culture than on Christ.[49]

Parker's departure was the culmination of several years of discussion about whether his salary ought to be covered by the ABCFM or if he could secure funding through another organization focused on medicine.[50] It was not only his political work, then, that Anderson thought took him outside of the proper concern of the American Board.

Other missionary organizations were more supportive of their missionaries engaging in political work in addition to institution building. The Presbyterian Board of Foreign Missions had no such concerns about Divie Bethune McCartee's combination of missionary, medical, and political work, even as his political duties occasionally required absences from his missionary work. "Going into civil or political life" was not a disqualification for missionary labor here. Presbyterian missionary Stephen Mattoon similarly combined the roles in Siam, although his appointment as consul aroused some early concerns. In his journal, Mattoon reflected that he had not sought out his diplomatic and political work, and hoped that he would "not forget my higher duties while engaged in them. In this as in everything I shall await the indications of Providence and seek to be guided accordingly as to the path of duty." His missionary colleague Daniel Bradley had been shocked at the very idea of a missionary consul, reflecting that "such a thing would scarcely be possible."[51] Yet Mattoon found a way to work out his diplomatic and missionary work, and he was followed by many other Siam missionaries in combining the roles.

But some individuals did find the choice to be impossible. Dr. James T. Barclay, a Disciples of Christ missionary with the Christian Missionary Society, managed to combine his medical practice with a geographic study of Jerusalem but twice refused the position of consular agent in that city. He apparently could not imagine combining his work as a missionary with the duties of a consul.[52]

By 1869, at least some within missionary circles were beginning to question the close relationship between missionaries and consuls. In the *Chinese Recorder*, missionary "H. G." suggested to his colleagues that the "policy of Consular interference" that many missionaries had turned to as a default when they encountered local opposition or persecution "may be a mistaken one." Turning to consuls for protection may have allowed missionaries to expand their reach in China, he argued, but at what cost? The practice, he argued, was unscriptural, and it contributed to a bad image for Christian missionaries. The greatest risk, H.G.

found, was that it could "lead the Chinese to look upon our religion and great guns as inseparable." If missionaries turned to consuls, and even to gunboats, for protection in going about their work in places where they were not wanted, "one is led to inquire whether we are preachers of the gospel of peace, or merely propagators of the religion of a dominant power." It was an existential question that would come up repeatedly in the decades to come.[53]

American consuls around the world advocated for higher wages and a more professionalized system throughout this era. Peter Parker complained in 1856 that earlier consuls were "simply *commercial agents*," which put the entire US enterprise in China at a disadvantage. The Chinese, he reported, held their own commercial class in low esteem. For the United States to rely on commercial men for its consuls, and to have the consulates located in their "counting-rooms" made it hard for Americans to gain the respect of the Chinese.[54] This was especially important because in China, consuls had the care of far more than commercial relations. Extraterritoriality protected Americans, but it also demanded that US consuls fulfill their judicial and diplomatic responsibilities.

Even as Consul General George Frederick Seward asked Congress to professionalize the consular service in China, he praised missionary Edward Lord, then serving as consul in Ningpo, and warned that Lord would soon leave the consulate if the salary was not raised.[55] Similar concerns had previously been attributed to Divie Bethune McCartee's refusal of another consular post. In order to attract and retain reliable and skillful consuls, changes were needed. Samuel Wells Williams found this situation to be a blight on America's reputation abroad. In his thirty-two years of service in China, he reported in 1865, he had known of only one non-missionary US consular officer who was able to speak Chinese.[56] This was not good for US diplomatic interests and, perhaps, was getting in the way of missionary interests as well. But until reforms were made, the United States in China would continue to depend on missionary labor.

These critiques and calls for action saw a slow response in Washington. Peter Parker first suggested special language training for US consuls to reduce their reliance on missionaries in 1846; twenty years later, the problem had still not been addressed. While reforms in the 1860s brought salaries to many of the China consulates, reducing the need for consuls to make the bulk of their income through business, the amounts were well under what those with experience in China recommended. Most frustratingly, perhaps, were the comparisons to salaries at other consulates. China consuls earned less than those in England, even though the British consulate did not have diplomatic or judicial responsibilities.[57]

So long as missionaries depended on consuls for protection in, and occasionally access to, the places they wanted to evangelize, they would exert as much influence as they could over consular efforts. Later in the century, when calls for consular reform and professionalization were finally heeded, the missionary relationship to consuls would shift. In the meantime, consuls in missionary lands could expect to spend a lot of their time on what they came to call "missionary troubles."

CHAPTER 5

Victims

In the summer of 1862, a group of US missionaries on Tanna in the South Pacific barricaded themselves in their home. They were terrified. Their Canadian colleagues had just been murdered by a group of islanders, and the Americans feared that they would be next. They hid in their home for ten days, praying for salvation before escaping to the bush, where they nearly starved waiting for rescue. Finally, they were able to signal a passing ship and leave for Sydney, where they would wait for a while. Soon, they hoped, they would be able to return. The US press described their story as "the perils of missionaries."[1]

Ten years later, another missionary murder captured American attention. ABCFM missionary John L. Stephens was killed in Mexico just three months after he began his work in Ahualulco, a town some sixty miles from Guadalajara. Stephens had had been invited to the town by a group of Catholics who had been reading the Bible and wanted instruction in Protestant doctrines. In his short time in the town, Stephens established schools and preached to growing congregations who gathered from the nearby ranchos and pueblos. But he also generated fierce opposition.[2]

The day before Stephens died, the local Catholic priest preached a fiery sermon. In it, he told the crowd that "it is necessary to cut down even to the roots the tree that bears bad fruit. You may interpret these words as you please." The *New York Times* informed its readers that in so doing, he had "advocated the extermination of the Protestants." That night, a crowd of two hundred armed men surrounded Stephens's home, shouting "Long live the priests!" and "Death to the Protestants!"[3] Though there were Mexican soldiers nearby, they did not protect him. Stephens attempted to hide in a hayloft but was soon found by the crowd. He was shot in the face and the chest, after which he was stabbed with swords and knives and his skull was divided into pieces. His dead body was robbed of its clothing, and his books, including his English Bible, were burned in the public plaza.[4]

The Mexican government reacted swiftly. On the same day as the attack, the governor sent soldiers to quiet the mob and arrest the guilty. Upward of thirty were arrested and brought to trial, and the governor sent police protection for the remaining missionaries. They remained nervous. Missionary Daniel Watkins was convinced that "the priests are intent on killing us." He claimed the priests could activate criminals to rise against the Protestant missionaries at any time.[5]

One of Watkins's first actions after the murder had been to cable John Foster, the US minister to Mexico, for help. Foster jumped to action, calling in person on the Mexican minister of foreign affairs. It was, Foster summarized, a "brutal" murder with "revolting barbarities." He attributed its cause to "religious fanaticism." He expected the Mexican government to investigate the crime and punish the offenders, and in this he was not disappointed. By the time he met with the minister of foreign affairs, order had already been restored. Two priests and the "principal assassins" had been arrested. A judge was in place and ready to conduct a speedy trial. But no one could predict how the trial would progress.[6]

Stephens's missionary board, too, reached out to the State Department to ensure that the perpetrators were punished. After hearing from Secretary of State Hamilton Fish that the murderers had been arrested and at least seven had been condemned to death, the ABCFM secretary expressed the board's thanks for the actions of both the US minister to Mexico and the Mexican government. He fully expected the execution of the assassins to "do much to secure protection to the lives and property of US citizens in that country."[7] Several months later, five of the condemned had been executed.[8] But missionary supporters grumbled that others awaited appeal and one had even been set free by a jury.[9]

At the time of his death, Rev. Stephens was hard at work managing day and evening schools. His fellow missionaries reported that he was gaining both students and congregants, and had earned the affectionate nickname Don Juanito.[10] After his death, the missionaries reported a new atmosphere of great fear and religious intolerance. Protestants claimed that Catholics were issuing death threats to anyone attending Protestant worship. School attendance dropped as a result, with only eight or ten students in the classroom each day.[11]

The American Protestant press was explicit in their anti-Catholic coverage of this case. This was a "brutal murder" committed by a "mob frenzied by priestly harangues and denunciations" that ought to indicate "what ideas of religious liberty are entertained by the Roman Catholic Church" in Mexico.[12] Earlier in the century, US Protestant missionaries had been reluctant to send missionaries to Latin America, fully expecting that the well-established Catholicism there would not allow for successful Protestant evangelism. But Mexican law promised religious liberty. Stephens should have been within his rights to publicly exercise his Protestant religion, they insisted. Within the United States and Mexico, the murder was condemned as a violation of this principle.[13]

Stephens was far from the only missionary victim of physical violence in these decades, and not all governments would be as responsive to US appeals for justice as Mexico had been. By the early 1880s, discussions of "missionary troubles" began to appear regularly in the State Department's correspondence when missionaries and their US supporters requested government assistance in confronting the various perils that they faced. The phrase appeared in dispatches about Turkey, Bulgaria, Mozambique, Egypt, the Caroline Islands, Russia, China, Mexico, Liberia, Colombia, Persia, Portugal, Turkey, Belgium, Haiti, Ecuador, and Japan.[14] In all of these places, missionaries worried about their physical safety and the protection they could expect from the US government. Difficulties seemed to follow the missionaries wherever they went. In some places, they faced violent attack. In others, they came into conflict with local governments. Their evangelism could put them at odds with those in power. None of these conflicts were new. With several decades of experience behind them, missionary organizations after the Civil War could be pretty sure that they could call on the US government for support in their troubles. And call on them they did.

Between the US Civil War and the Boxer Uprising, missionaries appealed to the government with ever more frequency. In part, this was due to the increasing presence of consuls that missionaries could reach out to. More help was available, and missionaries took it. But if there were more consuls in the world, there were also more missionaries. After the Civil War, the numbers of missionary organizations and the missionaries they sponsored grew. Perhaps trusting that the government would follow in their wake to protect them, they went to new communities, faced new risks, and confronted more resistance. Over these decades, the State Department and the foreign mission movement negotiated a new relationship. Missionary diplomacy shifted its form in these years as the professionalization and expansion of the diplomatic corps allowed for missionaries to approach their government more frequently as citizens in need rather than partners in shaping the US presence overseas.

Missionary Murders in Turkey

The troubles in the Ottoman Empire began almost as soon as missionaries had arrived there. Questions of religious tolerance, liberty, and freedom—what these various terms meant and how far the US government ought to go to protect missionaries' ability to work wherever they went—had been relentless. After the Civil War, the government had not reached any answers. But these were not the only problems missionaries faced. The far graver issues, and the ones that had a much clearer call to action for US diplomats, were physical attacks. Missionaries reported thefts, beatings, and even murder in the late 1860s, 1870s, and 1880s. Even when the perpetrators were identified and arrested, there seemed to be no response from local officials. To American observers, this seemed to create a pernicious cycle. If punishments were not enforced, more crimes would be committed. American diplomats called for harsh punishments against perpetrators to bring about a "wholesome terror" throughout the Ottoman Empire that, they hoped, would protect Americans.[15]

This violent language was a direct response to the missionaries' understanding that they were under threat in the Ottoman Empire. These attacks were generally not a response to missionary activities. Instead, missionaries, like many other foreigners, fell victim to brigands while traveling throughout the region. The first of these cases was Jackson G. Coffing, an ABCFM missionary at Hadjin (Saimbeyli, Turkey) who was murdered in 1862 as he traveled to Aleppo to attend the annual meeting of the mission. After he and his servant were shot, they were attended by the English vice consul, who was also a physician, and taken to the home of the US vice consul. In spite of the consuls' best efforts, they did not survive.

Observers believed the murder to have been premeditated. As the obituary in the *Missionary Herald* explained, it was believed to be the work of Armenians who "were known to be exceedingly bitter against him, or rather . . . against the gospel which he preached." The *Herald* praised the consul at Beirut, Mr. Johnson, for his energetic efforts to bring the killers to justice. Coffing's fellow missionaries refused to be afraid. After all, they reflected, they had been in the region for years and this was the first time a missionary had been attacked.[16]

Two months later, though, another missionary was killed. The Reverend William Meriam, of the Western Turkey mission, was murdered in July as he returned from the annual meeting of the mission. The missionaries had been warned of violent gangs on several of the roads, so Meriam and his family took what they believed to be a safer route. But soon they heard that armed horsemen were on the road. Meriam refused to delay. He was armed with "one of Colt's best revolvers, and expressed no fear," as his obituary would later report. Robbers stopped the Meriam family's wagon train and killed three of the travelers. Meriam was shot twice and, eyewitnesses claimed, one of the robbers then jumped forward and "stamped on his face and head." Meriam's death did not seem to be premeditated, and it did not seem to be at all motivated by enmity toward the mission. Rather, the missionaries understood it to be the effect of a much broader story of violence and criminality in the region. One of Meriam's brethren, in fact, hoped that the death "may prove a public good" in drawing attention to the issue. "If these murderers are apprehended and brought to speedy justice—*executed*—we may hope for immunity in traveling." Anything short of that, however, and the surviving missionaries felt travel would be unwise.[17]

The missionary societies in the United States were accordingly quite interested in the outcome of these cases. Here were two Americans killed within a single summer. The ABCFM, the sponsor of both Coffing and Meriam, demanded swift action. When nothing had yet been accomplished by August, the ABCFM complained to the State Department about Mr. Morus, the minister at Constantinople.[18] The ABCFM had more praise for the consul at Smyrna, whom the missionaries appreciated for his faithful support of their work.[19]

Secretary of State William Seward had worried that the murders would lead to alarm and "disturb the growing kindness of sentiment which exists, and the confidence and faith which are everywhere entertained in this country toward the government of Turkey, as administered by the new, humane, and enlightened head of the empire." He had, accordingly, urged the US minister at Constantinople and the consul at Beirut to do their utmost to work with the Turkish authorities to seek justice.[20] By October, the consular agent at Adana was happy to report that justice had been done in the Coffing case. He witnessed the beheading of one of Coffing's killers alongside consular agents from France, Russia, and Italy, the governor of the province, and a crowd of at least five thousand observers. It was an event, he hoped, that would "make a lasting impression on the public mind."[21]

Merriam's killers, meanwhile, were still at large, and the Americans blamed this on the "delinquency" of Turkish police. But Seward understood that US diplomats were in a "very peculiar and trying" position as they navigated conflicts between missionaries and the Turkish government.[22] For years, US officials had complained that the promises of religious toleration and protection from Constantinople were nearly meaningless in provinces where the governors were unsympathetic. Corruption, crime, and robberies were, Minister Morris explained, the result of this order of things.[23]

Morris, Seward, and the men who followed them in their roles responded to this situation with bloodlust. The only way to make it clear that Americans should be protected from violence was to respond with violence in turn. Two of the brigands who had murdered Merriam were never arrested, but Morris was "gratified to be able to inform" Seward that they had "both met violent deaths" through other means.[24] In 1880, the US minister argued that life in prison, rather than execution, was "virtually an acquittal" in a case involving the death of a Russian military attaché. For all observers, these events were revealing of Islamic-Christian relations in the region.[25]

In July 1880, another US missionary was murdered on the road. J. W. Parsons had been itinerating and distributing religious texts when he stopped for the night to make camp under the trees with a servant. While they were sleeping, a group of men came upon them, shot them, stole their belongings, and hid their bodies. When the corpses were discovered a few days later, officials had very little trouble in locating the criminals. The three men were quickly arrested and confessed. Yet US diplomats found themselves still discussing the case months and years later, frustrated by what they described as the failure to act on the part of the Ottoman government. Justice, they fumed, had not been done.[26]

Missionary supporters at home were horrified by the danger that missionaries seemed to be facing and turned to their government. The cause of the danger, some articles were careful to acknowledge, was not "religious fanaticism" or opposition to missionaries, but rather "wholly different causes, for which the [Turkish] government is mainly responsible."[27] Mission boards in the United States wrote to the secretary of state over the summer of 1880 to call for US efforts to ensure that justice was done.[28] The *Chicago Daily Tribune* called for a US fleet to "take position off the Sultan's Palace in Constantinople and blow it into flinders if instant reparation is not made for the infamously brutal murder of the American missionary, the Rev. Mr. Parsons." In order to defend its missionary citizens, the government needed to act. Summarizing the arguments of missionary Henry Dwight, the paper explained that the case for intervention was really quite simple. The law in Turkey was insufficient to protect US citizens there: "To kill a Christian in Turkey is no more an offense than to kill a sheep or a dog. In this case the Christian who has been killed is an American." It was time, they argued, for the United States to respond.[29]

By the fall, the ABCFM reported their pleasure with the response of the State Department in the pages of the *Missionary Herald*. The government had promised "vigorous measures" to protect US citizens going forward. Naval vessels were on their way to Turkish waters.[30] Americans wanted the criminals punished and the missionaries protected, even as they doubted that the Sultan would approve the use of capital punishment for a Muslim who had killed a Christian.[31]

The secretary of state at the time was William Evarts, who had deep ties to foreign missions. His father was Jeremiah Evarts, one of the most important leaders of the ABCFM earlier in the century. Now, his son was in a seat of power and the younger Evarts was clear that the death of a US citizen must be "avenged."[32] As he understood it, the "existing state of lawlessness" in Ottoman lands was such that all travelers were in "constant danger" of sharing Parsons's fate. There were at least a hundred US citizens serving as missionaries in Ottoman territories, but this was not simply a missionary concern. After all, Parsons had not been killed because of his missionary activity.[33] American officials in Turkey took these matters seriously, meeting with the judges for two hours before the trial began, and following up with the minister of foreign affairs repeatedly both in person and in writing. They made it clear that the US government demanded that the guilty be sentenced to "the severest penalty of the law." Failure to do so would result in "a very painful impression in the United States."[34]

These attacks did not seem to be religiously motivated, making the government's defense of the missionaries a far easier stance than in cases that involved missionaries' rights to evangelize. Missionaries could frame the danger as a business issue. Because of the risk of violence, "the business interests of all this region remain paralyzed," as missionary Rev. Pierce complained after he had been attacked. "Shall I relinquish my business," he asked, referring to his missionary work, "or may I hope for protection from the government?"[35] American minister Heap did his best to provide the desired protection, working with the minister of foreign affairs to have the robbers found and Pierce's stolen property returned. It was an issue of concern all the way up to President James Garfield, whose letter to the US residents in Turkey assured them of his care and attention, and whose message to the Turkish foreign minister minced no words about the "intolerable" "state of perversion of the sense of truth and justice in the administration of the judicial power in Turkey."[36]

When Rev. Barnum was robbed as he traveled from Harpoot (Harput) to Sivas in 1881, Heap reported to the State Department that the root of the problem was "the failure to punish malefactors who have been captured, tried, and sentenced." This was one of three robbery cases that the minister had dealt with in only ten days. The region was in "a state of anarchy."[37]

Ten years later, missionaries continued to take great risks when traveling throughout Turkey. Miss Anna Melton, a teacher at the Presbyterian mission school in Mosul, was attacked while she slept on a journey through Koordistan (Kurdistan). Two men with clubs beat her, while accomplices fired their guns to frighten away any villagers. The missionaries described Melton as "a delicate little woman, although very brave." Her injuries were extensive. She had been beaten severely on the head and had bruises over her body. Melton defended herself fiercely, grabbing the stick away from one attacker and binding his hands to prevent him from attacking her further. "It seemed to me he was Satan himself," she later reflected, and she fought back even as she felt "stunned and terrified as if in some terrible nightmare."[38] When the men left, they did not steal anything. She was covered in blood but would recover.

When her fellow missionary, Edward McDowell, went to the local official to search for and arrest the assailants, they made little progress. A week later, the official had not taken further action. The missionaries concluded that "he does not intend to do anything." McDowell echoed the same complaint that missionaries in the Ottoman Empire had been making for decades: "Our common word is that our Government is so far away that it can not reach us." The Americans needed more protection.[39]

The US minister at Constantinople quickly worked to obtain redress, convincing the grand vizier to urge the governor-general to action. This attack, he informed his counterparts, would be particularly troubling to Americans. The "assault and beating [of] a woman" was sure to create a "deplorable impression" in the United States. Yet some of the details from this story did not sit right with the minister. While he waited for a response, he reflected to the State Department his surprise that "two men armed with clubs and having a frail woman in their power, did not inflict more serious injury." He wondered why she had not been robbed, given that the place was "notorious for robberies." Perhaps the attack had not been random.[40]

The missionaries agreed. They assured the minister that they had given no offense to anyone. But as the weeks went on without any arrests, the missionaries reported that the people were being intimidated. Even though they suspected who the guilty parties were, no one would come forward. Some of the villagers even felt the need to deny that they had become sympathetic to Protestantism, or that they had welcomed the missionaries into their village.[41] The minister was sure that someone of high rank had been involved. The mission board was convinced that the attack had been "deliberately planned and executed by quite a body of men" to force the missionaries away. It was an attack on Melton, but it was also an attack on the mission as a whole.[42]

It mattered to all of these writers that Melton was a woman. Both the missionaries and the government officials emphasized again and again that it was an "American lady" who had been assaulted. Her attackers needed to be punished; the US government would not stand for anything less. Even though the Ottoman government eventually made arrests, Americans continued to complain for months about delays in the trial.[43] The minister believed this was due to insufficient evidence.[44] But the missionaries were convinced that only "a wholesome fear of our Government" would protect American missionaries from violent attack.[45] But just how far the United States could or should go to facilitate such a fear of US intervention was far from settled. In this moment, at least, there was little that the minister felt the Americans could do.

Rumors and Anti-Christian Violence in China

In 1868, the time had come for a renegotiation of the treaty between the United States and China. The Burlingame Treaty, as it would come to be known, would form the structural basis of US diplomatic responses to the missionary troubles that emerged in the coming decades. At its heart, the treaty set out the principle that the United States would recognize Chinese sovereignty. The Americans in China would, as Secretary of State Hamilton Fish insisted, respect all of the "prejudices and traditions of the people of China." Or at least they would do so as long as those "prejudices and traditions" did not "interfere with rights which have been acquired to the United States by treaty."[46]

Respecting the sovereign right of a foreign power to rule over its own people is a foundational principle of diplomacy that US ambassadors around the world would happily recognize. But in China, as Fish noted to the new US minister Frederick Low, "Christian" powers had been far more likely to turn to "force" to get their way.[47] Over the twenty-six years since China had been forced to allow Western residents and traders in to four port cities, European and US influence had been steadily growing. Chinese anti-foreign sentiments were significant. The Burlingame Treaty, Fish expected, would mark the beginning of a new era of Sino-American relations in which the United States respected China as an equal peer. This respect, it was hoped, would in turn lead to a greater acceptance of a foreign presence in China.

This was challenging to put into practice. Much of the trouble centered around missionaries and the opposition—at times violent—that they faced. It could be difficult for missionaries and diplomats alike to determine if this opposition was primarily about religion or the Western presence in general. Missions, both American and European, often became the focus of Chinese opponents of Western incursion into the country.

In Yang-tchoo (Yangzhou), there had been rumors of coming violence against the Protestant missions for days when a mob attacked British and American missionaries in 1868. No one died, but there were injuries and the mission premises were burned to the ground, forcing several of the women of the mission, who had run upstairs to escape the violence, to jump out of the windows to save themselves. Following established procedure, the missionaries reported the violence to their consuls, and it fell to the US and British officials to determine how to respond.

The British consul's response revealed a deep mistrust and disrespect for the Chinese government's authority. He quickly visited the site of the violence and called on local officials to respond by punishing the offenders and paying reparations to the missionaries. But he did not expect that this would be enough. He did not trust the Chinese government to act unless forced, and so he quickly called a fleet of six British naval vessels to come to his aid. While civilized states must respect "the broad principles of justice, of right and wrong, which underlie the international code of nations," he wrote, this was not appropriate in China. Instead, "an over-scrupulous pedantry" to the law of nations in Asia would only "do mischief, and bring on the very evils it is intended to avert." Force was needed, he believed, when dealing with "an Asiatic race."[48]

Seward, for his part, felt that the British response was uncalled for. The foreign countries in China needed to "give the regular proceeding at least a trial." The proper response, he thought, would look like this: any dispute should be brought to the local consul, who should investigate alongside a Chinese officer. If this did not lead to "justice," the consul should turn to the legation at Peking (Beijing), where the US minister could address the central Chinese government and, if necessary, seek out instructions from their home government. Only if all this failed might the possibility of force be hinted at. Such a method, Seward was sure, could not fail.[49] George Seward's multistep plan did not seem to have much faith in local Chinese officials to get the work done, either, but his call for patience and process was shaped by a generalized optimism about the changes that were occurring in China as a result of interactions with the West.

Seward's theory would soon be tested. In the summer of 1870, reports reached Washington about an ever-increasing "feeling of insecurity and peril" resulting from a massacre in Tientsin (Tianjin). Many months later, it was not clear what, exactly, had happened in June, or why. Most importantly for Minister Frederick Low and for the American missionaries he was unsuccessfully trying to calm down, it was not at all clear how much of a risk remained. What they did know was this: sixteen French subjects, three Russians, and an unspecified number of Chinese Christians had been killed at the French consulate and missionary establishments in Tientsin. The consulate had been destroyed, as had a Catholic cathedral and the orphanage and asylum operated by a group of French nuns, the Sisters of Charity. Beyond that, there were many rumors, and few known facts. Was this an anti-French and anti-Catholic riot? Low thought so. Or was it a part of a more generalized anti-foreign conspiracy? The US missionaries and many of their Chinese converts were convinced this was the case. For years, the echoes of Tientsin and its unresolved questions would shape missionary diplomacy in China.

Whether the events in Tientsin were specific to the French and Catholics or not, the rumors about the missionaries and their practices mirrored those that plagued US Protestant missions in China too. Chinese observers accused the Sisters of encouraging kidnapping by paying bounties for children. Once a child was delivered to their orphanage, it could not be returned to the family. Suspicions ran wild. What were the Christians doing with those children? Community concerns were especially heightened because of stories circulating throughout China that missionaries harvested the brains, eyes, and hearts of children for the making of medicine. Was this what the Sisters of Charity were really up to?

Early in June, an official proclamation in Tientsin repeated these rumors as if they were an accurate description of missionary activities. Calling the kidnapping of children for the harvesting of their organs "detestable in the extreme," it urged "instant measures" to punish those responsible.[50] Ambassador Low believed that this proclamation was one of the primary catalysts of the riot. Tsang-Kwoh-fan, the Chinese official responsible for the investigation into the events in Tientsin, largely agreed. Suspicions, he concluded, led to hatred, which had led to "this serious catastrophe." After interviewing all 150 boys and girls who had been taken from the asylum, he found that every one of them had been brought to the Sisters by their relatives. None had been kidnapped or coerced. The rumors were untrue. But like most rumors, their veracity had nothing to do with their power.[51]

No Americans were harmed at Tientsin. This put Low in a difficult position. He joined together with other foreign representatives in Peking to consider the matter. They regularly cooperated to coordinate relations with China, and this was no different. Together, they asked Prince Kung, the Chinese minister of foreign affairs, to provide more support for foreigners throughout the empire. The Chinese government, Low assured the secretary of state, wanted to help foreigners, but it was ultimately "weak and effeminate," and in need of the "constant advice and aid" of these foreign powers.[52]

Low seemed content to conclude that what had happened in Tientsin was a specific response to French misbehavior. He believed reports that the French consul, who was killed in the riot, had opened fire on the crowd, thus fanning the flames and making things much worse. He believed, too, that part of the problem in this case had been the Chinese belief that the French government was actively supporting the Sisters of Charity mission. That sense of a united religious and political interest, Low thought, had contributed to the anti-French passions that erupted in Tientsin.[53] He did not believe that any particular risk existed for

Americans beyond what had been the case before Tientsin. The missionaries, however, disagreed with both his approach and his conclusions.

The American missionaries based in Tientsin had been absent from the city on the day of the massacre. Unsatisfied with Low's report, they conducted their own investigation and published the results in the local press. Missionary C. A. Stanley of the ABCFM insisted in the *Shanghai Courier* that this outbreak was not just about the Catholics. He pointed out that the mobs had also attacked the eight Protestant chapels in the city, taking valuables and tearing down many of the walls. Stanley urged his government to take a firm response: "America has lost no children," he admitted, "but others have, and we should stand by them in demanding a full investigation, impartial justice, and determined punishment of the guilty." In this sentiment, Stanley echoed the feelings of British missionaries Jonathan Lees and William Hall who explained to their consul that "we are not crying for war and vengeance, but we do claim justice, and we hold most firmly to the belief that the path of safety and of honor, no less for individual Englishmen than for our government, is to stand by our fellow-sufferers in the hour of trial."[54]

Low was not pleased. He marveled that these missionaries "appear to be impressed with the belief that they are somehow specially charged with diplomatic functions by their governments, in addition to their self-imposed task of taking care of the spiritual welfare of the Chinese." This was ridiculous and presumptuous, he implied, as well as dangerous. Their anxieties were only spreading rumors further and increasing anti-foreign sentiments, as well as urging a war between China and France.

Over the summer, more and more reports of coming violence circulated. W. Ashmore, a missionary serving as vice consul in Swatow (Shantou), reported that the news of Tientsin had circulated very quickly throughout the region, leading to the rise of "a bitter, malicious rancor towards foreigners." It was not that the anti-foreign sentiments were new. Rather, Tientsin had allowed "a long-cherished but suppressed ill-will" to finally see the light of day. Even Low had to admit that "there is no sentiment of regret or sorrow among the people over the result of the riot." By the end of August, one could purchase fans illustrated with scenes of the attacks. Missionaries reported ongoing threats and rumors of violence to come.

Stanley, for example, reported a warning his mission had received from a Chinese informant about a "general rising against foreigners" scheduled for later that month. He wrote to Captain B. B. Tailor of the *Asuelot*, urging the US fleet to take "precautionary measures" to defend

American lives.[55] In September, missionaries in Tunchow (Tongzhou) had become so concerned about rumors of a coming attack that they had abandoned their station and sought shelter on a British vessel. According to the rumors, two thousand troops were marching toward them, determined upon "the extermination of the missionaries." Missionary H. C. W. Matteer described the decision to leave as "the greatest trial I ever met with." After seven years in residence, he had to weigh whether the mission was in actual danger, or if they were simply afraid. He could not tell, but ultimately decided not to risk it.[56]

Low was disappointed by the Tunchow missionaries. He was humiliated that they had relied on a British ship to carry them and was furious that the consul had not consulted with him early on about any rumors of coming violence. But he was also frustrated that the missionaries had "felt compelled to abandon, even temporarily, a field that had cost such a struggle to win." The long-term effects, he feared, would not be good. The retreat would suggest that violence and threats of violence would be effective at getting missionaries to leave, which Low thought would only make the situation worse.[57] This concern about holding on to hard-won fields sounds more like a member of a mission board that the US minister to China. For all that Low had criticized the French for aligning the interests of the state too closely with those of the mission, he was not immune to such slippages either.

When former secretary of state William H. Seward arrived in China in the fall of 1870 as part of his world tour, he noted the anxiety that continued to plague the foreign community.[58] Many of the foreign legations were currently decamping from the capitol to seek safety in Shanghai, where the gunships of their respective nations were ready to respond if needed. European residents had begun drilling in preparation for a feared Chinese attack.[59] Seward celebrated Low's calm consideration of events, writing that he and Samuel Wells Williams seemed to be "almost the only persons in China who take a rational and statesmanlike view of the political situation."[60] William Seward, like Low, was satisfied that the Chinese had done all that they could and should to rectify the situation. Eighteen of the rioters had been beheaded. The Chinese paid indemnities. Nevertheless, the resident Americans and foreigners he met seemed united in their belief that nothing good could "come out of China, except through blockade and bombardment."[61]

Seward and Low shared a great deal in their perspectives on China and the troubles that missionaries brought with them. Both diplomats felt that Christianity was necessary for the transformation of China.

The Chinese Empire was in decline, Seward wrote, at least in part as "a result of the imperfect development of religious truth."[62] For his part, Low was convinced that missionaries were needed to educate the masses, just as foreign diplomats would have to enlighten Chinese officials on the proper functioning of diplomacy. Neither wanted to turn to force to "open" China to full Western commercial and diplomatic relations, and both agreed that missionaries were partners in the work of preparing China to open itself peacefully. But they agreed, too, that Christianity alone would not be enough.

Although Seward found the missionaries he met to be "earnest, true, and good men and women," Low had real apprehensions about their approach.[63] Neither Seward nor Low felt missionaries could or should expect the government to act aggressively in their defense. It was "right, just, and wise," Seward wrote, "that all the Christian nations shall mourn together over the victims, sympathize with the survivors, and unite in demanding such satisfaction from the Chinese Government as would afford security against a recurrence of persecution." This, however, had already happened. No more action from the government was needed or appropriate. Low complained that the missionaries had begun to endorse force as a way to open China for their own work. Force, they believed, was "absolutely necessary to break down the barriers of ignorance, conceit, and superstition, and that the use of armies to compel submission is only adding an auxiliary force to reason to accomplish the great work of the Master." Low did not agree. "The arguments against such a theory," he continued, "are so obvious that it is not necessary to repeat them here."[64]

Missionary work was, by its very nature, dangerous. William Seward reflected that missionaries would do well to remember that in Matthew's gospel, the Great Commission to go out and teach all nations was accompanied by a warning. Missionaries were sent out "as sheep in the midst of wolves," and accordingly needed to be as "wise as serpents and harmless as doves."[65] This scriptural allusion spoke to the contemporary political moment, Seward believed. Missionaries needed to pay attention to the perils that they might face and not expect the government to leap to their defense at all times. They might have been doing God's work, but this did not guarantee them the backing of the US government.

But this did not mean that the United States would not, in fact, back them when they were at risk. When the Chinese government issued a circular in response to Tientsin that blamed the missionaries for the violence, US diplomats joined with their European peers to object. The Chinese said that missionaries made themselves "odious to the principal men and people" in the places where they settled and were at fault for the violence they faced.

The Chinese government proposed a series of regulations for missionary activity that, they hoped, would resolve some of the tension: orphanages would operate with more transparency, women would not be allowed to enter the churches, missionaries would be required to "conform to the laws and customs of China," missionaries would cease protecting converts from trial, passports and missionary property would be more closely monitored, and missionaries would not allow any criminals to become Christians.[66] The French, British, and US governments were united in their opposition to these resolutions, which seemed to fly in the face, not only of their understanding of Christianity, but perhaps more important, of the protections guaranteed in earlier treaties. Women made up the majority of missionaries in the field at this time. The idea that missionaries might prevent women from coming into the churches was laughable.

In Washington, the president and secretary of state took comfort in knowing that nothing in Tientsin concerned the behavior of US missionaries. President Ulysses S. Grant supported Low's statements and actions, and confirmed that the US government had no interest in treating missionaries different in any way from any other US citizen abroad. If earlier in the century, missionaries used the principle of their equal rights of citizenship to make the government protect them abroad, increasingly diplomats and politicians were using it to argue that missionaries deserved no additional privileges not enjoyed by other Americans abroad. "We stand upon our treaty rights," Secretary Davis wrote. "We ask no more, we expect no less."[67]

Consuls and Violence in Persia

The State Department certainly grew in these years, but missionary activity continued in regions that were far from the centers of US diplomatic interest. There was sparse diplomatic coverage in the Ottoman Empire, but in Persia (Iran), there was no US diplomatic presence at all. This had not stopped American missionaries from working in the region, establishing a mission in the 1830s. By 1865, they believed the time had come for a formal US presence that could provide them with greater protection in times of trouble.

The Reverend Samuel Rhea appealed to President Andrew Johnson, using the same sort of reasoning that missionaries had adopted for decades to make these arguments. He pointed to the country's dedication to protecting its citizens abroad who were "engaged in lawful and laudable pursuits." This described the missionaries in Oroomiah (Urmia). He hoped that Johnson would agree that establishing a consulate or legation would be a beneficial way to inform the Persian government that the United States was "not unmindful of the well-being of its citizens, removed so far from the aegis of its own protection."[68] This request was not granted. By the 1880s, political difficulties in the region put the missionaries at risk without any US aid.

The missionary troubles in Persia were not the result of a misunderstanding about religious liberty or opposition to missionary evangelism. In some ways, they resembled the threats of attack by brigands that missionaries encountered in Turkey, but they were more complicated. The missionaries here were in physical danger as the result of ongoing warfare in the region. When Oroomiah was attacked during a Kurdish rebellion, there were rumors that the missionaries had been informed in advance. They denied this. During the siege, the missionary college sheltered some three hundred local Christians as well as a "large number" of Muslims in the area. Their longstanding good relations with local officials, largely due to the appreciation for the college, had kept them relatively safe. But when it had looked like troubles might arise, they were forced to rely on the British government for protection.[69]

Would the US government have considered representation in Persia at this time if it were not for the presence of missionaries? Probably not. Congressman Rufus Dawes, the brother of a Persia missionary, had brought the issue to the attention of the US government in 1880. As had been the case in Turkey, it was the physical attack—or the possibility of the attack—of American missionaries that created a clear duty for the United States. Missionary troubles led the United States to send its first representative to Tehran in 1883.[70] Yet even this was insufficient to missionary needs.

In May 1890, Shusan Wright was stabbed in her home. She was a Persian Nestorian by birth, but a US citizen by marriage—a fact that the missionaries were sure to point out when they approached the government for assistance in seeking justice for her murder. For five years, she had been married to Rev. John Wright, a Presbyterian missionary. The couple had spent their married life living in Persia and the United States. At the time of her death, she was the mother to a son and a daughter, and was expecting to give birth again shortly. The couple made their home in Salmas, where there was an American mission school but no nearby consulate.

This attack was different from what missionaries tended to worry about. The motive was not theft or anti-foreign opposition to the missionary movement. It was far more personal than that. Minas, Wright's attacker, was a graduate of the mission college who had been employed as a schoolteacher. For several months, he had been staying at the mission. The missionaries considered him "a gentle, nice-appearing fellow." But the Wrights became concerned that he was "too intimate" with their maidservant. They rebuked the servant and sent Minas to a different home, but found this made little difference. When she took the children out for a walk, or when she went onto the roof of the building, he was there. Matters seemed to come to a head after Mrs. Wright noticed the nurse was absent from her usual spot next to the baby in the middle of the night and saw Minas pass through a gate from the mission to his own yard. The Wrights were convinced that the two were having an affair and decided to dismiss him. The next afternoon, when John Wright went to gather the balance of his wages, Minas took the opportunity to attack.

John Wright's description of the scene was bloody. Minas had drawn a dagger from his sleeve and jumped on Shusan Wright, who was bent over her sewing. He tried to cut her throat, and sliced her chin, jaw, shoulders, and hands. He cut an artery and "the blood spurted as from a fountain." He pierced her lung. Even though her husband had come running the moment he heard her scream, the attack was too fast. Minas ran away, Wright gave instruction for the villagers to arrest him, and immediately called for another missionary to come and help him attend to his wife. In the half hour that he waited, he held the gashes on her back shut with his own hands. They feared for her life and for her pregnancy.[71]

Wright survived for several weeks, though she remained weak. Dr. Mary Bradford attended to her care, finding her "dangerously ill" on account of her wounds. In the days after the attack, her husband's attention was torn between caring for her and attempting to bring Minas to justice. This was challenging. John Wright had informed the government at Salmas of the attack at the same time that he had telegrammed for a doctor, but he was met with a refusal to act. It was Ramadan, and neither the governor nor his men could leave until they had broken their fast in the evening. Wright sent a messenger to bang on the door and demand redress, but no one would answer his call. From Wednesday until Sunday, the government would not take any action to arrest Minas. Wright offered a reward, but still nothing was done.

It was only when the British consul general happened to pass through town to visit with the missionaries that things began to change. The consul demanded action and informed the governor of Salmas, Hadji Khan, that he would inform both the British and US ministers of his negligence. Now "fully scared," Hadji Khan began "vigorous measures" to capture Minas, who had passed into Turkish territory. Within a few days, Minas was in custody. It was through the British consul that the US minister in Tehran learned of the events in Salmas. Without any US government officials nearby, the missionaries relied on British protection.[72]

Once John Wright learned that Minas had been captured, he declined to state his preference for what punishment the would-be assassin ought to face. "I leave the matter of his punishment entirely with you and Colonel Stewart," he wrote to the U.S. minister, "feeling sure that justice will be done and that he will be made an example, so that other evildoers may fear the results of their crimes." This was "premeditated and deliberately attempted murder," and Minas needed to face the consequences.[73] Unless his wife died from her wounds, Wright did not think that Minas should be executed for his crime. On the first of June, Shusan Wright delivered a stillborn baby boy. Several hours later, she died.[74]

After Wright's death, the Americans and British called for Minas's execution, but the British consul was worried about unrest in the region. The Armenians asked the missionaries to forgive Minas.[75] In the United States, the Presbyterian mission board demanded that the government work to ensure "an adequate punishment in this case." Leniency, they agreed, would endanger the lives of all Americans and Europeans living in Persia.[76] The case proceeded to trial, where the Americans and British insisted that, under Islamic law, Minas should be held responsible for two murders—of Wright and of her unborn child.[77]

At the end of the trial, Minas was sentenced to a life in prison. Spencer Pratt, the US minister at Tehran, called on the Eminé Soultan to challenge this decision. Pratt argued that only capital punishment could "meet the exigencies of the occasion."[78] The Presbyterian mission board agreed and asked the State Department to take action. Any discomfort they might have had in seeking "the execution of a poor deluded creature" could be cast aside. This was a man who had "deliberately murdered a noble wife and mother." On behalf of the US citizens working as missionaries in Persia, they asked the government to ensure that "the ends of justice be not defeated, lest the lives of those who remain may be jeopardized."[79]

This situation highlighted the dangers that American missionaries faced when they worked away from the protective arm of the US state. Foreign intervention was necessary to secure justice, it seemed. But the United States could not act alone. It was the British consul who forced the Persian government to act and who attended the trial.[80] And when the death penalty was not pursued, the Americans considered uniting with the British in protest. But Pratt was not sure about the international implications of such a move. Would this bind the United States to future actions?

The United States was a "disinterested power" in Persia, whereas Britain was "one of the powers directly concerned in Persia's politics." Joining together might force the United States out of its neutral position. Accordingly, Pratt believed it best to either ask alone, or else join with not only the British, but also the French and Russian ministers in protest. Pratt believed that if he were to make "a formal demand in the name of the Government of the United States for this criminal's execution," the Persian government would comply.[81] The United States, however, would make no such demand.

William Wharton, the acting secretary of state, agreed that life in prison was insufficient to the situation. But this was not just a question of justice for Mrs. Wright. It was also a matter of international relations between the United States and Persia. Because of the "high respect" that the United States had for the Persian government, the State Department remained confident that Persia would, upon "a full consideration of the case in all its aspects," act "wisely and courageously" in punishing the criminal. No formal demand was necessary.[82]

Attacks on missionary employees provide a case in point for how one type of trouble could lead to another. Physical violence followed missionary activity, but it was not the Americans who were hurt. In a case such as this, what was the duty of the US government?

In the same year that Stephens was murdered in Mexico, missionaries in Syria complained to the State Department about the violence that they faced. The Reformed Presbyterian Church mission requested immediate government intervention to give them redress. In the middle of the night, a group of soldiers had surrounded the mission building, mounted the roof, and broke down the doors of the school, where they bound and seized the people sleeping within. Because the building was American property, and because two of the five captives were employees of US citizens, they hoped that the government would act.[83] In Siam, too, missionaries requested the support of the US government when converts were hurt during an attack on the mission building in 1870.

In neither of these cases were US citizens harmed (though their property was damaged). Yet the missionaries hoped that the protection that they expected from their government might be extended to cover their employees and converts as well. These sorts of cases emerged naturally out of the missionary troubles that demanded government intervention and out of expanded understandings of extraterritoriality that included protection for American employees. Missionaries and consuls had long worked together, and it was easy for the missionaries to expect support in these situations just as they had in those where missionaries had been more directly victimized.

After decades of missionary troubles, the mission boards and the State Department were already in contact about the protections that missionaries required around the world. Why not seek help in these other types of trouble as well?

One type of missionary trouble, in other words, led easily to another. Soon, the missionary troubles were not only about missionaries who had been attacked. They also included the type of trouble that missionaries could drag the US government into and diplomatic crises that were entirely unexpected. Some diplomats began to wonder if the missionaries were victims after all, or if they might be better understood as troublemakers.

CHAPTER 6

Troublemakers

George F. Seward did not trust the missionaries. In 1867, the nephew of the secretary of state was serving as the US consul in Shanghai, and he did not like the practice of hiring missionaries as interpreters. Seward was convinced that the US legation and consulates were far too dependent on these missionaries. Though missionaries were the people usually available, they could not be counted on to know the court dialect or to understand official forms. They were distracted by their missionary work. They could not be expected to dedicate the time needed to prioritize government work. Yet even after decades of interactions with China, no US consuls could speak or read Chinese—unless they had been connected with the Protestant missions. The situation, Seward bemoaned, was humiliating. The time had come for the consuls to train up their own interpreters: young men who could be sent out especially for government work.[1]

A decade later, in 1877, Seward was appointed US minister to China, and he noticed something that worried him. Not only had the consuls been too dependent on the missionaries, but the missionaries had been expecting quite a lot from the consuls and the legation. In fact, the majority of cases that came before the legation had something to do with missionaries. This made sense, of course. Missionaries had long enjoyed a symbiotic relationship with US diplomats, and they made up the majority of US citizens living in China. Seward worried, though, that missionary diplomacy may have gone too far. He was not convinced that it was appropriate for diplomats to intervene on missionaries' behalf as much as they did.

In a circular letter, Seward warned the China consuls about this tendency of missionary troubles to appear in the legation's business. To some extent, he understood that such problems were inevitable. Missionary work was, by its nature, disruptive. If missionaries wanted to transform religious cultures, they could hardly expect to do so without facing resistance. Seward summarized the many forms of these missionary troubles bluntly: "They are assaulted, their converts maltreated, their mission-houses, chapels, dispensaries, and book-shops are pillaged and destroyed, or if none of these things happen, they find difficulty in securing houses and lands from which to carry on their work." To find redress for all of these wrongs, missionaries turned to the consuls or the legation.[2]

These conflicts between the missionaries and their host governments could be, as Seward put it, "awkward" for the government of the United States. Things were changing for Americans in China and around the world. American missionaries could be a troubling presence, forcing themselves into challenging situations and then expecting the US government to fix things. As Seward set out to articulate policy regarding missionaries, he walked a delicate line.

Seward reminded the consuls that the missionaries had the "sympathies of the American people," and that they did important work toward the "moral and physical advancement of the people." But part of the professionalization of the diplomatic corps after the Civil War meant distinguishing between the government's foreign policy priorities and the crises of foreign missions. Church and state were, and had to remain, separate. The rights that the government had to protect were the civil rights of missionaries as individual citizens; the government would not and could not "bring the power of the state actively into the advocacy of the Christian system." This seemed clear enough. In practice, however, it was not always easy to determine where to draw the line between the rights of missionaries as citizens and the rights of missionaries as missionaries.[3]

Seward's frustration was based on the kinds of missionary troubles he encountered through much of his work in China. Here, it seemed, missionaries were not always innocent victims. Rather, driven by religious ardor and confident that God and the United States would protect them, they pushed against the limits of foreign restrictions, trying to do as much as they could get away with. "Missionary troubles," it turned out, not only described the troubles that missionaries could find themselves in. It could also describe the problems that missionaries caused for the US government. In China and elsewhere, missionaries could be troublemakers. Seward and his peers were faced with an important question: Just how much should the government respond to the troubles that missionaries seemed to create in their wake?

Treaty Rights in Interior China

In the fall of 1872, Chinese officials in Hangchow (Hangzhou) began arresting people who had sold or leased land to missionaries. Missionaries were concerned. The punishments seemed extreme: up to "one thousand stripes," as they informed the consul. These were punishments designed to scare anyone away from helping the missionaries set up in the area, and they wanted the consul, stationed at Ningpo, to intervene. He did so, noting that it was his duty to protect the missionaries, as US citizens, from both "danger and annoyance" as they went about what he called their "benevolent work."[4] He was sure that these efforts were motivated by anti-foreign, rather than anti-mission, sentiments, a distinction that was ever-important after Tientsin and seemed to justify government intervention. The goal was nothing less than to rid the city of foreign residents. But one thing did worry the consul: Did the missionaries actually have the right to be in Hangchow?

Successive treaties between China and the various Western powers had gradually opened more and more coastal cities to trade. Under the terms of the treaties, foreign governments could send consuls to what became known as the "treaty ports" to help facilitate international trade. Alongside consuls and merchants came missionaries, whose right to purchase land and reside in these cities was explicitly permitted in the treaties. Missionaries were also permitted to obtain passports to travel throughout the Chinese Empire. Herein lay the challenge. Over the course of the 1860s, missionaries claimed not only the right to itinerate in the interior, but also to reside there and to establish the schools, chapels, and medical institutions that were part of their work.

In that decade, American missionaries established stations outside of China's treaty ports. In justifying this move, they relied on an 1860 treaty between France and China that, they believed, had guaranteed the right of missionaries to reside inland—a right denied to merchants and diplomats. The most-favored-nation status that the United States had acquired through their treaty with China meant that Americans, too, could claim this privilege. But by 1870, US diplomats had come to the opinion that the missionaries had been misinterpreting the treaty. There were discrepancies between the French and Chinese translations of the treaty, leaving it unclear whether any missionaries had the right to live away from the ports. George Seward, then the consul at Shanghai, noted in that year that the ability of missionaries to reside inland had been "wrung from the Chinese by war" and had left a bad feeling among many of the Chinese. As a result, he mused, "the record of murdered ones is a long one."[5] He was, in short, not inclined to help when missionaries encountered opposition at their inland stations.

Hangchow was 140 miles inland from the consulate at Ningpo, and it was in that port city that Americans had secured the right by treaty to reside. Missionaries had moved inland regardless. As the consul reflected on this, he concluded that whatever the treaties said, the fact was that "missionaries were here, and they had been here for many years."[6] The missionaries, in other words, had secured their right of residence not through treaty, but through practice. The missionaries had come, no one had stopped them before, and now the consul would work to secure their ability to remain.

Two years after the Ningpo consul's intervention, the missionaries were still in Hangchow, and community leaders adopted a different method to address missionary property. Now, they approached the missionaries and the consul with a petition requesting the migration of the mission buildings. The problem was not the missionaries as such—it was merely their specific location, which interfered with the feng shui of the city. Residents of the city paid to move the mission premises to a new location and reimbursed the missionaries for their trouble. Samuel Wells Williams, now working for the legation, rejoiced that this seemed to present a new era in US missions in China. Clearly, the American missionaries had made a "good name" for themselves in the seven years they had been in Hangchow. The "ugly rumors" that missionaries faced in places like Tientsin could be neutralized because the community knew and trusted the American missionaries. Conflicts could be handled simply and respectfully, and the missionaries were welcomed. It was not quite so simple as Wells made it seem—there would be a number of negotiations between the missionaries, the consulate, and the local officials in Hangchow before everyone was satisfied. But all recognized that they were on a path toward good relations.[7]

Williams's delight at how things worked out in Hangchow might be explained by the fact that elsewhere in China, consuls continued to report attacks on missionaries living away from the treaty ports. In 1872, Rev. Isaac Pierson was attacked in Yu-Cheu (Yuzhou). In 1874, consuls reported attacks on missionaries in Hoochow (Huzhou), Soo-chow (Suzhou), Kiu-kiang (Jiujiang), and Chi-mi (Chimi).[8] In 1875, two more missionaries were attacked in Shui Chang (Shuicheng).[9] Many of these situations echoed the earlier concerns in Tientsin.

There were conflicting accounts of what actually happened in Chi-mi. Missionary Rev. H. Corbett had been traveling from his home there to a nearby village where a group of Christians had invited him to preach. Something happened when he passed through a market town on his journey. According to Corbett, he was beset by a crowd of men chanting "hit him, hit him" and "kill him, kill him" while attacking him with stones. A few weeks later, he was again met by a crowd who attacked him from all sides and threw stones at him. Corbett escaped, but some of the Chinese Christians he was with were not so lucky. One received a bad gash on his head; another was so severely wounded that he could not walk. Corbett's home, too, was attacked. Corbett went to the consular agent at Chefoo (Yantai), 130 miles away, who approached a local Chinese official, the *taotai*, with a request for an investigation. The investigation, however, reported a very different series of events.

According to the taotai's report, Corbett had never been attacked at all. Instead, the crowd had gathered on the first day in response to a Chinese Christian kidnapping a young boy and announcing to a theater that he would take the child to the Catholic church and force him to become a Christian. The crowd had rescued the child. Corbett had been at the theater with his own children, who had attracted the interest of the gathering. Corbett had "rebuk[ed]" the crowd and left. "There was certainly no such thing as attacking and stoning him." As the taotai remarked: "What a discrepancy between these two representations!"[10]

The US consul faced a potentially complicated situation here. The missionary, a US citizen, claimed that he had been the victim of assault and theft. The Chinese officials, however, denied outright that anything of the sort had happened. The taotai had further reminded the consul of the challenges that missionaries faced in the interior, where their treaty rights were unclear. Good relations were possible, he suggested, but only if missionaries were "peaceable" in their interactions with the Chinese. Friendly relations, clearly, were not being maintained. But whose fault was it, and what actions should the United States take?[11]

No one at the consulate or legation appears to have doubted for a moment Corbett's version of events. When the consul was not satisfied with his correspondence with the taotai, he asked the legation to reach out to the Chinese foreign office. Williams did so, and the foreign office urged another investigation, this time with the governor of Shantung. This was not sufficient for the Americans, however. Williams sent Eli Shepherd, the US consul at Tientsin, to conduct his own investigation. Shepherd's report referred to these events as a "serious disturbance"—the first since Tientsin—that revealed the existence of real hostility against missionaries, even one who "had been peaceably living and quietly pursuing his calling in their midst."[12]

Shepherd found that the same rumors that had circulated in Tientsin had now come to Chi-mi. He reported that a mob of three thousand had assembled at one point, riled up by anti-foreign sentiments and the accusations that missionaries kidnapped children to use their body parts in medicine. Shepherd demanded the arrest of forty-two rioters, all known by name. This demand was backed with the threat of force: it was only when a US gunboat appeared and promised to stay until the affair was settled that the taotai agreed to bring charges against some of the accused. By June, Sheppard and the taotai came to a final settlement. At the meeting, the officers of the US gunboat *Saco* attended in full uniform. The four leaders of the mob who had been convicted of stoning were to be beaten with bamboo. Local constables would be dismissed from their office. Corbett would be repaid for his pecuniary losses. And, at Sheppard's request, the rest of the criminals would be pardoned after agreeing to a bond to "keep the peace" and guarantee Corbett's safety in the region.

Sheppard's report had two conclusions. First: that many of the people of China, and even many of the officials, did not know, or else did not understand, the provisions of the treaties between the United States and China that protected missionaries' work. And second: the involvement of the US Navy was ultimately essential for the keeping of the peace.[13]

It was no accident that many of these attacks occurred at the mission stations in the interior. As Secretary of State Hamilton Fish explained, missionaries took a risk when they move inland, and these risks affected more than just the missionaries themselves. American diplomats faced "embarrassment" when missionaries assumed "privileges which cannot be claimed or defended under the treaty."[14] But missionaries continued to push the boundaries of the treaty, and local officials continued to reveal a wide range of interpretations of the legality of the missionary presence. No one could agree on what, exactly, the treaties had to say about missionaries outside of treaty ports. Missionaries described this as "ignorance of the most basic provisions of the treaty." The effect of this was clear. Without officials proclaiming the right of missionaries to live in the interior, they faced strident opposition from those who saw the missionary presence as "an unauthorized intruder." Missionaries in the mid-1870s wanted the Chinese authorities issue proclamations about the missionaries' rights to reside and evangelize in China.[15] Seeing the same problem, the US diplomats puzzled over how best to respond.

Benjamin Avery, the new US minister in 1875 explained this dilemma to a consul: "The difficulty," he wrote, was that "our missionaries have advanced their stakes and cannot be left in the lurch; yet it would be wrong to encourage them to make any new ventures beyond treaty-limits in the present unsettled and somewhat threatening aspect of the question." He advised the missionaries to "learn to wait and labor where they are," and not to rush into fields where they could not legally reside.[16] To the Chinese government, he promised to advise the missionaries to avoid communities known to be hostile to their presence, even as he maintained that the missionaries did, in fact, have the right to reside where they wished. He had every reason to believe the missionaries would be "duly cautious in their movements."[17]

But even with those concerns, Avery was quite clear that if missionaries came into trouble, it was the job of the government to protect them. He defended missionaries against Chinese officials who blamed them for the troubles they encountered. If a missionary did break the law or exceed treaty limits, he argued, extraterritoriality provisions in the Sino-American treaties guaranteed that missionaries should face US, not Chinese, justice.[18] Whether or not the missionaries had the right to reside wherever they chose, this was a right that they possessed everywhere they went. He merely hoped that the missionaries would allow their "sense of prudence and patriotism" to prevent them from testing this.[19]

Avery clearly understood the missionary position to be important for the US cause more generally. Adopting militaristic language as he described the situation to the secretary of state, Avery worried about the "general retreat of all missionaries, of whatever nations, from the advanced posts they are now occupying." To the Chinese, such a retreat would seem to be evidence of "a weakening of foreign influence and power," which could "react disastrously upon other interests than those of religion."[20]

All Avery wanted was for the missionaries to use tact and delicacy and to avoid unnecessary conflict. For the most part, this seemed to be precisely what happened. But the conflicts that did arise suggested deeper concerns festering under the surface. Avery's letters about missionary troubles existed among other dispatches to the State Department about a rising anti-foreign sentiment in China. The challenge facing US diplomats was significant. As Avery explained to the secretary of state, they had to simultaneously support the "prestige and opportunities" of missionary citizens without "engaging indirectly in religious propagandism," while still "dealing justly and honorably by China." It was a tricky balance, and one that missionaries were not making any easier.[21]

These were the concerns echoing in his mind when Seward wrote his reflections on missions in 1876. His primary concern was that the missionaries not draw the government into difficult situations. Echoing his uncle's use of biblical allusions a few years earlier, he advised missionaries to adopt the "wisdom of the serpent."[22] Seward urged them to be "forbearing and long-suffering, to avoid places which are dangerous, to deal respectfully with cherished beliefs, erroneous though they be," and finally "to arouse the least possible animosity, and to draw the Government as little as may be into the arena of discussion and conflict."[23] Seward's use of the Bible to make his case for how missionaries should maintain the separation between church and state was indicative of the challenges diplomats like himself would continue to face.

Seward instructed all the consuls to gather the missionaries residing in their area together and read his letter aloud to them. The missionaries, he felt, needed to be reminded of what they could and could not expect from their government. As he outlined the ways that they ought to avoid conflict, he asked that they "not embarrass us unduly." When troubles did come, as indeed they would—in China and elsewhere—the agents of the US government would do their work to learn the facts of the case, present them to the local authorities, and to procure settlements promptly. They, like the missionaries, should use "discretion and tact," taking care not to add to any difficulties. Whenever possible, consuls should handle difficulties locally, but always keep the legation at Peking informed of what they were doing.[24] The government was committed to protecting missionary interests. Seward just hoped that the missionaries would not drag the legation into unnecessary conflict.

It did not take long for Seward's new policy to be tested. Seward's circular was penned in March; by April, the Wuchang (Wuhan) consul and Episcopalian missionaries had an opportunity to exercise tact and delicacy in facing local opposition. On the afternoon of the fourteenth, the mission station at Fukai was busy. In the chapel, a small group gathered to hear a native convert give an address about his faith. In the dispensary behind the chapel, Dr. A. C. Bunn was hard at work seeing to his patients. His work was interrupted, however, when he heard a disturbance outside. A crowd descended on the chapel, led by two distressed women. The women, he wrote, threw themselves at Bunn's feet, begging him to return their missing children to them. Two children, it appeared, had disappeared, and the crowd believed that the missionaries had taken them.[25]

It was a tense afternoon, the kind of situation that could go badly very quickly. By the end of the day, as things calmed down, some five hundred people remained crowded in the street outside of the chapel. They only caused "but little annoyance," Bunn reported, although the missionaries received threats. Bunn explained to the diplomats that the suspicions against him could be traced to the same sorts of rumors that had long plagued Christian foreigners. In addition, tensions were already high in the community because of rumors of a coming war or insurrection.[26]

Bunn had no doubt that the women genuinely believed he had the children on the premises, and he allowed the crowd to make a thorough search. Throughout, he continued to see to his patients, who continued coming through the crowd to receive care. He exercised precisely the sort of delicacy and tact that Seward had hoped for. In the end, this was a crisis averted. The crowd, encouraged by the constable that Bunn eventually called, dispersed. The children were located elsewhere. When the local officials learned what had happened, they issued a proclamation that the missionaries were there "only to do good," and thus should not be attacked by any crowds.[27]

Seward was quite pleased with how this all played out. Well aware of how things might have gone differently, he was grateful and relieved by the behavior of the missionaries, the consul, and the Chinese officials alike. He sent his congratulations to the consul and informed the secretary of state that the missionaries had been "very discreet" and the Chinese officials had demonstrated "good will and favorable action." At no point did the consul or the US minister have to get involved at all, although clearly, they were keeping track of events. Bunn only wrote his summary of what had happened because the consul requested it. The report then made its way all the way to Washington, where it appeared among the papers relating to the foreign relations of the United States that Congress received in December 1876. Though he was grateful not to get involved, Seward was keeping a close eye on what was happening to those he called "our missionaries."[28]

Religious Toleration and Printing in the Ottoman Empire

Missionaries in the Ottoman Empire, too, required government attention. The empire was a place of incredible religious diversity, and the Ottoman government had made religious toleration an important part of its legal code in the 1850s. While Islam remained the state religion, the government recognized the rights of its subjects who practiced other religions. Tolerance, the Ottoman government understood, was the key to maintaining rule over such a large group of people. What this policy might mean for US missionaries was not immediately clear, however, especially considering the different ways that Americans understood religious freedom from the ways that the Turks defined religious tolerance.

Edward Joy Morris, the US minister resident at Constantinople in 1865, accordingly understood that it was important for Americans to grasp what, exactly, religious tolerance meant. To this end, Morris sent documents to the State Department explaining the Turkish government's views on the subject so that US Christians could understand how much Christian practice and Christian evangelism would be welcomed in the sultan's territories.[29]

American Christians who celebrated the religious toleration of the sultan may have been surprised to learn that this toleration demanded an extreme wariness toward missionaries. Christians were allowed to enter Turkey and faced no "restraints in the exercise of their spiritual ceremonies." But proselytism was something different—especially proselytism directed against Islam, the religion of the state. "The principle of religious toleration," a Turkish official explained, "cannot, in our view, be reconciled with open aggression against any religion whatever." Proselytism was, in this understanding, a "contradiction in the principle of religious liberty, for by its very existence it attacks that liberty in others, and that respect for the conviction of others, without which religious tolerance would be but an empty form." Missionaries who complained that they were facing intolerance when they faced restrictions on their evangelism were, he argued, willfully misinterpreting the law.[30]

And missionaries did complain, especially after a new restriction on the importation or publishing of certain books in 1875. The policy targeted "improper books, pamphlets, and writings," and required significant oversight of missionary operations. All works to be published in Constantinople or imported for sale from foreign countries or the provinces had to be inspected. Unpublished material would need to first be approved in draft form, and then have the printed copy rechecked to ensure that no objectionable material had been added. It also required all texts to prominently display on the title page whether the book was of a religious or scientific nature. The goal, in part, was to clarify which publications were evangelistic and to keep problematic materials off the market. In the words of US minister Horace Maynard, this had the effect of "carr[ying] us backward centuries."[31]

Shortly after hearing of these new regulations, American missionaries made their protest known to the US minister at Constantinople. Identifying themselves not as a missionary group, but rather as a large institution of book publishing and importing, they argued that the new procedures were "needlessly burdensome." They worried that they would have books seized throughout the provinces. In practice, they expected that it would make book publishing in Constantinople nearly impossible. They complained about existing delays that groups like the American Bible Society had faced in getting written permission to publish biblical translations (the effort of ten years of missionary labor). In their forty years in the region, the missionaries emphasized, they had never before been censored. But, they acknowledged, they faced opposition and mistrust because of the "impression" that they did, in fact, publish objectionable material.[32]

Enclosed with the missionaries' protest was a catalog of the more than three hundred books and tracts that US missionaries in Constantinople printed in Arabic, Armenian, Greek, Bulgarian, Spanish, and English. Some of these would have been quite easy to categorize as either religious or scientific, as the regulations required. Titles like *Beatitudes and Lord's Prayer*, *Notes on Matthew and Mark*, *Belief and Worship*, or *Sin and Salvation* would all have clearly been "religious." Similarly, the arithmetic and algebra textbooks (with multiple editions of each), as well as other classroom texts like *Physiology* would have been "scientific." But many of the titles on the list would have been difficult to categorize, precisely because they reflected the ways that US Christians so often collapsed the categories of "religious" and "scientific."

How would textbooks on moral science or geography be sorted? These were academic subjects and books intended for the schoolroom, but their content reflected a clear religious point of view with commentary on the religious character of various populations. So too would the multiple readers intended for classroom instruction, the *Magazine of Knowledge*, and even the many memoirs and biographies that the missionaries published. The regulations sought to make it easier for readers and consumers to identify when they were looking at a book that was talking about subjects of belief or subjects of fact. But the missionaries' way of thinking defied this categorization. For them, all knowledge would lead to a better understanding of God and God's world.

In the decades after the new regulations were enacted, missionary organizations complained about texts being seized and the US government not doing enough to stop it. In June 1881, the American Bible Society reported that authorities in Gallipoli had seized Bibles that were prepared for distribution in the region. Although the government was attentive to this issue, it would take nearly two years to reach a resolution that the Bible Society would find satisfactory.[33] By the summer of 1884, US officials in Turkey were still working to reach a "favorable adjustment" in what had become a ban on the sale of Bibles in Turkey.[34] At the same time, the American Bible Society reported similar bans of Bible sales in Russia and Greece. There, too, they wanted the government to intervene to allow them to conduct their missionary efforts.

For missionaries and their supporters, after all, this was not just about some books that had been seized. It was about their rights. It is telling that the missionaries framed their appeals as business concerns. They were not just evangelists—they were publishers and booksellers. As missionaries had been doing for decades, they called on their government to support them in the pursuit of their legitimate business. Accordingly, when a rumor reached the ABCFM in Boston that the Turkish minister in Washington had persuaded Secretary of State Frelinghuysen to waive the $100 indemnity for the Gallipoli case, the ABCFM objected. In a letter to the secretary, the mission board explained that Turkish authorities seemed to have "very little respect for the rights of our missionaries," which required a strong response from the US government.

Missionary groups approached these cases as if they were the same as those in which missionaries were the victims of physical attack. "Any failure to secure indemnity and punishment of wrong doers is speedily known everywhere," the ABCFM warned, "to the great inconvenience and possible injury of American citizens in the Empire." Backing down, in other words, was not a viable option.[35] The government did not, however, see the situations as the same. The American Bible Society and the

ABCFM, frequent collaborators, accused the State Department of providing insufficient protection for missionaries and their work.[36]

Though diplomats referred to both sorts of cases as missionary troubles, this group was more frustrating. Evangelical missions were clearly at odds with the religious tolerance demanded by Ottoman law, and it was harder to frame them as innocent victims. As much as missionaries tried to limit their work to non-Muslim populations, their long-term goals were clear. Missionaries had long compared their publishing work to the planting of seeds. In due time, they expected a harvest of profound cultural transformations. How, then, was the US government to respond to the publishing crisis? They did work to protect missionary investment and recuperate seized material, but as in China, their support of the missionaries could not seem to endorse the mission itself.

Religious Freedom in the Caroline Islands

The missionary troubles in the Ottoman Empire and China challenged US diplomats in part because the United States had other interests in both regions. Protestant missionaries were a vocal and powerful group of US citizens in both places, but they were not alone and diplomats did not want to put other groups at risk by prioritizing missionary interests too much. It was a rather different situation on Ponape in the Caroline Islands. The island had been home to a small group of US missionaries for thirty-five years when, in 1887, one of them was arrested by the new Spanish colonial government. Here, too, missionary troubles required US government action. Within a decade, the Caroline Islands would have their first US consul—a direct response to missionary demands for assistance in navigating foreign empires and questions of religious freedom.

The Rev. E. J. Doane first arrived at Ponape in the 1850s and had led the ABCFM missionaries in building schools and Protestant churches as they worked to "civilize" the people of the islands. A year before his arrest, Doane had held up Ponape as a tremendous example of America's benevolent "influence upon the world." In an article in the *Missionary Herald*'s children's column, Doane described the celebration of the Fourth of July on the islands. "Our Ponape natives," he crowed, "have taken up the day as almost one of their own." Doane and the missionaries did not celebrate with fireworks and parades, but rather with a great celebration that brought together the children of ten Sunday Schools. In the packed church, adults gathered to pray, sing, read Scripture, and listen to orations from Christian converts. For Doane, this was evidence of the true influence of America on the world. As the *Herald*'s editors noted, American Christians should celebrate that the "glorious Fourth is now honored the world around," not only in the homes of foreign ambassadors, but in mission houses. "True it is," Doane concluded, "that the kingdom of Christ gives both political freedom and freedom from the poverty and savageness of heathenism." American missionaries, linking their country's legacy of political independence with their religious commitment to evangelism, embraced both sides of this project.[37]

This influence could not last. Once Spain asserted its control over the islands, the US missionaries quickly faced opposition from the new governor. At least some of the conflict was religious in nature, as the Spanish worked to encourage Catholicism on the islands and limit the influence of Protestantism. Doane and his missionary colleagues were frustrated by what they saw happening. Schools closed. Church attendance decreased. Alcohol seemed more prevalent. The US missionaries saw all this as evidence of Spain's negative influence.[38] When officials arrested Doane on vague charges and sent him to Manila, his missionary sponsors demanded US action. In the correspondence between the ABCFM and the State Department, it was clear that the government was sympathetic to these "missionary troubles," as they were again called. The nearest US representative was Julius G. Voight, the consul at Manila. He began an investigation in August and met with the governor-general and Doane, and quickly sought reparations for the difficulties Doane had endured and a guarantee of the protection of American missionaries and their work in the Caroline Islands. The United States dispatched a naval vessel in support of the imprisoned American missionary citizen that remained there to guarantee the missionaries' protection.[39]

Doane was released, and even received the approbation of the Spanish governor-general Emilio Terrero, who called the missionary work in the islands an "extraordinary service to humanity and civilization."[40] Terrero granted the missionaries the right to "preach, teach, catechize, distribute Bibles, hold schools, make proselytes to the Protestant faith, and, in short, to pursue the missionary and other work precisely as heretofore." They retained the right, too, to own real estate on the island if they could provide clear titles from the original native owners. They were ordered to obey all Spanish laws and to respect the "opinions of others in all matters, especially of religion"—the particular concern here was that Protestant American missionaries not interfere with the work of Catholic friars and priests who were also establishing churches and schools on the islands.[41]

Missionary supporters at home were cautiously optimistic about these results. Terrero's support was important, but it did not necessarily mean anything about what would happen on Ponape. After all, more than two thousand nautical miles separated that island from Terrero and the US consul in Manila, and it was the local officials who had arrested Doane in the first place. "Whether this officer can or will control the subordinate officials throughout the Spanish possessions," as a writer for the *Missionary Herald* put it, "remains to be seen."[42] In the meantime, the supporters waited for news of an indemnity. Ongoing negotiations would be needed between the Spanish and US governments.

At least one of the missionaries in the Caroline Islands felt that US missionary presence ought to have some relation to US power there. Missionary Miss Fletcher argued that even if it was indisputable that Spain had the "right of discovery," the question needed to be asked: "How about those thirty-four or thirty-five years of labor and expense which America has given?" In the intervening years, Spain had not "even looked at" the islands; it was only when Germany attempted to claim the islands that Spain became interested. Now she asked if American missionaries were really expected to "step aside and see all this come to naught."[43] The missionaries were not being sent away, which made her concerns all the more compelling. Sharing the islands with the Spanish Catholics felt like being asked to step aside. While the United States had never claimed the islands, the missionaries had come to think of them as their own.

The logic of empire underpinned much of the ways that both the United States and Spain reacted to these events. The arrest had occurred in Ponape, but the important diplomatic conversations were not with the people of the islands, but rather between officials in Washington, Madrid, and Manila. It was in these centers that US and Spanish officials conferred about the proper relationship between American missionaries, islanders, and local governors. And the Spanish officials in Manila and Madrid agreed that the US missionaries were doing good work on the islands. The tensions between Catholicism and Protestantism were set aside in the interest of promoting the more general goals of "civilization." For more than thirty-five years, US missionaries had transformed the Caroline Islands in ways that, Spain understood, ultimately benefited their colonial interests.

The view from Washington, Madrid, and Manila, then, seemed rosy. But Doane's release did not change the fact that he had been falsely arrested in the first place. The American missionaries and their organizations in the United States wanted more of a US presence on the ground. They wanted a guarantee of extraterritoriality—common in US treaties in Asia and the Middle East, but unheard of in US treaties with European powers. The problem for the State Department was that after 1886, the government on Ponape was not a non-Christian one; it was Spanish. It was obvious within diplomatic circles that the ABCFM's request was absurd. Spain required more respect and deference than China, and could be counted on to take the concerns of the Americans and their missionaries more seriously.[44]

Yet Spain did not respond as fully as the Americans, missionaries or diplomats, had wanted or expected. Government officials in Madrid were saying the right things, but action was slow. Yes, the Spanish agreed, Doane's arrest had been unjust. When the Spanish began to "actively" occupy the Caroline Islands, the US government was given "specific assurance" that the "rights and privileges of citizens of the United States" in the islands would not only not be infringed, but would in fact "be fully protected and secured." But two years after Doane's release, reparations remained unpaid. The new governor had taken the deeds to Doane's property, and it seemed likely that Doane would be removed from the land he had owned for more than three decades. For the missionaries, this was unacceptable. In a letter to Secretary of State James Blaine, Judson Smith of the ABCFM reflected that the missionaries enjoyed better protection at their missions "in the midst of the Turkish Empire, in China, and among many tribes of Africa."

If the missionaries could expect protection "even of heathen kings and rulers," there was no reason he could understand why their protection could not be demanded of Spain.[45] If the Spanish would not respect the rights of Americans, Smith suggested that the government send a man-of-war to Ponape and show a "distinct protest" against the actions of the Spanish government on the island. A show of strength was required. The Spanish needed to "understand that the American Government stands behind the American citizens who reside there, and guards their welfare and their just claims with all its wealth and strength."[46]

Doane never did receive his indemnity. The Spanish government concluded that none was actually necessary. Neither the ABCFM nor the US State Department would leave it at that. Throughout the whole incident, the ABCFM linked its concerns about Doane's rights and the proper respect that the US government deserved. Unlike in China or Ottoman territory, Americans had no major competing interests at play here and were able to interpret this incursion of missionary rights as an affront to American standing. In the American Board's initial call for indemnity in 1887, Judson Smith had made it clear: the "honor of our Government" was at stake.[47] When asked to quantify the damages that Doane needed to be reimbursed, Smith came to a figure of $5,000 by adding the amount that the Board had to spend as a result of Doane's arrest ($1,000) to the value of the land the governor had seized in Ponape ($2,000). The remainder was a rough estimate of what was needed to recognize both the interruption of Doane's work and "the indignity to our Government" as a result of Doane's ill treatment.[48] Smith regularly described the missionary interests on the islands as "American interests," and the State Department did not take issue with this interpretation. Indeed, they adopted it. The crisis in Ponape mattered to the US government not only because of the arrest of a US citizen, but also because of the interest that the United States had in supporting the civilizing work that missionaries had undertaken on the island.

William Wharton, the acting secretary of state, had to walk the delicate line that so many State Department officials had walked before and since in explaining this US interest in missionary work. The US government "can take no cognizance of the relations of these missionaries to any sect or church," he explained to the US chargé d'affaires in Spain H. R. Newberry. That would be clearly inappropriate. But at the same time, the United States "has felt a deep interest in their efforts to ameliorate and improve the condition of the natives." For Wharton, the decisive factor in determining whether and how to respond was the recognition that "these missionaries are citizens of the United States and entitled to the intervention of this Government for the protection of their persons and their property."[49]

It was as a result of these struggles between the Spanish governor and the missionaries that the United States decided to send a consul to Ponape. The ABCFM had made this suggestion when the conflicts seemed to them to demand additional pressure that was more local than Madrid, Washington, or even Manila. While missionaries served as consuls elsewhere, it did not seem wise for a missionary to serve in that capacity in this case. Strategically, it would be far better to have someone who could not be accused of taking the missionary side out of self-interest. Although the missionary board's suggestion of a US citizen already resident in Ponape was not taken up, the desired consul was on his way in 1890.[50]

But then, somehow, things got even worse at Ponape. In the summer of 1890, missionary Lucy Cole wrote that "we are in great trouble here." A new anti-Spanish uprising on June 30 had led to the death of more than thirty of the military forces from Manila, including a lieutenant and two corporals. Cole described the Ponapeans as "hunting them down like pigs." Cole and Anne Palmer were the only missionaries on the island at the time. They were two single women with a school full of girls to care for. One of the local teachers for the mission, Nanpei, had saved the two Catholic priests by bringing them, along with five other men from Manila, to be hidden at the mission residence. The women kept them in the house for two days and two nights, in constant fear that they would be discovered. In the midst of the conflict, Cole would escape with some of the girls on the boat of a friendly American; Palmer felt the need to stay at the house until the priests were safe. Though they were only in her house from Wednesday morning until midnight on Thursday, Palmer reflected, "It seems as if it must have been at least a week."[51]

Under cover of darkness, Nanpei eventually snuck the men to the Spanish man-of-war that waited in the harbor to retreat to Manila. The missionaries knew that it was only a matter of time before the fighting grew worse. Four Spanish ships were expected in a matter of weeks, with the promise that they would begin shelling Ponape as soon as they reached the island. The missionaries feared for their lives, convinced that they would be caught in the crossfire. The US fleet in the Sandwich Islands was too far away to reach them in time to do any good, and so the missionaries anxiously awaited the *Morning Star*, the ABCFM ship that was usually tasked with transporting their mail and provisions.[52] But the Spanish ships arrived first and brought with them the expected firepower.

When they were done, the American mission was in tatters. The mission church, built in 1870, had been burned. So, too, were the homes of four missionaries, the dormitories for the girls' school and the training school, and the school building. The church bell was destroyed, as were the books, household goods, and medicines that the mission relied on. All told, the damages amounted to $11,114.

The Spanish would later insist that this attack on American property had been a necessary act of war. The rebels, they claimed, were seeking asylum in the mission buildings and needed to be routed out. In effect, they were treating the missionaries as more Ponopean than American. Their sympathy for the rebels outweighed their status as US citizens. The missionaries, the Spanish believed, were troublemakers.[53]

In a panic, the ABCFM wrote to the State Department that things were dire. Could the government do anything to hurry the consul along? He had never been needed more than he was right now.[54] By October, the governor had refused to allow the missionaries to leave the island and forbade them from holding any meetings. Commander Taylor, of the USS *Alliance*, arrived on the islands in the middle of the month. He reported that the Spanish now accused the missionaries of "inciting the natives to rebellion."[55]

Taylor's investigation into the events in Ponape presented a rather different picture than what the Spanish were suggesting. His arrival provided precisely the "moral effect" that the navy had expected: missionaries were reassured that the government would send protection when it was needed, and the Spanish would be reminded that "the Government of the United States stands by its citizens wherever they may be."[56] Taylor negotiated between the governor—once friendly, but now deeply suspicious—and the missionaries. Coming into a space he described as "in a condition of active war," he worked to assess the damage to the mission property and secure the ability of the missionaries to leave the island safely and quickly. He determined easily that the missionaries were innocent of all the charges leveled against them, and managed to do so without upsetting the governor.[57]

This was somewhat remarkable, given the charges that the governor was leveling against the missionaries. Governor Cadarso was convinced that the missionaries were behind the uprising. The rebels were "the missionaries' best friends," he ranted to Taylor. Their entrenchments, he was sure, had been "planned under the advice of missionaries, or of their native assistants, who had been to Europe or America." None of this was true. Yet Taylor did believe that the mission had an important influence that set the stage for rebellion. For decades, the American Protestant missionaries had worked to educate and "civilize" the Ponapeans. "It may be supposed," he granted, "that the ideas, religious and political, imbibed by the natives in long association with these missionaries, would not predispose them to ready submission to Spain and its religion." By its very nature, in other words, mission work helped to raise this community to a level of civilization that chafed at the sort of colonialism that the Spanish hoped to enforce. "But," Taylor argued, "no act unfriendly to Spain has been committed."[58]

Taylor received permission to remove the missionaries, along with a number of their students, from Ponape until peace was restored. They left very reluctantly. It was only with Taylor's assurances that they were truly in grave danger, and the realization that they could not rely on the protection of the local government, that they agreed to leave. They boarded the USS *Alliance* and were escorted off the island.

The ABCFM hoped that the US government would take swift and decisive action. Smith urged Secretary Blaine "to exert the authority of the Government in defence [*sic*] of these defenceless [*sic*] Americans." Such defense was, Smith argued, "the glory of the American Government."[59] But it was more than this. Smith was clearly worried about the safety of missionaries at Ponape and elsewhere—if Spain could get away with this, then what might missionaries in other spaces expect? For now, this was a unique situation. "The heathen Emperor of China does nothing of the kind," he noted; nor did "the pagan kings and chiefs of Africa." What Spain was allowing to happen in Ponape was beyond the pale. The US government simply had to respond. If they did not, the effects would quickly spread beyond missionaries. "It is more than a question of protecting a few men and women at the island of Ponape. It is a question of the honor and dignity of our Government."[60] The State Department agreed.

Writing to the US minister to Spain, Acting Secretary of State William Wharton expressed the frustration of the US government. Enough was enough. It was "inherently inconceivable" to Wharton that either of the female missionaries could have had anything to do with the uprising, and yet they faced a "spirit of hostility" from the local government and were "virtually held as prisoners" on the island. What was at issue, Wharton suggested, was the method of Spain's colonialism. When the Spanish arrived in 1886, they had only "purely historical" claims to justify their possession of the islands. Neither they nor the Germans, against whom the Spanish had vied for control of the Carolines, had any actual presence on the island. At the time, "the only foreign influence they had known was the quiet, peaceful, and beneficent [*sic*] effort of the American missionaries to educate and civilize them." The American missionaries, he suggested, brought the benefits of colonialism with them: civilization and education. As a result, they were loved. Spanish colonialism brought only oppression and division.[61]

While he came close, Wharton never directly questioned he legitimacy of Spain's presence in the Caroline Islands. Instead, he closed his instructions to the minister with the usual diplomatic niceties. At this moment when officials in Ponape displayed a "ruthless disregard" for the rights of US citizens, the honorableness of the Spanish government was taken for granted.[62] As fellow members of the community of nations, the United States and Spain would be able to come to an arrangement, the diplomats were sure. The United States was not about to challenge a colonial power for the control of this distant island. Yet the missionaries had brought Ponape, and Spanish colonial governance, to the close attention of the State Department.

Two years later, the State Department was still corresponding with its legation in Spain about the missionary troubles at Ponape. The new minister to Spain, A. Loudon Snowden, received extensive instructions about how to proceed with this delicate matter in the face of Spanish unwillingness to accept the missionary version of events.[63] Snowden would prove to be the sort of advocate missionaries had long been looking for: firm and insistent, apparently as deeply sympathetic to missionary work as he was eager to defend the interests of his country.

Snowden bluntly dismissed the Spanish claims that the missionary property had been insufficiently marked as American at the time when it had been destroyed. This was willful destruction; to pretend otherwise was counterproductive. After all, Snowden was sure that he and the Spanish could agree, missionaries deserved "especial sympathy and protection." They did not make trouble. They were "self-denying" women and men "who, to extend the civilizing and ennobling influence of Christianity, cross wide seas, penetrate heathen lands, face innumerable dangers, suffer untold hardships in an unselfish desire to spread the gospel of Christ."[64]

In the end, Snowden negotiated a settlement of $17,500, the absolute minimum that the US government was willing to accept. It was significantly less than the $25,000 that the ABCFM had requested, and was paid as a lump sum, as the Spanish government refused to concede any of the specific points that the Americans had raised about who, exactly, deserved repayment. Doane's original deed to the property he claimed remained contested; the Spanish continued to insist that the destruction of the mission buildings was a necessity of war. But they paid. In late May 1893—some six years after Doane had first been arrested—the missionary troubles at Ponape came to a close. The Spanish government still would not guarantee the safety of the missionaries if they were to return to the islands, but the honor of the United States seemed to have been respected at last.[65]

One of the more telling moments in the Ponape crisis can be found in one of John Foster's letters to Snowden. The Spanish had been regularly referring to the missionaries as Methodists, and from time to time the Americans bristled at this specificity. The missionaries themselves were working with the American Board of Commissioners for Foreign Missions—primarily a Congregational missionary organization, but this was not the issue. For the Spanish, "Methodist" seemed to stand in for "Protestant." This, they were. Was this, then, a conflict between a Catholic and a Protestant state? Not so, Foster claimed. The Spanish believed that the missionaries had acted politically; this was the root of their complaint. But Foster insisted that they had not. After all, the ABCFM "expressly forbid all interference by the missionaries with the political affairs of the country where they dwell." But more than this: the US government "cannot take into consideration the particular sect of these missionaries." It did not matter that they were Protestant, he claimed. If they had been Catholic, "the relation of this Government to them would be precisely the same." Speaking of the position of the United States to the missionaries, he explained: "It sympathizes with their work because Christian. It accords them protection because American."[66]

This distinction between sympathy and protection was, in many ways, what Seward had been getting at in China. The challenge for diplomats at the end of the century was precisely how to determine whether missionaries in trouble were acting as Christians or as Americans, and how far the government ought to go to act in their defense.

CHAPTER 7

Workers

On the fourth of July 1871, former secretary of state Henry Seward was in Constantinople (Istanbul). Among the other celebrations of the day, Seward joined the formal opening of the new buildings of Robert College. It was a grand edifice of stone on a prime location overlooking the Bosporus. After years of difficulty securing the right to build these new expanded premises, the building now stood ready to welcome in a larger class of eager students. Above its roof flew the US flag.

This was the first time that a building had been granted permission to fly a foreign flag on the Bosporus, a fact whose significance was not lost on the school's founder, Cyrus Hamlin. Hamlin had first come to Turkey as a missionary for the ABCFM in 1840. After two decades at the head of Bebek Seminary, and almost as long in conflict with the ABCFM over how a mission school should operate, he left his formal missionary career to focus his attention on a new endeavor. He would create the "first Christian college in Turkey." True, he would later recall, the Jesuits had previously built institutions that they called colleges. But those were not what he was talking about. His school would be, he explained, an "American college," and therefore could lay claim to the title of a Christian college in a way he thought that the Jesuit schools

Figure 7.1.   Front view of Robert College, Istanbul, with the US flag.
Source: Hamlin, *My Life and Times*, facing 461.

never could. Within this idea was the claim that to be an American was, in an important way, to be Christian.[1]

Robert College was founded to be an American Christian college in Turkey. Although he was no longer officially connected to a missionary body, Hamlin believed this to be a missionary endeavor. Missionary organizations had long debated the proper combination of "secular" and "religious" subjects in mission schools. Now Hamlin was free to embrace the kind of educational model that he understood to be best suited to help the future of Protestant Christianity in Turkey. It was not just, or even primarily, about evangelism and preparing a native ministry—the narrower goals of some missionary bodies. Rather, his school offered a high-caliber liberal arts and scientific curriculum that allowed its graduates to seek employment in a range of fields.

When William Seward helped celebrate the opening of Robert College in 1871, he endorsed the vision of America's role abroad that supported close connections between missionary and diplomatic goals. There was a reason that the college's new buildings were opened on July 4, just as there was a reason that the initial cornerstone had been laid on July 4 a few years earlier. There was a reason, too, that the school flew the US flag. The college would become the most prominent US institution in the Ottoman Empire. Because of Hamlin's missionary history and his commitment to creating a Christian school, it was an emblem, too, of the ongoing difficulty of parsing "religious" from "secular" subjects in both missionary and diplomatic contexts. Americans and Turks alike celebrated the school.

The "secular" work of missionaries invited a new sort of missionary troubles as the century drew to a close. The 1880s and 1890s were years of great expansion for both the missionary movement and the State Department. The numbers of both US missionaries and US diplomats abroad had been steadily increasing since the 1870s. On the part of the mission movement, this growth was largely thanks to the formation of women's mission boards. The number of American foreign missionary organizations had ballooned from sixteen at mid-century to ninety in 1900. By the end of the century, American women outnumbered men in the mission field.[2]

This demographic shift among missionaries necessarily affected the dynamics between missions and the State Department. Missionary women, unlike men, did not easily move between government and evangelistic work, though many of them prided themselves on representing their country through mission work. Since they were not ordained ministers, their presence also heightened ongoing discussions with US religious communities about the proper methods for mission work. At the same time, reformers within the State Department and the consular system sought professionalization and a shift away from the systems that allowed for so much missionary diplomacy in earlier decades.

Robert College established Hamlin's legacy as a missionary, an educator, and as many of his obituaries insisted, a diplomat. When Hamlin died in 1900, the press celebrated him as a "missionary diplomatist" for his skillful handling of the Sublime Porte. He had obtained permission to build on the Bosporus in the face of Turkish and Russian opposition and had further gained the right to fly the US flag and claim the protection of the United States over his college—a right that no English, French, German, or Russian institution along the strait could claim.[3] Hamlin was no diplomat in a formal sense. He was a booster of a certain kind of American presence with enough connections to help make that vision more of a reality. Hamlin's American college was just one example of the type of "secular" and humanitarian work that emerged out of the missionary movement at the turn of the century.

Hamlin almost failed to get permission to build his college. It was the perceived connections between the missionary and US officials that eventually led the Sublime Porte to allow Hamlin to build his school. A simple question from a visiting US admiral—why can't the American college be built?—seemed potentially threatening in the context of Ottoman resistance in Crete and American seeming sympathy for the Cretan cause. "Better build a hundred colleges for the Americans with our own money," a Turkish gentleman would later explain to Hamlin, "than to have one of Farragut's monitors come into the Mediterranean!"[4]

When he was naming the school, Hamlin had considered calling it the American College, only rejecting that title out of a concern that it was "too much tainted with democracy."[5] Two decades later, the Women's Board of Missions had no such concerns about identifying their school in this way: The American College for Girls joined Robert College in 1871 as the leading US institutions in the city. The word *American* in the school's name signified something. It said something about the kind of education that would be provided, the values that its curriculum would inculcate, and the changes that it hoped to inspire throughout the region.

Though the curriculum at the American College for Girls was not evangelical, it was a mission school through and through. The board of trustees were all members of the Women's Board of Missions, led by Augusta Smith, president of the Women's Board of Missions (affiliated with the ABCFM). Within Constantinople, five of the six members of the college advisory board served as missionaries.[6] The school was necessary, as its most conservative supporters believed, to create a pool of eligible brides for future missionaries and ministers. But the supporters of the American College for Girls had much more ambitious aims. As teachers and as mothers, women were the key to transforming Ottoman culture. This was a very old idea for American women's educators, who had used similar arguments in favor of advanced women's education for decades. In the mission field, women missionaries continued to embrace this maternalist justification for women's education, suggesting that teaching women was the surest way to advance non-Christian cultures.[7]

It was this aspect of the American College for Girls that attracted the approval of both the US and Turkish governments. At the 1891 graduation ceremonies, for example, students listened to celebratory addresses by representatives of both the US legation and the Turkish Department of Public Instruction.[8] Both governments found much to praise in the school's project of educating women to educate the nation. For the Ottoman government, the advanced curriculum seemed to be educating modern women who would help build Ottoman culture. For the United States, the school represented the sort of positive cultural influence that Americans wanted their country to have in the world. The college, like many similar institutions, positioned the United States as a civilized and benevolent power on the world stage that had much to offer to the people of the world. That it did so without the official sponsorship of the US Government was an important benefit. It allowed the United States to represent itself as lacking in self-interest or imperialist ambitions, in contrast with European powers. Politically, then, both governments found much to praise in the mission schools. As they did so, neither focused on the religious goals or identity of the school. To both, it was primarily a secular institution, despite its missionary credentials.

The missionary leaders of these schools embraced the secular effects of their institutions, fully expecting that in due time they would result in spiritual and religious shifts as well. Later in life, Hamlin would reflect that this educational work had "some permanent value in the intellectual and spiritual changes then taking place."[9] He might have added political changes to that list. The students who came to Hamlin were, he remembered, leaving everything behind in order to advance their education. Hamlin called them "patriotic," as they "fervently desired to do something for the emancipation of their people."[10] He took pride that some of the leaders of the Bulgarian nationalist movement had graduated from his schools.[11] His son would later claim that Bulgaria owed "her emergence from a virtual serfdom into practical independence" to Robert College's "liberalizing and uplifting tendencies." The college, he wrote, was "an unassailable lighthouse of progress in a benighted empire."[12]

The mission schools, hospitals, and presses staffed by American women and men were institutions with significant symbolic value. That value could look slightly different for diplomats, missionaries, foreign governments, patients, students, and their families, depending on their needs and goals. The resulting questions in the mission field, American churches, and in Washington over the political and religious meaning of mission work set the stage for profound debates about the nature of the missionary diplomacy that had operated for nearly a century.

The Secular and the Sacred in Education and Medicine

By the 1880s, missionary supporters had gotten used to debates over missionary methodology and the proper relationship of evangelism and "secular" work. Naysayers had criticized the monthly prayer concerts of the 1830s for being too earthbound when they included maps and geographical lessons as part of their efforts to attract attention (and funds) to missions. From the 1840s onward, missionary leaders like Rufus Anderson critiqued mission schools for becoming too "secular" and focusing too much attention on preparing students for careers other than ministry.[13] These debates were far from resolved by the 1880s. The wide range of missionary organizations at work throughout the world allowed for considerable variation of approach to education. All of the missionary organizations sought to spread the gospel and create Christian societies. The differences in method represented both the range of visions of what a Christian society could look like and the different priorities of various mission groups. These debates would have important implications for the relationship between missions and foreign relations.

American missionaries had emphasized the importance of education from the very beginning of their work. From the 1810s forward, establishing a school was one of the first activities of many American missions. This impulse came from a number of motives. American Protestant missionaries felt it was essential for all Christians to be able to read the scriptures. Accordingly, they prioritized literacy training and primary-level education. For missionaries coming from denominations that valued an educated ministry, secondary and higher educational institutions were necessary to prepare Christian converts for work as evangelists and preachers. But there were other reasons that missionaries founded schools too.

Missionary educators knew that schools could do more than train future pastors. They could attract people to the mission who otherwise would not have come. Families who were interested in the social and economic mobility that Western education could offer in many of the colonized spaces where missionaries worked were willing, sometimes even eager, to have their children educated at the mission. This could provide a captive audience for the evangelizing work of missionaries. Many of these missionary teachers welcomed this sort of work, as they found education to be an important part of the civilizing work that they believed was essential to their mission. Finally, mission schools could be a way for the mission to financially support itself when funds from the United States were slow or irregular. These motives were no less religious in nature, but critics would, over the course of the century, raise questions.

It was this second cluster of motivations that caused debate about mission schools as early as the 1840s. Hamlin embraced the value of a secular education to the mission movement. Training in the sciences, literature, and even the English language could prepare students for new opportunities. At Bebek Seminary, Hamlin experimented with pairing an industrial workshop with the school in order to allow his impoverished students to earn money for clothing and other necessities. This had religious value, he was quick to note. Protestant converts faced persecution and, with it, real financial risks. Creating economic opportunities was essential, both as a humanitarian impulse and as a means to remove a major disincentive to conversion.[14] Yet some of his missionary brethren joined the ABCFM's Rufus Anderson in criticizing Hamlin's work as "Americanizing" the students and making them more focused on their financial situation than on spiritual concerns.[15]

For these critics, educational institution building seemed to serve the needs of the state more than the kingdom of God. Such schools emphasized culture over Christ and, as anti-foreign and anti-imperial movements grew in many missionary regions, identified missions too closely with Western power. Missionaries like Hamlin debated strategy with leaders like Anderson in arguments that were about both theology and politics. These two camps could not decide how or where to draw the lines between the secular and the sacred, or between the mission and the country. At times, they even argued over whether such a line was necessary or even possible.

Medical missions attempted to strike a similar balance and relied on several explanations for how their work was a legitimate part of the missionary project. In the first place, there was real need. Missionaries described non-Western medical care as decidedly inferior to what medical missionaries could provide. They emphasized painful treatments and "cruel" practices that had their roots in what one medical missionary described as "inherited religious beliefs and hoary prejudices." The "bad medicine" of the East was, in part, a religious problem; it had to be solved through the Christian application of scientific knowledge. It was this humanitarian explanation that diplomats embraced. Missionary hospitals exemplified the benefits that could come with connections with the United States. They helped make the United States appear to be a benevolent force in the world.

But it was more than this. Medical missionaries also insisted that the justification for medical missions could be found in Jesus's role as a divine healer. Medical care was sacred work. Focusing on the themes of healing in many of the miracle stories of Jesus, they found a scriptural basis for the connection between medical care and missionary work. Medical missionaries, as one explained it, were prompted both by "our humanity, as well as our Christianity."[16]

Medical missionaries worked evangelization into their medical practices. People came to the hospital to receive medical treatment, not to be evangelized. But the missionaries did not lose any opportunities to evangelize the sick. They hired local Christian teachers, known as Bible Women, to preach in the waiting areas of their hospitals. In some hospitals, missionaries and Bible Women conducted daily worship services and brought the Bible with them to visit hospital patients at noon. Some printed scriptures on prescriptions. Waiting rooms served as libraries of Christian texts. When medical missionaries visited patients in their homes, they not only checked on the progress of their healing, but prayed with them and taught them hymns.[17]

The missionaries found that few objected to the evangelizing in the waiting rooms. Some former patients even returned with neighbors and family to hear the Bible Women speak of the gospel. Like mission schools, mission hospitals were places that the community understood to be capable of providing a clear benefit. Both could be just the beginning of a longer relationship with the mission. And because of their involvement in "nonreligious" life, they could invite unexpected sorts of missionary troubles.

Religious Freedom and Japanese Mission Schools

When the Japanese responded to foreign pressure in 1873 and lifted the laws prohibiting Christianity, Protestant missionaries flooded into the country, sure that their understanding of religious freedom would now be embraced by both the Japanese government and the Western powers. In that single year, eighty-seven Protestant missionaries began their work in Japan.[18] They found a country in the midst of a profound political and cultural transformation, and the missionaries were optimistic about what that might mean. Somewhat similar to the Ottoman government, the Japanese government seemed to recognize benefits in the Western education that American missionaries offered, even as proselytization remained illegal.[19] Starting in 1872, when the government urged universal primary education for boys and girls, through the 1889 adoption of the Meiji constitution, missionaries embraced the opportunity to build Christian schools that benefited Japanese families and the government alike. Because the government did not have the resources to fund the wide-ranging educational program that it planned, private missionary schools filled an important gap at the primary and secondary level in these years. Missionaries were particularly important in the education of girls and women, with schools offering a range of curricula from industrial to academic subjects.

A group of these early missionary teachers, employed at the government-sponsored college, had emphasized that it was only "fear of the government" that kept people from listening to their gospel message more broadly. They described the students as "very desirous to be instructed in history." Though the missionaries were told to leave Christianity outside of the classroom, they found this impossible. The history of the West was, they argued, "to a great degree, the history of Christianity." If they were to teach Japanese students about the history, law, and culture of the West, they would simply have to teach them about Christianity. And as they encouraged their students to embrace the legal and commercial culture of the West, the missionaries would necessarily encourage them to embrace the Christianity that they believed was its inspiration. Missionaries taught their students that it would be "vain for them to strive to enter the light of modern civilization and reject the light of Christianity."[20] To the missionaries, they were one and the same.

It was into this context of new possibilities that the Woman's Foreign Missionary Society of the Methodist Episcopal Church sent Elizabeth Russell to Nagasaki in 1879. Russell, too, would start a school that would have her thinking about the line between Christian and secular education. Russell's school emphasized the academic subjects. She taught reading, history, arithmetic, and algebra in English, which she identified as "the language of civilization, the language of progress." The school also offered courses in Latin, Greek, and after 1885, the sciences. From 1888, she offered a collegiate degree. Her goal was not only to teach her students content, but to wake up "powers that would forever lie dormant under the mental enervation" that was the result of studying only in Asian languages and less rigorous subjects. These branches were, she insisted, "indirectly religious work" that would result in "the students' steadily broadening views on all subjects."[21] This explanation was typical of those who celebrated the religious benefits of academic study.

By this point, missionaries claimed that in practice, the Japanese had the free ability to practice Christianity. While anti-Christian prejudices may have remained in some areas, missionaries argued that it was often sufficient to show authorities the recent regulations that supported Christian practice, and the problems resolved themselves.[22] In remarkable contrast to the records from China, Korea, or the Ottoman territories in the 1880s, the diplomatic correspondence of the Japan legation revealed no missionary troubles. This did not mean, however, that the missionaries were not active in political affairs. Their educational work, in fact, brought them very close to political debates in the country.

As in Turkey, women missionaries in Japan understood their work to be training women to become the mothers and teachers of their nation. At such a transformative time in Japanese history, this was an important role. The Japanese Education Ministry released guidelines in 1882 that called for distinct curricula for male and female high school students. Girls were to be trained to serve their family and the state through participation in the national economy, with industrial education as a component of all schools. Missionaries worked to ensure that their educational program conformed to the state guidelines, though leaders like Russell bristled against the expectation that women's primary identities should be as wives and mothers.

Some Japanese observers criticized missionaries for encouraging political dissent among their female students. Government-sponsored newspapers as well as statements from the Ministry of Education argued that the curriculum of these US missionary schools had led Japanese women down the wrong path, encouraging Western values like individualism and equality, which did not fit easily with the submissive role that Japan was hoping to inculcate in its young women. Leading Meiji feminists had connections to the mission schools and faced government repression for their advocacy for women's rights.[23] In response, the government began prioritizing public secondary schools for girls, removing much of the audience for the missionary institutions.

Once the Meiji constitution was finalized in 1889, missionaries faced a new period of crisis. Japan had lost its earlier expectation that embracing aspects of US culture would result in increased American respect for Japan. Instead, Japanese political leaders endorsed a new nationalist era. Most of the mission schools dropped the study of English around this time, not because of domestic American debates about missionary education, but because of Japanese demands for a less Western approach to education.[24] By the end of the century, new treaties brought mission schools under the direct oversight of the Japanese government. Soon, religious instruction was banned in primary

schools and government-recognized middle and high schools, requir-
ing the missions to give up many of their schools and renegotiate the
curriculum and status at those that remained.[25]

What stands out across these debates over missionary education
is the difficulty in defining such work as religious or nonreligious.
The Japanese government, like the Turkish government that embraced
US mission schools, sought to benefit from the scientific and literary
teachings of US missionaries without allowing their religious influence to spread. American government officials, too, could celebrate
the educational work of Protestant missionaries as if it was a secular
project that was wholly disconnected from their evangelistic goals. Yet
missionaries blurred these lines at every turn, taking full advantage
of any benefits of being seen as secular while always insisting to their
supporters at home that their work was religious.

Korea, Medicine, and Politics

In the 1880s and 1890s, Korea emerged as another field of great interest to missionaries, but of little interest to the Department of State.
A tributary of both China and Japan, Korea seemed to have little to offer
independently as a trading partner. Around 1870, the US government
had unsuccessfully attempted to open relations with Korea. This first
attempt to force relations with Korea emerged when the United States
became troubled about the fate that could await sailors stranded on
Korean shores due to storms or wrecks.

Frederick Low, the man sent by President Ulysses S. Grant to negotiate the matter, admitted that he knew very little about Korea or its
people. But he was sure that it was an uncivilized country with a racially
inferior populace. After sending initial communications of his intent to
negotiate a treaty through the Chinese, Low arrived in Korea with five
heavily armed warships staffed by 1,230 marines and sailors. As the US
ships advanced up the river from Chagyak to Seoul, they received warning to turn back. When they did not, the Korean cannons opened fire.
In the initial skirmish, some thirty Koreans were killed. The Americans
advanced further upriver, opened fire, and landed ground forces. After
two days of fighting, at least 250 Koreans and three Americans were
dead. Low withdrew without even getting the meeting he had sought
with a high-ranking Korean official to negotiate.[26]

It would take another decade, until 1882, for the United States and
Korea to reach a treaty of amity and commerce. Among the negotiators

was Chester Holcombe, a diplomat based in China who would later become one of the directors of the ABCFM.[27] American interests in the region remained the same: the United States wanted protection for stranded sailors and a commercial relationship. Korean interests, however, had shifted slightly in the years since the fighting in 1871. Watching developments in China and Japan, the Koreans were increasingly worried about the imperialist designs of the West, especially given its own tributary position in relation to the Chinese and Japanese. Considering their options, Korean leaders wondered if an alliance with the United States might be a possible way to keep other, more invasive countries, at arms' length.[28]

Missionaries, keenly interested in Korea as a mission field, followed these developments closely from China, Japan, and the United States. As American missionaries understood the situation, the Korean king would "gladly welcome" the "influence and friendship" of the United States. "It is bad enough to be ground between the upper and nether millstones of China and Japan, but to see England and Russia waiting to circumvent not only China and Japan, but each other, is a still darker outlook," on missionary periodical explained. "There is only a choice of masters."[29]

With the treaty signed, the United States sent its official representative: a minister resident and consul general. This official was lower in rank than the leading diplomats in China or Japan, and he served alongside a small staff that only rarely included another US citizen. Outside of Seoul, there were no US representatives at all.[30] This small legation reflected the relative insignificance that the State Department expected Korea to have for US affairs. And in a commercial sense, this was the case. Korea presented only a small market for Americans, and did not generate much excitement among the commercial classes. But for missionaries, it was another matter entirely. Missionaries from the Presbyterian and Methodist mission boards soon arrived on the peninsula and established what would become a significant missionary establishment in Korea.

American Protestants heralded this moment as the "hour for Korea." They expected great opportunity there. Not only had Korea become open to political and economic interactions with the West, it also welcomed US technologies and institutions. Korea began to institute a new postal system in 1885, and soon reports came to the United States about the spread of steam, rail, and telegraph. And the Korean people seemed receptive to Protestant missionaries.[31]

In 1886, there were five US missionaries in Korea, with more to come. Within two years, the missionaries claimed to have baptized more than a hundred Korean converts.[32] By 1909, there were nearly three hundred Protestant missionaries in the country.[33] In Seoul, Pyeng-yang (Pyongyang), Mokpo, Kwngju (Gwangju), Chunju (Chungju), and Kusan (Kunsan) US missionaries worked to build up evangelistic, medical, and educational projects. The main missionary hospital reported treating more than ten thousand patients in 1886, and missionaries founded schools at all levels from elementary through medical training.[34]

The missionary enthusiasm for Korea in the 1880s and 1890s is, at first glance, surprising. Proselytization was not legally sanctioned in the country, and the missionaries did not officially possess the right to reside in the interior of the country. The Korean government did not revoke anti-Christian laws that could potentially endanger not only converts but the missionaries themselves if they practiced their religion publicly. One might have expected the missionary troubles of China and the Ottoman Empire to emerge here too. While the first US minister to Korea did occasionally discuss religious freedom as a general principle of the United States, he did not push the issue, and the United States would decline to join France in a request to remove anti-Christian laws in 1893.[35] It was France, far more invested than the United States in providing government support for evangelization, that opened the door for American missionaries by obtaining permission for noncommercial travel in the interior of the country with passports.[36]

Yet here, as elsewhere, American missionaries took a lack of explicit opposition to their work to be tacit acceptance. Relying on a higher authority than earthly states, they went where they could and pushed against the limits of the permission granted them in treaties. Some of the missionary work, particularly in the education and medical fields, was welcomed, even celebrated. Here, as elsewhere, missionaries faced a challenge of categorizing and describing their work. Missionaries' "religious" work was problematic; their "nonreligious" work was praised by Koreans and US representatives alike. But as missionary discussions about methods and secularization suggest, none of the work of the mission was actually nonreligious. The stage was set for another string of missionary troubles.

Dr. Horace Allen arrived in Korea from China in 1884 as the doctor attached to the US Legation. He had missionary goals, however, and hoped to establish a hospital in the country. Within a year, he had done so: the Korean Government Hospital of Seoul. As its name indicates, the hospital was paid for by the Korean government, which made for an unlikely partnership for the American missionary. The only costs that Allen's missionary supporters faced was that of the medicines themselves and his salary.

It was either luck or coincidence that brought Allen's proposal to open a hospital before the crown. Shortly after Allen's arrival in the country, a political uprising rocked Seoul. The return of the king's father, the former regent, sparked a rebellion that erupted into violence in December. The US minister, Lucius Foote, described it as a "political revolution." At the height of the uproar, Prince Min Young Ik, gravely wounded, stumbled into a dinner party that Foote had been attending. Foote called for Allen to attend to the prince and several of his injured companions. It was an auspicious beginning for the missionary relationship with the royal family. From then on, Allen served as the king's doctor.[37]

Soon thereafter, George Foulk, the interim chargé d'affaires, assisted him in working with the Korean government to get the hospital started. The Americans had every hope of success. The year before, an American missionary had visited Korea to begin exploring the establishment of a mission hospital. Minister Foote had hosted the missionary and discussed the matter with the king. There seemed at the time to be "no serious objection," and in fact Foote thought that "a mission school and hospital at Seoul will be tacitly encouraged."[38] When he returned to the matter, Foulk stressed the missionary's humanitarian and altruistic goals in his communications with both the Korean and US governments, regularly referring to the fact that Allen offered "gratuitous service" and did not ask to be paid for his medical work by anyone but the mission board.[39]

Foulk presented Allen's proposal to the crown in January of 1885; by May, Foulk triumphantly wrote to Washington to announce the successful opening of the hospital, serving patients every day but Sunday.[40] The hospital was a great success. Allen was joined by another medical missionary, and soon they opened a school through the hospital that trained a small class of Korean students in medicine. Before long, the king named Allen as his private physician, which gave Allen significant access to the palace.

Allen was not the only missionary to enjoy such access. The queen, too, named an American missionary as her physician: Dr. Lillias Horton Underwood. Horton had been sent to Korea in 1888 by the Presbyterians in response to a request for a female medical missionary.

After the establishment of Allen's hospital, it became clear that there was a real need for a dedicated women's hospital. Though women were treated at the government hospital, male doctors reported some difficulty in providing care to female patients.[41] Korean society, Americans understood, was deeply segregated along gender lines for all but the lowest classes.[42] Allen had even told US readers about a time he had provided medical care for the queen, only to find that she had been veiled and covered so completely that he was only able to see "one square inch" of her skin.[43] American women's mission boards well understood the need for women doctors and nurses throughout the mission field. The purpose was to provide opportunities for American women to serve the needs of women around the world, and they eagerly sent women like Dr. Horton to advance the dual causes of medicine and the gospel among women.

Horton had been a doctor in Chicago prior to her entry into the mission field, and she brought with her not only medical expertise, but a passion for education. She managed the care of the women of the royal family, ran a dispensary for lower-class women, and also taught mathematics and English in the mission school and ran a Bible class for women. In Seoul, Horton met and married missionary Horace Grant Underwood.[44]

Horton's description of her first meeting with the queen reflects the uneasy position that missionaries held in the country. She recalled feeling incredibly anxious as her "chair coolies" carried her through the city. The gowns that she had packed in order to attend events in full court dress had been ruined on her journey across the Pacific. But it was not only her dress that concerned her. Far more concerning was the ways in which she had been warned not to mention religion. The other missionaries reminded her that they were only in Korea "on sufferance," and though their preaching "may be overlooked and winked at" when they focused only on "the common people," they expected grave results if they should raise the subject in the palace. "I saw the logic of these words," Horton remembered, "though my heart talked hotly in a very different way; but I went to the palace with my mouth sealed on the one subject I had come to proclaim."[45]

Horton did well, despite her fears, and served as the queen's doctor until her assassination in 1895. After that, she, Allen, and her husband found themselves enmeshed in a new type of missionary trouble in Korea. By the end of the year, the US Department of State would be issuing increasingly frustrated statements about their inappropriate behavior and ultimately removing the US minister from office for failing to control the missionaries.

The murder of Queen Min in 1895 and the subsequent confinement of the king to the palace by Japanese-backed conspirators shocked the Americans in Seoul. John Sill, a former Episcopal priest serving as the US minister to Korea, first reported the event in October. The assassination, he explained, was part of an attempt by Japan to exert more control in the region. He expected the United States to take swift action to restore the king to power. "It is absurd," Sill reflected, that the Americans could be expected to recognize the new Korean government. He hoped to join representatives from England, Russia, and France in taking action to restore the king to power. These hopes were dashed, however, when Washington responded.[46]

The rebuke from the State Department on November 11 was blunt: "Intervention in political concerns of Korea is not among your functions." This would be the first of many warnings that Sill received from Washington in the coming months. All of the news reaching the United States suggested that the Americans in Seoul were very closely involved in the ongoing political crisis.[47] Sill tried to justify his actions by insisting that US interests were indeed at risk as a result of the political upheavals in Korea—instability created risks for the US residents.[48] But Olney was far more concerned about reports that "irresponsible persons" among the Americans had been "advising and attempting to control, through irregular channels, the Government of the country."[49] Since the Americans living in Korea at the time were missionaries, this was a critique on missionary involvement, and particularly of Sill, Allen, and Underwood.[50] After several decades of missionary troubles around the world, the State Department was very concerned about the kind of problems that missionaries could create for US foreign relations—not only in Korea, but in US relations with China and Japan.

The relationship between a small group of missionaries in Seoul and the king during these difficult months was quite close. King Gojong, suspecting that the Japanese would not act against him with foreign witnesses present, called on US missionaries to remain near the royal chamber at all times. Missionaries took turns sleeping at the palace, and they came armed.[51]

The missionaries' protection of the king took multiple forms. The king was reportedly so concerned about poisoning that he would not eat any food prepared in the palace and was subsisting on condensed milk and hard-boiled eggs that arrived to him still in their shells. This,

Dr. Underwood concluded, would not do. She and the wife of the Russian minister began to prepare special meals for the king, delivered daily to the palace by her husband in a locked box. Her care for the king suggests a kind of intimacy that was quite unusual in missionary experience with foreign leaders, particularly when the leader in question was not Christian.[52]

Not only did the male missionaries sleep by the king's chamber while the female missionaries prepared the king's food, the men accompanied some US military advisors in protecting the king from an attempted kidnapping by the pro-Japanese prime minister and acting minister of war. Lillias Underwood later recalled multiple visitors coming to their home to speak of schemes to free the king from his confinement. Horace Underwood, she claimed, did not participate in the planning—he did not know who to trust, and further assumed that as a missionary, he ought not take part. But on the day in question, he joined the others in storming the palace to free the king, and he carried a revolver. During the ordeal, the king clung to Underwood's hand. The missionaries later sheltered the king's second son and sponsored his journey to the United States, promising the support of the Presbyterian Board of Missions.[53]

The Underwoods insisted that Horace had not been involved in the planning, but rumors continued to follow them for years. Many of the missionaries in Korea began to gain a reputation as political meddlers. In practice, most missionaries in the country did not create problems, but the Japanese press frequently criticized them and suggested that they were acting out of turn. Missionaries in Japan and China accordingly reported back to Washington about the political meddling of the Korea missionaries, concerned that it would have negative implications for their own work and for the reputation of the United States in the region. It was out of this context that Olney's instructions to Sill in 1895 and 1896 were so insistent that missionaries "strictly confine themselves to their missionary work" and leave politics alone.[54] It was not only US political interests, but also missionary interests around the world that were at stake.

Even though the State Department was frustrated by Sill and the missionaries' activities in 1895, these concerns did not lead to a complete abandonment of missionary diplomacy. By the time of the assassination, Allen had become the secretary of the US legation; he would be named US minister to China only a few years later, under President McKinley. This turn to diplomatic work did require Allen to formally step away from his affiliation with the missionary society, but his interests in the cause of missions never disappeared.

Though these missionaries clearly became involved in local politics, they also revealed some level of discomfort with it. They did not want to be seen to be political, regardless of what they actually did. So Dr. Allen, in 1885, declined an invitation to make a public address welcoming the new British consul because he "thought it best to stay out of politics." Yet in the very next sentence of the letter where he explained this decision to American supporters, he described a successful petition he had sent to the government regarding his hospital.[55] This dynamic is perhaps most revealing of the debates within missionary circles (and even within the missionary community in Korea) over the appropriateness of such political connections. When government alliances served the cause of missions, they were commendable, Allen and others seemed to conclude. But in a nod to those who critiqued such closeness, and in the face of inconsistent policies among mission boards that neither particularly trusted foreign governments, nor wanted to pay for programs whose costs the government might cover, Allen maintained some boundaries between political and mission work.[56] When his work took on a more explicitly political dimension, he stepped away from the mission.

The events of 1895 and 1896 were far from typical. Yet, as Horace Allen reflected in 1901, "Scarcely a day passes in fact, when I am not called upon to assist a missionary."[57] Like consuls and ministers throughout missionary lands, he faced the challenge of missionary troubles as part of his regular work. As elsewhere, the cases largely emerged away from the capital, when local officials bristled against the seeming invasion of Western influence. The same rumors of foreigners taking the bodies of babies and children to turn them into medicine that had plagued missionaries in China earlier followed missionaries with their entry into Korea, occasionally leading to what Lillias Underwood called "the baby riots." These did not reach the level of violence as had been experienced in Tien-tsin, but the US minister warned the missionaries that if violence did seem likely, they should seek immediate refuge at the legation.[58]

Missionary Humanitarians and the 1895 Armenian Massacres

In 1895, missionary teacher Mary Barnum opened a letter home with the haunting phrase: "Written after the dreadful massacres of Nov. 12." She was in Harpoot in late November 1895 and witnessed one of the many attacks that would collectively be known as the Hamidian massacres. Barnum, like a number of other American, British, and Armenian witnesses, sent accounts of the violence to horrified readers who wondered how the European powers had failed to prevent such atrocities. "The dreadfulness of the situation around us grows more and more appalling," she explained. "We seem to have gone back to the dark ages."[59]

After Sultan Abdul Hamid II suspended the new constitution in 1878, much of his focus was on how to maintain power over the vast lands of the Ottoman Empire in the face of nationalist movements within and Russian pressure without. Armenian nationalists bristled at the increasingly restrictive and oppressive reforms as Hamid sought to create religious, cultural, and ethnic uniformity throughout the empire. Among other things, Hamid sought to unify the empire through Islam. By the mid-1890s, the sultan's response to oppositional movements was to orchestrate brutal attacks on the Armenian Christian population throughout the empire. The death count is imprecise, but over the course of the Hamidian massacres, somewhere between 100,000 and 200,000 Armenians died.[60]

Within weeks of the attack at Harpoot, only thirty-two girls and teachers remained at Barnum's school. Many of the students had learned of "fathers and brothers killed, homes plundered and burned, and saddest of all, that their friends have denied Christ." As a missionary, Barnum was particularly troubled by the idea of Christians being forced to abandon their faith, and she thus framed part of the crisis as a religious liberty issue. The victims were religious martyrs, in this framing, and Christian Americans could and should sympathize with their fellow Christians in their time of suffering.

This was also a political and humanitarian issue. On their own, there was little the missionaries could do to help in a practical way. Barnum distributed the needles and thread that had been unharmed after the mission buildings had been set on fire, but she had little else of use to share. Deeply frustrated to see so much suffering without the ability to help, she wrote of her desire to light a "grand bonfire" to destroy the unnecessary articles that remained in the house. It felt a "mockery" to have what little remained when it could do no practical good. How could she expect to clothe people with only the "hats, collars, (especially soiled gentlemen's paper collars), belts and gloves" that remained? "And how would pictures do for beds and quilts?" The needs were great, and the missionaries did not feel prepared to meet them.[61]

The only way to change that was to raise the alarm throughout the international community. Aid was needed, and American missionaries planned to make sure that Americans understood their duty. In the United States, Cyrus Hamlin, now retired from Robert College, got to work. When he addressed a church in Lexington, Massachusetts, on what was becoming known as "the Armenian Question," the *Boston Globe* covered the event and spread Hamlin's missionary intelligence far beyond the walls of the church. Hamlin, relying on reports he had received from a missionary in Bitlis, reported that two Armenian villages in that region had been sacked. The Turks carried off the livestock, leaving the people to starve. The missionaries denied the sultan's claims that the soldiers were there to put down a rebellion. There was no rebellion in that region; the Armenians were unarmed and outnumbered. As Hamlin explained to his US audience, the sultan's command was nothing short of "an order to destroy the Armenians." Some two and a half million Armenians were living "in terror and distress" in the Ottoman Empire, fearful of "a general assassination" against them. In case anyone missed the religious significance of the attacks, the title of the article was blunt: "Killed Because Christians."[62]

Hamlin was not the only missionary to spread news of the massacres. Former missionary Frederick David Greene compiled an assortment of letters from missionaries like Barnum and Knapp to create *The Armenian Crisis in Turkey*, an early entry into the American reporting on the Armenian massacres. One reviewer found that the collection of missionary letters provided evidence of "a gigantic and indescribably horrible massacre of Armenian men, women, and children" in Sassoun (Sason) in early September 1894.[63] In the two years that followed, the crisis only grew.

Missionary troubles had, of course, long drawn the US government into more involvement in the region. Now, missionaries hoped that the intelligence they provided might inspire intervention. They worried about their own safety, and they worried about the safety of their fellow Christians. They wanted the United States to act. The US press echoed their denunciation of the Ottoman government. Mass rallies across the country protested the violence.[64]

In the face of the public uproar over the Armenian massacres, two problems faced the US government: how to provide safety for the US citizens in the region (almost all of whom were missionaries, many working in schools and hospitals that provided vital services) and how to respond to the international humanitarian crisis. To the first point, the government did not need to do much differently from its earlier responses to missionary troubles. But at least some in the government seemed to be fed up with the demands of missionaries. The 1890s were the early days of a debate over the value of missionaries, and at least some argued that the government should not intervene on the missionaries' behalf. "If our citizens go to a far distant country, semi-civilized and bitterly opposed to their movements," Senator John Sherman wrote, "we cannot follow them there and protect them." To respond with force would only make matters worse, and lead to the deaths of the missionaries and probably also their converts and sympathizers. But it was not only this. Other politicians argued with missionary reporting about the state of affairs in Turkey. When missionary Dr. Grace Kimball claimed that the United States flag was not respected and provided no protection for American missionaries in Turkey, Secretary of State Richard Olney publicly refuted her in the *Washington Post*. Olney urged her and the other missionaries to stop spreading such rumors, claiming that "intemperate expressions of public opinion excited by appeals to sentiment, regardless of facts, endanger American missionaries at the hands of revolutionists in Turkey more than anything else."[65]

Hamlin refuted both ideas in the pages of the *Washington Post* and the *North American Review*. The problem was not the missionaries, Hamlin argued, but the US government's unwillingness to forcibly protect the treaty rights of its citizens. If the United States had done this earlier, "the massacres that blot with innocent blood the last pages of the century would never have been perpetrated," he argued. Like so many missionary defenders, he carefully parsed the religious and the secular work of the missionaries. The government had promised to protect mission schools and presses, but had failed to do so. "No penalty was ever exacted, no promise was ever fulfilled." Now, Hamlin claimed, the sultan felt free to act on his most extreme desires: "The extermination of all Armenians who will not Islamize, the expulsion of the American missionaries, the destruction of their property, and the showing of himself as superior to all treaties and to all claims of truth, justice, and humanity towards all men of the Christian faith."[66]

Missionary writings about the crisis continually relied on Islamophobic tropes as they described the sultan, his troops, and the suffering of Armenian Christians. At least in part, missionaries and their supporters argued that US interests were properly aligned with suffering Christians around the world in the face of Muslim oppression. Their humanitarian arguments were inflected with religious and racial specificity.[67]

Hamlin went far beyond the earlier missionary arguments that the US government needed to protect their treaty rights around the world because this was the meaning of US citizenship. It was not only, or even primarily, US citizens who had been harmed in this case. By failing to uphold US treaty rights, Hamlin claimed, the US government had set into motion the steps that resulted in the massacre of somewhere between 100,000 and 200,000 Armenian men, women, and children.[68] Intervention of some sort was now necessary.

But what kind of intervention was possible? The foreign powers who had the greatest interests in the region were Great Britain and Russia, neither of which supported foreign action. The United States had no tradition of such intervention. The Hamidian massacres in Armenia, which were both a humanitarian crisis and a political quagmire, would be an important turning point.

United States government officials attempted to maintain a distinction between US and Armenian interests as they navigated the crisis. In his 1895 address to Congress, President Grover Cleveland attempted to carefully balance the competing interests at play, both expressing his concern for the safety of American missionaries in the region while also refusing to let the United States intervene directly. When it came to the dangers that missionaries faced, or the damages to their property as a result of the violence, the government should use "official energy and perseverance," as missionary Henry Otis Dwight explained in the *New York Tribune*. But more tact and discretion was necessary for US action on the humanitarian crisis.[69]

To some observers, though, this distinction was far from clear. The missionary presence, they argued, demanded a broader US duty in the region. After all, missionaries were doing important work beyond evangelization. As one article in the *Union Signal* had explained, it was the influence of the American mission schools that had inspired "the Armenian spirit of independence."[70] Americans should, accordingly, send help. Meanwhile, petitions poured into Congress asking for warships to be sent to the region, at least in part to protect the American missionaries in the region.[71] Cleveland worried that any show of force would impede the ability of American aid to reach those who suffered.[72] Instead of gunboats, the United States sent money. Missionary and Armenian immigrant networks created the National Armenian Relief Committee, with Greene serving as secretary. Between 1894 and 1897, they raised approximately $300,000 to support the work of the Red Cross and missionaries in the region.[73]

The Armenian Crisis of the 1890s revealed a shift in US international engagement. At the beginning of the century, the Greek Revolution had inspired a similar US interest in Christian nationalist struggles against the Ottoman Empire, with similar turns to anti-Islamic rhetoric. But if the earlier situation had resulted in a firm government insistence that the United States would not intervene in European affairs, that was no longer the case. Congress not only debated intervention, it adopted a resolution in support of US intervention to "stay the hand of fanaticism and lawless violence."[74] When, by 1900, the Ottoman government had still refused to offer an indemnity to American missionaries for the property that had been destroyed in the violence, President McKinley sent a Philippines-bound warship to Smyrna (Izmir) to provide a demonstration of strength and support to the missionary interests in the region. The ship, and the warships that would continue to patrol the region in the coming decade, would also inspire Armenian hopes for future US intervention.[75]

As they taught, healed, and wrote in the final decades of the century, missionaries found that their work had political implications, both in the places where they worked and at home in the United States. American and foreign governments alike tried to parse out the religious and the nonreligious aspects of their work, suggesting that educational, medical, and civilizing efforts could somehow be divided from evangelism. But the missionaries themselves had a hard time distinguishing along these lines. Their work, they understood, had secular effects in addition to religious ones, and sometimes required political efforts. But they never lost sight of their religious motivations, or the ultimate religious effects that they hoped to see.

The first decade of the twentieth century would see some important shifts in the relationship between missions and the US government, all of which had their roots in these turbulent years. American empire entered a new phase with the wars of 1898, and both the missionaries and the government had to reevaluate their ability to partner in the work of spreading US culture and values around the world. The missionary troubles of the late nineteenth century exploded into the Boxer Uprising of 1900, resulting in a vigorous debate about the relative benefits and threats of missionary work for US diplomacy. And mission-ary appeals to American humanitarian concern would take on a new meaning with the coming of the first world war. The nineteenth-century debates about missionary methods and their political impact would set the stage for a new century with a much stronger State Department.

PART III

Diplomatic Missions, 1890s–1920s

When twenty-five-year-old missionary Ellen Stone was abducted in Macedonia in September 1901, the US government encountered missionary troubles of a sort they had not faced before. Stone was, it seemed, both a victim and a troublemaker, and her involvement in nationalist politics presented new challenges for the government that hoped to save her. At first glance, this was not unlike the earlier set of troubles that missionaries faced in what had been Ottoman territory. Brigands had attacked a group that Stone was traveling with for her Bible class. Stone had always rejected concerns about the dangers of this sort of travel for any American, but especially for a woman, as alarmist. She felt herself to be protected by the Bible she carried and the US flag she always wore as part of her dress.[1]

Yet this was not a mere crime of opportunity. As it soon became clear, it was a planned attack designed to bring in a high ransom to fund the revolutionary movement in Macedonia against the Ottoman state.[2] It was not clear where the women had been taken—were they in Turkey? Bulgaria? Quite quickly, the US consul in Salonica demanded action from the Turkish government. Within the month, Charles Dickinson, the US consul general, arrived in Sofia from Constantinople.[3]

Throughout October, telegrams in cipher zipped across the Atlantic as Americans in Washington and Bulgaria sought to determine what to do next. The US and British press covered the story in detail for a captivated audience. When readers learned that Stone's companion Ella Tsilka was pregnant and might even be forced to give birth in captivity, the panic grew. But there was no precedent for the government paying ransom for a kidnapped citizen. The missionaries and their US supporters were quite clear that the State Department needed to act. Judson Smith, of the ABCFM, requested a meeting with President Theodore Roosevelt to discuss the issue.

Roosevelt's response revealed some of the complicated issues involved in determining what to do. "Of course everything that can be done must be done to try to rescue Miss Stone," he wrote to Alvey Augustus Adee, the second assistant secretary of state who was handling the Stone case. The problem was, however, that not much *could* be done. The government simply did not have the ability to pay the ransom. If Stone had been a man, this would have been much less complicated. All missionaries, Roosevelt explained, had to know that they had "no kind of business to venture to wild lands with the expectation that somehow the government would protect him as well as if he stayed at home." If and when troubles arose, a missionary "has no more right to complain of what may befall him than a soldier has in getting shot." Yet Roosevelt found it impossible to apply this standard to women, whom he believed needed more protection. He fumed in a postscript to Adee that "women have no earthly business to go out as missionaries into these wild countries." But Stone had already been sent, and she had already been kidnapped. It was too late for such thinking now.[4]

At the meeting between Roosevelt and Smith, Adee was shocked by the missionary insistence that the government take a more active role to protect the missionaries. He described Smith's mind as "virgin soil on all matters of fact, law and history," and found the missionary director to be "appalled at the intricacies of the international questions involved." This was a far cry from an earlier era when the mission boards claimed more expertise about the places where they worked than the State Department. Now, the diplomats were frustrated that the missionaries could not wrap their heads around the complicated mess that the missions found themselves in.[5]

Raising money to pay the demanded ransom was tricky. The Turkish government refused to contribute, and the US government was unable to do so. The ABCFM, Stone's missionary agency, was reluctant to pay out of fear that it would encourage brigands to kidnap their other missionaries for ransom. The only choice, then, was to appeal for donations from friends and sympathizers in the United States.[6] Stone's brothers raised six thousand dollars from the American public through an appeal in the *Christian Herald*, a leading evangelical periodical.[7] When she finally was freed and found shelter at the mission house in Salonica, Stone reflected that she felt safe "under the folds of the stars and stripes." The mission space was, importantly, an American space.[8]

What had prompted Ellen Stone's capture was not immediately clear. Some observers, attentive to the Macedonian revolutionary movement, accused Stone and Tsilka of participating in their own capture. As a US citizen, Stone insisted that the Turkish government had no right to demand her testimony about the ordeal. She left the country and returned to the United States. Both women wrote about the ordeal many times in the years after, and they always refused to name their captors or to criticize the Macedonian revolutionary movement that their captors participated in. Stone placed the blame on Turkey and the political situation that the government had allowed to unfold. If Turkey had only lived up to the Treaty of Berlin's promise to bring about reforms to benefit her Christian subjects, she mused to readers in *McClure's* magazine, none of this might have happened.[9] Stone, like so many others, was unable to live and work as a missionary without becoming affected by the political world around her.

Stone's ordeal came on the heels of a tremendous shift in US political life. It was only three years earlier that war with Spain had ushered in a new era of US imperialism and humanitarianism that built on nearly a century of missionary diplomacy. And Ellen Stone would not be the only missionary whose experiences raised new questions about how missionary diplomacy ought to function in a new century.

Across the country, the sinking of the *Maine* in the middle of February 1898 was front-page news. As Americans worried about what had happened—an accident? a torpedo?—and what would come next—war?—supporters of the foreign missions movement found themselves furious about a short piece buried in the letters to the editor of the *New York Times*. "Missionaries as Hostiles," ran the title, and the author did not hold back. Opening with a quotation from the 1796 Treaty with Tripoli, the letter reminded readers that the United States, from its very first official relations with the Islamic world, had declared itself "not in any sense founded on the Christian religion" and having "no character of enmity against the laws, religion, or tranquility" of Muslims. American missionaries at the turn of the new century seemed to be flying in the face of that tradition of religious freedom and toleration.

Islam was an established religion in Turkey, the article went on to say. Missionaries traveled from the United States "to undermine that law, to seduce families from allegiance to it, to declare the head of Islam (the Sultan) an infidel." They were "engaged in acts of hostility against that nation." Accordingly, they should not expect the defense of the US government in any disagreements with the Turkish government. Bristling with frustration at missionary troublemakers, the author insisted that missionaries could not "expect us to propagate their faith by the sword." The letter was signed under the pen name "Equity."[10]

Alfred Dwight Foster Hamlin's response appeared in the paper three days later. Hamlin, the son of missionaries, had been born in Turkey. Now a professor of architecture at Columbia University, he took it upon himself to set the record straight for the *Times'* readers. Equity had it all wrong, fundamentally misunderstanding the work of the missionaries, their relationship with the Turkish government, and the nature of their requests for support from the United States.[11] His defensiveness was clear. Missionaries were not asking for the US government to act on their behalf in any inappropriate way, he insisted. Their religious freedom was granted under Turkish law; their rights were being denied by Turkish administrators. For Hamlin, the time had come for the US government to receive "not a curb, but a whip and spur, in its dealings with the monstrous and unpublished outrages of the last twelve years by Turks upon law-abiding American citizens."[12] James L. Barton of the ABCFM agreed. His letter to the editor was unpublished, covering as it did many of the same points that Hamlin had raised. Barton could not believe how "unfair and unjust" Equity had been to American missionaries. Missionaries were not breaking any Turkish laws. If they had, they could be tried and convicted. Instead, they had spent nearly eighty years building schools, hospitals, medical dispensaries, and presses, working with the full knowledge and approval of the Turkish government.[13]

This back-and-forth on the opinion pages was a hint that the missionary troubles the State Department had been noting for nearly two decades was emerging as a broader issue in US politics. Hamlin's father, Rev. Cyrus Hamlin, had already written on the subject in the *North American Review*.[14] Increasingly, missionary troubles extended beyond their interactions with foreign governments. At home, too, missionaries were in trouble. American observers like Equity increasingly argued that missionaries created problems for themselves and their country, getting themselves into situations that could have been avoided if only they had followed the rules. Missionary troubles were their own fault, the critique went, and they were trying to drag US diplomacy into unnecessary conflict.

In February 1898, as the Hamlins and Barton stewed over the ways that Americans misunderstood missionaries, their work, and what they wanted from the US government, their country entered a new war for empire. The destruction of the *Maine* began the war that would remove the Spanish from Cuba and the Philippines; by the end of the year, the United States would claim its own territories.

For students of US history, 1898 is a significant year. After at least a century of colonial expansion across the continent, the Spanish American War resulted in the first US overseas territories in Puerto Rico and the Philippines. In that same year, missionary descendants were key players in the US annexation of Hawai'i. After decades of using different words to describe US imperialism—Manifest Destiny, expansion—a new terminology seemed to threaten core ideas about what America was seemed difficult to escape. The islands of Puerto Rico, Hawai'i, and the Philippines seemed different from western territories: did America now have colonies? Had it become an empire in the same way as the European powers it had previously defined itself against? The map of the United States was changing, and along with it, new arguments emerged about the role of the United States in the world.

As in earlier years, missionary boards gathered in meeting rooms surrounded by maps that measured their progress around the world. And those visual aids continued to perform their own work. Presbyterian women attending the Annual Union Meeting of the Women's Mission Board agreed that missionary maps could have "preached a sermon of their own." As they gazed over the maps, looking for the familiar stations that they had long read about but never visited, they had to work. As much as mission supporters felt like they knew the world, the geography could feel unfamiliar, the stations on the map never seemed to be where they were supposed to be. And yet there they were. Once located, the women found the black dots representing missionary stations were "loud, insistent, beckoning, persuasive, looking down into your heart . . . until you grow tender and wistful, anxious and determined."[15]

Determined to accomplish what, though? If missionaries at the start of the century had dreamed of the conversion of the world, the missionaries at the end of the century were now dedicating themselves to the evangelization of the world *in this generation*. It was a goal that was both optimistic and naïve. They were animated by a sense of new possibility

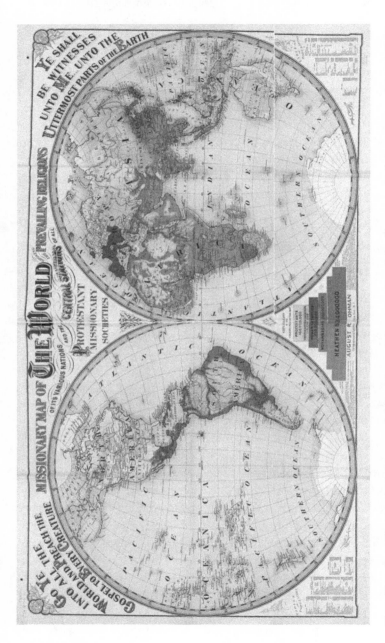

Figure III.1. Map of Protestant missions around the world, 1902. This map was intended to demonstrate both the progress made by missionaries in the previous century and the significant work still ahead. The chart at the bottom center tabulated the numbers of Protestants, Orthodox Christians, Catholics, Muslims, and "Heathen" across the globe.

Source: August R. Ohman, *Missionary Map of the World Showing Prevailing Religions of Its Various Nations and the Central Stations of all Protestant Missionary Societies* (New York: August R. Ohman, 1902), https://www.loc.gov/item/2017586281/, Library of Congress, Geography and Map Division.

and potential shaped in part by changes in global politics and in part by changes in American religious life. The expansion of American colonialism seemed poised to open up new lands for missionary endeavors.[16]

The final decades of the nineteenth century saw the rise of a Protestant movement known as the Social Gospel, and it ushered in changes in the ways that missionaries and their supporters approached their work. Proponents of the Social Gospel responded to the changes of a modernizing and industrializing world by turning their attention to social, not individual, sin. As they tried to realize a more Christian society, they sought systemic changes in political, economic, and social institutions, and often paid attention to problems like class and racial inequality. Within the mission movement, this shift provided theological justification for educational and medical institution building while encouraging subtle shifts in the logic behind the work of "civilizing" the world as a part of evangelization. The Social Gospel was not without its critics, and the debates within American Protestantism over this movement would eventually create a split between these modernists and those who would adopt the label fundamentalists in the 1920s. These Protestants, too, continued to be engaged in mission work, though they prioritized conversion and proselytizing over institution building.[17]

Even as American missionaries responded to these religious shifts, they also had to contend with the new goals of the US government. Missionaries were not the only ones to greet the new century with an optimistic vision of expansion and global connection. By the close of the nineteenth century, the United States had developed a far more robust and professionalized diplomatic infrastructure. Diplomats debated new reforms to the consular system, so long at the heart of missionary diplomacy. And with the defeat of Spain in the wars of 1898, the US government not only began to impose rule over overseas colonies but confronted a robust domestic anti-imperialist movement. Anti-imperialists forced the United States to examine the question of the meaning of American national identity and the true mission of the United States in the world.

Americans debated whether this was a disturbing break with their traditional position in international relations or the fruition of a long-promised destiny. But the war with Spain and the struggle for control in the Philippines that followed it was far from the only event that challenged American thinking about empire at the turn of the twentieth century. The Boxer Uprising in China and the crisis in the Congo both struck US anti-imperialists as excellent examples of the dangers of empire. But humanitarian crises around the world—in Cuba, in Congo, in Armenia—brought missionaries into partnership with other Americans who saw the benefits to the whole world of a more interventionist United States. Missionary diplomacy was part of all of these stories.

As Americans debated what global role they should play in the new century, the value of missionaries was subject to debate. Did missionaries represent the best of the United States, or did they distort US interests? Could their educational, humanitarian, and medical work be separated from their evangelism?

CHAPTER 8

Imperialists

Theodore Roosevelt had questions, and Arthur Judson Brown seemed like a man who might have answers. In 1902, Roosevelt was president and needed more information on the Philippines. He had William Howard Taft's commission report, but Taft was still on the other side of the world. Brown, on the other hand, was in Washington, just recently returned for a tour of Presbyterian missions in Japan, Korea, China, the Philippines, Siam, India, Egypt, Syria, and Palestine. Why not ask the missionary secretary for his impressions of the United States' new colonial territory?

The two men had known each other since 1900, when Brown invited then-vice president Roosevelt, President William McKinley, and former president Benjamin Harrison to take part in the opening exercises of a missionary conference in New York. After McKinley and Harrison delivered their ten-minute prepared speeches, Roosevelt entertained the gathered crowd with extemporaneous tales of bear hunting in the Rockies.[1] Roosevelt and Brown continued a friendly correspondence after the event, and when Roosevelt heard that Brown had recently returned to the country from the Philippines, the new president invited the missionary to the White House.

Brown would later remember Roosevelt's conviction that US diplomacy needed be sure to prioritize "fairness and friendship" in its relations with Asian people now that the United States had "been brought into such close contact" with Asia. Roosevelt's use of the passive voice was telling. He and Brown both agreed that the time had passed for any questions about why or how the United States had come to the Philippines. The important thing now was that the United States was in power. The question on both of their minds was not whether they should withdraw, but as Brown put it, "in what spirit should we remain."[2]

In the coming years, Brown sent along his books and articles, urging Roosevelt to read them for information about not only the Philippines but other missionary lands as well. Roosevelt responded with appreciation. In October 1904, Roosevelt thanked Brown for sending his new book and scrawled at the bottom of the page, "When can you get to Washington? I wish you to lunch with me."[3]

For Brown, it was essential that Filipinos always understand that the Protestant missionaries were not "agents of the US government or affiliated with it in any way." The Philippines had known centuries of religious governance under Spanish rule. Brown and the missionaries he represented wanted to be clear that US occupation meant a separation of church and state for the Philippines. The Protestant missionaries would be there, but they wanted conversions to be based on religious conviction, not political pressure. So naturally, missionaries and their supporters at home spent a good amount of energy talking about politics.

Diplomats and missionaries both served as sources of information and as strategists for the US-Filipino relationship. Brown's report to the Presbyterian Board of Foreign Missions repeatedly cited William Howard Taft's commission and included a page-long quotation from President William McKinley.[4] American occupation meant religious freedom, these leaders all agreed. Religious freedom would open the way for American missionaries. It was an interesting formulation, made only the more interesting when the president of the United States mined the director of the Presbyterian Board of Foreign Missions for information, and the director of the missionary society in turn relied on government sources.

The Protestant missionary response to the wars of 1898 was, in a word, complicated. There was significant missionary support for the war, and for the occupation of the Philippines that followed it. This was true even as Filipino resistance made it clear that US governance was not welcome. American rule opened up a new mission field and Protestant missionaries welcomed the opportunity to "civilize" the islands. But two facts made the US missionary experience in the Philippines different than what they had experienced elsewhere. First, the majority of Filipinos were Catholic. And second, they were ruled not by a European or Turkish power, but by a conquering United States. Together, these facts challenged the existing dynamics of missionary diplomacy.

The US occupation of the Philippines ushered in a new era of American Christian imperialism. As had been the case throughout the nineteenth century, missionaries looked to empire as a potential tool for evangelism. With empire, they hoped, missionary access could follow. In the Philippines, this hope would be realized. Here, more than anywhere before, missionaries were acting at the pleasure of the US government.

Cuba and Humanitarianism

Long before the United States declared war on Spain in 1898, Americans had been concerned about Spanish colonial rule. Americans had observed, and often sympathized with, the early nineteenth-century independence movements in South and Central America that had removed much of Spanish power in the hemisphere and replaced it with new republics.[5] But what was happening in Cuba as the island fought for its independence from Spain drew American attention in new ways, and it was Cuba that would eventually open the door to the Philippines. A new language of humanitarian concern animated US observers, both inside and outside the mission movement.

Cuba had been fighting for its independence since the 1860s. The latest stage of the war between Cuba and Spain emerged in 1895, and observers in the United States watched closely and with rising alarm. Spain began a policy of "reconcentration" in 1896 in an effort to quash the guerrilla tactics of the revolutionaries. Under this program, the colonial government moved Cuban civilians from their homes to centralized locations under military rule. The results were horrifying. Sanitary conditions were terrible in the camps, and many residents could not access adequate food or medical care. Reports in the United States estimated civilian deaths between 300,000 and 500,000 (though the actual deaths were probably closer to 100,000).[6] Americans were particularly struck by stories of suffering women and children that inspired a chivalric desire to intervene and protect innocents from abuse at the hands of supposedly rapacious Spaniards.[7] In the summer of 1897, the *Christian Herald* reported that every piece of news they received from Cuba brought "some new and startling story of brutality inflicted upon the helpless Cuban peasantry by the Spanish troops under the name of military law."[8]

Missionaries helped to spread the news of Cuban suffering while also suggesting that Cuba would make an excellent mission field. The Baptists, Episcopalians, and Southern Presbyterians had already sent missionaries to the island, only to be removed by the Spanish. There, they found a populace that had been "lying for centuries at our very gates, crushed beneath the tyranny and superstition of the Romish Church." As one article in the *Christian Observer* suggested, missionary-minded Americans found themselves with the opportunity to act like the Good Samaritan. Cuba had been left "stripped, wounded, and half dead" by Spain. Now American Christians had to ask if they would pass by, or take action to help their neighbor.[9] The *Boston Globe* reported in early April that American ministers were enthusiastic about the possibility of intervention in Cuba precisely because they thought it would open the way for a more aggressive missionary project.[10]

With the increasingly upsetting news from Cuba, the US State Department, too, began to urge Americans to take action. On Christmas Eve, 1897, Secretary of State John Sherman issued a press release urging Americans to donate funds and provisions for Cuba. President McKinley created a Central Cuban Relief Committee, adapting a model that the government had previously used to manage aid in the Armenian crisis. McKinley appointed Louis Klopsch of the *Christian Herald*, the leading evangelical periodical of the era; Stephen Barton of the American Red Cross; and Charles Schieren of the New York Chamber of Commerce to oversee the work. Soon they sent nurses along with a hundred hospital beds and five thousand dollars in food for Cuban children. The needs were great, and they urged Americans to give generously.[11]

The Golden Rule inspired the Christian and philanthropic organizations to take an interest in humanitarian issues. But US diplomats had not previously embraced this role, instead preferring to leave philanthropy to private citizens and nongovernmental organizations such as the mission boards. In the 1820s, John Quincy Adams had insisted that the United States did not go out into the world in search of "monsters to destroy." But by the 1890s, that seemed like a policy that had outlived its relevance. Americans were deeply enmeshed in global networks. Whether they went searching or not, they found monsters abroad. Increasingly, some government officials suggested that the only appropriate response was to destroy them when they were found.

Destroying monsters, after all, was not only philanthropic. It also made the United States look good. It signaled America's position as a < civilizing and benevolent country ⟩ Sending donations to Cuba, the *Christian Herald* argued, provided "a striking and memorable object lesson to the entire world" about what kind of country the United States was.[12] Economic interests were also at play, as the United States searched for new markets for US manufactured goods. But the emphasis in public statements all focused on the humanitarian issues at hand. Pamphlets and petitions called on the US government to "rescue" Cuba. One such pamphlet declared that "the cause of freedom in Cuba is the cause of God and man."[13] In the congressional debates about intervention, Rep. Harry Skinner of North Carolina argued that God had given the United States to Cubans "as their guardians, defenders, and protectors."[14] The White House and the State Department both insisted that the United States cared about the fate of the Cuban people and wanted to bring relief and safety to the island nation.

To be a guardian and defender, these politicians argued, the United States would need to go to war with Spain. That was certainly the theme of President William McKinley's 1898 war message. The "Cuba question," he insisted, had an "intimate connection" to the state of the American union. Ongoing fighting had challenged the United States in enforcing neutrality laws, caused losses to US trade, and "by the exercise of cruel, barbarous, and uncivilized practices of warfare, shocked the sensibilities and offended the humane sympathies of our people," the president argued. There were multiple grounds for US intervention, he continued. But first, McKinley argued that "in the cause of humanity," the United States ought to "put an end to the barbarities, bloodshed, starvation, and horrible miseries" existing in Cuba.[15]

McKinley's claims for humanitarian motivations were supported by his call to continue the distribution of food and supplies, and his request that the Congress appropriate funds from the national treasury "to supplement the charity of our citizens."[16] Congress agreed, and the war in Cuba lasted from April to December 1898. Cuba was not the only front in the "splendid little war" between the United States and Spain. After fighting began in Cuba, McKinley ordered a US squadron to Manila, where another group of Spanish colonial subjects were at war for their independence. Within hours, the United States claimed victory.

None of this interest in intervention meant that the United States planned to claim Cuba as its own colonial territory. McKinley said such a move "cannot be thought of." Forcible annexation "would be criminal aggression."[17] The Teller Amendment to Congress's resolution for war codified this vision, declaring that the United States had no intention of ruling over Cuba once victory was obtained. But this did not mean that the United States recognized Cuban independence yet. That would wait until the US government was satisfied that Cuba was prepared to self-govern.

The war would have profound effects on the shape of US imperialism. At the Treaty of Paris, Spain lost its possession of Cuba, Puerto Rico, Guam, and the Philippines. With the exception of Cuba, all of these Spanish colonies became US territories. It was in the Philippines that the war would most clearly usher in a new era of US foreign relations and missionary diplomacy. As one writer in the *Christian Observer* urged, missionaries might "overcome the evil of war with the good of the Gospel. Let us remember the Maine and give them hot shot from our Gospel guns."[18]

Missionary Opportunism in the Philippines

As in Cuba, the Philippines had seen many years of anticolonial protest and warfare by the time the Americans arrived. Spanish rule on the archipelago was repressive; the Filipinos had little political power within the empire. Instead, the Spanish ruled the islands through the military and the Catholic friars. By 1898, a resistance movement to increase Filipino representation in Spanish governance had developed into a revolution that sought independence.

At first, Filipino revolutionaries had hoped that the United States might be an ally. Revolutionary leader Emilio Aguinaldo met with the US consul in Singapore before the United States entered the war, and he left that meeting assured that the United States would support the independence of the Philippines. Admiral George Dewey, the hero of the US naval attack on the Spanish, arranged Aguilaldo's return to Manila. With the Spanish defeated, Filipino revolutionaries got to work building a new Philippine Republic. It would not last long.

The negotiations over the Treaty of Paris did not include any Filipinos. The treaty named the Philippines as a US territory, reflecting the understanding of the Euro-American powers that the Filipinos were racially and culturally unprepared for self-government. The fighting in the Philippines soon shifted from a war for independence from Spain into a war for independence from the United States. As the US government and the American missionaries debated how they would respond to the new opportunities presented to them by this new colony, the Filipinos themselves did not plan to make colonial rule easy for the United States.[19]

One of the first tasks facing the US government was simply to learn more about the place and the people. Accordingly, President McKinley appointed a commission to travel to the Philippines and report on its political, social, and cultural conditions in the interest of setting up a new colonial government. William Howard Taft, a well-respected lawyer, was selected to lead this important project. In this role, Taft would create legislative and judicial policies for the islands and would soon replace the existing military government as governor-general. In June of 1900, Taft and his commission arrived in the Philippines.

The Philippine Commission's report set out to describe conditions on the islands at this pivotal moment between colonial regimes. There was little that they did not consider worthy of study: the report covered public health, the civil government, the military, the economy, the liquor trade, sugar farming, mining, forestry, transport, taxation, education, and more. Appendices included extensive tables on the climate, ethnographic reports from different regions throughout the islands, and a lengthy history of the judicial system throughout the history of the Philippines. It provided, or at least the government hoped it provided, a roadmap for US colonial rule.[20]

Taft knew from the beginning that religion would be an important theme for US rule. Spain had ruled the islands largely through Catholic friars who had monastic orders based on the islands. These religious leaders were Spanish, not Filipino, and owned a huge amount of the land. Americans believed that much of the resistance to Spanish rule was resistance to the friars. Getting rid of the friar system was accordingly a priority. What would replace it, however, was up for discussion.

For some American Christians, the humanitarian rhetoric meant that the war in Cuba could be embraced as a Christian cause. Yet the humanitarian questions were different in the Philippines. For many observers, war in the Philippines seemed much more about territory and colonization. The Women's Christian Temperance Union, for example, had embraced the cause in Cuba, but had questions about the Philippines. So, too, did many US clergy.[21] William Jennings Bryan, McKinley's opponent in the presidential race of 1900, joined his voice to those Christians who balked at the imperialism of America's entry into the Philippines with the reminder that the Great Commission "has no Gatling-gun attachment." American missionaries, he warned, needed to keep their

distance. At risk was the too-close identification of the missionary project with the colonial one. How would it look, he wondered, if missionaries seemed to be part of a conquering force? "Let it be known that our
missionaries are seeking souls instead of sovereignty," he urged. "Let it
be known that instead of being the advance guard of conquering armies,
they are going forth to help and uplift."[22]

This warning was needed, for many American Protestant missionaries and their supporters viewed the US occupation of the Philippines as
an act of God.[23] For these Christian observers, the ease with which the
United States had triumphed in the Philippines could be nothing short
of Providential. Over and over again, they emphasized the accidental
nature of occupation, and the ways in which the United States was duty
bound to govern there. As Arthur Judson Brown of the Presbyterian mission board explained, the country had gained this new territory through
"no scheming of our own."[24] The ABCFM believed that the US victory
was "the will of God, and we stand in awe as we think of it." It was so
swift, with no cost of life—how else could it be explained?[25] Methodist
bishop William Oldham claimed that the "roar of the American cannon
was the voice of Almighty God announcing that the Philippines should
be free."[26] Methodist bishop James Thoburn, too, attributed the US possession of the Philippines to divine intervention when he testified before
the US Senate.[27]

Despite this enthusiasm, it was not initially clear what the
United States could or should do after the victory in Manila. President
McKinley would later describe the islands as having "dropped into our
laps," leaving him with the question of "what to do with them." The
war there had begun, as it had in Cuba, as an independence movement.
But many US observers insisted that the Philippines could not possibly
be independent. Racist assumptions about who could or could not self-
govern structured these discussions in the United States. At the same
time, many Americans believed that to take possession of an overseas
colony would be a break with the American past and its core values.

Missionary supporters, meanwhile, were noting an opportunity "second to none that has ever been offered them," as one article in *The Independent* explained. The Philippines were "an immense territory hitherto
closed" to evangelism and now "open and ready for occupation."[28] The
Methodist Woman's Missionary Society put it a bit less militaristically:
if the islands were "providentially opened to the society," they wanted
to send along their missionaries. According to a report on the society's
meeting in the *Washington Post*, there was "no mistaking the feeling of

the delegates on the question of the retention of the islands." They had every expectation that once the Philippines were brought within the United States, they would make "a fruitful and advantageous field" for missionary labor.[29] The Presbyterian Board of Foreign Missions, too, felt that the hand of God had been at work in these "political and military relations into which the United States has been so strangely forced." Moral and religious responsibilities, they argued, necessarily followed. By late June, that mission board had already received letters from five states urging Presbyterian missions to the Philippines, with one pastor having raised more than a thousand dollars to support the first missionary to be sent there even before the mission board agreed to appoint one.[30] American Protestants, in short, were excited by the opportunity that empire seemed to offer.

Julia Ward Howe agreed. The peace advocate, reformer, and poet addressed a congregation on the subject of victory in the fall of 1898. Victory, she noted, was "the joyous word of this hour," but the difficult task would be to turn the momentary success of Admiral Dewey at Manila into a lasting victory in the Philippines. That victory would not come from the military, but from a band coming from "clean Christian homes." Instead of weapons, "their ammunition is the spelling book, the grammar, the psalms of David, the promises of Christ." In time, she hoped, the missionary would say to the soldier, "Your business was to destroy men; mine is to create citizens, which is far better." Howe's address noted the long-standing work that US missionaries had done around the world to fight against oppression, but noted that "in all its noble record missionary labor has never had before it a scope so vital, so important as that opened by the late military operations." They now had the opportunity to "make whole races free with the freedom of the 19th century, the freedom of intelligent thought, of just institutions, of reasonable religion—what a prospect is this!"[31]

Would the United States take up the "white man's burden," as Rudyard Kipling so famously phrased it, and govern a colony of nonwhite subjects in apparent need of civilizing rule? Or would it hold on to what some Americans considered its anti-imperialist traditions and leave the islands to self-rule? Was that even an option? For American Christians who had not given much passing thought to these islands before, it was a dilemma indeed.

As debates over what to do with the Philippines echoed in the halls of Congress, from church pulpits, and in the columns of newspapers across the country, President McKinley paced the floors of the White House late into the night, wondering what to do. When he later described this time to a group of fellow Methodists, McKinley claimed that the answer came to him through prayer. He knelt down to pray, asking God for guidance on this monumental decision. And finally, the answer came. The United States could neither return the Philippines to Spain—it would be "cowardly and dishonorable"—nor turn them over to another imperial power such as France or Germany—this would be "bad business." But they also could not leave the Philippines alone—"they were unfit for self-government and would soon have anarchy and misrule worse than Spain's was." Only one choice seemed to remain. The United States would simply have to "take them all, and to educate the Filipinos, and uplift them and civilize and Christianize them, and by God's grace do the very best we could by them, as our fellow-men for whom Christ also died."[32]

McKinley's language here is striking. Whether or not he had literally fallen to his knees to pray for God's guidance in the Philippines, he articulated a Christian diplomacy that was in accord with the commitments of missionaries and their US supporters. After all, missionary diplomats had advocated more or less similar goals for decades: uplift, civilization, and Christianization were all watchwords of the late-nineteenth-century mission movement. The sorts of schools, hospitals, and presses that Protestant missionaries had established at their various stations elsewhere around the world seemed like they would fit in well with the administration's vision of US rule in the Philippines. And McKinley's justification for this—to serve "those for whom Christ also died"—was an explicitly Christian call to action. To have the president of the United States advocating not only for a civilizing and uplifting form of empire, but to directly link those goals to the work of Christianizing was an exciting development for McKinley's Methodist audience. In his rhetoric, at least, McKinley was a powerful ally to missionary diplomacy.

If earlier generations of Christian imperialists had sought to direct US political and economic interests overseas in ways that would benefit the mission movement, here now was a US empire that seemed ready for missionary activity. One Episcopal priest described how, standing on the Pacific shore in North America and looking out over the ocean, his "heart thrilled at the thought of that great field now open for the church in the Philippines" as he "pray[ed] earnestly that the Holy Ghost may direct us in occupying it."[33] The government had acted first, and now missionaries could respond.

The churches quickly did so.[34] By the end of the decade, American missionaries had arrived in the Philippines from the YMCA, the Methodist Episcopal Church, the Presbyterian Church (USA), the Episcopalian Church, the American Baptist Missionary Union, the Christian and Missionary Alliance, the United Brethren in Christ, the Foreign Christian Missionary Society of the Disciples of Christ, the ABCFM, the Seventh-Day Adventists, the Free Methodist Church, and the Christian Science Society.[35] The missionaries went about their work, dividing the land among the various mission boards and adopting the colonial language of "unoccupied territory." This wording of occupation is at once striking and unsurprising. They were, after all, part of a colonial force.

These missionaries believed themselves to be joining with the government of the United States in a single project: bringing civilization, the gospel, and religious freedom to the Philippines. They saw the US flag as "the glorious symbol of liberty and a Christian civilization," and they saw themselves as important bearers of both of those concepts.[36] Bishop Charles Brent, of the Episcopal Church, insisted that it was time for Americans to realize their duty "not merely as a Churchman, but also as a citizen" to support these missions wholeheartedly.[37] As they had done for many years around the world, missionary organizations again walked the delicate balance between celebrating the importance of religious freedom and expecting the US government to aid missionaries in their evangelistic project. The war simply brought a new attention to these long-standing concerns.

Imperial Governance

If Protestant missionaries were excited by the possibilities of partnering in the colonial governance of the Philippines, American Catholic observers were horrified. Protestant missionary anti-Catholicism was no secret, and McKinley's language of Christianizing the Philippines was alarming. After all, the Philippines were majority Catholic. Christianity had come to the Philippines long ago. The problem for Protestant missionaries and their supporters was the type of Christianity that had flourished on the islands. Catholic Americans were accordingly watching closely to ensure that the "religious freedom" that the United States promised the Philippines was not simply anti-Catholicism in disguise. Both groups waited anxiously to see what William Howard Taft, the newly appointed governor-general of the Philippines, would do.

In the 1900 US presidential election, various questions raised by the Philippines were at the heart of McKinley's battle against William Jennings Bryan for the White House. While Taft governed a colony that was actively resisting US rule, a vibrant anti-imperialist movement emerged in the United States that set off a debate not only about the specifics of US governance in the new territories of the Philippines, Hawai'i, Puerto Rico, and Guam, but also about the nature of American national identity. No one could afford to be complacent about the challenges of US empire.

American anti-imperialists argued that the United States had been founded in an anti-imperialist revolution and had, throughout its history, embraced values in opposition to colonialism and empire. These values, they claimed, were at the heart of their understanding of American national identity. Thomas Jefferson had called for the United States to become an "empire of liberty," spreading its freedoms wherever the flag flew. Any new territories, under this approach, would need to eventually become states with full and equal membership in the American union. Such a future, anti-imperialists insisted, was not possible for the far distant and nonwhite spaces of the former Spanish empire. The United States simply could not incorporate them as colonies (or, in the American terminology, "territories") without fundamentally changing its character.

Protestant and Catholic Americans could be found in both the pro- and anti-imperialist camps. While the Christian stance on humanitarian questions seemed clear, it was far cloudier on the question of colonial governance. Anti-imperialists worried about the corruption and oppression that so often followed colonial rule. Pro-imperialists focused instead on the opportunities that empire provided for evangelism and benevolence. Both sides could look back on a century of US missionary engagement with empires and colonized people to find evidence for their arguments.

To prove that imperialism had been at the core of America's history since its beginning, pro-imperialists pointed to more than a century of US imperialist rule over Native Americans. Whatever anti-imperialists had argued about the meaning of US history, the fact remained that the United States had controlled colonial territory throughout its history. It had always been both a republic and an empire. For the entire history of the United States, the government had not only sought to claim the lands of Indigenous Americans, it had also imposed significant changes to Indigenous culture, often through the work of missionary societies.

Missionaries and US empire went hand-in-hand. This history was not lost on anyone. For pro-imperialists, it was clear that the United States had long been imperial.[38]

Mission boards largely agreed, but in 1904, the Methodists raised an interesting question. If the Philippines were an American space, could the denomination still refer to the Philippines as a "foreign" mission? Foreign missions were, by definition, in countries outside of the United States and its governing power. A minority report to the General Conference raised this question, arguing that the Philippines ought to be considered a "home" mission, just like the missions to the various Native American nations in North America. But the conference as a whole disagreed. "The power to classify its missions and direct their administration is in the Methodist Episcopal Church, and not in the government of the United States," the decision read. Allowing US colonization over "an island beyond the seas" to change the classification of its missions would be to allow the US government inappropriate power over the missionary organizations. For these Methodists, distance and race mattered more than political governance in determining a space's identity as "foreign" or "home." Could the government's relationship to the Philippines determine the missionary relationship to the Philippines? "We think not."[39]

In spite of this wariness about giving the government too much control over how the mission societies categorized their work, many missionary leaders celebrated the opportunity to work within this US colonial space. Arthur Judson Brown was particularly enthusiastic. He came into his role as general secretary for the Presbyterian mission board with a commitment to the progressive movement known as the Social Gospel, and he considered social service and human welfare to be just as important to missionary work as evangelism. Brown traveled with his wife, Jennie E. Thomas Brown, to the Philippines in 1901 as part of a delegation to study the viability of Presbyterian missions and the path forward. He took this role seriously, studying the available reports on Philippine history and culture and interviewing Governor-General Taft, Catholic bishops, Board of Education officials, public school teachers, and of course the missionaries themselves. He would later describe these visits as "crowded with interviews, conferences, addresses, and visits to institutions."[40] The trip would be the source of several publications for various audiences: a 1902 report, intended for the Presbyterian mission board, and a book, *The New Era in the Philippines*, which went through multiple editions in 1903.

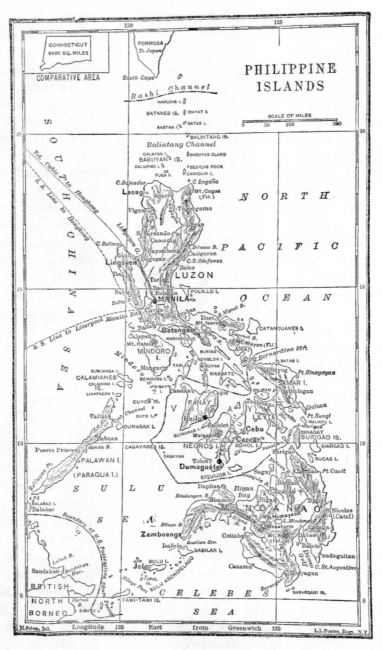

Figure 8.1. Map of the Philippines, 1903. This map accompanied one of Arthur Judson Brown's publications on the Philippines for US missionary audiences. Note the use of Connecticut in the top left of the map to communicate scale to readers in the US mainland.
Source: Brown, *New Era in the Philippines*, 306.

Brown's reporting identified the Filipinos as a "naturally intelligent and kindly" people who were not ready for self-government. Brown estimated that it would take "some decades" before they would be prepared, and even then only if they received the sort of cultural reform that he believed necessary. He found most of the "common people" to be "ignorant and superstitious," but he believed that could be easily explained by their history. "What else could be expected after nearly four centuries of corrupt and oppressive Spanish rule?"[41] American sovereignty, he was sure, would change things.

The state and the mission alike agreed that what Filipinos really needed was character development. Brown insisted that missionaries were uniquely positioned to do this work. The problem was, he argued, that the Filipinos were idle and undisciplined. They needed to learn the industriousness of "the Scotchman, the Yankee, or the Chinese." This industriousness could be taught by the missionaries, he believed, even as he associated industry with particular racial groups over others.[42]

The methods and institutions that guided mission work elsewhere would need tweaks in the Philippines due to the related work of the colonial government. The United States had taken charge of health care within Manila, but left the rest of the Philippines to be cared for by the missionaries. As public health was a major concern in the colony, this would be an important task. Government control of elementary education freed the missionaries to focus on the higher branches. The missionaries debated naming their new college after President McKinley.[43]

Protestant missionaries generally approved of the state control of education, seeing it as an important marker of the separation of church and state that would diminish Catholic influence while subtly supporting their own power. Brown, for example, celebrated the 1901 school law that removed religion from the public schools as part of a fight against the Catholicism of the islands, identifying "intellectual freedom and enlightenment" as the "death to the type of Romanism which prevails in the Philippines."[44] Certainly this was how William Jessup, a missionary in Syria, understood the situation. Reading Brown's book on the Philippines, he was struck by the ways that the public schools would lift "an immense load" off the missionaries. "To think of being on a 'Foreign Mission Field' with the enthusiastic backing of the whole United States in giving the people a true education! Why the idea is superb!"[45]

Missionaries and their supporters embraced the language of responsibility and duty that drove the "white man's burden" approach to the Philippines. Accordingly, missionary reporting on the moral effects of empire did not shy away from harsh critique, either of Filipinos or of the "irreligious" Americans they encountered on the islands. Missionaries had long worried about the bad influence of immoral Euro-Americans on potential converts' ideas about Christianity. Here, the sheer numbers of Americans unaffiliated with the church seemed a major threat. Accordingly, the missionaries built an American church for the colonizers in addition to Filipino churches for the colonized, effectively segregating worshippers.

Missionaries also organized opposition to the sale of alcohol at military canteens and the government regulation of prostitution.[46] Speaking in front of the Christian Alliance Convention, missionary Bessie White reported that before the Americans took Manila, there were only two saloons in the city. One year later, there were four hundred. Reports like this, shared first with missionary audiences but then reported in mainstream publications like the *New York Times*, spread missionary critiques to a wider audience.[47]

Both of these topics hit on the core question of what kind of influence US rule would have. Was the United States a moral force in the world? And if so, how could it justify these policies that, to their critics, seemed to encourage immoral behavior? Missionaries and their supporters asked these questions with deep earnestness, and they were met with similar passion from their audiences. When Rev. Homer C. Stuntz, the superintendent of the Methodist missions in the Philippines, spoke to the General Methodist Missionary Convention on reasons to oppose the canteens, it was, according to the *Baltimore Sun*, "one of the hits of the address."[48]

Though missionaries benefitted from and identified with aspects of the US political project in the Philippines, they well understood themselves to have a distinct role. As missionaries regularly insisted, they were not political. Brown, for example, claimed that mission boards "would prefer to have no relations with governments," though this claim was belied by the activities of many mission boards throughout the century.[49] Indeed if this were true, why had he invited Roosevelt and McKinley to the 1900 missionary conference? The connections between the missionaries and the government was complicated in the Philippines. This was not a space where missionary diplomacy played out in the ways that it had earlier in the nineteenth century. Though their contemporaries in other parts of the world continued in consular work, and though mission boards continued to remain in contact with the State Department, Philippines missionaries did not fill diplomatic roles. They did, however, understand their presence to be an important part of US influence on the islands, particularly because they saw themselves as embodying a particular American virtue: religious freedom and the separation of church and state.

Religious Freedom

When Taft arrived in the Philippines, he, like so many American observers, noted that it had no tradition of separating church and state. Under Spanish rule, much of the civic life of the islands had been administered by Spanish friars in the Augustinian and Dominican orders. By the time of American arrival, the friars had become unpopular among the Filipinos. The hostility, as Taft understood it, came from several sources. Perhaps most important, there was "a cleavage between the native clergy and the friars" due to the exclusion of Filipinos from the religious orders. This was a lesson that should have struck Protestant missionaries as well—problems emerged when the leaders of the religious hierarchy were perceived as outsiders. But American missionaries focused on a different lesson: the friars, Americans understood, had too much power and had been corrupted. They were major landowners in the Philippines, controlling access to 420,000 acres of land. They had also long controlled the public school system. Unraveling the connections between the state and the Catholic church in the Philippines would be one of the most sensitive tasks that Taft would face in the Philippines.[50]

The challenge was heightened by American missionaries and politicians trumpeting the ways that US rule would bring religious freedom.[51] Methodist Bishop William Oldham had claimed that God's purpose had "clearly" been for the United States to colonize the Philippines in order "to give the Filipinos freedom of religion." The Methodist Foreign Missionary Society echoed this idea, praising the "guarantees of religious liberty" that would come with peace and US rule.[52] Religious freedom was, in fact, specifically mentioned in the Treaty of Paris that established US sovereignty over the islands. It was at the heart of the American project, but its meaning was unclear.[53]

In both its domestic and foreign applications, religious freedom was a concept with multiple meanings. Protestant missionaries had long been skilled at simultaneously using several—at times contradictory—definitions in order to support their own work. American religious freedom depended on the separation of church and state, but also assumed that, in some general but important sense, the United States was a

Christian nation. American religious freedom demanded that the law recognize an individual's freedom of conscience, but in this colonial context it operated alongside a system that required imperial rule when the people did not exhibit proper "civilization"—including the embrace of the right kind of Christianity.

In their many stations around the world, Protestant missionaries had long used a flexible definition of religious freedom that prioritized their right to evangelize. They continued to present themselves as the embodiment of religious freedom now that the way was opened for their work in the Philippines. Religious freedom to them meant the ability to choose one's religion. Protestant missionaries truly believed that once people had the free choice to become Protestant, its obvious benefits would bring them to the church. Arthur Judson Brown, for example, explained that the problem with Filipino Catholicism was that it had been forced by Catholic friars who controlled religious, political, and civic matters. The people had not been given a choice.

Although Protestant missionaries also combined civic and evangelistic work, they insisted that their work was different because they understood their own religious outlook to be most conductive to the improvement of the islands and of individual Filipinos as well. From there, not only true Christianity but also civilized culture and democratic politics would follow. This complicated logic explained how Brown could proclaim his support for the separation of church and state while still insisting that "every true American patriot" ought to support Protestant missionaries.[54]

Catholic Americans, unsurprisingly, took issue with such an idea. For even though Protestant missionaries were anxious to "Christianize" the islands, the fact remained that the majority of the islands' inhabitants, were, in fact, Christians. They just weren't Protestants. Looking at a century of Protestant missionary diplomacy and their own experiences of anti-Catholicism in the mainland United States, these observers were quick to notice Protestant anti-Catholicism masking itself as religious freedom. They worried that the removal of the friars and the secularization of the schools would decimate the Catholic church on the islands. Archbishop John Ireland voiced these concerns in the pages of *The Outlook*, where he was interviewed on the subject of how Catholics and Protestants might cooperate in the "religious reconstruction" of the Philippines. He rejected any efforts of Protestant missionaries in the islands. The Catholics were "in complete control" there and to remove Catholicism would be to "throw them into absolute religious indifference." As an American, too, Ireland objected to Protestant missions. "Do your Protestant missionaries realize," he asked, "that they are doing the greatest harm to America by making her flag unpopular?" By making it appear to Filipinos that US rule would result in the removal of Catholicism, he claimed, missionaries were damaging the entire colonial project.[55]

Protestant missionaries responded to these attacks quickly. Presbyterian James Rodgers insisted that Filipinos saw the United States as the bearer of religious freedom. The mission was not creating bad will toward the United States. Rather, Filipinos understood the Protestant missions to be part and parcel of the project of religious freedom.[56] Such assurances were not entirely comforting to American Catholic audiences.

Within the government, McKinley, Taft, and Roosevelt were all attentive to the concerns of these Catholic Americans, at least in part in the interest of defending themselves in electoral battles. But the attention to Catholic concerns was not merely self-interested. Many writers who tried to explain the Philippines to readers in the United States emphasized that while individual corrupt friars may have caused problems, Catholicism itself had been an important and valuable tool of colonization and civilization on the islands. Just as Protestantism could serve the colonial interests, in other words, so too could an American version of Catholicism.[57]

Taft, for his part, had a genuine respect for Filipino Catholics and the civilizing power of Catholicism in general. His speeches on the subject of religion in the Philippines in front of Presbyterian, Episcopalian, and Catholic audiences were respectful of the Catholic past and present of the Philippines. While he shared missionary discomfort with the rule of Spanish friars, he understood that the problem was not Catholicism itself, but particular dynamics within the friar system. The solutions to the problems of church and state were relatively simple, at least in theory. First, Taft would work with the Catholic hierarchy to replace Spanish friars with other Catholic leaders who would not generate such opposition from the Filipino people. Then, he would transfer the power of major institutions that had been run by the church into the hands of civil government.

Taft worked with the Vatican to ensure these transitions would be smooth, and his communications with the US public were respectful of Catholicism, both in the Philippines and in the United States. The contrast with Protestant missionary rhetoric was evident. Where they saw innate problems with Catholicism itself, he saw particular issues that emerged out of a particular colonial context.[58]

Though Taft won accolades for his diplomatic visit to the Vatican, the implementation of his plan was far more challenging in practice than it had been in theory. The schools presented a particular challenge. After the Treaty of Paris, the US government took control of Filipino schools. At first, a Catholic army chaplain served as school superintendent, partly in the hopes that this would ease the transition from the schools being run by priests during the Spanish era. The government banned religious instruction and removed religious emblems from the walls. Catholics in the mainland United States and the Philippines alike were concerned by what they saw happening. To quiet their fears, Taft allowed priests and nuns to provide after-hours religious instruction to those children whose parents requested it. But rumors spread that teachers and administrators were largely being staffed through Protestant mission boards and the YMCA. Protestant missionaries, for their part, complained about an unstated preference for Catholic instructors. Neither of these claims had merit.[59]

Demand for public school teachers was high, and a good deal of care went into selecting who might serve in this capacity. In 1903, the superintendent of schools reported examining 1,500 applicants to make 500 appointments as teachers. All applicants were required to be a college or normal school graduate with at least two years' experience in the classroom and two references that could attest to "moral character and personal habits," in addition to a certificate of good health and a successful examination in a range of subjects. Successful applicants signed a contract for two years and were required to serve at whatever location the Civil Service Board sent them to.[60] In time, the government hoped to employ as many Filipino teachers as they could train. In the meantime, teachers came from the United States.

If the Protestant missionaries struggled at times to justify their work in the Philippines among Filipino Catholics, they had considerably less trouble in explaining their work among other groups in the Philippines. Americans understood there to be roughly three religious groups in the Philippines: the Catholics, the Moros, and the Negritos. As Brown phrased it, the Moros were "fanatical Mohammedans" and the Negritos were untouched by Spanish colonialism, having maintained "their primitive paganism." None of these, he argued, were civilized "according to Anglo Saxon standards."[61] The government mirrored this three-way classification, governing the Catholic, Muslim, and pagan sections of the Philippines differently. While colonial officials believed that all three groups were markedly superstitious and in need of modernization, they also understood that these religious identities were the most important factors in understanding how to rule over them.[62]

In the face of the violent opposition to US rule in the northern part of the archipelago, the initial strategy of the US government in the southern Moro territory was to rule indirectly. Working with local leaders, such as the sultan of Sulu, seemed to be an ideal way to rule this new colonial possession. But by 1902, the American approach changed. With the anti-American resistance elsewhere in the archipelago seemingly more controlled and rebellions in the Moro Province on the rise, the United States turned its attention to the Moros. Here the government's goal of being the bearer of civilization seemed ever more important. Protestant missionaries positioned themselves as key partners in this work, just as they had done in other regions of the Philippines and around the world. Soon, the government welcomed missionaries into the region.

Leonard Wood, appointed the new governor of the Moro Province in 1903, traveled to the Philippines by way of Constantinople, and his experience of the Ottoman Empire shaped his approach to the Muslims he met in the Philippines. He was convinced, even before his arrival, that the sultan of Sulu would be "degenerate, dishonest, tricky, dissipated, and absolutely devoid of principle." He ruled with an iron fist, and led the Americans to respond to Moro resistance brutally, often interpreting their resistance as religious fanaticism rather than anticolonial rebellion. In the first decade of American rule in the region, more than ten thousand Moros were killed.[63] Missionaries endorsed Wood's approach. Henry Otis Dwight, an ABCFM missionary, had even suggested that displays of violence would be essential to maintaining colonial authority in this new American Muslim territory.[64]

Wood welcomed missionaries into the region, hoping that their work to civilize and evangelize would have broader effects on the Moros' willingness to succumb to colonial rule.[65] Missionary hospitals, in particular, were heralded as an important tool of colonial rule. They served as the colonial carrot next to the stick of brutal violence. Missionaries, allied with the government, hoped that the civilization they brought with them would lead to better times in the future.

The missionary experience in the Philippines provided early hints that a new era in missionary diplomacy had begun. The United States based the legitimacy of its power on the idea that it brought civilization and religious freedom to its new colonial subjects. Missionaries were both an asset and a challenge to that claim. As complicated as it could be, it was far easier for the US government to come to a compromise with the missionary movement in other empires. In the Philippines, it was clear that the missionary definition of religious freedom as the right to evangelize was not fully compatible with the government definition of religious freedom that respected the right to have one's religious beliefs respected and left alone.

The turn of the century in the Philippines presented a moment to rethink some of the central components of US missionary diplomacy. As the US position on the world stage evolved, did the earlier relationships between missionaries and US foreign relations still work for the benefit of both groups? While many US officials continued to unthinkingly assume at times that Protestant missions would be an important and obvious partner in the work of civilizing the world, there were increasing challenges to this long-standing opinion. Missionaries were not driving the conversation here; rather, their ability to participate in US diplomacy was fully reactive.

The missionary role in religious freedom as an international relations issue would go on to be an important continued connection between the mission movement and US politics into the twentieth century. As part of the Foreign Missions Conference of North America's Committee on the Relations of Missions and Governments, Arthur Judson Brown regularly traveled to Washington, DC, to meet with presidents, secretaries of state, and chairmen of the House and Senate committees on foreign affairs. "We were invariably received courteously," he would later remember, because the politicians understood that the missionaries had "no political or personal interest to serve," being only interested in "matters affecting religious freedom and friendly international relations." Left unexamined in Brown's reflections, though, was the extent to which religious freedom was itself a political interest.[66]

As Taft's career in US politics continued, he would become, if anything, a stronger advocate of foreign missions. At a 1908 speech before the Laymen's Missionary Movement in Carnegie Hall in New York City, Taft spoke of how traveling abroad taught him "the immense importance of foreign missions." He learned that "Christianity is the hope of modern civilization, for Christianity is the true democracy." Unlike many of his Protestant listeners, he continued to include Catholicism as a civilizing force, but they agreed with him that the influence of the churches "upholds the hands of the civil governor for the maintenance of the peace and order." This was not, he suggested, about any sort of inappropriate union between church and state. Rather, he explained that he was "talking practical facts upon the effect of religion on government, and I know what I am talking about."[67] Missionaries, he insisted, did not cause trouble for the government. Instead, they were valuable ‖ partners.

As president, Taft welcomed a group of Methodist bishops to the White House in 1910. Again, he praised the work of missionaries and reflected on his time in the Philippines. There were some at the time, he recalled, who had opposed US rule there, claiming that "we were reaching out with a greed of territory and a greed for power, rather than with the desire to advance the cause of civilization and help our fellow-men." But in the intervening years, those critics had been proven wrong, Taft argued—thanks to the efforts of Protestant missionaries. The results of a decade of missionary labor had shown that "we are all working in the same field—you in one way and those of us who conduct the civil part of the Government in another; but it is all for the glory of God and the promotion of Christianity among men."[68]

Taft's comments were about the Philippines, but they could just as easily have been about China as well. There, too, missionaries and their relationship to the government and imperialism had been a major political issue for the past decade. There, Christian missionaries were increasingly identified by a group of anti-Western Chinese men and women as part and parcel of the attempt to control their country.

Brown's visit to the Philippines had been part of a broader trip to visit Presbyterian missions around the world. Upon his return in 1902, Brown would be called on not only as a recent witness of things in the Philippines, but in these other countries as well. His reflections on China in particular would be important to a new series of discussions about missions and foreign relations in the first decades of the new century.[69] As Brown euphemized in his memoirs, there were "conditions in China which called for the personal presence of an officer of the Board." Those conditions were the Boxer Uprising and its aftermath, a crisis that would raise a new set of questions about missions and foreign relations for the new century.

missionaries as civilizing partners

CHAPTER 9

Boxers

"What kind of thing is the law of nations?" Scribbling in his notebooks on China and Japan, William Rankin recorded this question, underlined it, and noted that to fully answer the question would "require the space of a large book." Rankin, the son of China missionaries, had returned to the United States for his education and had become a historian of East Asia. Now, in notebook after notebook, he compiled and indexed his notes: names of missionaries and diplomats and a long list of subject headings. His notes on missionaries were so extensive that they required several subcategories: missionaries, as interpreters; missions and science; missionaries and good faith; Prot. missions not political; political affairs; heroism; vindication of missions; objections to missions; and more. The questions on the law of nations were part of his notes on an 1857 interview with Townsend Harris, "the first formal instruction ever received by Japan in international law," as Rankin explained.[1] In the first decade of the twentieth century, Rankin was reviewing these notebooks for his next big project: a biography of his uncle, Divie Bethune McCartee. He would need all of these notes to advance his overarching thesis.

McCartee, Rankin argued, was a model missionary. His career, which took him from the United States to China and then Japan, revealed "all of the principal kinds of work likely to be done by a foreign missionary," but it did more than this as well. For McCartee was not just a missionary, he was also a diplomat. To Rankin, this meant that McCartee revealed "the international functions and uses that often make a missionary the most indispensable nexus between the Orient and the Western world."[2] This was a bold statement, and one that not everyone agreed with. For all his confidence about the significant role of missionaries in diplomatic history, he found difficult audiences in editors, diplomats, and missionaries alike, all of whom had doubts about the true importance of missionary diplomats by the turn of the twentieth century when Rankin was writing.

No wonder he was taking notes on international law. Harris had been asked: "What kind of treatment is a minister entitled to from the country to which he is sent?" and the answer was: "He must be treated according to the law of nations."[3] As Rankin argued about missionaries as the "indispensable nexus" between Asia and the United States, it was essential to understand this concept and the ways that it shaped missionary experiences abroad: what they did, where they went, and how they acted. But missionaries were never just missionaries, Rankin insisted. For all that missionaries represented their faith, Rankin knew they also represented their country. McCartee, after all, was only one of many missionaries who had served both his God and his country, working for the US consulate in China in addition to other diplomatic positions on behalf of the Chinese and Japanese governments.

By the time that Rankin was writing, the Boxer Uprising had fundamentally altered the way that Americans viewed the role of foreign missionaries, particularly in East Asia. In his article, "Political Values of the American Missionary," Rankin joined with others who were insistent that missionaries should not be blamed for anti-Western sentiments in China or anywhere else. Rankin's arguments were not always consistent, but they were passionately made.[4]

East Asia, as the place of his birth and the scene of so many of his family's adventures, held a particular fascination for Rankin. His ten volumes of research notes on Asian history and politics were self-indexed and reveal a systematic mind that read widely and attentively. Such notes would eventually help him tell his uncle's story and place Asian missions within the history of US diplomacy. But first, they would help him write articles such as "The Hour of China and the United States," his attempt to describe Sino-American relations and the role of America in China's future. The article, published in July 1899, included a postscript referencing the "momentous events" that had occurred in China since its writing. In this immediate pre–Boxer Uprising moment, Rankin recognized some of the tensions that would soon lead to that explosive event, but like so many other missionary supporters, he was blind to the possibility of missions as a contributing factor. Debates over Asian immigration and the Philippine War were the immediate US political contexts in which Rankin was writing in 1899. China's recent loss in the Sino-Japanese War and its resulting indebtedness to Russia made up the Chinese political context. "A new page of history opens with the virtual invasion of China, not by barbarous horde, but by the governments of Europe," he warned. It was a portentous moment.[5]

Rankin was not an anti-imperialist. His sense, coming out of the war in the Philippines, was that the United States needed to remain there and assume "the responsibilities of victory." This meant spreading American civilization and freedoms: "Wherever our flag has gone, there the liberty, the humanity, and the civilization which that flag embodies and represents must remain and abide forever," he wrote. Now, China was at the brink of change. Rankin reported political and educational reforms, even as Russia attempted to extend its influence in the north. It was a time for America to take a stand. For Rankin, the obvious choice was to unite with the British and back either "a native government" or a British protectorate that would "encourage, assist, and require development on lines of freedom and light." With schools, commerce, and churches, England and America could help China to achieve its destiny.[6]

In time, Rankin hoped, the Chinese government and Christian missionaries could spread schools, colleges, and churches throughout the country. "Then how long need it be to make the English language as prevalent in China as it is in India to-day, or even in Japan; and how long to bring the quickening message of Christianity to every hamlet of that empire?" Rankin insisted that the United States had more than a commercial interest in China—it had a moral interest, too. The same duties that he felt called the United States to the Philippines also demanded its attention in China.[7]

Within a year, the American conversation about China changed dramatically. The Boxer Uprising—an outpouring of anti-foreign and anti-Christian violence culminating in the arrival of foreign troops into Peking and a siege on foreign legations—set the stage for an American reconsideration of its position in China. Observers at the time, like historians ever sense, puzzled over the multiple causes of these violent events. Who was to blame? What was the way forward? Because of the centrality of missionaries and Chinese Christian converts to the events, the foreign mission movement, too, was a subject of debate. Had missionary troubles gone too far? Were missionaries at the heart of anti-Western sentiment in places like China? As Rankin explained, the question on everyone's mind was "What is a missionary good for anyway?"[8]

The Boxer Uprising

Edwin H. Conger, the US minister in China, began warning Washington about the newest set of "missionary troubles" in early December 1899. By that point, missionaries in northern China had been sending increasingly concerned notices about the Spirit Boxers and the Big Sword Society for almost a year. Sometimes described as secret societies, sometimes as militias, these groups worried the missionaries for their threats to foreigners and Christian converts.[9] The Boxers, as they came to be known thanks to their use of martial arts practices, seemed to be motivated by a number of concerns, but missionaries found them to be united by an opposition to Christians. Churches and Christian communities in China had faced isolated incidents of violence for years. The Boxers, though, seemed to be an escalation of what had previously seemed like localized issues. As Tungchow missionary Luella Miner explained, the movement had broken its anti-Christian specificity and become "general and anti-foreign."[10] By its end, the Boxer Uprising would claim the lives of more than two hundred foreigners and many thousands of Chinese Christians.[11]

The Boxer Uprising emerged in northern China, in Shandong, where the Big Sword Society and the Spirit Boxers had been active since around 1895. The Chinese defeat in the Sino-Japanese War in that year shook Chinese confidence, and the presence of foreign powers continually anxious to extend their economic and religious reach into China was not helping. Northern China was experiencing an economic depression. The increasing dependence on foreign imports over the second half of the nineteenth century had challenged the region's economy, particularly in cotton production.

Away from the port cities, the most palpable embodiment of these foreign powers were the missionaries. And the missionaries, of course, had long been active participants in the imperialism that the Boxers wanted to challenge. The tradition of Protestant missionaries serving diplomatic roles within US foreign relations existed alongside troublesome missionary involvement in political matters in other national contexts. German Catholic missionaries were particularly aggressive

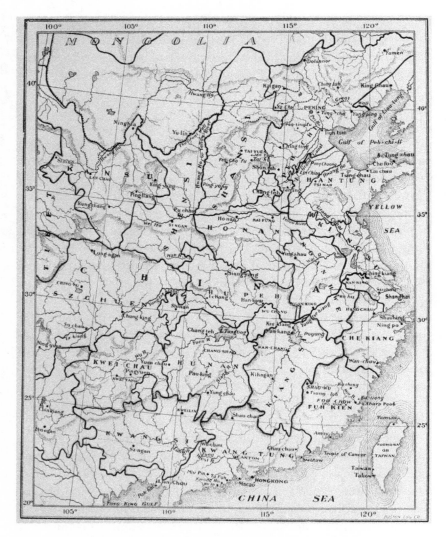

FIGURE 9.1.   Map of China, 1898. This map shows the extent of missionary presence in the interior of China in the years before the Boxer Uprising.
Source: ABCFM, *Maps of Missions of the American Board of Commissioners for Foreign Missions* (Boston: The Board, 1898), 7.

in legal matters, bringing lawsuits on behalf of their converts. Americans, for their part, occasionally expressed concerns about these actions, acknowledging that these missionaries' extension of extraterritoriality over their converts "practically removes this class from the jurisdiction of their own rulers," which had the doubly bad effects of encouraging conversion for economic motives and encouraging opposition from non-Christian Chinese subjects who objected to such treatment.[12]

It was in this context that the initial attacks on churches, Chinese converts, and missionaries emerged. But the groups who would become the Boxers had other roots as well. The Spirit Boxers were first motivated by appeals to return to traditional values in order to restore harmony in local communities.[13] Some of the groups active in the 1890s were focused on spirit possession, others on physical prowess. The anti-Christian conviction of different groups seemed to vary earlier in the decade. By late 1898 and early 1899, though, as missionary Luella Miner described, these local groups began to converge, changing their names to a unified title of the Boxers United in Righteousness. They began to use the same slogan: "Fu-Qing mieyang," or "Support the Qing, destroy the foreign." They spread their geographic reach across North China. When they were shut down after violent clashes with Chinese forces in one place, they reemerged elsewhere. Attacks on Christians spread and became increasingly violent. In 1899 and early 1900, the Boxers, the foreign powers, and the Chinese government were caught in a triangle of struggle and anxiety.

As the Boxers expanded, Western observers demanded a strong response from the Chinese government. Missionaries worried for the safety of their converts and themselves. Qing officials worried about the direction that Western reactions would take. The situation deteriorated as the Boxers moved toward Peking.

Over the first half of 1900, Conger's dispatches and telegrams to the State Department related a rapidly escalating situation in northern China and, soon, Peking as well. The US missionaries were his informants, cabling him with the news of attacks on Christian converts and threats against the missions. Church members were attacked starting in November 1899. An English missionary was killed in January 1900. While the delegations in Peking were reluctant to sound the alarm, many of the Western diplomats recognized that the missionaries were "the only foreigners . . . really at all in touch with Chinese native feeling."[14] And missionary reports were alarming.

The missionaries reported that local government officials would not listen to their concerns; it fell to Conger to communicate with the Chinese and try to demand that attention be paid to the situation in Shandong. His communications with the Tsungli Yamen, China's foreign relations body, relayed stories of attacks, beatings, and even murders of Chinese Christians. Over time, his reminders about China's treaty obligations to protect Christian converts went from subtle to explicit as he sought to protect US citizens in inland China. By March, the situation had deteriorated to the point that Conger asked for a naval response. The missionaries concurred. They had wanted US warships as early as February.

As Conger saw it, the problem was that the Empress Dowager herself had "very strong anti-foreign sentiments," and so had little motivation to actually enforce the treaty protections of foreigners and Christians in China.[15] Local officials at best looked the other way, or at worst sympathized with the Boxers in their attacks on Christians. Conger coordinated his interactions with the Tsungli Yamen with the European powers in the region: Germany, England, France, and Italy. All were concerned about the safety of their missionaries. Many worried, too, about commercial access to inland China. The Boxers attacked telegraph wires and railroad tracks, leading to worries that Westerners would be stranded and unable to evacuate or call for help. Though the US State Department worried about too much coordinated effort with other foreign powers, assuming that the best way forward with China was to work alone and to appear as conciliatory as possible, when the situation was dire, Conger was ordered to join with the Europeans.

In April, Conger reported that warships had arrived: two British, one French, two Italian, two German, and one American. They were ready to suppress the Boxers and bring "peace and quiet again" to the area.[16] American marines made their way into Peking in late May to defend the US legation. As Secretary of State John Hay reassured the foreign secretary of the ABCFM, the United States was "ready and willing to do its utmost to protect its citizens in China and everywhere else."[17]

All of these actions and worried reports preceded any actual attacks on US citizens or property. On May 8, a stone was thrown into the Presbyterian mission compound in Peking, narrowly avoiding striking a servant in the head.[18] Later that month, American missionaries based thirty-five miles east of Peking reported that open threats of violence against missionaries there had become a daily occurrence. When some Methodist converts at the US mission were murdered at the end of May, Conger demanded a full investigation and swift punishment of the criminals. The obsequious formality of all of Conger's official correspondence with the Tsungli Yamen barely masked his anger when he wrote that the crime was "all the more outrageous and the responsibility therefore the more direct because the Chinese Government has been repeatedly informed of the presence and operation of the Boxers in that vicinity." He had written about this countless times, having "insistently demanded protection for these poor people against just what exactly has happened."[19] Things only got worse from there.

June saw a flurry of correspondence between Peking and Washington as Conger reported that missionaries were being personally threatened alongside foreign railway employees. Conger reported that more railways were destroyed. Foreign troops were needed. The Chinese appointed new, anti-foreign members to the Tsungli Yamen.[20] Bricks were thrown into an American chapel. Boxers seized one US missionary station, giving the missionaries the choice to "recant, or flee and leave their property to be looted, or stay and be killed." Another American mission was burned to the ground. Eleven church members were killed, and their houses, too, were destroyed. An English missionary was murdered. Missionaries evacuated their stations. One US marine, watching the scene in Peking, would recall that they came "with only such articles of clothing as they could carry in their arms, as they had to flee for their lives."[21]

The evacuees came together at the Methodist compound in Peking, half a mile down the road from the US Legation. Seventy American men, women, and children gathered there, alongside Chinese Christians and a number of US marines. Frank Gamewell, the senior Methodist missionary at that station, estimated that up to 1,500 people were crammed into the missionary compound.[22] It quickly became a garrison: missionaries and their converts built stronger brick walls, laid out barbed wire, dug ditches, and carried guns.

For months, Conger had called on the Chinese government to suppress the Boxers, with only lukewarm response. The show of Western force seemed to turn the tide, but not in the direction he had hoped for. When an imperial edict of June 21, 1900, embraced the Boxers as patriotic soldiers and declared war on the foreign powers, the situation went from bad to worse. Just over a week later, Conger sent his last message out of Peking until the end of the conflict. Two messages reached Tientsin via courier pleading for help. The telegraph wires were cut, and the legation was cut off from contact with the United States.

The missionaries moved from the Methodist compound to the US Legation, but even that was not safe enough when the threat of siege came closer and closer. The US Legation was too close to the city walls, and so they relocated to the British Legation, where they joined the entire foreign community of Peking. They would be there for over a month. It was overcrowded and undersupplied. Female missionaries soon tried to find ways to make horse meat appetizing to the crowd. They could smell human and horse corpses just outside the complex walls, rotting in the June sun.[23] They waited and they worried while John Goodnow, in Shanghai, took over the role of negotiating with China on behalf of the Americans.

Anxious observers in the United States and Europe worried about the fate of these besieged Westerners. The *London Daily Mail* and the *New York Times* reported (incorrectly) that hundreds in the diplomatic legations had been murdered. The media assumed that Conger was dead, along with who knows how many other Americans.[24] Stories of the Boxers had appeared in foreign papers since the late fall of 1899, with missionaries reporting the movement's rapid spread.[25] "BOXER REBELLION IS SPREADING; AMERICAN LIVES IN GREAT DANGER" proclaimed one front-page headline in the *Chicago Daily Tribune* from June 1900. The US media reported that missionaries needed protection urgently. Women and children at the mission stations, in particular, were in danger. "Missionary work in north China has been crushed for years to come," the article predicted.[26] The secretary of state wired to hear if the press reports were true; US missionary supporters were anxious to know if they were safe. In response to this perilous state of affairs, the secretary of state sent William W. Rockhill to act as commissioner to China. He reached China at the end of August and remained until September of the following year, when a resolution was finally reached and signed by China and the foreign powers.

Even after the resolution of September 1901, there were still many lingering questions. The press had reported the echoing of the chant "support the Qing, destroy the foreign!" through the streets during the uprising, and American observers nervously noted the seeming equation of this problematic foreignness with Christian evangelism.[27] In the aftermath of the fighting, the role of missionaries in US relations with China continued to trouble observers. On the one hand, missionaries were recognized as victims of the uprising. Memorials, such as that at Oberlin College, celebrated those who had fallen. But even after the fighting was over, the negotiations to set the terms of peace were complicated.

Indemnities, in particular, became the subject of intense debate, as the Western powers set a price on the losses that they had suffered. In these negotiations, missionaries were again important. Churches and missionary premises, after all, were high among the property of foreign citizens that were destroyed by the Boxers. But far more significant was the damaged property of Chinese converts that some wanted to claim for indemnities, as well. Once again, the goals of the mission movement and the goals of diplomacy were uncomfortably blurred.

Conger's thought was that including Chinese Christians in these claims would be "a most humane act and would give to missionary work great prestige for the future," but would ultimately be unproductive. The investigations would be "almost limitless," and the missionaries themselves should be able to settle the losses of their converts within their villages.[28] Missionaries were not so sure. These conversations continued for months. When the questions were raised about how much the Chinese would actually be able to pay, the debates became even more complicated.

The US position was that securing trade was much more important than imposing indemnity on China. In the long term, trade would benefit the United States much more than repayment for any lost property from the Boxer Rebellion. As Conger and Rockhill negotiated with the European powers and China about how best to resolve this crisis, they were also weighing the interests of different groups of Americans against each other. Merchants and missionaries had always had sometimes overlapping, sometimes conflicting priorities in China. Now, when the United States was again taking stock of its position in Asia, those competing claims came up again.[29]

Were the Boxers anti-foreign, anti-Christian, or both? The difference was not one that Conger felt the need to parse too carefully. The American missionaries were "our missionaries." He and Hay had both initially called these events "the missionary troubles" until they became "The Boxer War" in their correspondence.[30] Conger's correspondence with the Tsungli Yamen discussed both issues, noting the banners inscribed with "exterminate the foreigners" and simultaneously calling for the defense of Chinese nationals who happened to have converted to Christianity.[31] Because the treaties between the United States and China protected (non-American) Christian converts as well as American missionaries, there was a certain fuzziness to the categories at issue here. Though no Americans were attacked in the first months of the uprising, their converts and church members were. Since the treaties promised protection of Christians, Conger could interpret the lack of protection for these converts as a breach of Chinese treaty obligations.

Meanwhile, the Boxers blurred the lines as well. When German engineers planned a railroad near the American Presbyterian mission at Chefoo (Yantai), the missionaries and Conger worried that a general anti-foreign sentiment stoked by the railroad would ultimately harm the mission.[32] After decades of Western nations mixing commercial and religious entries into China, the Boxers had responded with a generalized opposition that reacted to the seemingly encroaching imperialism of some states and the missionary presence of Catholics and Protestants as if they were all the same thing. With US missionaries calling for warships to protect them, perhaps the Boxers had a point.

Reconsidering the Missionary Presence

In the aftermath of the Boxer Uprising, not everyone was so sympathetic with the missionary side. If the Boxers were, at heart, anti-Christian, was this an example of foreign missionaries dragging US foreign relations into another difficult situation that was unnecessary and dangerous? Critiques of missionaries were easy to come by in the United States in those years. Stories about missionary greed, prejudice, intolerance, and narrow-mindedness were common. Reports on the Boxer indemnities suggested that missionaries lied about the valuation of their destroyed property and stated that the State Department needed a "ruthless hand" in evaluating the legitimacy of missionary claims.[33] Even as the mission movement continued to grow and to send an impressive number of American Protestants abroad, Americans at home could be forgiven for feeling ambivalent or even critical about their role in the world. American diplomats in China, too, could be quite critical of the missionaries.

Some, such as Anson Burlingame Johnson, the US consul at Amoy (Xiamen), seemed to blame the Boxer's anti-foreign stance entirely on the missionaries. "It is well-known here that the ill-feeling toward the foreigners in this province is entirely confined to the missionaries," he reported in August 1900. Missionaries had been stepping beyond their evangelistic roles and inappropriately "meddling" in "secular matters." To avoid another situation like the Boxer Uprising, missionaries needed to be restricted to purely spiritual work, he argued.[34]

After the uprising, missionaries did not retreat; if anything, they expanded. The numbers of Protestant missionaries in China, including Americans, increased during the following decade. And they did not confine their efforts to spiritual work. Education and medicine continued to be part of their agenda. In addition, missionaries collected indemnities that were issued as part of the peace negotiations. For this, they were roundly criticized in the US press, particularly after reports of missionary Dr. Ament of the ABCFM taking part in the post-uprising looting in northern China. Newspapers debated these reports and raised doubts about the virtues of missionaries. As one piece in the *Detroit Free Press* put it, the stories from China and elsewhere had begun to pile up to the point that missionaries "can hardly expect that judgement will be suspended forever."[35]

For Mark Twain, the missionary response to the Boxer Uprising was inherently intwined with the whole story of US imperialism. Reflecting on the missionary claims of indemnity in China, Twain painted a picture of missionaries as greedy and callous, demanding retribution from a peasantry that could hardly afford to pay the exaggerated claims of the Western powers. This, in Twain's telling, was the blasphemy at the heart of the missionary movement—and the hypocrisy at the heart of US foreign relations. It revealed that there were "two Americas" and two versions of the American civilization that the missionaries preached: one for export, and one for domestic consumption. The version for export was considerably adulterated, and this, Twain wrote, was becoming obvious to those whom Americans imagined were "sitting in darkness," awaiting the enlightenment that missions and empire could spread. For Twain, the story of the American response to the Boxer Uprising was the same as the American experience in the Philippines, and he criticized the missionaries with the same venom that he criticized US imperialists. Twain's argument did not fall on deaf ears.[36]

These critiques became common enough that they merited a small flurry of defenses of mission work in the first decades of the century. Some of these came from missionaries and their supporters, of course. Arthur Judson Brown addressed these concerns directly in his 1907 book for church and college mission studies, *The Foreign Missionary: The Incarnation of a World Movement.* Brown sought to answer the charges of any missionary critics who might pick up his book or (the more likely scenario) to provide supporters with tools to do so themselves. He expected that his readers would have a few key questions about missionaries at the front of their minds: "Is he wise in his dealings with proud and ancient peoples and their social and religious customs? Does he make unnecessary trouble for his own and other governments?"[37]

If supporters early in the nineteenth century focused on "the salvation of the heathen" as the justification for foreign missions, this was less emphasized by the beginning of the twentieth. The same religious motives drove American missionaries of this later era, but they often phrased their concerns differently. Brown was quite clear that "secondary" motivations were essential to understanding the missionary movement of his day. Philanthropic, intellectual, and commercial motives joined civilizing and religious motives for missionaries serving abroad. In other words, missionaries spread hospitals and schools, learned about the world and brought that knowledge back to their home communities, and created markets for Western goods and technologies as they went about their missionary work. To understand the missionary of the early twentieth century, Brown suggested, meant appreciating the ways in which they had "vastly increased the world's store of useful knowledge."[38]

Missionaries had to face criticism from all directions, Brown observed. Some of it was legitimate, but much of it was built on false assumptions about mission work and missionaries. Brown was very concerned about the ways in which the new ease of travel meant that more and more Americans were touring the world, but not always interacting with it beyond port cities, clubs, and foreign enclaves that kept travelers from getting to know much about the places where they traveled, the people who lived there, or the missionaries who served them. The problem here, so far as the reputation of missionaries was concerned, was that these "globe-trotters" spent their time around the sort of Americans abroad who did not much like missionaries and thought they were getting the full story.

Merchants, in Brown's telling, disliked missionaries because the missionaries would not drink with them at the club, or because the missionaries might offer resistance to their more oppressive plans. If someone comes home from abroad and "maligns missionaries," Brown explained "it is safe to assume, either that he has been making a fool of himself so that he had to be rebuked by the missionaries" or that he had been spending his time with those who had. Their "slanders" would be "sensationally paraded in the newspapers, and eagerly swallowed by a gullible public" that did not have much of a taste for earnest Christian folk anyway. Or at least, this was how Brown framed the main thrust of the problem.[39] But, of course, it was not so simple as all that. Particular concerns arose with enough regularity that Brown could list them off one by one and discount them each in turn. Missionaries are inferior men? Missionaries live in luxury and idleness? Missionary administration is costly and unbusinesslike? Converts only care about economic gain, and are not motivated by genuine faith? Not so.[40]

But other questions took longer to answer and spoke to more particular political concerns. Among them were questions motivated by the theological transformations that had been occurring within American Christianity in the past several decades. With the rise of liberal theology came an increasing likelihood of tolerance for, and even celebration of, other religions. Non-Christians might not "want our religion," and that lack of interest might be justified.[41] This philosophical point had even more weight after the Boxer Uprising, as Americans wondered if perhaps missionaries were to blame for anti-foreign sentiments after all. Brown was ready to disprove this point, too, but he could not stop the critiques from coming with increasing frequency. The uprising had led American missionary critics to wonder if missionaries got involved in political questions too often, interfering in lawsuits and making themselves "universally hated" by local people. Critics claimed that "missionaries make trouble for their own governments," too, drawing them into conflict with foreign powers wherever they went.[42]

Defending Missionary Diplomacy

It was not only missionary figures who defended missionaries. Defenders also turned to sympathetic diplomats who reported that missionaries caused them much less trouble than other categories of Americans abroad. Having the endorsement of political figures was extremely valuable in this debate. In October 1900, the *Missionary Herald* responded to what they categorized as "many flippant utterances" critiquing missionary work in China by publishing quotations from five diplomats supporting missionary work. John Foster, a former secretary of state, joined former U.S. ministers to China James Angell, Charles Denby, George Seward, and a former minister to Siam, John Barrett, in responding to the ABCFM's questions with enthusiasm.

The ABCFM was sure that this eminent group of men would silence their ignorant critics. Foster was sure that "the presence of missionaries in China had little to do with these troubles," and that China remained an important missionary field. Angell blamed the Boxer Uprising on "the aggressive policy of certain European powers" and conflicts within China over reform policies. Denby declared missionaries to be "benefactors of the people among whom their lives are spent, and forerunners of the commerce of the world." Seward, in a passage that would also be published in the *Boston Herald*, declared that "for every enemy a missionary makes he makes fifty friends." Barrett informed readers that the king of Siam (Thailand) felt that missionaries "had done more to advance the welfare of his country and people than any other foreign influence." In this moment of tension, Americans should remember that their country was, as he put it, "a Christian as well as a commercial nation" that accordingly could not "think of withdrawing the messengers of Christianity from Asia until we are ready to withdraw the merchants of commerce and the ministers of diplomacy." If the United States was to have any relations with Asia, in other words, Barrett felt that it needed to send missionaries. They were an essential part of US foreign relations.[43]

Barrett went further in his article in *The Outlook*, a weekly news and opinion magazine, "Some Truths About the Missionaries." Barrett found anti-missionary stories to be unfair. He argued that they seized on a few negative examples and ignored the good that the vast majority of missionaries were accomplishing. He himself had arrived in Siam with a "slight prejudice against missionaries," but had been entirely converted after his experience working with more than one hundred missionaries in Siam and seeing the good they were doing in China, Japan, Korea, and elsewhere in Asia.[44]

The "truths" Barrett shared with American readers focused on a few themes. First, that missionaries were doing important work, particularly in the fields of education and medicine. In rural areas especially, missionaries were creating institutions that mattered. Their good influences were creating "better men and women." Graduates of mission schools were an "earnest, energetic, and ambitious body of men who want[ed] to see their own country advance along lines of modern civilization." In this evaluation, Barrett insisted that he did not stand alone. "Nearly every Minister or Consul of the United States who has lived many years in Asia" would agree with him, he was sure. While missionaries had their "faults and weaknesses," the world should not "overlook their virtues and their strong points."[45]

In addition to this, Barrett complicated the picture of anti-Western sentiment in Asia. This was not simple opposition to missionaries. Rather, it had emerged out of economic and political contexts in which the missionaries played only one small part. Barrett himself had found that he had much more trouble from "tactless and selfish business agents and promoters" during his tenure in Asia than from missionaries. Meanwhile, foreign nations had committed "unwarranted seizures of Chinese territory," leading to an understandable mistrust of foreigners, and "dishonest local officials" inspired fear and hatred of missionaries out of a hope that they might expel the foreigners from their country. Missionaries, then, were not to blame.[46]

Rankin, too, joined in this defense of missionary diplomacy. The uprising, he insisted, was misunderstood by Americans. "It is not the western creed but the western greed which has made most of the trouble between China and the Occident," he explained.[47] To those who argued that missionaries destabilized the places where they worked, Rankin argued that, on the contrary, missionaries were essential to the stability of any Western presence in Asia. They created good will; in contrast to those who only came to Asia for profit and self-interest, missionaries came to help. In addition, missionaries had the double effect of both supporting colonial governments by stabilizing the colonized population while also preparing that population for eventual independence and self-government.[48]

This last point was a complicated one. Citing the shift over the course of the nineteenth century that British officials had made in their thinking about missions, Rankin pointed to the ways that missionaries, in fact, helped to sustain Western empires. While they supported self-government, they did not do so universally. In India and the Philippines, for example, missionaries could be expected to support the British and US colonial governments, respectively. In neither place, Rankin believed, was the population prepared for self-governance. Missionaries, out of their desire for what was truly best for the peoples they hoped to serve, thus supported colonial governments as preferential to any alternatives. It would only be when "Christian ideals of the social order have made a far more vital and general impression upon the native mind" that imperial control could decline. Accordingly, missionaries were needed to help "make a new moral climate" to transform the world.[49]

If the goal of missions was to transform the world into God's kingdom, Rankin suggested, evangelism was not the only way that missionaries could accomplish significant changes. Important, too, was the consular and diplomatic work that some missionaries did for their governments. "Times without number," Rankin insisted, missionaries had served as ideal civil servants.[50] The reason missionaries were so well-suited to this work was that they always sought a "genuine reciprocity" for their work. They were guided by the Golden Rule, and let those values shape their interactions with foreign powers.[51] Missionaries promoted "the social harmony of the races" wherever they went.[52] They possessed a deep "knowledge of the language and people."[53] At his best, Rankin concluded with tremendous bluster, a missionary was "always a statesman, who takes a high and cosmic view of the duty and destiny of nations."[54]

In China specifically, Rankin argued that missionaries were key because what the Chinese really needed was not "new furniture and machinery," but "a new conception of their own best good, and how to attain it, in their ideals of life." This message was what missionaries could bring, working alongside the US government, with whom they were "entirely at one."[55]

The idea that missionaries were always guided by the Golden Rule, as Rankin suggested, was an open question; that they were "statesmen" at all seemed absurd to many observers in the years after the Boxer Uprising. After decades of missionaries working alongside diplomats in relative comfort, the uprising forced the question of how appropriate such relations were at precisely the moment that the State Department itself was undergoing a new series of reforms to professionalize the consular service. Missionaries and their supporters had to answer a new set of questions about the proper connections between their own work and that of the state. After decades of missionaries being able to argue persuasively that they knew the places where they worked better than any other Americans, now in the early years of the twentieth century that seemed less true. In the aftermath of the Boxers, all of those earlier tensions in American missionary diplomacy came to the fore like never before. It would be hard to imagine the career of someone like Divie Bethune McCartee emerging in quite the same way ever again, even as missionary leaders like Brown could still claim the ear of the president.

When Brown returned to the United States from his world tour in 1902, he had much to say about America's place in the world. The Golden Rule, he—like Rankin—was sure, should go on to guide US foreign relations. But the United States was not always eager to take action in the face of humanitarian crises. Experience in China had provided a strong example of the risks the government took when it let missionaries lead. And missionaries continued to see the whole world as their field—including places that the State Department did not deem a high diplomatic priority. Such would be the case in Congo, where another group of American missionaries attempted to shape diplomacy, this time in the interest of averting humanitarian catastrophe.

CHAPTER 10

Witnesses

In 1903, British consul Roger Casement began his investigation into reports of ongoing atrocities in the Congo Free State. He boarded the *Henry Reed*, the American Baptist Missionary Society's steamer that would carry him on his three-month journey. Casement hoped—as did his Protestant missionary guides—that his choice of missionary transport would allow him to be independent from the colonial authorities. It would be harder for officials to monitor his progress and control what he saw. Local officials would not be warned in advance of his arrival. Casement hoped that this would allow him to witness things as they really were.[1]

It was challenging for outsiders to access unfettered information about the Congo Free State. For more than a decade, there had been competing narratives about what was happening in this colony. King Leopold II's government insisted that it was a benevolent colonial project dedicated to spreading civilization in "Darkest Africa." But others claimed that agents of the state committed horrible atrocities. They reported an oppressive "rubber tax" that kept the people practically in a state of slavery. They reported horrific violence against those who would not—or could not—comply with government demands for rubber. Readers living far away from the Congo were not sure whom to trust. The European and US press published these accusations as well as government rebuttals. Casement's trip was designed to be independent and unbiased. He wanted to get to the truth, and to share what he learned with the governments in Britain and the United States—both of which he currently served as a consul. And so he turned to the missionaries for help.

Casement rode on a mission steamer, was accompanied by missionary translators, and stayed in missionary homes. Missionaries connected him with Congolese informants and shared with him their own observations. Though many missionaries had long kept quiet about what they had witnessed in the Congo Free State, they assisted the consul in his efforts to set the record straight. Some of these missionaries would become among the most important American witnesses to atrocities in Africa, working alongside humanitarian allies to demand international intervention.[2]

Casement's report, published in England and the United States in 1904, provided a stark and disturbing picture of King Leopold's rule. Casement fully endorsed the claims that atrocities were rife in the Congo Free State. Among other harrowing examples, he told the story of a young boy named Epondo, whose hand had been cut off at the wrist in an effort to intimidate his neighbors to collect more rubber for the state. Epondo's story, Casement wrote, was not an isolated incident. He and the missionaries met other boys with similar injuries and described similar atrocities throughout the colony. Writing to the governor-general, Casement summarized his findings about the violence and oppression of the rubber system: if it continued, it would inevitably lead to the "final extinction" of the Congolese people, as well as the "universal condemnation of the civilized world."[3]

In the Congo Free State, Leopold and a small circle of select companies held a monopoly on rubber. The incredibly high profits, Casement's readers learned, were the result of oppressive and coercive conditions that amounted to a kind of state-sanctioned slavery. In key regions, taxes were paid in rubber, and the quantities were outrageous. Leopold's government claimed that the amount of rubber was reasonable and comparable to the taxes that any government could legitimately charge their subjects in support of government services, ignoring the issue of whether the colonial subjects in Congo were the beneficiaries of those services in any meaningful way. But Casement and his missionary informants argued that the government was being disingenuous. It was impossible to harvest sufficient rubber while also making a living: it was simply too demanding. There was no time for anything else. The effects were wide ranging: houses were in disrepair and fields were untended. But that was not all. Failure to pay the impossibly high rubber tax could result in horrific violence against one's person, family, or entire village.

King Leopold was in violation of the agreements that had been reached at the Berlin Conference of 1884 and the Brussels Conference of 1890, Casement informed his readers. Those international conventions placed Leopold as the sole ruler of the Congo Free State on the understanding that he would be a benevolent leader. He had pledged to end the practice of slavery and to spread Christian civilization in Africa. But these promises were never realized. It was clear that Leopold could not be trusted to reform matters. Some other political body needed to intervene. Britain was the most obvious choice, but American missionaries hoped that the United States, too, could take some sort of action. They would be disappointed.

Africa was not a high priority for US diplomacy at the turn of the century. The United States did not yet have its own consul in the region, and so Casement provided aid to Americans in the Congo as well.[4] In 1903, those Americans largely consisted of Protestant missionaries. After Casement's report, the US missionaries' requests that the State Department send them a consul of their own were finally answered. Soon a US consul and vice consul would arrive in the colony at Boma, though they and the missionaries would continue to work with their British colleagues—particularly when it came to sharing information with the world about atrocities.[5]

The American missionary community in the Congo Free State consisted of a mix of white and Black missionaries of multiple denominations. Ever since the first American missions to Liberia in the 1820s and 1830s, Black American Christians had taken part in the civilizing and evangelizing work of American Protestant missions in Africa. Due to the racism of both the US government and white-run American missionary organizations, they had not generally been a part of the network of missionary diplomats with access to US political power. The missionary experience as witnesses to Congo atrocities would begin to shift this, however slightly.

Rumors of bad things happening in the Congo had circulated in the 1890s, but it was not until 1904 that people in the United States really paid attention. When the missionaries began their work in the region during the 1880s and 1890s, international crises all over the world attracted American attention, and one might have expected that Congo atrocities would have generated a similar public outcry. Americans were responding to humanitarian crises in Cuba and fighting a war in the Philippines. They were attempting to navigate the complicated politics of the Boxer Uprising in China and the Hamidian massacres in Turkey. But the early missionary reports of Congo atrocities in the 1890s attracted little public notice. Perhaps Americans were distracted by the pressing concerns of the Gilded Age. But white Americans seemed comfortable ignoring the charges of violence against African men and women—especially when the stories were so forcefully denied by Leopold's supporters.

At a time when hundreds of African Americans were lynched in the United States annually, it was unsurprising that the news of Africans being killed in the Congo attracted little attention among white Americans.[6] But a small number of Black and white missionaries began to draw American attention to the inhumane treatment of Africans under the Congo Free State. As they had in so many earlier moments of missionary troubles, they demanded action from their government. But humanitarian crises alone would not be enough to motivate the US State Department to respond. It would take a direct attack on missionaries in 1909 to get the state involved after many years of reluctance.

The Congo Free State and Empire

In 1884, shortly after recognizing Leopold's rule in the Congo, the US government appointed an agent to the Congo Valley to investigate the potential for US commerce in the region. American knowledge of the Congo was limited. In the mid-1880s, Henry Stanley's writings about his explorations were the main source of information. Stanley, the adventuring journalist whose search for David Livingstone had fascinated readers on both sides of the Atlantic, had given Americans reason to believe that the region was "a territory of inexhaustible resources." It was not immediately clear, however, how Europeans and Americans would be able to access those resources. Secretary of State Frederick Frelinghuysen summarized Americans' understanding of the Congolese when he described them as "wild, savage and cruel," people who had just begun to "find civilization dawning upon them." He suggested that it might be an "inviting" field for African American outreach. Black Americans, he argued, were well positioned "to educate and civilize fifty millions of blacks" in the Congo Free State.[7]

It was Stanley's map that King Leopold had used in 1884 as he began to draw the contours of what would become a unique colony in Central Africa. Unlike colonies that were controlled by a metropolitan

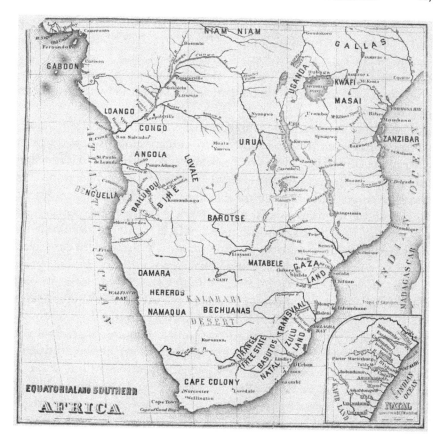

Figure 10.1. Map of equatorial and southern Africa, 1898, including the region covered by the Congo mission. Note the minimal detail in central Africa.
Source: ABCFM, *Maps of Missions of the American Board of Commissioners for Foreign Missions* (Boston: The Board, 1898), 1.

government, the Congo Free State was the domain of a single man: King Leopold II of Belgium. But it was similar to other colonies in many ways. The borders were somewhat arbitrary (as the colonies were made to serve the metropole rather than the communities on the ground), and Leopold tried to expand his territorial possessions beyond what his agents could actually control. The colony maintained its power through a colonial army called the Force Publique. Soldiers from Zanzibar, Nigeria, and Liberia served along with growing numbers of Congolese soldiers under white officers.[8]

The promise of a benevolent civilizing empire in the Congo Free State drew missionaries to the region. Although King Leopold was Catholic, he had promised to welcome Protestant missionaries into his colony and embrace freedom of religion.[9] At Berlin and then again at Brussels, he had made it quite clear that the goal of the colony was to bring the blessings of free trade and Western "civilization" to the region. Missionaries, whether Catholic or Protestant, would serve an important role in that project.

The Berlin Conference heightened the expectation among missionary supporters that the time had come for great evangelistic progress in Africa. The United States sent representatives to Berlin, but did not sign on to the important agreements that came out of that convention. This strategic choice reflected the tumultuous US political debates about empire and foreign intervention in the last decades of the century. By not signing, the United States signaled its lack of interest in colonizing Africa, even as the presence of US diplomats in Berlin revealed American hopes to benefit from the fruits of African colonization by European powers. In the mid-1880s, America's interests in Africa were twofold: commercial possibility and humanitarian civilization. The United States was pleased with the promise of new trade opportunities that colonization seemed to present in Africa and welcomed the supposed embrace of benevolent measures like the end of the slave trade within the continent. Yet some members of Congress saw participation in Berlin as a break in a US diplomatic tradition of noninterference and anti-imperialism.[10]

Because they saw new evangelistic possibilities, American missionaries were supportive of these developments. Missionaries had, in fact, begun planning for new stations near the Congo River shortly after Stanley's reports were first published. Many of these missionaries agreed with the author in the *Missionary Herald* who argued that the United States and Europe owed a great debt to Africa because of the history of the international slave trade. Now, they believed, the time had come for a concerted effort to civilize and evangelize this region that was simultaneously poised to transform the world economy due to its natural agricultural and mineral wealth and degraded by slavery, polygamy, and witchcraft. Protestant evangelism would bring the gift of civilization and pave the way for Africa to grow into its full potential as a major contributor to "the wealth and culture of mankind."[11] American missionaries, both Black and white, responded to the call.

While the United States was not a signatory in Berlin, it did play an important role in the early colonial history of the Congo Free State. In February 1884, the United States became the first country to formally recognize Leopold's rule over the country—announcing its "sympathy with and approval of the humane and benevolent purposes" of the government there. This recognition opened the way for France and Great Britain to follow suit and recognize Leopold's power in advance of the Berlin Conference. When American missionaries later called on their government to take action in the Congo Free State, they would cite this early recognition as grounds for US intervention. Recognition, the missionaries and their humanitarian allies would argue, gave the United States a stake in how the colony was run.[12]

During the early years of the Congo Free State, the US government's interactions with the colony were not extensive. The government sent no consul, though it would work as best it could to support American missionaries when they came into conflict with the local government. The first of these missionary troubles emerged in 1888, when Stanley, working for Leopold's government, seized the American Baptist mission's steamer by force. In August, the missionaries appealed to the nearest US consul—stationed at St. Paul de Loanda (Luanda) in Angola, nearly five hundred miles away—and the complaint made its way to Washington and Brussels over the next several months. As US officials rose to defend the rights of their missionaries, they relied on the old language of missionary diplomacy. The missionaries, they understood, were doing important work that would make commerce and progress possible. These were "unselfish and self-sacrificing men who, braving the dangers of climate and the privations incident to a savage and unsettled country, have posted themselves there as aids of humanity and religion." As such, they were invaluable to the colonial government, and deserved both protection and consideration.[13] The United States, however, continued to believe that this protection could be safeguarded well enough without a direct representative there, despite ongoing missionary pressure to appoint a consul to the Congo in the following decade.

The United States was more directly involved in the Brussels Conference of 1890, signing on to the Brussels Act's documents that defined the colonization of the Congo as a benevolent effort to spread civilization and end slavery. Certainly this was how missionaries and humanitarian reformers understood the documents. As they saw it, the US government made itself duty-bound to protect the rights of the people of the Congo and to defend them against any abuses they might face from the colonial government. In theory, the agreement pledged its signatories to ensure that colonization would be a benefit to the colonized.

One year after Brussels, the Southern Presbyterians established their first mission station in the Congo. This organization had been founded when the Presbyterian denomination split over slavery prior to the US Civil War. The Southern denomination's mission board, now run by former slaveholder and missionary to Liberia John Leighton Wilson, was eager to evangelize this newly accessible part of Africa. The first two missionaries, Samuel Lapsley and William Sheppard, traveled to Luebo and began their work of learning languages, exploring the region, building schools, and providing very basic medical care.[14] Sheppard, an African American graduate of the Hampton Institute, had long hoped to go to Africa as a missionary. The denomination, however, was not prepared to send a Black man as the sole missionary anywhere. It was only when Lapsley, a white Presbyterian minister, presented himself as a potential missionary to Africa that the Presbyterians began their Congo mission.

The missionaries preached to whoever would listen and enrolled "recaptured slaves," some of whom they had purchased, in their schools. They hoped that Congo would soon become "a colony of the emancipated." When Lapsley died in 1892, Sheppard remained as the sole missionary and continued his three-pronged work of teaching, preaching, and healing alongside hippopotamus hunting, artifact collecting, and exploring Central Africa until the denomination could send additional missionary laborers. In 1893, Sheppard was initiated into the Royal Geographical Society in recognition of his contributions to Euro-American knowledge of Africa.[15]

At the same time that the Presbyterians were setting up their mission, another Black American was traveling through the region. George Washington Williams, a former Baptist minister who was traveling in the Congo to consider sites for a possible African American mission, would become the first of many witnesses who would go on the record about atrocities he had seen in the Congo. Williams, like other American and European missionaries, had at first been quite optimistic about the possibilities of the Congo Free State. He had met with King Leopold himself on his way to Africa. But he was quickly disillusioned. He wrote an "open letter" to Leopold, soon published in both the United States and Europe, accusing the government of murder, slavery, expropriation, and sexual crimes. Upon his 1889 return to Washington, DC, he met with President Benjamin Harrison and the secretary of state. Williams wrote that he had seen "crimes against humanity" in the Congo Free State—an early use of the phrase that was designed to highlight the extreme nature of the crisis. He called on the United States to take action. Williams's writings circulated in the US and British press, but his appeals did not result in much action. Few listened to what he had to say. Williams would die before the international movement for Congo reform really got started.[16]

Atrocities

The rubber tire was invented in 1888. Between bicycles and automobiles, new transportation technologies in the 1890s created a seemingly endless market for rubber, and King Leopold was determined to get as much out of his colonial holdings as possible and levied a demanding rubber tax. To reach the rubber vines, some people had to travel significant distances from their homes. If the people were to provide the state with all the rubber it demanded, they simply would not have time to labor for their own benefit and support. Leopold's land policy further exacerbated matters. The Free State had decreed that any "unoccupied land"—meaning land not being cultivated or inhabited, and any produce of that land—belonged to the state. This included land used for hunting, farming, and fishing. Leopold turned much of that land over to a few privileged companies—the concessionaires—most of which thanked Leopold with a majority share of their profits.

Conditions were bad enough when Williams witnessed the rubber system in the early 1890s, and they only got worse. In 1899, Leopold ordered his officials to bring in even more rubber. He instructed them to "enjoy gentleness first" but if the people were unable or unwilling to harvest the amount that the state required, they might "employ the force of arms." And they did.[17]

Rubber taxes had to be delivered to either the Force Publique or armed sentries, depending on whether one lived in Crown or concessionaire territory. In violation of the humanitarian pretentions of the Berlin and Brussels agreements, the Congo Free State armed these groups to police their neighbors. The rubber system thus provided fire power and state legitimacy to longstanding animosity. Since the sentries themselves would not receive payment unless they delivered the expected amount of rubber, they were highly motivated. The results were disastrous.[18]

American Baptist missionaries had protested conditions in the Congo since the late 1880s, to no avail. Local officials did not reform, and the US press opted not to publish their protests.[19] In an effort to defang his early critics, Leopold created a Commission for the Protection of the Natives in 1896. This group of six consisted of three Catholic and three Protestant missionaries, all tasked with informing the administration of any abuses that they learned of. Yet the commission was ineffectual—and likely was so by design. The commissioners lived far enough away from each other to make regular meetings impossible, and they all lived far enough away from the areas that faced the worst atrocities to make it unlikely that they appreciated the full scope of the violence.[20]

In 1899, the American Presbyterian mission decided to investigate formally the rumors of massacres and violence. They well understood that state officials would do nothing if the missionaries simply reported what they had heard from visitors to their mission. Only firsthand accounts could have any hope of making a difference and forcing change. And so, four years before Casement began his investigation, missionary William Sheppard prepared to see for himself.

By the time Sheppard began to look into the atrocity allegations, he had been in the Congo for nearly a decade. His language skills were good enough that he had made friends and allies among the Bakuba people. But he was nervous as he made his way toward the Zappo Zap camp. They were working for the state to collect the rubber tax, and Sheppard had heard terrible things, including reports of cannibalism.[21] He did not know what to expect.

As he made his way north, Sheppard passed villages that should have been bustling with people. He knew them to house a thousand people in earlier times. Yet they were empty. In one village, he saw the corpse of a woman who had been left leaning against the wall of a house. Sheppard and his guides met only fifteen people, and these were "very much frightened" and "ready to fly into the bush" to escape. From the few villagers he met, he learned of people who had been killed, others who had been shot and wounded, and even more villages abandoned or burned. The Zappo Zaps were nearby.[22]

After a few days of walking, they met a group of the Zappo Zaps, one of whom recognized Sheppard from Luebo. This man would become his informant, not only pointing out the smoke from a burning village the Zappo Zaps had just left, but answering Sheppard's questions about what, exactly, was going on. He showed Sheppard the bodies of two men he had shot and welcomed the missionary into the camp.

As Sheppard described their conversations, he was sure to emphasize his own shrewdness as well as the dangers he faced. Though his "heart burned," he worked to control his emotions and get as much information as he possibly could. The Zappo Zaps spoke to him not only about their actions, but also about how the colonial Free State had demanded that they claim slaves, rubber, ivory, and food from the villagers. "I don't like to fight," Sheppard remembered one man saying, "but the State told me if the villagers refused to pay to make fire." Sheppard described the men sitting around the fire with hands "dripping with the crimson blood of innocent men, women, and children." They showed him their weapons (Sheppard estimated that he saw five hundred guns) and the sixty women they had taken as prisoners. They led him to see the bodies of some eighty or ninety people they had killed that day: corpses with portions of flesh cut off, some with heads removed. But the image that would be most often repeated in later reporting on the atrocities was the pile of eighty-one right hands, severed from human bodies, and roasting over a slow fire. The hands, he learned, were removed so that the men could prove to the State that they had, in fact, killed the people as they had been ordered, and not used the bullets for their own purposes. It was a horrible story, full of violence and terror. And even as he described the Zappo Zaps as cruel, Sheppard was clear where the blame ought to rest: with the colonial Free State.[23]

Sheppard and his missionary colleagues now faced the challenging question: what should they do about it?

Missionaries in general and Congo missionaries specifically had long had to confront the question of how involved they ought to be in local political questions and humanitarian crises. In the decade and a half since the American Presbyterians began their work in the Congo, they had said very little about the atrocities that they saw emerging in the Free State. Missionaries had largely been silent in the 1890s, concerned that the government would expel them from the country if they spoke out. By the end of the decade, as Sheppard returned from his investigation, they had begun to regret that silence.[24]

Missionary silence was the result of both political realism and moral cowardice. Reporting the atrocities they witnessed would be costly, and those who chose to speak up did so at considerable risk. Missionaries in the 1890s were generally too afraid to pay that price. Sheppard in particular worried that, as a Black man, his testimony against a white government would not be taken seriously.[25] But he did not have to act alone. With the partnership of William Morrison, his fellow Presbyterian missionary, his report eventually reached a wide audience. Morrison's writings appeared before the British Parliament. Sheppard's writing appeared in the US and British press. Word was getting out.

King Leopold had actively silenced his critics since the 1880s, paying for positive coverage of the colony and denouncing the witnesses of the atrocities. It would not be until the end of 1906 that Americans learned of the active lobby of journalists that Leopold had employed to control the depictions of the Congo in the US press and politics. In the face of such powerful propaganda and influenced by the ongoing questioning of the role of missionaries after the Boxer Uprising, it was quite easy for missionary opponents or skeptics to accept Leopold's insistence that the missionaries were meddlesome and speaking about complicated matters they did not fully understand.[26]

The US missionaries accordingly did all that they could to emphasize the accuracy of their reporting. After Sheppard's initial exploration, missionary Lachlan Vass conducted a second investigation, which confirmed everything that Sheppard had seen. At first, the mission had no desire to publicize their findings in front of a wide audience. Instead, they reached out to local officials in the Congo Free State and, when this did not result in any changes, Morrison wrote directly to King Leopold. The king dismissed their comments as inaccurate. The Belgian press claimed that any problematic behavior was the fault of the African tribes themselves, and that any bad actors had already been punished. Morrison decried the "whitewashing or indifferent responses" that the mission had received and wondered if the time had come for the missions to turn to the US government for assistance. Once again, missionaries insisted that the United States needed to send a consul to a region of missionary interest. And perhaps, Sheppard believed, the US press needed to cover these atrocities more directly.[27]

As the missionaries in Congo began to speak out more directly, their sponsors at home worried that they might go too far. Samuel Chester, the secretary of the Presbyterian Executive Committee of Foreign Missions, adopted a warning tone when he responded to Sheppard's 1899 report. The Executive Committee approved of the missionaries' decision to investigate and found Sheppard's conduct "courageous and prudent." But it was essential that the missionaries used the "utmost caution" in moving forward. After all, the missionaries had to avoid being accused of "doing or saying things inconsistent with [the mission's] purely spiritual and non-political character." In the midst of the turmoil over the Boxer Uprising, it was essential that the mission could be identified as wholly religious in its nature. They could not be seen as troublemakers.[28]

For several years, the missionaries followed this advice. William and Lucy Sheppard worked to establish their mission station at Ibanche. In 1900, the mission celebrated the arrival of a new printing press that would allow them to print their own classroom and periodical publications. They reported high rates of conversion, with nearly three hundred new members baptized into the church in 1903. The mission had grown in personnel, too, with new Black missionaries recruited by Sheppard. They opened new schools.[29] Though the missionaries complained that Congo officials continually denied their requests for new land to expand their reach, they were quiet about any other concerns they might have had.

But in 1903, both William Morrison and William Shepherd took furlough trips to England and the United States and began speaking directly in public about the state of affairs in the Congo. Morrison in particular became an important figure in the creation of the American Congo Reform Association (modeled on the organization E. D. Morel founded in England in the same year). Only when they had left the Congo were the missionaries able to claim the mantle of experts on what had been happening in the Congo Free State. They were witnesses to atrocities, and they would finally do their part to spread the word.

In the summer of 1903, US newspapers reported that Morrison joined a delegation petitioning the State Department. Their request, as the Baltimore *Sun* explained, was that the United States "call a halt upon the policy of monopoly and alleged inhumanity" in the Congo. The actions of King Leopold and his agents were "in contravention of the Berlin and Brussels treaties," and the United States, as the first country to formally recognize the Congo Free State, had both a right and a duty to intervene.[30] But the Roosevelt administration insisted that US nonparticipation in Berlin meant that the United States had no role to play. The US government, Roosevelt and Secretary of State John Hay insisted, must remain neutral. But the missionaries and their supporters were not deterred.

Throughout 1904, American and British Protestant missionaries worked with the American Congo Reform Society to draw public attention to the plight of Congo and to encourage state intervention on the part of the United States and Britain. In April, a group of missionaries presented a memorial to the US Senate with a request that the government push for an impartial inquiry. But the request was vague and conservative. They only asked the Senate to follow the inquiry with "such other action as may be found necessary and appropriate for the correction of the evils from which the State is suffering."[31]

Over and over, the missionaries had insisted that what they wanted was an impartial investigation—one that might set the record straight and make it clear to the world at large what was happening in the Free State. After that, they hoped, the United States would act with others to end the suffering. How that might happen, however, was unclear. This lack of an obvious course of action certainly did not help the Roosevelt or Taft administrations imagine a future in which they would intervene in this foreign crisis. The missionaries could only hope to convince a reluctant government that the situation was so dire, and that existing treaties were in such clear breach, that there was no choice but to act.

The missionaries' memorial opened with basic information: a history of the Congo Free State, the role of the United States in securing its international recognition, and a geographic and ethnographic survey of the region. But it quickly delved into the "catalogue of wrongs" that the memorialists found it their "painful duty" to relate to the Senate. They wrote about a wide range of atrocities—from forced labor to hostage taking, to burning villages and "the indiscriminate slaughter of people pursued and hunted in the forests to which they flee." They spoke of mutilation of living and dead bodies, of cannibalism, and more. "Horror is added to horror," they wrote.[32]

The general report was followed by the "reluctant testimony" of nine missionaries—American and British—who could provide firsthand testimony of what they had seen across different regions of the Congo Free State. All nine were published in the *Congressional Record* for general consumption. One missionary reported that he knew of forty-five villages that had been entirely burned to the ground; another reported seeing a pile of bones and counting thirty-six skulls. Altogether, the missionaries supported the assertion of Rev. John Weeks that the people "had their spirit crushed out of them by an ever-increasing burden of taxation that has taken the heart out of them and made life not worth living." They hoped that the United States could work with Britain to investigate and force a change.[33] Though the Senate would not take action in 1904, the publication of these reports contributed to the general spread of US interest in the Congo.

Morrison, joined by Samuel Chester, visited the White House to make their case directly to President Roosevelt. Like the president's other missionary visitors, the men left their meeting cautiously hopeful. Though Roosevelt could not promise to take any action—he insisted that the United States had no grounds to do so unless US citizens were mistreated—they saw hints that he was sympathetic. They had found the president to be an engaging conversation partner. Morrison noted that *Red Rubber*, the report on the Congo atrocities by E. D. Morel, lay on Roosevelt's desk.[34] Sheppard, too, would visit the president, bearing gifts of textiles and artwork to demonstrate "the abilities of the persecuted Congolese."[35] Secretary of State Elihu Root would later complain about these missionaries and their supporters in the Protestant churches who "were wild to have us stop the atrocities in the Congo."[36] For the time being, and despite Roosevelt's seeming sympathies, Roosevelt and Root would do nothing.

The missionaries did not only appeal to the US government. They also appealed to the public. In October 1904, Morrison took to the stage in Boston for the meeting of the Boston Peace Congress. His passionate speech accused the Congo Free State of failing to promote free trade, the civilizing mission, or the suppression of slave raiding as they had promised to do at the Berlin and Brussels Conferences. This was a "dark, bloody, and treacherous" era of history, he told his audience. When he came to describe the forced labor and forced military service that were at the heart of his complaints against the state, Morrison wanted to be sure that his audience could understand just how terrible conditions really were. "Words fail me," he said. It was simply "the most heartless and iniquitous [system] in the history of modern colonization enterprises."

To demonstrate this claim, Morrison went on to describe the things that he himself had seen. His descriptions were blunt. "I have seen the people, filled with terror, flee into the forests for safety," he told his audience. "I have seen villages, in which officers and soldiers had quartered for the night, pillaged and desecrated in the most shameless manner, and that, too, right under the eyes of the government officials." The apparent prosperity that the Congo Free State had brought its investors was only made possible by "the lash and the chains and the repeating rifles" that the state and the rubber companies relied on. Morrison painted a picture of destruction and terror with his words.[37]

Sheppard, for his part, relied not only on his words, but on his Kodak camera. Alongside images of mission buildings, students, artifacts, and wild game, Sheppard shared stark images of the victims of atrocities. One such picture shows three adolescent boys, bare-chested and wrapped in white cloth, holding out their arms for the camera. The pale cloth was a strategic choice to highlight their injuries. All three had their hands cut off.[38]

Images like this were an important part of the Congo reform toolkit. Technological developments had made cameras more portable and easier to use, and early twentieth century missionaries all over the world made use of them as a valuable way to record their experiences and share the mission field with their supporters at home.[39] But photographs took on a particular significance in moments like this. To all who suggested that missionaries were exaggerating or meddling in things they did not understand, Sheppard and his peers could present the seemingly unassailable evidence of a visual record. The photographs were proof in a way that even the missionary descriptions could not be. Sheppard's images, alongside those of British missionary Alice Harris, brought an emotional weight to the written and oral descriptions of Congo atrocities. Readers who might have been tempted to skim past the words were stopped in their tracks by the striking images.[40]

The Congo reformers fought an uphill battle in the United States for political, historical, and diplomatic reasons. Opponents pointed out that there was little precedent for US intervention on humanitarian grounds. They wondered if these reformers were being duped by British imperialists who simply wanted the Congo for themselves. They accepted the claims that the missionaries were meddlers who did not fully understand what they were talking about, and they accepted the excuses and explanations from Brussels that minimized problems in the Congo Free State.[41]

Not everyone was satisfied with these excuses. Senator Morgan, whose former law partner had been Lapsley's father, worked to bring the missionary reporting on Congo atrocities before the Senate several times, including a 1906 memorial signed by fifty-two Congo missionaries, nineteen of whom were US citizens.[42] Edwin Denby, a congressional representative from Michigan and the brother of Charles Denby, the US minister to China during the Boxer Uprising, was just one example. Denby wrote to the secretary of state about his constituents' demands that the government needed to do "something to bring about an international inquiry" into the conditions in the Congo. The State Department refused. Secretary of State Elihu Root went so far as to suggest that accusations of atrocities under colonial rule were inevitable. "If the United States had happened to possess in Darkest Africa a territory seven times as large and four times as populous as the Philippines," he mused, "we, too, might find good government difficult and come in for our share of just or unjust criticism."[43] While Congo reformers saw these atrocities as uniquely horrific, Root's frank comment was a reminder that violence was common to all colonial projects. If the United States intervened here, where would it stop? And, importantly, Root suggested that US colonial rule might not withstand humanitarian scrutiny either. Root's letter to Denby was published in the Belgian press, where it was a welcome statement of support for the Congo Free State's representatives in Brussels.[44]

In time, it was missionary rights, not human rights, that inspired consular action. Protestant missionaries were having a hard time purchasing land, and framed this as a matter of religious freedom. Protestants believed that the government was more willing to provide land to Catholic missions, finding them to be more fully aligned with government interests. Yet the letter of the law demanded that Protestant and Catholic missions should be treated equally. Unlike missionary appeals about atrocities, the land question found a ready and willing audience in the State Department. This was a clear question of the rights of US citizens, and the government was happy to act.[45] The reply from the secretary-general of the Free State that the Americans had the right to purchase land, but not the right to compel anyone to sell to them, was less than satisfactory.

Slowly, the State Department began to reconsider its stance on neutrality in the Congo Free State. By 1907, the United States had its own consul in the colony. Toward the end of his term, President Roosevelt and his administration began to articulate a more expansive reading of its rights and responsibilities as a signatory at the Brussels Convention. Missionary troubles and missionary testimony had long demanded the United States take on a more interventionist role. Once missionaries' testimony about the atrocities they had witnessed got them into trouble with the colonial government, the government began to expand its understanding of how it could and should intervene—or not—in international humanitarian crises.

Missionaries on Trial

Sheppard and Morrison returned to the Congo from their American furlough in 1906 and were shocked by what they saw. William Sheppard would write about the drastic changes that only a few years had brought to the region for the *Kasai Herald*, the mission's quarterly magazine for American donors. Where once there had been a community of "great stalwart men and women" living "happy, busy, prosperous lives," there was now destruction and suffering, far beyond what had been present a few years earlier. Farms had turned to "weeds and jungles," homes were "half-built" and "much neglected." The streets were dirty. "Even their children cry for bread." What had changed? For Sheppard, the explanation was quite simple: it was the expansion of the rubber companies' activities.

The Bakuba had been besieged by "armed sentries of chartered trading companies" who forced the people to harvest rubber at a pay so low that it was practically slavery. They could not live on such pay, and they could not escape the companies. The result was obvious: they suffered.[46]

As far as the charges against the rubber companies in the Congo Free State went, Sheppard's article was quite tame. There was no mention of atrocities here: no severed hands or cannibalism. No villages burned or women kidnapped. No massacres. His claims were simple, and easily demonstrated: forced labor and pitifully meager wages. His reporting from several years earlier had been far more explicit and damning. But it was this article and the resulting legal action that would bring Sheppard and Morrison to trial for criminal libel. It was, in many ways, this article that would force the US government to take action in the Congo Free State. With the arrest of the missionaries, the State Department no longer faced only a humanitarian crisis. Now, they had to consider the rights of US citizens abroad.

On February 23, 1909, Sheppard and Morrison received a summons to the court in Leopoldville (Kinshasa), some nine hundred miles from their home in Kasai. The summons alleged that Sheppard's article had been "incorrect and highly damaging" to the Compagnie Kasai, "heaping on it reproach, sullying the honor of its operation and committing an offense against its authority." The company charged Sheppard, as the article's author, and Morrison, as the *Kasai Herald*'s publisher, with criminal libel. They demanded eighty thousand francs from the two missionaries (the equivalent of sixteen thousand dollars at the time) and a retraction in the next issue of the publication.[47] The charges were serious and the stakes were high.

The company had long denied any wrongdoing. Shortly after the article first appeared, the director of the Compagnie Kasai demanded a retraction. The company did not make use of armed sentries, he claimed, and the pay was not too low. If it was, he asked, why did people continue to work for them?[48] Another officer insisted that the company "works solely in accordance with the principle of supply and demand, and the natives are not forced to make rubber for us."[49] The missionaries, however, insisted that they knew better than these officials who did not even reside in the region. The missionaries had no doubt that an impartial investigation would demonstrate the veracity of their assertions. The company's denials could only be made "as a result of ignorance or dishonesty," Morrison asserted. When he responded to the company director, he enclosed a photograph.[50]

The missionaries did not expect to find justice in the colonial courts. The government held over half of the company shares—a fact which US and British newspapers continually cited as evidence that this was a case between the Belgian government and the mission. It seemed foolish to imagine that the missionaries could face impartial judgment. All earlier government investigations had seemed perfunctory and biased. When the most recent government investigator left the region shortly after his arrival, having made it quite clear that his interest was more in the exoneration of the company than the discovery of the truth, Morrison summed up his feelings bluntly: "So much for his investigation."[51]

The day after the missionaries received the summons, Morrison wrote to William Handley and Wilfred Thesiger, the US and British consuls at Boma, as well as to Samuel Chester, the director of the Southern Presbyterian Foreign Mission Committee in Nashville. This was, he explained to Chester, a test case. Local officials were trying to control what the missionaries could say about conditions in the Congo and to whom they could say it. The missionaries would need both "public indignation" and government support to support them through the trial.[52]

As soon as the Presbyterian Foreign Mission Committee learned about the prosecution of the missionaries, they informed the State Department. Chester's letter to Secretary of State Philader Knox echoed generations of earlier missionary pleas to the government to protect missionaries "in their rights as American citizens." There was "just reason to fear" that the missionaries would not get "a fair trial according to American ideas," Chester explained. Now that US citizens were being charged with libel for reporting that Belgian reforms had not been realized, would the government protect them and demand that their trial be fair and transparent?[53]

The mission's supporters expressed two main concerns: that the missionaries' case could be heard impartially, and that it would be held at an appropriate time and place. "Justice and fairness," the missionary society assumed, would only be assured if the Congo officials knew that the US government was watching. They asked the State Department to instruct the consul at Boma to attend the trial and report on "any departure from the principles of international law or from the customs and practices of civilized governments." The missionaries had already been depicted as "meddling." Their supporters were anxious that they would not be punished for speaking out.[54]

In Boma, missionary Lachlan Vass met with the consuls while his brethren in Kasai prepared for their long journey. Transatlantic cables made communication between Washington and its consuls much faster than it had been in earlier decades. The missionaries had found a sympathetic audience in Secretary Knox, who agreed that there was nothing inappropriate in Sheppard's article. By February 27, consul

Handley had already received his instructions to attend the trial and to keep an eye on matters. He, along with Thesiger, agreed that the charges were "ridiculous." After all, the article did not say anything that could not be backed up by multiple other reports. Thesiger's recent investigation into conditions in the region for the British government was far more damning than anything that Sheppard had written or Morrison had published.[55]

The international community, too, had begun to turn more decisively against Leopold's rule in the Free State. International pressure had already resulted in Belgium's annexation of the Congo in 1908. It would no longer be the sole property of the king; the Congo Free State would become the Belgian Congo. The Belgian government hoped that this change in rule would satisfy critics, but reformers were not so sure if the "Belgian Solution," as it was called, would create any real change.[56] At the time of the trial, neither the US nor Britain recognized Belgian rule in the Congo. They hoped the delay would force Belgium to put more meaningful reforms in place. As the trial loomed, missionaries hoped that this government stance would strengthen their bargaining power.

Missionary concerns were heightened by the seeming injustice of the timing and location of the trial, which was originally scheduled for May 25 in Leopoldville. As the dry season left part of the river unnavigable by steamer, much of this journey would have to be taken overland. The missionaries and any witnesses would have to expect to be away from home for at least five months. It was, at the very least, inconvenient and expensive. The missionaries and their supporters suggested that this was intentional. At such a distance, how could the missionaries be expected to have sufficient witnesses who could attest to the veracity of Sheppard's article?

The State Department's strategy to aid the missionaries was two-pronged, reflecting the particular challenges of this moment of colonial diplomacy. As Secretary Knox instructed the consul in Boma to work with the missionaries on the ground in the Congo, he also instructed the US ambassador in Brussels to do what he could with the Belgian government. In May, the United States requested that Belgium change the time and place of the trial, but these efforts were unsuccessful. Despite annexation, the Belgians informed the Americans that they were unable to force any changes in the Congo justice system.[57] For observers who had hoped that the Belgian government's attempts to increase oversight in the Congo would result in better conditions and more avenues for diplomacy, this development was unpromising.

If the Americans in Brussels failed, those in Boma succeeded. Consul Handley ultimately convinced the court to postpone the trial, arguing that the missionaries could not possibly reach Leopoldville in time for the original May date. They needed time to secure witnesses and a lawyer, as well as time to travel the considerable distance to court. It would be August before the missionaries made their way to Leopoldville. The trial date was first pushed back to July 31, then again to September 24. Throughout these delays, the transatlantic network of Congo reformers and missionary supporters kept the case and the US missionaries in the public eye.

The most dedicated promoter of the missionaries' cause was the *Christian Observer*, one of the official publications of the Southern Presbyterians. News of the trial first appeared in the April 21 issue; by the end of 1909, it had published twenty-six articles on the case.[58] For the readers of the *Christian Observer*, the stakes of the trial were very high. Its outcome would "set a precedent that will either retard or advance the cause of Congo reforms, and will either guarantee protection to missionaries of all denominations or will put the missionary in a position where he cannot claim or expect protection that is ordinarily given to the trader or the traveler."[59]

As they advocated for the missionaries, the writers in the *Christian Observer* drew on the long tradition of asserting the rights of missionaries as US citizens. Missionary citizens had the right to do their work, and the US government needed to protect that right; this claim had been at the core of missionary diplomacy since the middle of the nineteenth century. Now, that claim joined with the emerging humanitarian concerns that had complicated US foreign relations for several decades. The articles claimed a new missionary right: to bear witness and testify to the world about atrocities that they had seen. The *Observer* insisted that missionaries possessed "the right to expose and publish the wrongs inflicted on unhappy tribes by foreign nations who are exploiting them for gain." And this right required the US government to "back up her citizens who are unveiling and denouncing barefaced violations of an international treaty, and the justice and courage to enforce that right."[60]

Whether or not they read the *Christian Observer*, Americans could follow the progress of the trial in the secular press. An April 1909 article on the charges that first appeared in London made its way to multiple US papers on May 10. Readers across the country read that the trial "may be considered one of the Belgian government against the missionaries," and that the missionaries' accusations were confirmed not only from other missionary observations, but also by official reports from both the US and British consuls. As the newspapers explained the charges against the company, they repeated the basic claims of the Congo reform movement against the Free State. If the case had been intended to silence critics, it had the opposite effect and instead publicized the charges against Leopold.[61] As the summer progressed, the US press continued to cover the story, discussing both the trial and the atrocities.[62]

Readers throughout the country were kept up to date on the various religious groups who had reached out to request the intervention of the State Department and President Taft. The Presbyterians, for example, used the occasion of their General Assembly meeting in the summer to urge both the US and British governments to demand reforms in the governance of the Congo. Regional papers made sure to mention Sheppard and Morrison's connections to the American South. Some, but not all, specified that Sheppard was Black. Most made sure to mention that Sheppard was a member of the Royal Geographical Society, as if to clothe him with as much respectability as possible.[63]

The result of this coverage was twofold. It kept the pressure on the US government to act in the missionaries' defense while also broadening the network of support for these missionaries. Petitions in support of the missionaries reached the State Department from multiple missionary organizations and denominational bodies. In the *Boston Daily Globe*, the secretary of the Christian Foreign Missionary Society argued that "the Congo situation must be radically changed. Missionaries must be free to speak the truth. The people must be granted the rights of which they have been wrongfully deprived."[64] These conversations about rights could occasionally be blurry: whose rights were at stake? The rights of the Congolese, or the rights of the American missionaries?

If found guilty, the missionaries would have to pay a hefty fine. Sheppard, however, insisted that he would never pay. To do so, he believed, would be an acknowledgement of wrong. Instead, he declared that if the court found him guilty, he would choose to go to prison. This "testimony to the truth of his charges" would, he hoped, "be the best means of protesting against the oppressions and cruelties" of the Compagnie Kasai.[65]

On October 5, American Presbyterians learned of the outcome of the trial with the arrival of a one-word telegram from Morrison: "Acquitted." The charges against Morrison had been dropped first, and in early October those against Sheppard, too, were dismissed. The *Christian Observer* explained that the victory was for more than just these two missionaries. "The entire world is demanding that Belgium shall make her rule in the Congo just and beneficent," the journal remarked. The outcome of this trial should show Belgium that the time had come to "set her house in order."[66]

Sheppard's journal of their journey home, later published in the *Christian Observer*, reveled in the joy of reunion with his family after four months of separation, but also spoke of the profound costs that this legal victory had demanded. One of their witnesses—a young man—became sick with malaria and died on his journey home. He left behind parents, a wife, and children. The missionaries had been acquitted of libel. Their right to testify to what they had seen was enforced. But there was no guarantee of reform to come. Missionary rights had been secured, but not the rights of the Congolese.[67] That would require more than the testimony of missionaries. Diplomatic and station actions would be required to reform the Belgian Congo.

One piece of leverage that the United States had during the missionaries' trial was the possibility of not recognizing the Belgian Congo. Belgium had annexed the Congo Free State early in 1909, and neither the United States nor Great Britain had yet recognized the legitimacy of the new government. Both powers were waiting for the promise of reform. On the ground in Africa, missionaries and consuls were doubtful that the shift in colonial rule would make much of a difference. The Congo Reform Associations in England and America kept pressure on their respective governments to try and make sure that real change could happen. Sheppard and Morrison's trial provided the United States with an occasion to make this point to Belgium. If the missionaries could be persecuted for writing about what they had witnessed, and if the atrocities continued, how could the United States be expected to recognize the Belgian Congo as a legitimate colony?

Humanitarian crises demanded that missionaries serve as witnesses. Indeed, their witness could often publicize the crisis in the media and diplomatic spheres. For decades, US missionaries had positioned themselves as experts who shared the world with their supporters at home. Before the Congo, they prided themselves on sharing the bad along with the good—indeed, writing about the supposed horrors of foreign cultures could be a powerful fundraising tool to further the evangelical movement throughout the nineteenth century. But atrocities like what they witnessed in the Congo Free State demanded something new of missionaries and it demanded something new of their American supporters. These were not problems that could be solved through the spread of Christian civilization or missionary influence. They demanded political intervention.

As missionaries and their supporters petitioned the US government to respond to humanitarian crises, they forced an important question: How and when would the US intervene out of humanitarian concern? Which victims merited their attention? How much suffering was too much? When did political considerations supersede human rights?

The US government and its citizens had pondered these questions before, but in the 1890s and the decades that followed, humanitarian crises emerged all over the world: in Cuba, in Armenia, and in the Congo. The Congo Free State presented Americans with the question of how far they would go to protect the rights of oppressed people who were not white, and who were (largely) not Christian. An active group of reformers ultimately could not pressure the government to do much. When US citizens—missionaries—went toe-to-toe with the colonial government, US diplomats did their duty to protect them. Once the State Department decided to finally take action in defense of Americans' rights in the Congo Free State, they stood by the veracity of the missionary witness and demanded fair treatment and reform. With Sheppard's acquittal and the promise of some change in the colony, the United States was satisfied. But without the missionary trial, it is unclear if the government would have done even this much. Roosevelt had made it clear that the United States could only act if and when its own citizens were in danger. With the case against Sheppard and Morrison, the government finally got the opportunity to bring human rights into diplomatic policy. In 1911, the United States officially recognized the Belgian Congo.

The Congo missionaries were not the only missionary witnesses to atrocities around the world. In the Ottoman Empire, too, missionaries sounded the alarm starting in the 1890s about attacks against the Armenian people. These attacks would escalate to genocide. In the midst of world war, missionaries would once again work with other humanitarians to try to pressure the government to take action on behalf of those in need.

Chapter 11

Humanitarians

James L. Barton needed to get to the bottom of it. In 1915, the foreign secretary of the ABCFM had been receiving letters from his correspondents in Turkey that made him nervous. Something was going on, it was clear. The Armenian population around Harpoot (Harput), where he had previously served as a missionary for seven years, seemed to be in danger. The letters used coded language. They reported "unusual events" that seemed to parallel some that "had before taken place in the country." Clearly, the missionaries were trying to get news past the Ottoman censors who controlled the flow of information outside of the region. When Barton spoke to other Americans familiar with the region in the late summer, they expressed similar concerns. "No one had very definite information," Barton would later remember, "although all had grave apprehensions." When he received a telegram from Henry Morgenthau, the US minister at Constantinople, his worst fears were confirmed: "Destruction of the Armenian race in Turkey is rapidly progressing."[1]

Barton soon joined with humanitarian leaders to form the American Committee for Armenian and Syrian Relief (ACASR), an organization dedicated to providing aid in the region. On September 21, he was in Washington, DC, hoping that the State Department would support these humanitarian efforts. These requests were "unhesitatingly granted" by Assistant Secretary of State Alvey Adee. The government support first came in the form of information. Barton was taken to a private room and given all of the dispatches and reports that the State Department had received from Turkey in the past year. A clerk provided pencils and a large pad of paper, and assured him that no one would disturb his work. If Barton had any questions, or needed any further materials, the clerk was at his service.[2]

When Barton told the story of that day later in his life, he was sure to describe the unfettered access he had been granted. Even cyphered telegrams were at his disposal. The government had no qualms with sharing what they knew with the missionary and authorized him to make use of whatever networks he had to share the information even more broadly.[3]

What he found was shocking.

Barton had gone to the State Department expecting to read horrible stories of violence against Armenian Christians. It had happened before, in the 1890s. The Hamidian massacres in that decade inspired a new era in US humanitarian activism. Twenty years later, Europe was at war, and the Ottoman Empire had joined on the side of Germany. There had been no reason to expect anything but bad news, but Barton was still taken aback. It was much worse than he had imagined. The Armenian population was forced to live "under most cruel conditions," he summarized. In fact, he had learned that the Turkish government was attempting nothing less than to "annihilate an ancient Christian race."[4]

That very night, Barton was on a train back to New York, where he took a room at the Hotel Roosevelt and began writing. By midnight, he had reports ready for the American papers, where they would cause a sensation. He provided a "vast collection of absolutely authentic material from Turkey" that told the story of the "regimented and designedly inhuman deportation of an entire race of men, women and children, from their ancestral homes towards the desert." As war erupted around the world. Barton worked to ensure that the story of the Armenian Genocide would be "spread upon the first pages of practically every journal in America."[5]

The Armenian crisis brought together missionaries, politicians, and humanitarian activists in a common cause. Initially, Barton had hoped to raise $100,000. Between 1916 and 1918 ACASR (later renamed Near East Relief) had raised nearly $14,000,000.[6] Adee was not Barton's only ally in the US government. Barton served as an advisor for President Woodrow Wilson, as did several other prominent missionaries and missionary supporters, which made it possible to bring the mission movement's priorities close to the heart of US strategy during the First World War.[7]

The Wilson administration seemed to present new opportunities for the mission movement. Wilson, the son of a Presbyterian minister, seemed to share many of the values of missionary leaders. Speaking before the Young Man's Christian Association in 1912, Wilson claimed to great applause that "it is Christianity that has produced the political liberty of the world," and he celebrated the work of missionaries in creating educational institutions around the world and setting the stage for the spread of democracy.[8] His vision of American internationalism aligned well with what missionaries had long advocated. This intellectual affinity was further helped by Wilson's close prewar relationship with many missionary leaders. Over the course of the war years, American missionaries positioned themselves as key partners in the new internationalist vision of the United States. They expected to be able to partner with their government in this new era.

For the missionaries, the Great War was the culmination of a century of international engagement. Violence that would have been almost unimaginable in their earlier experience perversely created opportunities to place missionaries close to the seat of diplomatic power. The modern era that the war ushered in presented new challenges for missionary diplomacy. After the robust debate over the value of missionary work a decade earlier, missionaries in Turkey could now clearly show their usefulness to their fellow Americans. But increasingly they went about this work alongside partners who embraced the humanitarian aspects of their work without the same dedication to the evangelical cause.

The Armenian Genocide again united the mission movement and the government in their visions of America's role abroad—and again revealed the fractures in that unity. Political realities, including waging war and attempting to build a lasting peace, made the Wilson administration at once reliant on missionaries and wary of committing completely to their influence.

World War and Armenian Genocide

In 1914, the assassination of the heir to the Austro-Hungarian Empire set off a chain of events that engulfed the European continent in war. The Ottoman Empire joined the war as one of the Central Powers allied with Germany, and the fighting would initiate a new phase in the nationalist movements that had plagued the empire for decades. These struggles were political, cultural, and religious. Ottoman attempts to create a shared Turkish identity over the past decades had emphasized assimilation for religious, ethnic, and linguistic minorities, including the Armenian Christians with whom US missionaries had long worked. With Turkey at war with the Allied powers, diplomats from Russia, France, and Great Britain all had to leave the region. The US diplomats, representing a neutral government, remained in place.

War touched the missionaries in the region quickly. At first, pressing military needs prompted government seizure of missionary property—especially hospitals. When medical missionary Dr. W. S. Dodd described the Turkish takeover of his hospital—"nurses, physicians, and all"—he did not seem disturbed. It was quite likely that the mission would have offered the premises to the Red Crescent, anyway. Using the mission hospital to tend wounded soldiers seemed in keeping with missionary goals.[9] In other locations, however, the effects of the war seemed less benign. In Moush (Muş), the Turkish army had seized food and fuel in addition to impressing all men between the ages of twenty and forty-five, leaving in their wake "many families without food and only the women and children to care for the fields."[10] In Harpoot, missionaries were "very apprehensive" about what might follow. They pledged to stay beside the people through whatever was to come.[11]

It soon became clear that the war against the Allied Powers was not the only battle that Turkey was engaged in. From their various bases across the empire, American missionaries and consuls began to report horrific atrocities to Ambassador Henry Morgenthau in 1915.[12] Something needed to be done. But once again, it was not at all clear what type of action the United States might take.

Missionaries were major figures in Morgenthau's letters to the State Department throughout 1915 and 1916. Morgenthau had come to Constantinople expecting the missionaries to be a bother. He thought they would be merely sectarian, primarily concerned with the supremacy of their own religious practices and beliefs. Instead, he was surprised to find the missionaries to be valuable partners in his work. They were, he wrote, "agents of civilization" whose work greatly benefited the interests of the United States in the region.[13]

Early in 1915, Morgenthau's letters to Washington about missionaries largely resembled those that his predecessors had written for decades. He and the missionaries were concerned about changing Turkish regulations that might affect the mission schools. The schools would soon

FIGURE 11.1.   Map of Turkey, 1898, including the region of the Armenian massacre.
Source: ABCFM, *Maps of Missions of the American Board of Commissioners for Foreign Missions* (Boston: The Board, 1898), 5.

face higher taxation and more oversight, most of which focused on religious instruction and the Turkish language. In March, he secured a delay in the new regulations and reported that he and the missionaries intended to comply with Turkish oversight. By September, however, he reported that the embassy had decided to protest the policies.[14] In just a few months, the situation had changed. Morgenthau no longer talked only of educational policy. Now, his concerns about the mission schools were connected to the ongoing violence against Armenian Christians.

"Owing to general deportation of Armenians in Asia Minor, accompanied by massacres, atrocities, and starvation, schools in those provinces may not open, or will open under greatest difficulties," Morgenthau telegrammed the Secretary of State on September 4. In light of everything else he mentioned, the question of whether or not the schools would open seemed of minor importance. But the missionary connection would be an important avenue into US action. "Inform Barton, Boston; Dodge, Crane, Brown, New York," Morgenthau signed off.[15] These were Rev. James Barton, of the ABCFM; Cleveland Dodge, a philanthropist and trustee of Robert College; Charles Crane, a Wilson supporter with an interest in the Middle East; and Arthur Judson Brown, of the Presbyterian Foreign Mission Board. These missionary leaders would lead the US humanitarian efforts to aid the Armenians throughout the war years.

Eyewitnesses described arrests, looting, stabbings, stoning, and rape. Some of the victims were thrown into wells while they were still alive. In an attempt to escape the violence, crowds of Armenians attempted to flee on foot. Many died on the journey from hunger or cold. The US missionaries eventually received permission to bury some of the dead. They found mutilated corpses that were missing eyes, ears, lips, or noses.[16] But news was slow to spread. Missionaries were cut off from easy communication with consuls, and it would take months for missionaries in one portion of the empire to learn of the violence that their peers faced in other regions. Slowly, missionary reports of this new wave of atrocities began to reach consulates, the embassy, and eventually, Washington. Across the empire, Armenians were exiled from their homes, forced to relocate to unfavorable locations, and faced with brutal attacks that amounted to nothing short of genocide.

In Ourmiah (Urmia), for example, it was the departure of Russian soldiers that created the opportunity for some thirty thousand Turkish and Kurdish soldiers to descend on nearby villages.[17] The Turkish government understood the Armenian Christians here and elsewhere to be a threat on multiple levels: they were a threat to the ethno-religious unity of Turkey as well as a potential military threat if their nationalist ambitions led them to join arms with Russia. And so they attacked. Missionary Mary Platt recorded these events in her journal using stark anti-Islamic language: "Evil-minded Moslems all over the plain began to plunder the Christian villages."[18]

Secretary of State William Jennings Bryan first contacted Morgenthau about the humanitarian crisis in February. He had heard rumors of potential unrest and instructed the ambassador to ask the Turkish government to take action to protect the "lives and property of Jews and Christians in case of massacre or looting."[19] Morgenthau was already attuned to the matter.[20] By late May, there was word of massacres of Armenians in Erzerurm (Erzurum), Dertchun (Datsun), Eguine (Egin), Van, Bitlis, Mush, Sassun (Sason), Zeitun (Süleymanli), and Cilicia.[21] Morgenthau described attacks of "unprecedented proportions" across "widely scattered districts." It was, he concluded, a "systematic attempt to uproot peaceful Armenian populations." The victims were sent out on foot to the desert regions of the empire, "herded like cattle," with no provisions for lodging or food. Most of them, he expected, would "doubtless perish by murder or slow starvation." The only exceptions might be those who "in desperation embrace Mohammedanism." In several places, he reported, aid workers were denied access to the refugees. The missionaries expected their schools to be shut down, but Morgenthau did not think they were in personal danger.[22] By September, Morgenthau had shifted from describing persecution to warning about absolute destruction.[23]

Missionary accounts agreed. In Van, American missionaries watched in horror as the violence erupted around them in April. The governor-general had ordered "a general massacre of his Armenian subjects," as the missionaries would later report. Since most men of fighting age had been drafted into the war, the Kurdish forces who came to smaller towns and villages throughout the province met little resistance. Missionaries estimated that 55,000 were killed in these attacks, with thousands more wounded and fleeing to the city for safety.[24] Missionary Grisell McLaren described listening to the rifles and cannons from inside the Van hospital, where she had been working with wounded Turkish soldiers. Soon, the government closed the hospital and the patients were transferred to Bitlis. McLaren accompanied them at the request of an Armenian patient who was sure they would die without the protection of an American escort.[25] On her journey, she described an Armenian community that was terrified of further violence and traumatized by what had come before, "rocking back and forth, and wringing their hands" as they told her their stories. McLaren recounted tales of babies who "had been killed and their bodies thrown into the lake and others had been thrown in alive," and of young women "carried off by the Kurds."[26] Thousands of Armenian refugees with similar stories poured into Bitlis, seeking protection. When McLaren reached the US mission, she was among approximately seven hundred refugees who sought sanctuary on the missionary premises.[27]

The missionary compound was "rather small," with only four buildings inside: a church, two schoolhouses, and the residence of one of the missionary families. But it was well fortified with a stone wall and iron bars that secured the gate every night. As they continued to hear of village after village under attack, terrified Armenians continued to pour into the city. Soon, the missionaries estimated that twelve thousand refugees had come to Bitlis. Many of these were cared for at the Armenian church; the American missionaries were responsible for eight thousand.

The available relief funds were insufficient, barely enough to keep any individuals alive. Soon, soldiers gathered the refugees and drove them out of the city. The missionaries later heard that many of those refugees were murdered during their travel.[28]

This was not the end. In late June, the mission premises were surrounded by soldiers and police who arrested every man and boy over ten years of age. After a week, the missionaries learned that the men had first been brought to an underground dungeon and then killed.[29] Soon thereafter, the women, too, were gathered together and forced to leave Bitlis. When McLaren asked that her female students be allowed to remain at the mission school, her request was denied. The government had ordered that no Armenians should remain in Bitlis.

The missionaries were allowed to take their students to Harpoot, but the mission premises there had already been turned over to the government for hospital use. McLaren planned to barricade the school building to protect her students if necessary, but was finally granted permission to keep them in place for as long as possible. No more Armenians could come into the compound, however. The missionaries "tried to keep this promise" to turn away the many suffering people who came by their gates "as their only hope of saving a few." The only exceptions to this prohibition came when the missionaries found old women "in a dying condition" or young children who were starving. These they were permitted to bring into the school building, but the police later claimed the children. "The screams of women and children could be heard at almost any time during the day," the missionaries would later recall. "The cries that rang out through the darkness of the night were even more heartrending."[30] By November, the missionaries, too, had been forced out of Bitlis.

The Bitlis mission was not the only one with such stories. American missionaries throughout the empire tried to do what they could, and sent word to Morgenthau in Constantinople that aid was desperately needed. This was a humanitarian crisis, but it was also about US interests, they reminded him. Some well-connected missionaries went beyond Morgenthau straight to Washington in their appeals for US intervention.

Missionary William Chambers had known President Wilson as a student at Princeton, and he had long followed Wilson's career with pride. In 1915, he was in New Jersey after a harrowing journey from Adana, Turkey, as part of a party of twelve missionaries. When he wrote to Wilson, he described a Sunday service that he had conducted on board the ship, one hand holding the Bible and the other on one of the guns of the USS *Des Moines*. It was a "startling" experience for Chambers to preach between these two objects whose purposes he felt were so different: "The one made for the destruction of men and the other revealed for their life and peace." The only way that he could resolve the tension was to recognize that "the world needs them both." Under the leadership of men like Wilson, Chambers was sure "the one would be used to restrain evil and the other to develop righteousness and good-will to men." The Armenian Genocide helped him to reach this conclusion. It was so horrible, he wrote, that he had come to hope that the United States "should become so strong on land and sea that such a government as Turkey would never dare to commit such a horrible crime." Humanitarian intervention—even, perhaps, military intervention—was needed.[31]

Morgenthau knew that Americans needed to act, but he was not sure how. The Ottoman government insisted that this was a domestic matter in which the United States had no right to interfere.[32] By August, he admitted that it was "difficult for me to restrain myself from doing something to stop this attempt to exterminate a race," but he knew that as an ambassador he was duty-bound to maintain a position of neutrality on the internal affairs of a foreign nation. He asked for the State Department to issue him with some orders—any orders—to make an "unequivocal protest on behalf of our government." Perhaps they might ask the Germans to challenge their ally's behavior. At the very least, he hoped, the United States might demand that the Ottomans allow Americans to provide relief to those who were suffering. "The advance of such assistance might be the means of saving thousands," he wrote.[33]

Morgenthau was not the only one asking. James Barton of the ABCFM telegrammed the secretary of state: "Cannot something be done to alleviate the horrors?"[34] By September, Morgenthau urged the secretary of state to create a committee to raise funds for Armenian relief that might allow for refugees to emigrate to the United States.[35]

American official appeals to humanitarianism did not move the Ottoman government to action. When Hoffman Philip, the US chargé in Constantinople, met with Talaat Bey, the Ottoman minister of war, Talaat insisted that US reports were an exaggeration and, further, that the American missionaries who had shared so much of the news with the world were a destabilizing presence. The "main effect" of missionary work with Armenian Christians, Talaat insisted, was to "stimulate their antigovernmental tendencies." Here was the familiar charge that missionaries were meddling in situations they did not understand, but Philip was unconcerned. Instead, he focused on how to get help to the suffering.[36]

Through the summer of 1916, Philip continued reporting that many were "dying of disease, starvation, and exhaustion" after being "shifted about from one place to another in the desert by relentless officials." The missionaries reported that somewhere between nine and eleven thousand men, women, and children in Aleppo and Adana had been massacred.[37] Thousands more were attacked later in the summer. "It is a complete extermination," Philip put it simply. "Everybody is in terror."[38]

But what was the US Department of State to do? Secretary Lansing asked Philip for ideas, but had few to share. Perhaps the United States should "flatly threaten to withdraw our diplomatic representative from a country where such barbarous methods are not only tolerated but actually carried out by order of the existing government." Such a threat would "have the effect of bringing the guilty parties to an appreciation of their true position before the world and of ameliorating the situation." But such a move would be risky, too. It would put US interests in Turkey—the missionaries—at risk, and could make it impossible to get the necessary aid to those who suffered.[39]

In the meantime, concerned Americans in the United States raised awareness and collected for Armenian relief. Foreign missionaries and their American supporters were at the center of this work: James Barton, foreign secretary of the ABCFM, served as president of ACASR, which quickly became a hub for missionary and government news from the region.[40] Barton worked with journalists to keep stories of the atrocities and appeals for relief in the news. Newspapers and more than twenty magazines ran stories on the Armenians in these years, many of which emphasized Islamic violence and the particular needs of women and children.[41] Inspired by their work, President Wilson set aside days of remembrance for the Armenians in 1916. Barton and other missionary leaders prepared his proclamation and traveled to Washington to deliver it by hand.[42]

As in the Armenian massacres of the 1890s, the most pressing concerns were how to stop the atrocities and how to get relief to those who were suffering. In 1916, US funding supported more than a thousand orphans in Aleppo, but this was hardly enough. The US embassy reported that hundreds more died of starvation. Many had only grass to eat.[43]

Relief took several forms: food for the hungry, specialized aid for exiles, medical aid, and finally, care for the many children who were left orphaned. By 1917, relief work also took the shape of employment: one thousand women in Erivan (Yerevan), for example, labored in a wool shop where they produced socks and blankets. Other workers produced bedclothes for local hospitals, sweaters for soldiers, or embroidery for export.[44] Missionaries, particularly from the ABCFM, were major distributors of this aid. After all, sixteen of the twenty cities that the Rockefeller Foundation's War Relief Commission had suggested for relief work were already the homes of American Board mission stations. The missionaries were on the ground and ready to help.[45]

To keep up this work, ACASR encouraged donations from the American populace. ACASR's aggressive public relations campaign kept Armenian suffering at the front of Americans' minds, encouraging even more donations. In 1916, the committee raised more than $2 million, and would raise double that in 1917. In 1918, they raised about $7 million.[46] But the need continued to outstrip donations. Armenia was, as missionary W. Nesbitt Chambers expressed it, "drenched with the blood of her sons and daughters." He urged US Christians to respond to the "piteous wail of a nation in distress."[47]

In the midst of humanitarian disaster, missionaries worried that their property, too, was under attack. Military authorities continued to seize missionary property, claiming that it was needed for military purposes. The Ottoman minister of foreign affairs assured the US government that these were merely temporary conditions, but the Americans were not so sure. In Marsovan (Merzifon), officials arrived without warning, ordered the fourteen missionaries out of their homes, and expelled their students from the school premises. The missionaries were prevented from contacting the ambassador and were told (incorrectly) that the embassy was closed and that a US declaration of war was "imminent." They were sent to Constantinople without being permitted to remove their personal belongings. When Philip inventoried the mission compound for the Turkish minister of foreign affairs, he listed some twenty-two buildings (schools, hospitals, residences) and "a library of 10,000 volumes, a museum with 7,000 objects," all on thirty-seven acres. Not counting the personal property of the missionary families, Philip valued the property at £50,000.[48] Mission properties at Sivas and Talas were similarly seized. It was not just the property that concerned Philip, however. Also of concern was the fact that the female students and teachers who were Ottoman subjects had been removed from mission premises and faced "strongest pressure" to renounce Christianity, embrace Islam, and take Muslim husbands.[49]

Philip had serious doubts about the military necessity of occupying missionary buildings, and he was furious about the way that the missionaries were treated. Missionaries and their supporters were upset that their buildings were being seized and their work stopped, but they were even more worried about their Armenian teachers and students who were killed or scattered. An article on the "martyred professors of Euphrates College" singled out four murdered Armenian teachers who had been taken from the school and tortured: one had been starved and hung by his arms, another had his finger nails pulled out by the roots. All were killed, alongside the majority of their students.[50] "American citizens, American property, and American enterprises have all suffered at the hands of the mad Turk," one article in the *Missionary Herald* summarized.[51]

Washington took this threat seriously. This was American property, and the rights of US citizens were at risk. It was not simply a matter of internal Ottoman politics. Acting Secretary of State Frank Polk ordered Philip to request that the Turkish government clarify its attitude toward the United States.[52] The United States was neutral in the war at this point; Americans should not be treated as belligerents.

Missionaries, Wilson, and War

That neutrality did not last long. In early April 1917, President Wilson asked Congress to declare war on Germany, marking the US entry into the European war. Wilson had won his narrow reelection with a slogan claiming that "he kept us out of war," but after continued German submarine warfare on neutral ships in the Atlantic and the discovery of the Zimmerman Telegram and its suggestion that Germany might ally with Mexico, the United States could remain neutral no longer. It was more than just submarines and German intrigue that brought Americans to the front. Wilson and many others had come to understand this as a war between democracy and absolutism, with nothing less than the "ultimate peace of the world and the liberation of its peoples" at stake.[53]

Woodrow Wilson was a sympathetic supporter of missionary interests. As had been the case for earlier generations of politicians, Wilson well understood that missionaries could have profound political importance. And he was enthusiastic about the positive effects missionaries could have in spreading not only Christianity, but also democracy. He said as much in an address to the YMCA in 1912, when he credited the organization with contributing to the recent revolution in China.[54]

The following year, Wilson wrote to Barton from the White House to celebrate the centenary of American missions in India. He praised "the great educational, christianizing and civilizing benefits" that the missionaries had brought about in that country.[55] It was his understanding of the missionary benefit to US foreign relations that made him nominate John Mott of the YMCA and Student Volunteer Movement as minister to China (Mott declined the appointment).[56] It should be no surprise, then, that when Wilson decided that the time had come to declare war, his description of the ideal world order and the US role within it resonated deeply with missionaries and their supporters.

As he addressed Congress on April 2, 1917, Wilson laid out the "motives and objects" of the United States in this fight. Americans would go to war to "vindicate the principles of peace and justice," which Wilson believed could only be maintained through "a partnership of democratic nations." Americans had no "selfish ends to serve," Wilson argued. "We desire no conquest, no dominion." Rather, they were fighting because "the world must be made safe for democracy." Americans would fight, too, for "the rights and liberties of small nations"—a claim that would raise the hopes of Armenians and others around the world that Wilson's vision of political self-determination would include them.[57]

In churches across the country, including the mainline and evangelical Protestant churches that supported foreign missions, US Christians generally embraced Wilson's call to arms. Wilson's own religious worldview emerged regularly as he described America's war aims and his hopes for the eventual peace. Through this war, he argued, providence had provided the United States with an opportunity "to show the world that she was born to save mankind."[58] Such a framing of America's role in the world echoed the patriotism of missionaries throughout the prior century.

Missionaries, too, supported America's entry into the war. Missionary Mrs. Douglas, in Tehran, wrote to the United States of the pride she felt when she learned that the United States had joined the war: "We feel so proud that our country has taken her rightful place among the nations to fight for righteousness and permanent peace."[59] The committee at the head of *Woman's Work*, a Presbyterian missionary magazine, showed their own pride in their country by investing one thousand dollars of the magazine's reserve fund toward a Liberty Bond. It was, they felt, "the duty of every Christian woman to back the Government of the United States in this way to the very utmost of her ability. In one way or another we are *all* in the war."[60]

Even before the United States entered the fight, missionaries began to use militaristic language to describe their work: the missionary lectures at a 1916 conference were referred to as "bugle calls from mission fields."[61] Missionaries embraced Wilson's internationalist vision and insisted that the war would ultimately further their larger goals. John Mott explained his support for the war simply, echoing Wilson's framing of the transformative effects of the peace that would follow. "At the close of the War there will be an unparalleled opportunity for reconstruction," he explained in 1917. The postwar era would be a moment of "incalculable plasticity." And the civilizing and humanitarian work that missionaries had long dedicated themselves to would, he assumed, be at the center of that reconstruction.[62] One missionary in Asia insisted that the defeat of Germany would be a tremendous boon to world missions. If more Americans understood this, he wrote, "there would not be a pacifist among them."[63]

Despite this enthusiasm, the war years presented challenges for mission work around the world. Prices went up. Communication became more challenging. Men who might have served as missionaries became soldiers instead.[64] Missionary societies across the country were insistent that they supported the overall goals of the war, and that their work was essential to both the war effort and the even more important reconstruction that would follow. The ABCFM urged its supporters not to "be drawn into any attitude of rivalry or competition" between mission work and the war effort.[65] Woman's Work appealed to its readers to "think a minute" about how to balance their support for the war effort with their support for missions: "Are YOU sacrificing for War Relief, or Are you asking your Missionary Magazine to sacrifice?" If you had to ask "the Red Cross or the Missionary Society—Which?" the magazine answered enthusiastically, "Both!"[66]

Missionaries were quick to remind their supporters that the realization of Wilson's grand vision would require the mission movement to act as an auxiliary to the war effort. "Certainly no organization is more vitally concerned with the American ideal which underlies our declaration of war than the American Board, which has been preaching and inculcating justice, humanity, and peace for over a century," the Missionary Herald appealed in its May issue. The only way to secure worldwide democracy and peace would be to support missionary work, Barton wrote. He claimed the full agreement of the president and the State Department in this assessment.[67]

While missionaries were not "political agents," Barton and the ABCFM took pride in the way that missionaries had helped to inspire "striking moral reforms" around the world through "the leadership of men and women trained in mission institutions." As the "confidential advisers of ambassadors, ministers, and consuls," missionaries had provided the kind of advice that was "helpful to sound, sane, and fraternal international relations."[68] These ideas were echoed in publication after publication. In *Woman's Work*, Mrs. Dwight H. Day wrote about the importance of convincing people that "the high purposes of the war positively cannot be achieved unless Christian principles are established among the nations of the world."[69]

However, missionaries and their supporters worried about what would happen to the US mission in Turkey. Since the Ottoman Empire and Germany were allied, would the United States go to war with the Turks? The other allied powers had done so. But missionaries and their supporters were sure that this would have grave effects. In the *Missionary Herald*, the answer to the question, "Should the United States declare war against Turkey and Bulgaria?" was "unqualifiedly and emphatically, 'No.'" The risks to the missionaries and the relief work they had undertaken were simply too great. And because the United States claimed that it had not entered the war out of aggression, it was "morally bound to limit its field of warfare to the utmost."[70] James Barton and Cleveland Dodge used their positions on the American Committee for Armenian and Syrian Relief and as advisors to President Wilson to urge the government to remain neutral toward Turkey, even as it declared war against Germany.[71] The *New York Tribune* went so far as to call the missionary lobby the "silent unofficial Cabinet" that was advising President Wilson on these matters.[72]

There were practical reasons for not going to war with Turkey. Most pressingly, the United States did not have a sufficient military force to dedicate to both the western and eastern front of the war.[73] The missionaries had a long list of reasons beyond the practical, and Secretary of State Robert Lansing echoed them in a memo to the chair of the Senate Committee on Foreign Relations. "The interests of the United States in Turkey are very large," he explained. These interests primarily consisted of the missionary institutions that had been built over the past century, with a total value of several millions of dollars. The missionaries themselves (numbering about three hundred in 1917) would also be in "great personal danger" if war was declared before they could leave the country.

Without a declaration of war, however, Lansing believed that the missionaries would be allowed to remain in place and tend to their students, whom Lansing estimated to number around fifty thousand. "As a final observation," he concluded, "it might be added that if we should declare war against Turkey, the Turks would be likely to retaliate by fresh massacres on the Christians and Jews in the Turkish Empire."[74]

The question of whether to declare war against Turkey was a difficult one. Britain and France both wanted the United States to do so, and General Tasker Bliss supported this plan. Former president Theodore Roosevelt loudly urged the United States to declare war on Turkey and Bulgaria in addition to Germany, and Republicans in Congress such as Senator Henry Cabot Lodge were also in favor.

But Secretary Lansing noticed "the failure to recognize the humanitarian side of the question" in these arguments for US belligerence. "Thousands of Armenians and Syrians are being kept alive today by the distribution of supplies purchased through funds sent to our missionaries in Turkey, which amount to one or two millions of dollars a month." While Lansing did not think that this issue should determine the US response, he did feel that it needed to be considered. "If a state of war is declared," Lansing understood, "that relief will come to an end, our missionaries will be expelled or interned and the great missionary properties will be confiscated."[75]

The United States did not declare war on Turkey, but the Ottoman government ended diplomatic relations with the United States regardless. Upon learning that the embassy would be forced to leave, Ambassador Abram Elkus recalled all the Americans in Turkey to Constantinople in preparation of their evacuation. More than fifty missionaries refused to abandon their posts and chose instead to remain at their stations and continue what missionary and relief work they could still perform, relying on the Swiss embassy for protection in case of emergency. They continued to serve tens of thousands of refugees, making good use of funding raised by ACASR.[76]

Missionary Ammunition and Planning for Peace

Missionary Ammunition began publication in 1916. The idea behind the series was much the same as had inspired publishers of missionary intelligence in the previous century: to encourage missionary enthusiasm by providing information to pastors and congregants about the world and the work of foreign missionaries.[77] But the language was new. This was not just missionary *intelligence*. Missionary *ammunition* implied that the pastors who read it were at battle. They were fighting against many of the same forces that they had struggled with for generations—apathy, localism. The Great War presented a new foe, even before the United States officially entered the fight. American missionaries were fighting for their place in the new world order, hoping to define the war and the US response to it in ways that would advance their cause and their vision.

The war itself brought Americans face to face with an unprecedented death toll and the horrors of trench warfare. By its end, more than a hundred thousand Americans had died, but this was nothing in comparison to the toll on their European counterparts. For some, the war challenged the basic premise that had undergirded a century of missionary diplomacy: the superiority of Western Christian civilization. What was the value of that civilization, really, if all of Europe seemed determined to kill each other?

In 1918, *Missionary Ammunition* took up the theme of "The War Test." In thirty-two short essays and prayers—by authors including political figures such as Woodrow Wilson and missionary leaders like John Mott, James Barton, and Robert Speer—the volume asked what the obligations of missionaries were during war. The "so-called Christian countries of Europe and North America," Mott explained with biting sarcasm, were in the midst of the most destructive war the world had ever seen. J. H. Oldham explained that "so complete an overturning of the established order cannot leave men's thoughts about Christianity unchanged."[78] But missionaries remained optimistic, insisting that "the non-Christian people themselves are coming to see that the type of Christianity which our missionaries represent is the only solution of the problems of the world."[79]

The missionaries identified this project with the goals of the United States in the war. The volume included excerpts from Wilson's addresses that defined US war aims as unselfish and humanitarian.[80] The missionary writings echoed this theme and urged America "to keep the flag and the cross close together."[81] Barton wrote about how the war had drawn missionaries closer than ever into diplomatic relations, particularly in Turkey. But even those who worked farther away from the center of fighting were affected. Missionaries, he wrote, "represent the true democracy which recognizes the right of the individual as well as the brotherhood of man." As a result, he was sure that whatever the end of the war would bring, it would require more missionaries to go out and serve.[82]

The war did not only present a crisis, missionaries argued. It also presented an opportunity. When calling for new volunteers in 1918, the ABCFM announced that it "believe[d] in Preparedness," adapting a watchword of the era. But they did not speak of military preparedness, but of *missionary* preparedness. They wanted to be ready for the new fields they hoped would open in the aftermath of war.[83] In 1918, Egbert Smith titled his report on the progress of Presbyterian missions "How the Battle Goes" and described the mission field as "the Front" and the United States as the "supply base." Though the war was not yet over, Smith already revealed some of the surprising optimism that many missionaries would bring to the postwar era. The war had changed everything. It brought untold destruction and suffering, but Smith hoped that it was "proving also a powerful promoter of the missionary cause." No longer could anyone focus on "petty" or "provincial" concerns. Instead, people were forced to realize that "world issues are the dominant questions of humanity." More and more, Americans would "eagerly scan the daily record of international developments."[84] The war, in other words, had the potential to draw American attention to the spiritual needs of the world, just as the foreign mission movement had been trying to do for over a century.

By the war's end, this sense of optimism was even more present in the pages of *Missionary Ammunition*. "The war is over! The battle for the ideals of righteousness, justice, and truth has been won," the writers celebrated. The war, further, had created "unparalleled opportunities." And the world needed these missionaries. "The war must be interpreted to the Nations of the World," the writers argued. "They must realize that spiritual forces are more powerful than material, that righteousness exalts a Nation, that Brotherhood and not rivalry must determine international relationships, and that sacrificial service is essential to the world's well-being. These truths are at the heart of the missionary message." The war had been won with armies, but "to keep it won," missionaries were needed.[85] After all, missionaries were "the great peacemakers between the most widely separated, unlike, and menacing nations."[86]

Both men and women were needed for this cause. The Reverend Stephen Corey described the "new thrill" that had come to "American manhood," marked by unselfish sacrifice for "sacred ideals, for human freedom, for the liberation of women and little children."[87] Lucy Peabody urged women, too, to heed the call for service. Women around the world needed to be "fitted for the new world democracy," and would need female missionaries to lead them. "Victory will not come to us," she urged. "We must win it and to win it we must have first a united campaign. We must recognize the necessity of working together, of praying together, and of presenting together the plan for the salvation of the women of the world."[88]

As the war ended, Wilson decided to travel to Europe himself to take part in the peace negotiations. He was the first sitting US president to travel to Europe, marking the start of a new era in US diplomacy. But the missionary diplomacy that had defined US interests in Turkey continued. As he prepared, Wilson asked Barton, Dodge, and some missionaries working in the Ottoman Empire to advise him. Barton's reports again emphasized that the only way to address the problems in Turkey was to spread Christianity there.

Missionaries greeted the peace with gratitude and optimism. "Turkey has surrendered," the *Missionary Herald* reported. "Her peoples are free from the yoke of their hated rulers." The time had come to "take up the work of rendering intelligent relief, of restoring and stimulating agriculture and industrial arts, and of heartening the several races to be found in the land, to reestablish themselves and to develop their life."[89] It was their dearest hope that the United States would be able to play a central role in the region after the Great War.[90] But this would be an uphill battle. Diplomatically, there was little that the Wilson administration was able to do to protect Armenia. When the Armenians declared the creation of a new republic in May of that year, the United States did not even recognize its independence.[91]

During the peace negotiations, the Great Powers faced the challenging question of what to do with the colonies and territories of their defeated foes. For the same reason that Americans had resisted independence in the Philippines in 1898, the Allies regarded the unrestricted independence of these former colonies as unwise. The people were not ready for self-government; Wilson explained that they were "not yet able to stand by themselves under the strenuous conditions of the modern world." They needed guidance, and the solution to this problem would be the creation of mandated powers responsible to the League of Nations that would prepare the country for true independence. This would be a "sacred trust of civilization," with a more powerful country providing varying degrees of oversight for these new and weaker countries.[92]

Religious freedom was one of several rights that Wilson hoped the mandates would guarantee. Since Wilson and many other American observers considered the Armenian Genocide to have been primarily religiously motivated, it was essential that the religious freedom of

minority groups would be guaranteed in the future. Religious freedom, Wilson believed, would be one way to prevent future conflicts,
atrocities, and warfare. But the old challenge of missionary definitions of religious freedom continued: What did religious freedom
mean, and who could claim it? The planned guarantees of religious
freedom that would shape the mandate system focused on two groups:
religious minorities, who should be granted freedom of conscience;
and Christian missionaries, who should be granted the freedom to go
about their business of building schools and hospitals, publishing,
and evangelizing.[93]

Among the countries that would need a mandated power was Armenia. The peace conference would not seat any Armenian delegates, leaving the fate of the new country in the hands of other powers. As Wilson
would explain to Armenian leaders, they could not join the negotiations
until they were recognized as members of the community of nations.
Left unstated was the fact that Wilson, and many other political leaders,
would not be willing to recognize the country until it had undergone a
period of oversight and modernization.[94] Wilson and the missionaries
hoped that the United States would accept this responsibility. In fact, he
told Cleveland Dodge, he had "set [his] heart on seeing this Government
accept the mandate for Armenia." It seemed to Wilson that the duty was
"plainly marked out for us." The question was only how to secure public
support.[95]

First, Wilson understood, he would have to get Americans to accept
the planned League of Nations. In 1919, Wilson returned from Europe
and began the hard task of convincing Americans that the League of
Nations was the only possible solution to the problems that had led to
the Great War.[96] To gain support for his plan, Wilson repeatedly invoked
Armenia alongside other small nations that he feared would be at risk of
destruction without the international protection of the League and the
mandate system it would create. "You poured out your money to help
succor Armenians after they suffered," he reminded a crowd in Boston.
"Now set up your strength so that they shall never suffer again."[97] In
Kansas City, he described one of the major war aims as "to see that helpless peoples were nowhere in the world put at the mercy of unscrupulous
enemies and masters" as the Armenians had been.[98] And to members
of the Democratic National Committee, he explained that Americans
"know more about Armenia and its sufferings than they know about
any other European area," not only because of the recent atrocities, but
because of a longstanding missionary interest in the region. "That is a

part of the world where already American influence extends—a saving influence and an educating and an uplifting influence." This was the sort of influence that Wilson hoped the United States might have on the world at large.[99]

As the political debates over the League of Nations continued, the suffering of Armenians continued as well, and US missionaries and humanitarians continued to serve them. Wilson made a public appeal at the end of 1918 for Americans to contribute to relief efforts, and Near East Relief collected $20 million the following year.[100] A delegation from Near East Relief in 1919 reported more than 500,000 refugees in the Caucuses. Aid continued to be desperately needed.[101] Missionaries who had been forced to abandon their posts were now beginning to return, and they reported horrible situations in the aftermath of war and genocide. As missionary Minnie B. Mills explained in Smyrna, the challenge that missionaries now faced was "what to do with all these children and young women, who have been the victims of such evil deeds, and how to save them from further unhappiness and wrong."[102] The Reverend Nesbitt Chambers, in Adana, echoed this image of dire suffering as he described the needs of those Armenians who began to return home after four years of exile and suffering. They had faced "indescribably diabolical and inhumanly cruel tortures" in that time and now were "in need of careful and sympathetic treatment with the necessary opportunity for recuperation and reconstruction."[103] Only additional giving from the United States could make it possible to help more and to prevent such dire suffering.

Missionaries were optimistic about the rumors of a potential US mandate in Armenia. In 1919, the *Missionary Herald* shared reports from Paris that suggested that the peace conference was urging the United States to assume this responsibility. Such a choice made sense, due to the longstanding American missionary presence in the region. And though such a move would be daunting, the *Herald* suggested it was necessary for the United States to rise to the challenge. "If there is anything in our talk about the brotherhood of nations," the article urged, "we cannot promptly refuse to act as the Big Brother when we are soberly called upon so to do." America had a duty toward the Armenians and could not shirk it. "Let us not hide in selfishness behind any Monroe Doctrine. America belongs to the world and will evermore; ours is a full-orbed world, not a hemisphere; that at least is settled."[104] Missionaries had been globally active for a century; it was time for their home government to catch up.

The crisis in Armenia created a duty for the United States, missionaries argued. It simply could not leave the country to "work out, unaided, her tremendous problems—social, religious, economic, national. No other country is in a position to render the same service, and we must not hesitate to respond."[105] As one departing missionary reflected, Armenia was "about to leap forward under the blessings of liberty, prosperity, and, it may be, under the protection of the Stars and Stripes."[106] The ABCFM was reluctant to officially take a political stand on the subject, but did avow that "justice demands that the Armenians shall be delivered from the atrocities of Turkish tyranny and misrule."[107]

Both the League and the mandate met with resistance in the Republican-controlled Congress. The primary conflict related to competing visions of the US role in the world and of the implications of international cooperation. But Wilson continued his appeal on behalf of a US mandate in Armenia. In 1920, the Senate passed a resolution congratulating Armenia on its independence in May, and Wilson informed Congress that he believed it was "*providential*," and not merely "coincidence" that on the same day he received a request for the United States to accept the mandate for Armenia. Wilson asked Congress to give him power to accept this mandate, with the expectation that it was the will of the people of the United States. After all, Wilson argued, Americans had sympathized with the Armenians "with extraordinary spontaneity and sincerity" that emerged from "untainted consciences, pure Christian faith, and an earnest desire to see Christian people everywhere succored in their time of suffering, and lifted from their abject *subjection and* distress and enabled to stand upon their feet and take their place among the free nations of the world."[108]

Ultimately, the United States rejected both the League of Nations and the Armenian mandate. In the Senate, the mandate vote was 23 in favor and 52 against.[109] Missionaries and humanitarians continued to work for Armenia regardless; Near East Relief remained active through the 1920s. In fifteen years, it spent $116 million in aid, serving more than a million refugees, educating 132,000 orphans, training 200 nurses, and building hundreds of miles of roads. The development work that missions had long undertaken continued under this mantle, introducing modern Western agricultural practices to the region alongside healthcare and education.[110]

These missionaries and humanitarians continued to promote US engagement with the cause through the creation of Golden Rule Sunday, the first Sunday in December. On this day, families were urged to eat simple fare like what might be served in an orphanage and to donate to Near East Relief. The Golden Rule was emerging as a nonsectarian ethos that Americans believed united all faith traditions. Because it was not specific to any particular religious group, it was presented as a civic idea as much as it was a religious one. Golden Rule Sunday quickly took off, with international participation and broad enthusiasm in the United States. Donors received letters from Presidents Coolidge and Wilson, in addition to governors, senators, and members of cabinet. Local schools and merchants sponsored connected events, which might feature Near East Relief promotional films or guest speakers alongside the simple fare.[111] The event's goal was nothing short of bringing together people from over fifty countries to try to envision a new world order in the aftermath of war.

The missionary movement emerged from the Great War secure in the righteousness of their country and of their churches. Yet under the surface, cracks were beginning to show. The connections that missionaries had made to humanitarian organizations provided new venues for Americans who were interested in serving the needs of others around the world. And for all that missionary leaders insisted that the church was stronger than ever, the horrors of war would profoundly challenge US Protestant denominations. Further, the rejection of the League of Nations brought the United States into a new period of conflict over its role in the world. The internationalist vision that missionaries had hoped the war would usher in was, in fact, defeated.

What that would mean for future of missionary diplomacy, only time would tell.

Epilogue
A New Generation

Among the US soldiers who died fighting the Great War was a young Chinese American man named Alexander Amador Eça da Silva Kin.[1] Kin had been born in Honolulu in 1895 and was educated in California and New York before he enlisted. His mother had hoped that he would return with her to China as an adult. Before they could plan that trip, they tried to secure proof of his US citizenship—no easy task in the era of Chinese Exclusion. As his mother described her own history of extensive travels between the United States, China, and Japan to the US officials, one thing was clear: Dr. Yamei Kin spent much of her life building connections between the United States and Asia.

As a child, Kin's travels were determined by the work of her adopted father: Divie Bethune McCartee, the Presbyterian missionary diplomat. As McCartee's career took his family from China to Japan to the United States and back again, Kin followed. When she was a teenager, however, it was her career that brought the family to America. Following in her father's footsteps, she became a medical missionary. She was one of the first Chinese women to earn a medical degree in the United States, and she put it to good use.

Like McCartee, Kin had a career that was eclectic and wide ranging. She is now best remembered for introducing Americans to the soybean through USDA-sponsored research in 1917, but she also carried on her parents' medical missionary work in China and Japan and was a celebrated lecturer in the United States. In China, she worked as a hospital director and founded a nursing school in Tientsin, the site of the missionary troubles that had spread rumors about the predatory nature of Western medicine. Armed with a letter of introduction from President Theodore Roosevelt, she garnered local support from the viceroy for her new school in China.[2] Like many missionary women, she toured the United States to lecture American women about the conditions of women in foreign lands.[3]

Unlike those missionary peers, however, she was not a citizen of the United States. She was born in China to Chinese parents, and her adoption by US missionaries had not changed her citizenship status. Kin's son, however, was able to claim his citizenship on the basis of his birth in the United States. After his death, he was buried at Arlington National Cemetery in recognition of his service to his country. But his mother traveled under a Chinese passport. In 1904, President Roosevelt apologized in an official letter that he had no power to change this fact, including a handwritten note at the bottom of the typed page offering his services to assist the "dear Doctor" in any way that he could.[4]

It is unclear when Roosevelt had come to know Dr. Kin well enough to call her "dear," but she counted him a friend, and she was well known in reform and society circles in the first decades of the century. The year after her US citizenship was denied, the *New York Times* described Dr. Kin as "the dainty little Chinese woman who has been charming American audiences with her addresses in defense of her people." At that time, she was asked what the Chinese think of Christian missionaries. Her response may have surprised those who knew of her family's background. The poor liked the missionaries: "They live in luxury, pay well, and are kind." But others did not share that high opinion. The "thoughtful" and many officials had "grave mistrust" of the missionaries. After all, "sometimes they meddle with politics."[5] McCartee's daughter knew this as well as anyone.

Dr. Kin's lectures in the United States covered a wide range of topics. During her 1904 tour, she revealed the full range of "missionary intelligence" that a modern woman could provide. Some of the lectures, like one she delivered to society ladies gathered in the Washington home of the mother of a New Jersey senator, focused on the theme "The Chinese Woman." Lectures like this covered domestic life and history, and amused the audience with stories of "henpecked husbands."[6] But she also discussed current political topics as a passionate and astute observer, as when she addressed the League for Political Education on the relations between China and Japan or when she was interviewed by the *New-York Tribune*. As she understood it, her task was to "interpret Orient to Occident." Decades after Samuel Wells Williams had taken on this work in his writings, Kin found that it was still a challenge. "The races are so different," she told one reporter. "I do not suppose it will ever be possible for Americans to understand the Chinese or for the Chinese to understand the Americans." Like generations of missionaries before her, though, she had to try.[7] By 1911, the *Los Angeles Times* described her as "one of the most extraordinary women in the world today," partly because "she understands the politics of the Far East as few others, men or women, and this fact is recognized, not by her government alone, but by the representatives of other governments."[8]

With the coming of the Great War, Kin's addresses frequently turned to two subjects: peace and soybeans. Her discussions of soy emerged from a similar impulse that had guided her earlier work: teaching the United States about Asian culture and helping Americans to understand the various gifts that Asia had to share. Soy, a key part of the Chinese diet, had much to offer Americans. An efficient, high-protein food, it had tremendous potential to transform the American diet. The US government agreed and sponsored her research in China.

But even as food science occupied much of Kin's attention, the war pulled at her heart. Her son enlisted. As she told one reporter, he was "doing his bit," and she wanted to do hers, too. After his death, she spent the rest of her life in China in relative seclusion. Her days of touring the United States were over. The McCartee tradition of missionary diplomacy—of combining service to God with service to America's global mission—was left to be continued by a new generation and new families.

After the war, changes in both US governance and the mission movement transformed [missionary diplomacy.] Twentieth-century pluralism, ecumenism, and cosmopolitanism all challenged the legacy of nineteenth-century confidence that missionaries and diplomats were ultimately in service of similar goals. After several decades of missionary troubles, nationalist and imperialist conflicts, and a world war, American observers and missionaries alike understood the relationship between missions and the US government differently than they had at the beginning of the foreign mission movement.

But Protestant missions, they understood, still had the potential to advance US interests. Missionary leadership in education and medicine, like the work of Dr. Kin and her many American peers, could advance humanitarian interests while also encouraging positive associations with the United States. Missionary colleges like Robert College and the American University Beirut remain to this day as lasting testaments of this earlier era of missionary diplomacy. Well into the twentieth century, missionaries could still serve as key figures in the exchange of intelligence between the United States and their mission fields. In these roles, missions enjoyed at least some support from the US government.

On January 28, 1925, President Calvin Coolidge took to the stage of the Washington Auditorium in Washington, DC, to address an audience of five thousand. It was the opening day of the Foreign Missions Conference of North America, and Coolidge had been invited to speak to the men and women from eighty-five missionary organizations in the United States and Canada who had gathered together for "information and inspiration." No major decisions were to be made over the six days of the conference. It was, rather, a purely educational event. The goal was to "enlarge the interest and deepen the conviction of the Christian people at the home base as to their foreign mission responsibilities and obligations."[9]

The convention's location in Washington made it easy to highlight the long connections between the mission movement and the US government. In a *New York Times* article advertising the event, the journalist made sure to note that the opening prayer would be delivered by former president Warren Harding's pastor.[10] Coolidge was not the first president who had addressed this sort of gathering. Twenty-five years earlier, Benjamin Harrison had served as honorary chairman of the Ecumenical Missionary Conference in New York, which Theodore Roosevelt and William McKinley also addressed.[11] The political presence was symbolic. Presidents and former presidents attended to indicate their approval of the mission movement and a generalized understanding of shared goals between the missions and the government.

Coolidge's address drew the audience's attention to the moment in which they were living: one in which there was "need for a revival of faith" and a "renewal of the spirit of brotherhood." In the aftermath of world war, there were new duties imposed on what Coolidge called "the Christian nations" of the world. In both "an intensely practical as well as a highly spiritual sense," those countries had been "charged with a great trust for civilization." Coolidge echoed what missionary diplomats and government officials had long argued: that the spread of Christianity around the world advanced important secular goals, including charity and benevolence, education, science, and industry. Christianity was, he insisted "a highly practical, as well as a profoundly spiritual mode of life."[12]

But Coolidge was not only celebratory. His address also noted, if vaguely, the negative impacts that missions could have. The important thing, he told his audience, was to embrace "true Christianity" and to approach the world with a spirit of "liberalism," "toleration," and "brotherhood." Missionaries should go out "into the twilight places of the world" and be open to learning new things that might transform and improve life in the United States. Missionary work, in other words, was not just about remaking the world in the image of American Protestantism. It could also transform the United States. There was, or there ought to be, some aspect of give-and-take.[13]

Coolidge was not the only one to come to this realization. Many missionaries agreed. Bishop Herbert Welch, a missionary in Japan, agreed that President Coolidge had spoken with "absolute accuracy" when he acknowledged negative consequences of Western influence. Welch told the conference that Americans needed to remember the weapons, the "vulgar films," and the drugs that had "been almost forced upon the Far East," as well as "the rum that went with our Bibles." Missionaries needed to come to terms with this darker side of their impact on the world. The West was not inherently superior to the East; US Christians had much that they could learn from the peoples and cultures they had set out to convert.[14]

By the mid-1920s, this cosmopolitan outlook was becoming a theme in some Protestant missionary circles. While James Barton was planning the Washington conference, Arthur Judson Brown of the Presbyterian Board of Foreign Missions had been hard at work planning the International Peace through Religion Conference that would meet in Geneva in 1928. Their goal was not comparison, but collaboration. Much like Golden Rule Sunday, the organizers and participants emphasized the points that various faith traditions had in common in the hopes of promoting peace and unity.[15]

The 1920s did not mark the end of mission diplomacy, but they certainly witnessed its transformation. The debates over the value of missions had left their mark, as had the disruptions of the first world war. But equally important, the US government profoundly transformed the machinery of US diplomacy during these years. The consular reforms that had begun to shift missionaries' relationship to the state at the end of the nineteenth century did not stop there.[16] In 1924, the Rogers Act combined the consular and diplomatic branches into a single US Foreign Service and marked the culmination of these decades of professionalization.[17] A new era had dawned.

In November of that year, Robert Speer of the Presbyterian Board of Foreign Missions wrote to Secretary of State Charles Hughes in the hopes that the US government might make a statement about religious freedom in Persia after a vice consul had been killed in that country. But Speer would be disappointed. While Hughes acknowledged the humanitarian concerns that motivated Speer, he would not push the government to take action. After all, as he reminded Speer, "The civil and religious rights of foreigners in their own countries are subjects concerning which the governments of those countries are not disposed to receive suggestions from other governments." This was not a matter for US intervention.[18]

Such a response from the State Department would have been much less likely several decades earlier. Hughes had to balance many concerns—protection of the American missionaries in the region among them. Pushing the Persian government to make a firm statement of support of religious toleration at a moment when they were already working together to bring the vice consul's killers to justice seemed unnecessary and unproductive.

Speer and his colleagues in the mission movement would continue to push their government in this way in the decades to come. After a century of cooperation, the mission movement had good reason to expect that they would find a friendly reception in the State Department. Though they did not always receive the responses that they wished for, they could expect respectful treatment and an attentive ear. The government continued to see missionaries as potential partners in their work around the world, particularly when regions that had long histories of missionary action became the subject of new diplomatic importance, as occurred during the Second World War.[19] Over the twentieth century, as humanitarianism and development work came to define more of US foreign policy, missionaries would continue to be a valuable resource to the American state.

The question of how far the US government could—or should—go to protect Protestant missionaries when they face troubles overseas remains unresolved. The missionary insistence that religious freedom ought to be a defining priority of US foreign relations was eventually enshrined in the 1998 International Religious Freedom Act, even if American Christians, the US government, and foreign governments can still disagree about how "religious freedom" ought to be defined.[20]

Modern-day American missionaries look very different from the missionary diplomats of the nineteenth century. Since 2000, approximately a million Americans annually take part in short-term service trips overseas—numbers that would have awed the leaders of nineteenth-century missionary organizations.[21] Programs like the Peace Corps have created government-sponsored secular options for Americans wanting to transform the world through development. Some evangelical Protestants follow in the footsteps of their nineteenth-century forebears by continuing to push against the boundaries of where they might be welcome—seeking out communities that have not yet been exposed to Western evangelical Christians. And sometimes, when they do, they get into trouble, as John Allen Chau did when he was killed in North Sentinel Island, India, in 2018. Although the US media largely concluded that Chau was a troublemaker who had ignored good sense and caused his own demise when he knowingly approached a community that did not welcome Christian evangelism, missionary Andrew Brunson received very different treatment from the press and politicians.

Brunson was not breaking the rules in the same way that Chau did when he was arrested after two decades in Turkey on vague charges of connections to a military coup. His imprisonment set off a diplomatic crisis, with the State Department only able to secure his release after two years of negotiations. The photo of Brunson kneeling in the Oval Office and praying with President Donald Trump accompanied news reports of the reception at the White House celebrating the missionary's safe return home. At the event, Senator Richard Burr of North Carolina described Brunson's work—"to spread the word of Jesus Christ"—as "a foundational thing about this country, the United States." Such a message should remind us that the many legacies of missionary diplomacy run deep.[22]

Notes

Prologue

1. Divie Bethune McCartee to Franklin Knight, Ningpo, Nov. 30, 1858. MFP, Folder 4.

2. Divie Bethune McCartee to Franklin Knight, Ningpo, China, July 13, 1860. MFP, Folder 4.

3. Haddad, *America's First Adventure in China*, ch. 8.

4. Divie Bethune McCartee to Franklin Knight, Ningpo, China, July 13, 1860. MFP, Folder 4.

5. No. 10 C. K. Stribling, Shanghai, May 28, 1861. MFP, Folder 3.

6. Anson Burlingame to D. B. McCartee, Peking, Feb. 20, 1865. Copy enclosed with No. 100 Anson Burlingame to William H. Seward, Legation of the United States, Peking, March 7, 1865. MFP, Folder 3.

7. McCartee, "Dr. McCartee's Reminiscences," 403.

8. Speer, *A Missionary Pioneer in the Far East*, 96.

9. Josephy Leidy, "Report of the Curators for 1850," *Proceedings of the Academy of Natural Sciences of Philadelphia* 5 (1850–1851), 130–131; "Aug. 26," *Proceedings of the Academy of Natural Sciences of Philadelphia* 8 (1856), 152, 154; "Sept. 8, 1857," *Proceedings of the Academy of Natural Sciences of Philadelphia* 9 (1857), 179.

10. Walter Hough, "Thumb Marks," *Science* 8, no. 185 (Aug. 20, 1886): 166–167.

11. On the American Oriental Society: Charles Folsom, "Additions to the Library and Cabinet of the American Oriental Society," *Journal of the American Oriental Society* 4 (1854), vi; "From a Letter from Rev. D. B. McCartee, M.D., of Ningpo," *Journal of the American Oriental Society* 5 (1855–1856), 260–262; "Proceedings at Baltimore, Oct. 29 and 30th, 1884," *Journal of the American Oriental Society* 11 (1885), cciv. On the American Geographical Society: "Additions to the Library and Map-Room, 1884," *Journal of the American Geographical Society of New York* 16 (1884), li.

12. Divie Bethune McCartee to Franklin Knight, Ningpo, April 21, 1854. MFP, Folder 4.

13. Divie Bethune McCartee to Henry Rankin, New York, Nov. 29, 1880. MFP, Folder 5. "Mixed Court," *The North-China Herald and Supreme Court and Consular Gazette* (May 26, 1877), 526; "Mixed Court," *The North-China Herald and Supreme Court and Consular Gazette* (June 23, 1877), 623; "Mixed Court," *The North-China Herald and Supreme Court and Consular Gazette* (July 14, 1877), 43.

14. Divie Bethune McCartee to Henry Rankin, New York, July 18, 1883; New York, Sept. 2, 1883; Divie Bethune McCartee to Samuel Wells Williams, New York, Oct. 13, 1883. MFP, Folder 5.

15. Divie Bethune McCartee to Henry Rankin, Washington, June 15, 1885. MFP, Folder 5.

16. Divie Bethune McCartee to Henry Rankin New York, June 21, 1884. MFP, Folder 5.

17. Divie Bethune McCartee to Henry Rankin, Tokyo, Feb. 23, 1897. MFP, Folder 5.

18. Divie Bethune McCartee to Henry W Rankin, San Francisco, Jan. 19, 1900. MFP, Folder 5

19. David Murray, "Divie Bethune McCartee MD: Pioneer Missionary in China and Japan," *NY Observer and Chronicle* (July 17, 1902), 73–74; Henry W. Rankin to Dr. David Murray, E. Northfield, Mass. Nov. 12, 1901, RFP, Box 1, Folder 22.

20. Henry W. Rankin to Dr. David Murray, E. Northfield, Mass. Nov. 12, 1901. RFP, Box 1, Folder 22.

21. Henry W. Rankin to Peter McCartee, Esq, E. Northfield, Mass., Dec. 16, 1901. RFP, Box 1, Folder 22.

22. For examples of work that focuses on this turn-of-the-century period as foundational, see for example Hollinger, *Protestants Abroad*; Preston, *Sword of the Spirit*; Curtis, *Holy Humanitarians*.

Part I

1. Matthew 28:19, King James Version.

1. Politicians

1. John Quincy Adams (JQA) Diary, Vol. 50 (February 28 and March 4, 1827); "American Missionaries at the Sandwich Islands," *North American Review* (January 1, 1828), 59–111.

2. Stewart, *Private Journal*. By 1839, the US printing was in a fifth, enlarged, edition.

3. JQA Diary, Vol. 50 (4 March 1827).

4. JQA Diary, Vol. 37 (22 March 1828; 28 March 1828).

5. Jonas King, quoted in Haines, *Jonas King*, 188.

6. JQA Diary, Vol. 37 (6 April 1828).

7. Matthew 13:38.

8. January 6, 1839, in Adams, ed. *Memoirs of John Quincy Adams*, 90–91.

9. Edel, *Nation Builder*.

10. Georgini, *Household Gods*, 47.

11. See, for example, JQA Diary, Vol. 35 (7 February 1824); and JQA Diary, Vol. 50 (8 March 1827).

12. JQA Diary, Vol. 31 (28 June 1819 and 8 October 1819).

13. JQA Diary, Vol. 36i (12 January 1829).

14. JQA Diary, Vol. 37 (28 May 1827).

15. JQA Diary, Vol. 37 (18 March 1828).

16. House of Representatives, 27th Congress, 3rd Session, Rep. No. 93, 2–3 (January 24, 1843).

17. Shoemaker, *Pursuing Respect in the Cannibal Isles*; Saunt, *West of the Revolution*, 209.

18. Lazich, "American Missionaries and the Opium Trade."

19. Whipple, *Relation of the American Board of Commissioners*, 20–21.

20. Adams, ed. *Memoirs of John Quincy Adams*, Vol. 10 (entry dated January 9, 1840), 188.

21. On information sources for American media coverage of the Opium Wars, see Norwood, *Trading Freedom*, ch. 4.

22. Quoted in Batson, "American Diplomats in Southeast Asia," 39–112.

23. Gulick, *Peter Parker*, ch. 3; Haddad, *America's First Adventure in China*.

24. Gulick, *Peter Parker*, ch. 6.

25. Gulick, *Peter Parker*, 98–99.

26. Adams, ed. *Memoirs of John Quincy Adams*, Vol. 10 (entry dated March 15, 1841), 444–445.

27. Gulick, *Peter Parker*, ch. 7.

28. Adams, ed. *Memoirs of John Quincy Adams*, Vol. 11 (entry dated June 2, 1842), 166–167.

29. Lazich, *E. C. Bridgman*, ch. 5.

30. Gulick, *Peter Parker*, 98–99.

31. Gulick, *Peter Parker*, ch. 8.

32. Rufus Anderson, quoted in Lazich, *E. C. Bridgman*, 222.

33. Haddad, *America's First Adventure in China*, 151–152: Lazich, *E. C. Bridgman*, ch. 5.

34. Gulick, *Peter Parker*, Ch. 8.

35. Quoted in Lazich, *E. C. Bridgman*, 10.

36. Adams, ed. *Memoirs of John Quincy Adams*, Vol. 12, 227.

37. John Quincy Adams, "Speech to the U.S. House of Representatives on Foreign Policy" (July 4, 1821), https://millercenter.org/the-presidency/presidential-speeches/july-4-1821-speech-us-house-representatives-foreign-policy.

38. Fitz, *Our Sister Republics*.

39. Walther, *Sacred Interests*, ch. 1; Santelli, *The Greek Fire*.

40. On the Islamophobia in US discussions of Greece, see Walther, *Sacred Interests*, ch. 1.

41. Treaty of Peace and Friendship, Signed at Tripoli, November 4, 1796, https://avalon.law.yale.edu/18th_century/bar1796t.asp.

42. Edel, *Nation Builder*.

43. On the early missions in the Ottoman Empire, see Heyrman, *American Apostles*; Walther, *Sacred Interests*, ch. 1.

44. Jonas King quoted in Haines, *Jonas King*, 188.

45. Haines, *Jonas King*, ch. 13.

46. "Greece: The President of Greece to Mr. Evarts," *Missionary Herald* (Feb. 1830), 41–47; "Letters from the Government," *Missionary Herald* (September 1831), 277–278.

47. Repousis, "The Trojan Women," 445–476; Boonshoft, *Aristocratic Education*; Kelley, *Learning to Stand and Speak*; Neem, *Democracy's Schools*.

48. "Missionary Intelligence: Greece," *Episcopal Recorder* (March 30, 1833), 207.

49. "Missionary Intelligence: Domestic and Foreign Missionary Society," *Episcopal Recorder* (July 28, 1832), 67.

50. Adams, ed. *Memoirs of John Quincy Adams,* Vol. 8 (entry dated March 28, 1830), 209–210. Adams records the preacher as Rev. Robinson, but this seems likely to be an error on his part.

51. JQA Diary, Vol. 31 (24 February 1819).

52. Daggar, *Cultivating Empire.*

53. On missionaries and the Cherokee, see, for example, McLoughlin, *Cherokees and Missionaries*; McLoughlin, *Cherokee Renascence;* Conroy-Krutz, *Christian Imperialism*, ch. 5. On US Indian policy in this era, see Satz, *American Indian Policy.*

54. On McCoy, see Mills, *The World Colonization Made,* ch. 3; Snyder, *Great Crossings*, 126–127.

55. JQA Diary, Vol. 37 (23 January 1828).

56. JQA Diary, Vol. 50 (8 March 1827). On Adams and US Indian policy, see Parsons, "A Perpetual Harrow Upon My Feelings."

57. Evarts, *Cherokee Removal;* Portnoy, *Their Right to Speak*; Hershberger, "Mobilizing Women."

58. *Cherokee Nation v. Georgia*, 30 U.S. 5 Pet. 1 1 (1831); *Worcester v. Georgia*, 31 U.S. 6 Pet. 515 515 (1832).

59. Adams, ed. *Memoirs of John Quincy Adams*, Vol. 8, 491–492. Entry dated March 11, 1832.

60. On slavery and expansion, see Greenberg, *A Wicked War;* Karp, *This Vast Southern Empire.*

61. Adams, ed. *Memoirs of John Quincy Adams*, Vol. 12 (entry dated July 7, 1845), 201–202.

62. Quoted in Pinheiro, *Missionaries of Republicanism*, 131.

63. "America," *Missionary Herald* (February 1841), 80.

64. "Baptist Home Missionary Society," *Missionary Herald* (June 1845), 208; "Methodist Episcopal Missionary Society," *Missionary Herald* (July 1845), 245. The Methodists reported significant growth in Texas: only three missionaries had been in the region in 1842. In 1845, they counted more than sixty-five preachers and more than fifty missionaries serving churches with 5,085 white and 1,005 "colored" members.

65. See, for example, "American Bible Society," *Missionary Herald* (June 1845), 210; "American Bible Society," *Missionary Herald* (June 1844), 209; "American Bible Society," *Missionary Herald* (July 1848), 242; "American Tract Society," *Missionary Herald* (July 1848, 242); "American Indian Mission Association," *Missionary Herald* (September, 1851), 314. In 1848, the ABS sent four thousand Bibles to Mexico. Fea, *The Bible Cause,* 70–71; 120–130.

2. Experts

1. Williams, *The Middle Kingdom*, Prologue. For more on Williams's writing of *The Middle Kingdom*, see Haddad, *The Romance of China*, ch. 6.

2. Translation of Title Page, Williams, *The Middle Kingdom*, xi.

3. Williams, *The Middle Kingdom*, xiii; 334.

4. Cayton in Reeves-Ellington et al., *Competing Kingdoms*, 69–93; Moreshead, "Beyond All Ambitious Motives."

5. Laurie, *The Ely Volume*, Appendix.

6. Carl Ritter, quoted in Laurie, *The Ely Volume*, 3.

7. David Greene to Mrs. Lydia Pratt, Boston, Sept. [1838], ABC 1.1, v.10.

8. On knowledge production empire, see Chidester, *Empire of Religion*, ch. 1; Susan Thorne, "Religion and Empire at Home," in Hall and Rose, *At Home with the Empire*, 143–165.

9. "Missionary Concert," *Boston Recorder*, Aug. 24, 1821; "Monthly Concert," *Boston Recorder*, Sept. 1, 1821; "Monthly Concert," *Boston Recorder*, Sept. 29, 1821. These articles were responding to a letter from December 16, 1820.

10. On the false binary between secularism and religion, see, for example, Janet R. Jakobsen and Ann Pellegrini, "Times Like These," in Jakobsen and Pellegrini, *Secularisms*, 1–38. For a discussion of similar dynamics in the publications of the American Tract Society, see Modern, *Secularism in Antebellum America*, ch. 1.

11. Malcolm, "The *Chinese Repository*," 165–178; Rubinstein, "The Wars They Wanted," 271–82.

12. Rouleau, *With Sails Whitening Every Sea*, ch. 4.

13. Haddad, *The Romance of China*, ch. 6; Malcolm, "The Chinese Repository," 165–178; Rubinstein, "The Wars They Wanted," 271–82.

14. Williams, *The Middle Kingdom*, xvi.

15. Williams, *The Middle Kingdom*, xiv–xv.

16. Imprints of the fourth edition can be found from 1859, 1861, 1871, and 1876, with a "revised edition" appearing in the market in 1883. This revised edition saw reprintings in 1883, 1904, 1907, 1945, and beyond.

17. Williams and Williams, *A History of China*.

18. Hayford, "China by the Book," 288; Haddad, *Romance of China*, ch. 6.

19. "The Middle Kingdom," *The United States Magazine and Democratic Review* (April 1848), 319–334.

20. W. J. Eustis, "The Middle Kingdom," *New Englander* (May 1849), 215–229.

21. "Williams' Middle Kingdom," *The Friend, a Religious and Literary Journal* (Feb. 10, 1849), 166–167; "The Middle Kingdom, by S. Wells Williams," *Holden's Dollar Magazine of Criticisms, Biographies, Sketches, Essays, Tales, Reviews, Poetry, etc.* (Feb. 1848), 121.

22. Haddad, *Romance of China*, ch. 6.

23. In Philadelphia, this could be seen in the creation of Nathan Dunn's Chinese Museum. See Haddad, *Romance of China*, ch. 6.

24. Essex Institute, *Books on China in the Library of Essex Institute*.

25. To contrast the holdings of the Athenaeum to that of the Public Library, see *Catalogue of the Library of the Boston Athenaeum* and Boston Public Library, *List of Books*. At the time the catalog was completed, the BPL held some 4,400 books in its total collection.

26. "The Book Trade: A Residence of Eight Years in Persia, among the Nestorian Christians," *The Merchants' Magazine and Commercial Review* (June 1, 1843),

577; "A Residence of Eight Years in Persia," *Graham's Magazine of Literature and Art* (April 1843), 261.

27. Rev. Rhea to President Andrew Johnson, Oroomiah, Persia, June 3, 1854. National Archives, RG 59 M179, Reel 226.

28. Perkins, *A Residence of Eight Years in Persia*, vi–viii.

29. "The Nestorian Christians," *North American Review* 57 (July 1843), 184.

30. Perkins, *Life of Justin Perkins*, 7.

31. "The Nestorian Christians," *North American Review* 57 (July 1843), 171.

32. "The Nestorian Christians," *North American Review* 57 (July 1843), 157.

33. "The Nestorian Christians," *North American Review* 57 (July 1843), 171. Smith and Dwight, *Researches*.

34. "The Nestorian Christians," *North American Review* 57 January 1843), 156–184.

35. "The Nestorian Christians," *North American Review* 57 (January 1843), 156–184.

36. "The Nestorian Christians," *North American Review* 57 (July 1843), 171–172.

37. "The Middle Kingdom," *North American Review* 67 (October 1848), 265–292; "The Nestorian Christians," *North American Review* 57 (July 1843), 171–184.

38. "The Middle Kingdom," *North American Review* 67 (October 1848), 266.

39. Circulation in 1830 was 3,200; by 1880 it would be 7,500 and by 1891, 76,000. Mott, *A History of American Magazines*, 218–261, quote on 232. See also Julius H. Ward, "The North American Review," *North American Review* 201 (Jan. 1915), 123–134; Taketani, "The 'North American Review,'" 111–127; Werner, "Bringing Down Holy Science," 27–42; Spann, "New England and Early Conservationism," 192–207.

40. "The Middle Kingdom," *North American Review* 67 (Oct. 1848), 266.

41. Religious topics would become more important within the *North American Review* beginning in the late-1870s. Mott, *A History of American Magazines*, 252–253.

42. "Brazil and the Brazilians," *North American Review* 85 (Oct. 1857), 533–549.

43. "Voyage of His Majesty's Ship Blonde to the Sandwich Islands . . . Narrative of a Tour through Hawaii . . . Review . . . The Rev. C.S. Stewart's Letters on the Sandwich Islands," *North American Review* 26 (Jan. 1828), 59–112. Ellis's narrative had been reviewed independently two years earlier. "Journal of a Tour Around Hawaii," *North American Review* 22 (Apr. 1826), 334–365.

44. *Memoir of Keopuolani.*

45. "Journal of a Tour around Hawaii, the Largest of the Sandwich Islands," *North American Review* 22 (Apr. 1826), 334–365.

46. "Stewart's Voyage to the South Sea," *North American Review* 33 (Oct. 1831), 484–507; "Anderson's Observations in Greece," *North American Review* 34 (Jan. 1832), 1–23; "Kay's Travels in Caffraria," *North American Review* 39 (Oct. 1834), 371–395; "India, Ancient and Modern," *North American Review* 82 (April 1856), 404–444; "Five Years in Damascus," *North American Review*

83 (July 1856), 30–53; "Grout's Zulu Land," *North American Review* 101 (July 1865), 274–276.

47. "Life of G.D. Boardman," *North American Review* 40 (April 1835), 376–410; "The Life and Letters of Mrs. Emily C. Judson," *North American Review* 92 (Jan. 1861), 269–270; "A Memoir of the Life and Labors of the Rev. Adoniram Judson, DD," *North American Review* 78 (Jan. 1854), 21–67; "Memoir of Rev. David Tappan Stoddard, Missionary to the Nestorians," *North American Review* 87 (Jan. 1859), 228–244.

48. "The Koran," *North American Review* 63 (Oct. 1846), 496–514.

49. "India, Ancient and Modern," *North American Review* 82 (Apr. 1856), 404–444.

50. Allen, *India, Ancient and Modern*, vii.

51. "The Crescent and the Cross," *North American Review* 65 (July 1847), 56–85.

52. "Ten Years on the Euphrates," *North American Review* 107 (Oct. 1868), 648–51.

53. Heyrman, *American Apostles*.

54. "Article III. Voyage of His Majesty's Ship Blonde to the Sandwich Islands. . . Narrative of a Tour through Hawaii. . . Review. . . The Rev. C.S. Stewart's Letters on the Sandwich Islands," *North American Review* 26 (Jan. 1828), 59–60.

55. W. J. Eustis, "The Middle Kingdom," *New Englander* (May 1849), 215.

56. "The Middle Kingdom," *North American Review* 67 (Oct. 1848), 266.

57. Williams, *Chinese Immigration*; Williams, *Our Relations with the Chinese Empire*.

58. W. L. Marcy, Dept. of State, to Hon. Nathaniel P. Banks, Jr., Washington, March 8, 1856, in House of Representatives "Interpreter to the Mission to China," 34th Congress, 1st Session. Ex. Doc. No. 49.

Part II

1. *New York Times* (July 4, 1862), 1.

2. J. G. Kerr, on behalf of US Missionaries at Canton, to Hon. W. H. Seward, Canton, China. July 8, 1862, National Archives, RG 59, M179, Reel 191. Emphasis in original.

3. Rev. Stephen Mattoon, "An Address Delivered at Bangkok on the 4th of July, 1865. The 89th Anniversary of American Independence" (Bangkok: American Missionary Association, Published by request of American Residents, 1865). RG 275.2.7, Presbyterian Historical Society.

4. "Letter from Mr. Smith, Dated Mount Lebanon, September 27, 1834," *Missionary Herald* (Apr. 1835), 136–137.

3. Citizens

1. "An Account of the Visit of the French Frigate L'Artemise," *North American Review* 51 (Oct. 1840), 503–513.

2. Laplace's letters to the American consul and his "manifesto" to Hawai'i were printed in several tracts including [Jones], *Suppliment* [*sic*] *to the Sandwich Island Mirror*, 49–50.

3. "Citizenship of Missionaries," *Christian Observer* (Oct. 1, 1841), 160.

4. "An Account of the Visit of the French Frigate L'Artemise," 505.

5. "An Account of the Visit of the French Frigate L'Artemise," 507.

6. "An Account of the Visit of the French Frigate L'Artemise," 509.

7. "An Account of the Visit of the French Frigate L'Artemise," 511.

8. On the negotiated definitions of American citizenship in the early republic and antebellum maritime world, see Herzog and Román, *Revoking Citizenship*, ch. 2; Hyde, *Civic Longing*, especially Introduction and ch. 1; Scully, *Bargaining with the State*, ch. 1; Perl-Rosenthal, *Citizen Sailors*, ch. 8; Rouleau, *With Sails Whitening Every Sea*, especially 98–99; Raffety, *Republic Afloat*, Part III.

9. On Hawaiian foreign relations in these years, see Arista, *The Kingdom and the Republic*; Thigpen, *Island Queens and Mission Wives*.

10. For an anti-mission perspective that went into great detail about violent attacks on Catholics, see [Jones], *Suppliment*. For a missionary account that admits to the existence of Catholic persecution, see Dibble, *History of the Sandwich Islands*, ch. 11.

11. Anderson, *A Heathen Nation Evangelized*, ch. 20.

12. The king to US Consul P. A. Brinsmade, Kauwila House, Oct. 28, 1839, in Castle, *An Account of the Visit of the French Frigate l'Artemise*, 4–6.

13. Dibble, *History*, 387.

14. [Jones], *Suppliment*.

15. [Jones], *Suppliment*.

16. [Jones], *Suppliment*, 20.

17. [Jones], *Suppliment*, 22. Emphasis in original.

18. [Jones], *Suppliment*, 18. Emphasis in original.

19. Dibble, *History*, 386.

20. [Jones], *Suppliment*, 31–32.

21. Dibble, *History*, 387.

22. The publication included a signed circular, a reprint of Samuel Northup Castle's article from the *Hawai'ian Spectator*, and the correspondence between missionaries, Read, the US consul, and the king. See Castle, *An Account of the Visit of the French Frigate*.

23. Rufus Anderson, "Citizenship of Missionaries and Their Children," in ABCFM Annual Report (1841), 36–38.

24. On the rights of merchants and mariners, see Rouleau, *With Sails Whitening Every Sea*, esp. ch. 4.

25. "Citizenship of Missionaries," *Christian Observer* (Oct. 1, 1841), 160.

26. Williams, "Report from Committee of Chief Justice Williams of Connecticut, Rev. Dr. Tucker, Thomas Bradford, Esq., Rev. T. T. Waterman, Rev. Lyman Strong," in ABCFM Annual Report (1841), 38–39.

27. Anderson and Williams, quoted in ABCFM Annual Report (1841), 36–39.

28. Daniel Webster to David Porter, Department of State, Washington, Feb. 2, 1842, in Shewmaker, ed., *The Papers of Daniel Webster*, Vol. 1, 280.

29. Anderson, *Memorial Volume*, 201.

30. Samuel Turell Armstrong had made a donation in Webster's honor to the American Board as thanks. Webster was "obliged and honored" by this gift, which he accepted "with pleasure." Daniel Webster to Samuel Turell Armstrong, Washington, Feb. 14, 1842, in Shewmaker, ed., *The Papers of Daniel Webster*, Vol. 1, 281.

31. David Porter to Jasper Chasseaud, US Legation, St Steffano, Oct. 14, 1841, in Shewmaker, ed., *The Papers of Daniel Webster*, Vol. 1, 279.

32. Eli Smith, William McClure Thomson, Samuel Wolcott, Nathaniel Abbot Keyes, and Leander Thompson to Jasper Chasseaud, Beyrout, July 20, 1841, in Shewmaker, ed., *The Papers of Daniel Webster*, Vol. 1, 274–277; for a discussion of the Druze and Maronite relationships with American missionaries in these years, see Makdisi, *Artillery of Heaven*, especially chs. 4–6.

33. Eli Smith, William McClure Thomson, Samuel Wolcott, Nathaniel Abbot Keyes, and Leander Thompson to Jasper Chasseaud, Beyrout, July 20, 1841, in Shewmaker, ed., *The Papers of Daniel Webster*, Vol. 1, 274–277.

34. Samuel Turell Armstrong to Daniel Webster, Washington, Jan. 31, 1842, in Shewmaker, ed., *The Papers of Daniel Webster*, Vol. 1, 279.

35. David Porter to Daniel Webster, US Legation, St Steffano, July 16, 1842, in Shewmaker, ed., *The Papers of Daniel Webster*, Vol. 1, 282.

36. "West Africa. Letter from Mr. Wilson, July 25, 1845," The Missionary Herald (Jan. 1846), 25–31; Conroy-Krutz, *Christian Imperialism*, ch. 6.

37. "West Africa. Letter from Mr. Wilson, July 25, 1845," *The Missionary Herald* (Jan. 1846), 25–31.

38. Juvenis, "Rights of Missionaries," *New York Evangelist* (June 22, 1848), 1.

39. On King's early career, see Heyrman, *American Apostles,* ch. 8; and Makdisi, *Artillery of Heaven*, ch. 4. See also Walther, *Sacred Interests*, 54–55.

40. On the Greek revolution, see Walther, *Sacred Interests* ch. 1; and Santelli, *The Greek Fire*, especially chs. 2 and 3.

41. George Marsh to Daniel Webster, Athens, Aug. 21, 1852 in 33rd Congress, 1st Session, Ex Doc 67, 44.

42. ABCFM, *Manual for Missionary Candidates*, 21–22.

43. For King's own telling of these events, see Haines, *Jonas King*, 311–314.

44. Haines, *Jonas King*, 311–314.

45. Anderson, *History of the Missions,* Vol. 1, 279.

46. Haines, *Jonas King*, 197.

47. Haines, *Jonas King*, 248.

48. Haines, *Jonas King*, 117.

49. Haines, *Jonas King*, 299

50. Haines, *Jonas King*, ch. 20.

51. John Henry Hill to Abbot Lawrence, Athens, Apr. 7, 1852 in Shewmaker, ed., *Papers of Daniel Webster*, Vol. 2, 198–200.

52. Shewmaker, ed., *Papers of Daniel Webster*, Vol. 1, 272–282.

53. Marsh to Webster, Gleichenberg, Oct. 9, 1852—enclosing a report written Athens, Aug. 21, 1852, Ex Doc 67, 47.

54. Daniel Webster to George Perkins Marsh, Department of State, Washington, Apr. 29, 1852, in Shewmaker, ed., *Papers of Daniel Webster*, Vol. 2, 202–206.

55. Thomas Scott Williams, quoted in Shewmaker, ed., *Papers of Daniel Webster*, Vol. 2, 204.

56. George P. Marsh to Daniel Webster, Athens, Aug. 21, 1852, in Shewmaker, ed., *Papers of Daniel Webster*, Vol. 2, 206–209.

57. Repousis, "The Devil's Apostle," 807–837.

58. Conroy-Krutz, *Christian Imperialism*, ch. 1. The financial agents in India for the board's early missionaries were all British. The United States had tried to send official consuls to India prior to this period, but when Benjamin Joy, the first American Consul to India, arrived in 1792, he was not recognized by the British government. It was not until the 1860s that the United States had a more reliable consulate in the country.

59. See, for example, Chancellor Woolworth; Hon. Charles Marsh; Walter Hubbell, Esq.; Rev. John W. Ellingwood; Rev. Lewis Bond, in ABCFM Annual Report (1840), 35.

4. Consuls

1. On Thayer's meeting with the viceroy, see Mr. Thayer to Mr. Seward, Alexandria, Aug. 26, 1861, *Religious Toleration in Egypt*, 5.

2. *Religious Toleration in Egypt*, 3–6. On the American mission in Egypt during these years, see Sharkey, *American Evangelicals in Egypt*, ch. 2.

3. *Religious Toleration in Egypt*, 5, 13.

4. Abraham Lincoln to Viceroy Mohammed Said Pacha of Egypt, Washington, Oct. 11, 1861, National Archives, RG 59, Series: Letters to Foreign Sovereigns and Heads of State, 1829–1877, File Unit: Communications to Foreign Sovereigns and States, Vol. 3.

5. Department of State, "List of Ministers, Consuls, and other Diplomatic and Commercial Agents of U.S.," in *Diplomatic and Consular Service of US* (1828, 1830, 1833, 1835, 1839, 1853, 1859).

6. *General Instructions to the Consuls and Commercial Agents of the United States*, 9–12.

7. "American Board of Commissioners for Foreign Missions: Recent Intelligence," *Missionary Herald* (May 1840), 187.

8. "Fuh-Chau: Letter from Mr. Peet, March 24, 1856," *Missionary Herald* (Sept. 1856), 277.

9. Burnet, *The Jerusalem Mission*, 164, 167, 170.

10. Burnet, *The Jerusalem Mission*, 180.

11. Kark, *American Consuls in the Holy Land*, 105; Dr. Barclay, quoted in Burnet, *The Jerusalem Mission*, 146. On Barclay's mission, see Blowers, "Living in a Land of Prophets."

12. On the consular system in general, see Nicole Phelps, "One Service, Three Systems, Many Empires: The US Consular Service and the Growth of US Global Power, 1789–1924," in Hoganson and Sexton, *Crossing Empires*, 135–158.

13. Rouleau, *With Sails Whitening Every Sea*, ch. 4.

14. Caleb Cushing to John C. Calhoun, Sept. 29, 1841 in Seward, *The United States Consulates in China*, 17–18.

15. "Letter from Mr. Maynard, July 4, 1849: The Teacher of the Missionaries," *Missionary Herald* (Nov. 1849), 403–404.

16. "Letter from Mr. Wright, July 4, 1856," *Missionary Herald* (Oct. 1856), 300–303.

17. Seward, *The United States Consulates in China*, 8.

18. Kark, *American Consuls in the Holy Land*, 101–102.

19. See, for example, Rufus Anderson to Lewis Cass, Missionary House, Boston, Mar. 1, 1860, M179, Reel 174; ABCFM Annual Report (1859), 111–115.

20. "Items of Intelligence," *Missionary Herald* (Jan. 1864), 13–14.

21. Batson, "American Diplomats in Southeast Asia in the Nineteenth Century," 39–112.

22. Batson, "American Diplomats in Southeast Asia in the Nineteenth Century," 39–112.

23. Quoted in Batson, "American Diplomats in Southeast Asia in the Nineteenth Century," 50

24. Lord, "Missionaries, Thai, and Diplomats," 413–431.

25. Harris, quoted in Batson, "American Diplomats in Southeast Asia," 51.

26. Margaret Landon to Miss Thomas, Washington DC, August 18, 1945, Mattoon Family Papers.

27. Lord, "Missionaries, Thai, and Diplomats," 413–431.

28. Quoted in Batson, "American Diplomats in Southeast Asia," 66.

29. "Japan: Historical Sketch. Recent Changes," *Missionary Herald* (Feb. 1864), 38. On Japan and religious freedom in the late-nineteenth century, see Thomas, *Faking Liberties*, ch. 1.

30. "Good News from Japan," *The Missionary Magazine* (Feb. 1859), 60–61.

31. "Japan: Historical Sketch. Recent Changes," *Missionary Herald* (Feb. 1864), 38.

32. "Recent Intelligence," *Missionary Herald* (Jan. 1859), 28.

33. "Japan—No. 2," *Missionary Herald* (Mar. 1864), 65–70.

34. This was Episcopal John Liggins, previously of the China mission, then sent to Nagasaki in 1859. "Japan—No. 2," *Missionary Herald* (Mar. 1864), 65–70.

35. "Japan—No. 2," *Missionary Herald* (Mar. 1864), 65–70

36. Paul Bagley to President Johnson, Balto, May 30, 1867. National Archives, RG 59, M179, Reel 258.

37. Quotes from "Missions of the Board: Mission to Japan," *Missionary Herald* (July 1871), 205–208; On missionary responses to Japan, see Nishioka, "Civilizing Okinawa," ch. 2.

38. See, for example: "Extraterritoriality in China," *The Continental Monthly: Devoted to Literature and National Policy* (Nov. 1863), 556–567.

39. Kark, *American Consuls in the Holy Land*, 99–102.

40. "Letter from Mr. Smith, Dated Mount Lebanon, Sept. 27, 1834," *Missionary Herald* (Apr. 1835), 136–137.

41. "Syria. Letter from Mr. Whiting, October 10, 1845," *Missionary Herald* (Feb. 1846), 37–39.

42. Rufus Anderson to Edward Everett, Dec. 1, 1852. Missionary House, Boston, National Archives, RG 59, M179 Roll 134.

43. ABCFM Nov. 11, 1859, National Archives, RG 59, M17, Reel 58.

44. American Board of F. Missions, July 30, 1860, National Archives, RG 59, M17, Reel 59.

45. Kark, *American Consuls in the Holy Land*, ch. 3.

46. "Syria. Mr. Smith's Account of the Rise of Protestantism in Hasbeiya," *Missionary Herald* (Jan. 1845), 14–21.

47. Gulick, *Peter Parker and the Opening of China*, 113.

48. Gulick, *Peter Parker and the Opening of China*, 139–141.

49. On Anderson's broader influences on the mission movement, see Harris, *Nothing but Christ*; and Hutchison, *Errand to the World*, 77–90.

50. See Gulick, *Peter Parker and the Opening of China*, ch. 9.

51. Quoted in Batson, "American Diplomats in Southeast Asia," 52.

52. Kark, *American Consuls in the Holy Land*, 124–126; Evelyn Edson, "An American Missionary's Maps of Jerusalem: Past, Present, and Future," in Kühnel, Noga-Banai, and Vorholt, *Visual Constructs of Jerusalem*, 285–295.

53. H G, "Missionaries and Their Consuls," *The Chinese Recorder and Missionary Journal* (June 1, 1869), 11–13.

54. Peter Parker to Mr. Marcy, Macao, June 14, 1856 in Seward, *The United States Consulates in China*, 23. Emphasis in original.

55. Seward, *The United States Consulates in China*, 4.

56. Williams to Seward, Peking, October 24, 1865 in Seward, *The United States Consulates in China*, 50–51.

57. Seward, *The United States Consulates in China*, 4–14.

5. Victims

1. "Perils of Missionaries," *New York Evangelist* (July 24, 1862), 7; see also "Missionaries Driven from Tanna," *Missionary Herald* (July 1862), 227.

2. "The Murdered Missionary," *New York Times* (Apr. 27, 1874), 5.

3. "Latest News by Cable. Mexico," *New York Times* (Mar. 17, 1874), 1; "The Murdered Missionary," *New York Times* (Apr. 27, 1874), 5.

4. "The Murdered Missionary," *New York Times* (Apr. 27, 1874), 5.

5. "The Murdered Missionary," *New York Times* (Apr. 27, 1874), 5.

6. John Foster to Hamilton Fish, Mexico, Mar. 7, 1834, FRUS 1874, 734–735.

7. N. G. Clark to Hamilton Fish, Boston, May 19, 1874, FRUS 1874, 751.

8. American Board for Foreign Missions, Apr. 29 1874; American Board of Foreign Missions, Oct. 3, 1874; American Board of Foreign Missions, Nov. 6, 1875, National Archives, RG 59, M17, Reel 62; The ABCFM published this letter. "Assassins Executed," *Missionary Herald* (Dec. 1875), 393.

9. "Western Mexico: Effects of Mr. Stephens' Assassination," *Missionary Herald* (Dec. 1874), 393–396.

10. "Western Mexico: Last Months of Mr. Stephens' Work," *Missionary Herald* (Oct. 1874), 303.

11. "Western Mexico: Effects of Mr. Stephens' Assassination," *Missionary Herald* (Dec. 1874), 393–396.

12. "The Mexican Tragedy—Who is Responsible?" *New York Evangelist* (Mar. 26, 1874), 4.

13. "Miscellany. A Mexican Paper on the Murder of Stephens," *Missionary Herald* (June 1874), 192-193; "Murder of Missionary Stephens in Mexico," *New York Evangelist* (Apr. 30, 1874), 1.

14. Missionary Society of the Wesleyan Episcopal Church, June 26, 1883, National Archives, RG 59, M17, Reel 64; ABCFM, Jan. 27, 1885, National Archives, RG 59, M17, Reel 64; ABCFM, Aug. 12, 1885, National Archives, RG 59, M17, Reel 64; ABCFM, June 15, 1886, National Archives, RG 59, M17, Reel 65; Presbyterian Board of Foreign Missions, June 28, 1882, National Archives, RG 59, M17, Reel 64; Presbyterian Board of Foreign Missions, July 24, 1882, National Archives, RG 59, M17, Reel 64; ABCFM, Sept. 11, 1885, National Archives, RG 59, M17, Reel 65. Scott, "The Government of the United States and American Foreign Missionaries," 81.

15. Morris to Seward, Constantinople, Nov. 27, 1862, in FRUS 1863, Part II, 1176.

16. "Rev. Jackson Coffing," *Missionary Herald* (June 1862), 196.

17. "Another Missionary Murdered. Rev. William W. Meriam," *Missionary Herald* (Sept. 1862), 266-268.

18. ABCFM, Aug. 15, 1862, Aug. 25, 1862, and Jan. 30, 1863, National Archives, RG 59, M17, Reel 59.

19. ABCFM, April 18, 1863, National Archives, RG 59, M17, Reel 59.

20. "Murder of an American Missionary in Turkey," *The [Baltimore] Sun* (May 12, 1862), 2.

21. Morris to William Seward, Constantinople, Oct. 16, 1862, in FRUS 1862, 791.

22. William H. Seward to E. Joy Morris, Washington, Sept. 19, 1862, in FRUS 1862, 784-785.

23. Morris to Seward, Constantinople, Nov. 11, 1862, in FRUS 1863, 1175.

24. Morris to Seward, Constantinople, April 30, 1863, in FRUS 2863, 1185.

25. G. H. Heap to William Evarts, Constantinople, March 26, 1880, in FRUS 1880, 975-976.

26. The issue was significant enough that President Arthur included a mention in his annual message to Congress. Chester A. Arthur, "Annual Message of the President of the United States," in FRUS 1881, v. For the diplomatic correspondence on the issue, see FRUS 1880, 983-987.

27. "Particulars of the Murder of the American Missionary," *Daily American* (Aug. 8, 1880), 1; For more coverage of the case, see "Murder of a Missionary," *Chicago Daily Tribune* (Aug. 26, 1880), 3; "The Murder of the American Missionary by Circassians," *The [Baltimore] Sun* (Aug. 24, 1880), 4; "The Murder of Dr. Parsons," *New York Times* (Aug. 8, 1880), 7; "The Murder of Missionary Parsons," *New York Evangelist* (Aug. 26, 1880), 4.

28. Clark, NY. Aug. 14, 1880 and May 27, 1881, National Archives, RG 59, M17, Reel 64.

29. "The Murdered American Missionary," *Chicago Daily Tribune* (Sept. 10, 1880), 4. Henry Dwight, "The Murdered Missionary," *New-York Tribune* (Sept. 7, 1880), 2.

30. "The State Department at Washington," *Missionary Herald* (Oct. 1880), 380.

31. See, for example, George Heap to William Evarts, Constantinople, Nov. 8, 1880, in FRUS 1881, 1174.

32. William Evarts to Heap, Washington, Oct. 15, 1880, in FRUS 1880, 992. On Jeremiah Evarts, see Andrew, *From Revivals to Removal*.

33. William Evarts to Heap, Washington, Aug. 21, 1880, in FRUS 1880, 986-987.

34. G. Heap to William Evarts, Constantinople, Oct. 11, 1880, in FRUS 1880, 991.

35. Pierce to G. Heap, Baghchejik, May 3, 1881, in FRUS 1881, 1178.

36. Blaine to Wallace, Washington, June 29, 1881, in FRUS 1881, 1184-1186; Wallace to Assi Pacha, Constantinople, Oct. 22, 1881, in FRUS 1881, 1190.

37. Mr. Heap to Mr. Blaine, Constantinople, May 14, 1881, in FRUS 1881, 1180-1181.

38. Anna Melton to Mr. Grant, Amadia Turkey, June 19, 1893, FRUS 1893, 659.

39. A. W. Terrell to Mr. Gresham, Constantinople, July 20, 1893, FRUS 1893, 642-647.

40. The Grand Vizier to the Governor-General of Mosul, July 3d-15th, 1893, FRUS 1893, 648; A W. Terrell to Mr. Gresham, Constantinople, July 20, 1893, FRUS 1893, 642.

41. A. W. Terrell to Mr. Gresham, Constantinople, Aug. 1, 1893, FRUS 1893, 652-656.

42. W. Q. Gresham to A. W. Terrell, Washington, Aug. 3, 1893, FRUS 1893, 656-665.

43. A. W. Terrell to Mr. Gresham, Constantinople, Sept. 23, 1893, FRUS 1893, 683; A. W. Terrell to Mr. Gresham, Constantinople, Oct. 11, 1893, FRUS 1893, 689-691.

44. A. W. Terrell to Mr. Gresham, Constantinople, Oct. 27, 1893, FRUS 1893, 695.

45. Edward McDowell to A.W. Terrell, Mosul, Oct. 2, 1893, FRUS 1893, 696.

46. Hamilton Fish to Frederick F. Low, Department of State, Washington, Dec. 3, 1869, in FRUS 1870, 303.

47. Mr. Hamilton Fish to Frederick F. Low, Department of State, Washington, Dec. 3, 1869, in FRUS 1870, 303.

48. Sir Rutherford, quoted in FRUS 1870, 350.

49. George F. Seward to Mr. Fish, Washington, Apr. 22, 1870, FRUS 1870, 339-355.

50. Proclamation of the Prefect of Tientsin, in FRUS 1870, 383.

51. Report of Tsang-Kwoh-Fan respecting the Tientsin Riot and its Causes, in FRUS 1870, 370-371.

52. Frederick F. Low to Mr. Fish, Legation of the United States, Pekin, June 27, 1870, in FRUS 1870, 358.

53. For a celebratory account of Low's handling of the Tientsin massacre, see Clyde, "Frederick F. Low and the Tientsin Massacre," 100-108.

54. Jonathan Lees and William N. Hall to W. H. Lay, in FRUS 1870, 376.

55. A. Stanley to Commander Taylor, Tientsin, Aug. 12, 1870, in FRUS 1870, 375.

56. Rev. C. W. Matteer to Mr. Holwill, Tungchow, Aug. 30, 1870, in FRUS 1870, 389; Frederick Low to His Imperial Highness Prince Kung, Pekin, Sept. 13, 1870, in FRUS 1870, 393.

57. Frederick Low to Rev. Edward P. Capp, Peking, Sept. 14, 1870, in FRUS 1870, 389.

58. On Seward's writings from this trip, see Sexton, "William H. Seward in the World," 398–430.

59. Seward, ed., *William H. Seward's Travels*, 110.

60. Seward, ed., *Seward's Travels*, 146.

61. Seward, ed., *Seward's Travels*, 114.

62. Seward, ed., *Seward's Travels*, 221.

63. Seward, ed., *Seward's Travels*, 221.

64. Low to Fish, Peking, Jan. 10, 1871, in FRUS 1871, 84.

65. Seward, ed., *Seward's Travels*, 212–213.

66. Extracts from British Blue Book, "China, No. 3, 1871," in FRUS 1871, 161.

67. Davis to Low, Washington, Oct. 19, 1871, in FRUS 1871, 155.

68. Rev. Rhea to Pres. Andrew Johnson, Oroomiah, Persia, June 3, 1865, National Archives, RG 59, M179, Reel 226.

69. *Protection of American Citizens in Persia. Message from the President of the United States, Accompanied by a Communication from the Secretary of State, In Response to a Resolution in the House of Representatives, Touching the Protection of American Citizens in Persia and the Establishment of Diplomatic Relations with that Country* Ex. Doc. No. 151, 47th Cong., 1st Sess. (1882).

70. Ghazvinian, *America and Iran*, 34–37.

71. Miss A. D. Van Duzse to Miss Holliday, Salmas, May 17, 1890, in FRUS 1890, 660–661; Mr. Wright to Mr. Pratt, Oola, Salmas, May 22, 1890, in FRUS 1890, 662–664.

72. Mr. Wright to Mr. Pratt, Oola, Salmas, May 22, 1890, in FRUS 1890, 662–664.

73. Mr. Wright to Mr. Pratt, Oola, Salmas, May 22, 1890, in FRUS 1890, 662–664.

74. Testimony of Dr. Mary Bradford, FRUS 1890, 682.

75. E. Spencer Pratt to Mr. Blaine, Teheran (Tehran), June 12, 1890, FRUS 1890, 666–668.

76. William Wharton to Mr. Pratt, Washington, Sept. 19, 1890, FRUS 1890, 691.

77. E. Spencer Pratt to Col. Stewart, Teheran, June 30, 1890, FRUS 1890, 673.

78. E. Spencer Pratt to Mr. Blaine, Teheran, July 26, 1890, FRUS 1890, 684.

79. John Gillespie to Mr. Blaine, New York, Sept. 16, 1890, FRUS 1890, 692.

80. On Col. Stewart's activities on behalf of the Americans, see enclosures in the following: Mr. Pratt to Mr. Blaine, Teheran, June 12, 1890, FRUS 1890, 666–669; Mr. Pratt to Mr. Blaine, Teheran, June 18, 1890, FRUS 1890, 669–670; Mr. Pratt to Mr. Blaine, Teheran, June 25, 1890, 670–674; Mr. Pratt to Mr. Blaine, Teheran, June 30, 1890, FRUS 1890, 672–673; Mr. Pratt to

Mr. Blaine, Teheran, July 5, 1890, FRUS 1890 673–674; Mr. Pratt to Mr. Blaine, Teheran, July 15, 1890, FRUS 1890, 674–683; Mr. Pratt to Mr. Blaine, Teheran, Aug. 8, 1890, FRUS 1890, 685–688; Mr. Pratt to Mr. Blaine, Teheran, Aug. 9, 1890, FRUS 1890, 689–690.

81. Mr. Pratt to Mr. Blaine, Teheran, Aug. 8, 1890, FRUS 1890, 685–686.

82. William Wharton to Mr. Pratt, Washington, Sept. 19, 1890, FRUS 1890, 691–692.

83. S. O. Wylie (Board of Missions for the Reformed Presbyterian Church) to Hamilton Fish, Philadelphia, Dec. 5, 1874, National Archives, RG 59, M179, Reel 428; Presbyterian Board of Missions, Dec. 7, 1874, National Archives, RG 59, M17, Reel 62.

6. Troublemakers

1. Seward, *The United States Consulates in China*, 6, 41, 50.

2. George F. Seward, quoted in Scott, "The Government of the United States and American Foreign Missionaries," 82–85.

3. George F. Seward, quoted in Scott, "The Government of the United States and American Foreign Missionaries," 84.

4. Edward Lord to Mr. Low, Ningpo, Sept. 21, 1872, in FRUS 1873, 120–122.

5. George F. Seward to Mr. Fish, Washington, Apr. 22, 1870, in FRUS 1870, 343.

6. Edward Lord to Mr. Low, Ningpo, Sept. 21, 1872, in FRUS 1873, 120–122.

7. Samuel Wells Williams to Mr. Fish, Peking, Jan. 23, 1874, in FRUS 1874, 232.

8. Mr. Benjamin Avery to Mr. Fish, Peking, Dec. 22, 1874, in 1875, 243–244.

9. Mr. Benjamin Avery to Mr. Fish, Peking, July 18, 1875, in FRUS 1875, 383–384.

10. The Taotai to W. A. Cornabé, Feb. 7, 1874, in FRUS 1874, 278–279.

11. The Taotai to W. A. Cornabé, Feb. 7, 1874, FRUS 1874, 278–279.

12. Eli Sheppard to Samuel Wells Williams, Tien-tsin, June 25, 1874, in FRUS 1874, 281.

13. Eli Sheppard to Samuel Wells Williams, Tien-tsin, June 25, 1874, in FRUS 1874, 281–287.

14. Hamilton Fish to Mr. Low, Washington, Dec. 31, 1872, in FRUS 1873, 138.

15. Rev. John MacIntyre to Mr. Cornabé, Che-foo, Oct. 15, 1874, in FRUS 1875, 237.

16. Benjamin Avery to Johnson, Peking, June 1, 1875, in FRUS 1875, 339.

17. Benjamin Avery to Hamilton Fish, Peking, July 18, 1875, in FRUS 1875, 386.

18. Benjamin Avery to Mr. De Lano, Peking, Dec. 28, 1874, in FRUS 1875, 335.

19. Benjamin Avery to Johnson, Peking, June 1, 1875, in FRUS 1875, 339. See also Benjamin Avery to Hamilton Fish, Peking, July 18, 1875, in FRUS 1875, 384.

20. Benjamin Avery to Hamilton Fish, Peking, June 1, 1875, in FRUS 1875, 333.

21. Benjamin Avery to Hamilton Fish, Peking, June 1, 1875, in FRUS 1875, 333.

22. Matthew 10:16 "Behold, I send you forth as sheep in the midst of wolves; be ye therefore wise as serpents and harmless as doves" (KJV).

23. George F. Seward, quoted in Scott, "The Government of the United States and American Foreign Missionaries," 84.

24. George F. Seward, quoted in Scott, "The Government of the United States and American Foreign Missionaries," 82–85.

25. George Seward to Hamilton Fish, Peking, June 19, 1876, in FRUS 1876, 53–55.

26. George Seward to Hamilton Fish, Peking, June 19, 1876, in FRUS 1876, 53–55.

27. George Seward to Hamilton Fish, Peking, June 19, 1876, in FRUS 1876, 53–55.

28. George Seward to Hamilton Fish, Peking, June 19, 1876, in FRUS 1876, 53–55.

29. E. Joy Morris to Mr. William Seward, Constantinople, Mar. 29, 1865, in FRUS 1866, 280.

30. Ali Pacha to M. Musurus, Sublime Porte, Nov. 30, 1865, FRUS 1866, 281–283.

31. Horace Maynard to Mr. Fish, Constantinople, June 30, 1875, FRUS 1875, 1298.

32. They suffered from the association of their work with that of the British missionaries who, the Americans claimed, did smuggle banned books for distribution. "Protest of American Citizens" in FRUS 1875, 1300.

33. American Bible Society, June 8, 1881, National Archives, RG 59, M17, Reel 64; American Bible Society, July 6, 1882, National Archives, M17, Reel 64; American Bible Society, Jan. 25, 1883 National Archives, RG 59, M17, Reel 64.

34. American Bible Society, July 11, 1884, National Archives, RG 59, M17, Reel 65.

35. N. G Clark to Frederick Frelinghuysen, Boston, June 29, 1882, National Archives, RG 59, M-179, Reel 612.

36. American Bible Society, Dec. 5, 1884, National Archives, RG 59, M17, Reel 65; American Board of Commissioners for Foreign Missions, Dec. 22, 1884, National Archives, RG 59, M17, Reel 65; American Bible Society, Feb. 24, 1885, National Archives, RG 59, M17, Reel 65. On the Bible Society's work in the region, see Fea, *The Bible Cause*, ch. 10.

37. E. Doane, "For Young People: The Fourth of July in Micronesia," *Missionary Herald* (Dec. 1886), 521–524. On children's missionary literature more generally, see Emily Conroy-Krutz, "For Young People: Protestant Missions, Geography, and American Youth at the End of the Nineteenth Century," in Nichols and Milne, *Ideology in U.S. Foreign Relations*, 211–230.

38. ABCFM, Aug. 6, 1887, National Archives, RG 59, M17, Reel 65; ABCFM, Sept. 3, 1887, National Archives, RG 59, M17, Reel 65; ABCFM, Sept. 5, 1887,

National Archives, RG 59, M17, Reel 65; ABCFM, Sept. 5, 1887, National Archives, RG 59, M17, Reel 65; ABCFM, Sept. 29, 1887, National Archives, RG 59, M17, Reel 65; ABCFM, Oct. 13, 1887, National Archives, RG 59, M17, Reel 65; ABCFM, Oct. 20, 1887, National Archives, RG 59, M17, Reel 65; ABCFM, Dec. 1, 1887, National Archives, RG 59, M17, Reel 65; ABCFM, Dec. 23, 1887, National Archives, RG 59, M17, Reel 65.

39. ABCFM, Aug. 6, 1887, RG 59, M17, Reel 65; ABCFM, Sept. 3, 1887, National Archives, RG 59, M17, Reel 65; ABCFM, Sept. 5, 1887, National Archives, RG 59, M17, Reel 65; ABCFM, Sept.5, 1887, National Archives, RG 59, M17, Reel 65; ABCFM, Sept. 29, 1887, National Archives, RG 59, M17, Reel 65; ABCFM, Oct. 13, 1887, National Archives, RG 59, M17, Reel 65; ABCFM, Oct. 20, 1887, National Archives, RG 59, M17, Reel 65; ABCFM, Dec. 1, 1887, National Archives, RG 59, M17, Reel 65; ABCFM, Dec. 23, 1887, National Archives, RG 59, M17, Reel 65; ABCFM, Feb. 7, 1888, National Archives, RG 59, M17, Reel 65; ABCFM, Feb. 11, 1888, National Archives, RG 59, M17, Reel 65. Liggins, *The Great Value and Success of Foreign Missions,* 132–134.

40. Liggins, *The Great Value and Success of Foreign Missions*, 132–134; also quoted in "The Case of Rev. Mr. Doane and the Spanish Government," *Missionary Herald* (Nov. 1887), 432.

41. Voight, quoted in "The Case of Rev. Mr. Doane," *Missionary Herald* (Nov. 1887), 431.

42. "The Case of Rev. Mr. Doane," *Missionary Herald* (Nov. 1887), 431.

43. Miss Fletcher, quoted in Liggins, *The Great Value and Success of Foreign Missions*, 133.

44. Bayard to Curry, Washington, Dec. 23, 1887, in FRUS 1892, 413–414.

45. Judson Smith to Mr. Blaine, Boston, Nov. 13, 1889, in FRUS 1892, 426.

46. Judson Smith to Mr. Blaine, Boston, Nov. 13, 1889, in FRUS 1892, 426.

47. Judson Smith to Bayard, Boston, Aug. 30, 1887, in FRUS 1892, 396–397.

48. Judson Smith to Mr. Bayard, Boston, Sept. 24, 1888, in FRUS 1892, 422.

49. Mr. Wharton to Mr. Newberry, Washington, Oct. 6, 1891, in FRUS 1892, 442–485.

50. Mr. Judson Smith to Mr. Bayard, ABCFM, Congregational House, Boston, Oct. 15, 1887, in FRUS 1892, 407–408.

51. Miss Palmer's Statement, Roukiti, Ponape, Oct. 29, 1890, in FRUS 1892, 464–466.

52. Mrs. Lucy M. Cole to Mrs. Cooke, Ponape, July 14, 1890, in FRUS 1892, 437.

53. Mr. Wharton to Mr. Newberry, Washington, Oct. 6, 1891, in FRUS 1892, 442–485.

54. James G. Blaine to Mr. Newberry, Washington, Nov. 4, 1890, in FRUS 1892, 435–436.

55. Commander H. C. Taylor to Rear-Admiral Belknap, USS Alliance, Ponape Islands, Jamestown Harbor, Oct. 31, 1890, in FRUS 1892, 450.

56. Rear-Admiral Belknap to Commander Taylor, Flagship Omaha, Yokohama, Japan, Sept. 22, 1890, in FRUS 1892, 450.

57. Commander Taylor to Rear-Admiral Belknap, USS Alliance, At Sea, Dec. 3, 1890, in FRUS 1892, 454.

58. Commander Taylor to Rear-Admiral Belknap, USS Alliance, At Sea, Dec. 3, 1890, in FRUS 1892, 457.

59. Judson Smith to Mr. Blaine, Boston, Nov. 3, 1890, in FRUS 1892, 436.

60. Judson Smith to Mr. Blaine, Boston, Jan. 8, 1891, in FRUS 1892, 478.

61. Mr. Wharton to Mr. Newberry, Washington, Oct. 6, 1891, in FRUS 1892, 445.

62. Mr. Wharton to Mr. Newberry, Washington, Oct. 6, 1891, in FRUS 1892, 448.

63. John W. Foster to Mr. Snowden, Washington, Nov. 3, 1892, in FRUS 1892, 504–513.

64. Mr. Snowden to the Marquis de Vega de Armijo, Madrid, Jan. 8, 1893, in FRUS 1894, 560–562.

65. Mr. John W. Foster to Mr. Snowden, Washington, Nov. 29, 1892, in FRUS 1892, 513–517; Mr. Snowden to Mr. Gresham, Legation of the United States, Madrid, May 28, 1893, in FRUS 1894, 582–583.

66. John W. Foster to Mr. Snowden, Washington, Nov. 3, 1892, in FRUS 1892, 506.

7. Workers

1. Hamlin, *My Life and Times*, 417.

2. Hutchison, *Errand to the World*, 91.

3. Hamlin, *In Memoriam*, 5, 7.

4. Hamlin, *Life and Times*, 472–474.

5. Hamlin, *Life and Times*, 434.

6. American College for Girls, *President's Report*, 2–3.

7. On republican motherhood and women's education, see Reeves-Ellington, *Domestic Frontiers*; Porterfield, *Mary Lyon and the Mount Holyoke Missionaries*, ch. 1.

8. The American was Mr. MacNutt, in the absence of Mr. Hirsch. Other speakers included the director of the Armenian High School in Scutari, Rev. C. H. Brooks, and a representative of the Bulgarian Exarch.

9. Hamlin, *Life and Times*, 255.

10. Hamlin, *Life and Times*, 256.

11. "The Sassoun Massacre," *New York Times* (Aug. 23, 1895), 12.

12. Hamlin, *In Memoriam*, 18.

13. Hutchison, *Errand to the World*, ch. 3; Harris, *Nothing but Christ*.

14. Hamlin, *Life and Times*, 295.

15. Cemal Yetinker, "At the Center of the Debate: Bebek Seminary and the Educational Policy of the American Board of Commissioners for Foreign Missions (1840–1860)," in Dogan and Sharkey, *American Missionaries in the Middle East*, 63–83.

16. Wanless, *The Medical Mission*, 18.

17. Ahn, *Awakening the Hermit Kingdom*, 247–303.

18. Seat, "Providence Has Freed Our Hands," 68.

19. Seat, "Providence Has Freed Our Hands," ch. 4.

20. "Missions of the Board: Mission to Japan," *Missionary Herald* (July 1871), 205–208.

21. Russel, quoted in Seat, *"Providence Has Freed Our Hand,"* 81.

22. Rev. C. S. Eby, "Christians in Japan," enclosed in Richard Hubbard to Mr. Bayard, Tokio, October 25, 1888, FRUS 1888, 1078–1079.

23. Seat, *"Providence Has Freed Our Hands,"* 90.

24. Seat, *"Providence Has Freed Our Hands,"* 102.

25. Seat, *"Providence Has Freed Our Hands,"* 102–112.

26. Chang, "Whose 'Barbarism?'" 1331–1365.

27. Chester Holcombe, ABC 77.1, Box 34, Folder 29:8.

28. Ryu, "An Odd Relationship," 261–287; Cohen, *East Asia at the Center,* 287–291. See also Duus, *The Abacus and the Sword.*

29. "Political Movements in Korea," *Foreign Missionary* (Oct. 1885), 229.

30. Ryu, "An Odd Relationship," 263–264.

31. "Japan and Korea," *Foreign Missionary* (Sept. 1885), 153; see J. R. Wolfe, "A Visit to Korea," *Foreign Missionary* (Sept. 1885), 161–163; Williams, *In Four Continents,* 120; Henry Loomis, "Changes in Korea," *Foreign Missionary* (June 1885), 34.

32. Williams, *In Four Continents,* 123.

33. "A General Survey of Our Fields," *Foreign Missionary* (Jan. 1886), 338–339; "The Value of Missions. Testimony from the American Consul General at Seoul. Korea," *Christian Observer* (Dec. 29, 1909), 2.

34. "Medical Work in Korea," *Foreign Missionary* (Oct. 1886), 215–217.

35. Ryu, "An Odd Relationship," 275. Interestingly, as Dae Young Ryu notes, there was some editing of the diplomatic correspondence about missionaries in the preparation of FRUS. Editors toned down critical language against the missionaries, perhaps to appeal to a pro-missionary US public (277).

36. Ryu, "Treaties," 174–203.

37. "Medical Work in Korea," *Foreign Missionary* (Oct. 1886), 215–217.

38. Lucius H. Foote to Mr. Frelinghuysen, Legation of the United States, Seoul, Corea, Sept. 1, 1884, FRUS 1884, 127–128.

39. See, for example, George Foulk to Frelinghuysen, Seoul, Mar. 5, 1885, FRUS 1885, 346.

40. George C. Foulk to Bayard, Seoul, May 30, 1885, FRUS 1885, 347–348.

41. "Medical Work in Korea," *Foreign Missionary* (Oct. 1886), 215–217.

42. See, for example, J. R. Wolfe, "A Visit to Korea," *Foreign Missionary* (Sept. 1885), 161–163.

43. Dr. H. N. Allen, "Korea: Only a Square Inch of Royalty," *Foreign Missionary* (Sept. 1885), 176.

44. Chung, "Her Name Was Lillias Horton Underwood," 56–71.

45. Lillias Underwood, *Fifteen Years Among the Top-Knots,* 18–19.

46. Mr. Dun to Mr. Olney, Tokyo, Oct. 14, 1895, FRUS 1895, 975.

47. "King of Corea: Scheme to Remove Him from the Palace," *The Nashville American* (Dec. 25, 1895), 3; "A Korean Sensation: Americans Accused of Violence," *Los Angeles Times* (Dec. 25, 1895), 3; Mr. Olney to Mr. Sill, Washington, Nov. 11, 1895, FRUS 1895, 975.

48. John M. B. Sill to Olney, Seoul, Jan. 20, 1896, FRUS 1895, 977–978.

49. Olney to Sill, Washington, Jan. 11, 1896, FRUS 1895, 975–976.

50. "Americans in Korea: The King Said to be Acting Entirely Under Their Influence," *Baltimore Sun* (Dec. 1, 1896), 1.

51. Ryu, "Religion Meets Politics," 113–133; Underwood, *Fifteen Years Among the Top-Knots*, 155.

52. Ryu, "Religion Meets Politics," 113–133; Underwood, *Fifteen Years Among the Top-Knots*, 156.

53. Ryu, "Religion Meets Politics," 113–133; Underwood, *Fifteen Years Among the Top-Knots*, 159–164.

54. Ryu, "An Odd Relationship," 282.

55. Dr. H. N. Allen, "Korea: Only a Square Inch of Royalty," *Foreign Missionary* (Sept. 1885), 176.

56. On these dimensions more broadly, see Gleeson, "The Stethoscope and the Gospel," 127–138.

57. Quoted in Ryu, "An Odd Relationship," 287.

58. Underwood, *Fifteen Years Among the Top-Knots,* 15–17. See also: Chung, "Her Name Was Lillias Horton Underwood," 59.

59. Mary Barnum, Nov. 25, 1895, William Goodell Papers, Box 1, Folder "Mary and Emma Barnum."

60. On the Ottoman and Armenian context for the Hamidian massacres, see Suny, *They Can Live in the Desert*, esp. chs. 1–4. On American responses to the Hamidian massacres, see Walther, *Sacred Interests*, ch. 7; Laderman, *Sharing the Burden*, ch. 1.

61. Unsigned letter to "My dear little Auntie," Nov. 26, 1895 William Goodell Papers, Box 1, Folder "Mary and Emma Barnum," Library of Congress.

62. "Killed Because Christians," *Boston Daily Globe* (Apr. 29, 1895), 9.

63. "The Armenian Crisis in Turkey," *The Woman's Journal* (Apr. 6, 1895), 1. This was not the only coverage of the crisis in *The Woman's Journal*. They continued reporting throughout the year. See "An Armenian Mother," *The Woman's Journal* (May 25, 1895), 162.

64. Laderman, *Sharing the Burden,* 21.

65. "Our Flag Respected in Turkey," *Washington Post* (Nov. 29, 1896), 12.

66. Cyrus Hamlin, "America's Duty to Americans in Turkey. An Open Letter to the Hon. John Sherman, United States Senator from Ohio," *North American Review* 163 (Sept. 1896), 276–281.

67. On racialized Islamophobia in the American response to the Armenian massacres, see Walther, *Sacred Interests*, 254–259.

68. Laderman, *Sharing the Burden*, 12.

69. Dwight, quoted in Laderman, *Sharing the Burden*, 31.

70. Frances Willard quoted in Tyrrell, *Reforming the World*, 104.

71. Laderman, *Sharing the Burden*, 22.

72. Laderman, *Sharing the Burden*, 29.

73. Curtis, *Holy Humanitarians*, 74–77; Irwin, *Making the World Safe*, 26; Tyrrell, *Reforming the World*, 111.

74. Quoted in Laderman, *Sharing the Burden*, 2.

75. Laderman, *Sharing the Burden*, 46.

Part III

1. Carpenter, *The Miss Stone Affair*, 15.

2. For a history of the Macedonian revolutionary movement and its connection to Stone's case, see Sherman, *Fires on the Mountain*.

3. Carpenter, *The Miss Stone Affair;* Sherman, *Fires on the Mountain*.

4. Roosevelt, quoted in Carpenter, *The Miss Stone Affair*, 30–31.

5. Adee quoted in Carpenter, *The Miss Stone Affair*, 33

6. Charles M. Dickinson to Miss Stone, Diplomatic Agency of the US, Sofia, Bulgaria, Oct. 26, 1901, Charles Monroe Dickinson Papers, Box 1, Folder Oct. 16–Oct. 31, 1901.

7. Charles Monroe Dickinson Papers, Box 1, Folder Oct. 16–Oct. 31, 1901.

8. Ellen Stone, quoted in Carpenter, *The Miss Stone Affair*, 185.

9. Stone, quoted in Roberta Wollons, "Writing Home to the American Board of Commissioners for Foreign Missions: Missionary Women Abroad Narrate Their Precarious Worlds, 1869–1915," in Mayer and Arredondo, *Women, Power Relations, and Education*, 114.

10. Equity, "Missionaries as Hostiles," *New York Times* (Feb. 17, 1898), 6.

11. ADF Hamlin, "American Missionaries in Turkey," *New York Times* (Feb. 21, 1898), 5.

12. ADF Hamlin, "American Missionaries in Turkey," *New York Times* (Feb. 21, 1898), 5.

13. James L. Barton ["Truth and Equity"] to the Editor of the *New York Times*, Feb. 23, 1898. ABC 11.4, Box 1, Folder 3.

14. Cyrus Hamlin, "America's Duty to Americans in Turkey," *North American Review* (September 1896), 276–281.

15. "Annual Union Meeting, Woman's Boards of Foreign Missions," *New York Evangelist* (June 2, 1898), 20.

16. Judson Smith and James L. Barton, "Annual Survey of the Work of the American Board," *Missionary Herald* (November 1898), 439–454.

17. Hutchison, *Modernist Impulse*, 164–174.

8. Imperialists

1. Brown, *Memoirs of a Centenarian*.

2. Brown, *Memoirs of a Centenarian*, 26–27.

3. Theodore Roosevelt to Arthur Brown, White House, Oct. 15, 1904, Arthur Judson Brown Papers, Box 2, Folder 76: Theodore Roosevelt.

4. Brown, *Report of a Visitation*, 87–89.

5. Fitz, *Our Sister Republics*.

6. McCartney, "Religion, the Spanish-American War, and the Idea of American Mission," 267.

7. Hoganson, *Fighting for American Manhood*, ch. 2.

8. Quoted in Curtis, *Holy Humanitarians*, 82.

9. Charles Ghiselin, "Our Mission in Cuba. Shall We Resume It?" *Christian Observer* (May 18, 1898), 467.

10. "Mission Boards Interested," *Boston Daily Globe* (Apr. 1, 1898), 7.

11. Curtis, *Holy Humanitarians*, ch. 3.

12. Quoted in Curtis, *Holy Humanitarians*, 89.

13. W.S. Rainsford, quoted in McCartney, "Religion, the Spanish-American War, and the Idea of American Mission," 268.

14. Quoted in McCartney, "Religion, the Spanish-American War, and the Idea of American Mission," 270.

15. William McKinley, "Message to the Congress of the United States" [war message], US Department of State, *Papers Relating to Foreign Affairs* (Washington), 1898, 750–760, https://history.state.gov/historicaldocuments/frus1898/ch83.

16. McKinley war message.

17. McKinley war message.

18. Charles Ghiselin, "Our Mission in Cuba. Shall We Resume It?" *Christian Observer* (May 18, 1898), 467.

19. On race and colonial governance in the Philippines, see Kramer, *Blood of Government*, ch. 1–2.

20. Department of War, *Reports of the Taft Commission*.

21. Preston, *Sword of the Spirit*, 220.

22. Bryan, quoted in Preston, *Sword of the Spirit*, 223.

23. According to a July 1900 poll, "Protestant clergy were the most ardent supporters of imperialism." Preston, *Sword of the Spirit*, 223.

24. Brown, *Report of a Visitation*, 1.

25. "Annual Survey of the Work of the American Board, 1897–1898," *Missionary Herald* (Nov. 1898), 445.

26. Quoted in Apilado, *Revolutionary Spirituality*, 56.

27. Quoted in Apilado, *Revolutionary Spirituality*, 66.

28. "The Missionary Problem in the Philippines," *The Independent* (June 16, 1898), 12.

29. "Philippines a Good Field," *Washington Post* (Oct. 29, 1989), 3; "They Would Keep Them," *Boston Daily Globe* (Oct. 29, 1898), 3.

30. "Cooperation in the Philippines," *New York Observer and Chronicle* (June 30, 1898), 916.

31. "To Redeem the Philippines," *Boston Daily Globe* (Sept. 12, 1898), 4.

32. McKinley, quoted in General James Rusling, "Interview with President William McKinley," *Christian Advocate* (Jan. 22, 1903), 17.

33. Wallace Gum to Brent, Florence, CO Oct. 23, 1901 in Charles H. Brent Papers, Box 5, Folder Oct. 1901.

34. This was a period of what historian Matthew McCullough has called "messianic interventionism," in which American Christians across denomination and region understood their nation's role in the world to be active engagement. McCullough, *The Cross of War*.

35. Clymer, *Protestant Missionaries in the Philippines*, 5–7.

36. "Annual Survey of the Work of the American Board, 1897–1898," *Missionary Herald* (Nov. 1898), 445.

37. Brent to Bishop W. A. Leonard, Oct. 26, 1901. Brent Papers, Box 5, Folder Oct. 1901.

38. On US relations with Indigenous nations as empire, see essays in *The Early Imperial Republic*, ed. Blaakman, Conroy-Krutz, and Arista.

39. Apilado, *Revolutionary Spirituality*, 76–77.

40. Brown, *Memoirs of a Centenarian*, 79–80.

41. Brown, *Memoirs of a Centenarian*, 80.

42. Brown, *Report of a Visitation of the Philippine Mission*, Introduction.

43. Brown, *Report of a Visitation of the Philippine Mission*, 46–63.

44. Brown, *Report of a Visitation of the Philippine Mission*, 54. See also 44–52.

45. William Jessup, in Arthur Judson Brown Papers, Box 4, Folder "New Era in the Philippines."

46. Tyrrell, *Reforming the World*, ch. 6; Paul A. Kramer, "The Darkness that Enters the Home: The Politics of Prostitution during the Philippine-American War," in Stoler, *Haunted by Empire*, 366–404.

47. "Talk on the Philippines," *New York Times* (Oct. 15, 1899), 3.

48. "Missions in Philippines," *The Sun* (Oct. 23, 1902), 2; See similar coverage in "Changes Discussed by P. E. Missionary Council," *Detroit Free Press* (Oct. 23, 1902), 2.

49. Brown, *Memoirs of a Centenarian*, 28.

50. Taft, *The Church and Our Government in the Philippines*, 17–20.

51. Wenger, *Religious Freedom*, ch. 1.

52. Quoted in Apilado, *Revolutionary Spirituality*, 56.

53. On the use of "religious freedom talk" by Protestant missionaries, Catholic leaders, Muslim Moros, and the US government, see Wenger, *Religious Freedom*, ch. 1–2.

54. Brown, *Report of a Visitation of the Philippine Mission*, 69–90.

55. John Ireland, "The Religious Conditions in Our New Island Territory," *Outlook* (Aug. 26, 1899), 933–934.

56. James B. Rodgers, "Religion in the Philippines: A Missionary's View," *Outlook* (Feb. 17, 1900), 404.

57. Moran, *The Imperial Church*, chs. 5–6.

58. Taft, *The Church and Our Government in the Philippines*.

59. Reuter, "William Howard Taft and the Separation of Church and State in the Philippines," 114–115.

60. Brown, *Report of a Visitation of the Philippine Mission*, 247.

61. Brown, *Report of a Visitation of the Philippine Mission*, 51–52.

62. Walther, *Sacred Interests*, ch. 6. On superstition, see Wheatley, "US Colonial Governance of Superstition and Fanaticism in the Philippines," 21–36.

63. Walther, *Sacred Interests*, 167.

64. Walther, *Sacred Interests*, 165.

65. Walther, *Sacred Interests*, ch. 5–6.

66. Brown, *Memoirs of a Centenarian*, 27–28.

67. "Taft Lauds Missionaries," *Washington Post* (Apr. 21, 1908), 2; see also "Missionaries: Lauded by Taft in Address in New York," *Courier-Journal* (Apr. 21, 1908), 2. The affection was mutual—an October 1908 article in the *New York Tribune* explained that Rev. Homer Stuntz, assistant secretary of the Board of Foreign Missions of the Methodist Episcopal Church, as well as Arthur Brown and John Mott, were all planning to vote for Taft in the 1908 election. "Missionaries Praise Judge Taft," *New-York Tribune* (Oct. 22, 1908), 3.

68. "Taft Talks to Bishops," *Baltimore Sun* (Oct. 28, 1910), 2.

69. On reception of his work, see Johnson, "The Legacy of Arthur Judson Brown," 71–75.

9. Boxers

1. Rankin Family Papers, Box 2, Vol. 3, Folder 8, pages 73–74.

2. Henry William Rankin, "Divie Bethune McCartee MD—Pioneer Missionary: A Sketch of His Career," *New York Evangelist* (May 22, 1902), 604.

3. Rankin Family Papers, Box 2, Vol. 3, Folder 8, pages 73–74.

4. Rankin, "Political Values of the American Missionary," 145–182.

5. Rankin, "The Hour of China and the United States," 561–578.

6. Rankin, "The Hour of China and the United States," 566, 570.

7. Rankin, "The Hour of China and the United States," 575.

8. Henry W. Rankin to Peter McCartee, Esq (of NY), E. Northfield, Mass., Dec. 16, 1901. Rankin Family Papers, Box 1, Folder 22.

9. On the question of secret societies vs. militias, see Papageorge, *The United States Diplomats' Response to Rising Chinese Nationalism*, 42–43.

10. Luella Miner, quoted in Preston, *Sword of the Spirit*, 36.

11. Cohen, *History in Three Keys*, 51.

12. In other words, the Catholic Church in China had become "an *imperium in imperio*." Quoted in Esherick, *The Origins of the Boxer Uprising*, 83–85.

13. Cohen, *History in Three Keys*, 30.

14. Clive Bingham quoted in Preston, *Sword of the Spirit*, 36.

15. Conger to Hay, Pekin, Mar. 13, 1900, in FRUS 1900, 109; Conger to Hay, Pekin, May 8, 1900, in FRUS 1900, 122.

16. Conger to Hay, Pekin, April 12, 1900, in FRUS 1900, 113–114.

17. John Hay to Judson Smith, Washington, March 27, 1900, in FRUS 1900, 113.

18. Conger to Hay, Pekin, May 8, 1900, in FRUS 1900, 123–125.

19. Conger to the Tsungli Yamen, Pekin, May 30, 1900, in FRUS 1900, 137.

20. Conger to Hay, June 4–10, FRUS 1900, 139–150.

21. Upham, quoted in Preston, *Sword of the Spirit*, 60.

22. Preston, *Besieged in Peking*, 60–61.

23. Preston, *Sword of the Spirit*, 111–112.

24. Preston, *Sword of the Spirit*, 1.

25. Cohen, *History in Three Keys*, 44.

26. "Boxer Rebellion is Spreading; American Lives in Great Danger," *Chicago Daily Tribune* (June 10, 1900), 1.

27. Cohen, *History in Three Keys*, 26.

28. E. H. Conger to Mr. Hay, Peking, Oct. 30, in FRUS 1901 Appendix: Affairs in China, 42.

29. John A. Kasson, "Report on Questions relating to Chinese Taxation, indemnity, and proposed conventional provisions" in FRUS 1901 Appendix: Affairs in China, 208–211.

30. Conger to Hay, Pekin, Mar. 9, 1900 in FRUS 1900, 102.

31. E. H. Conger to the Tsungli Yamen, Pekin, China, Jan. 27, 1900, in FRUS 1900, 96.

32. E. H. Conger to Mr. Hay, Pekin, China, Feb. 26, 1900, in FRUS 1900, 101.

33. See, for example, "China Indemnity on a Silver Basis," *Austin Statesman* (Jan. 1, 1903), 1.

34. Johnson was joined in this analysis by Consuls McWade and Wilcox. Anson Burlingame Johnson to David J. Hill, Amoy, China, Aug. 24, 1900, Consular Despatches, US Consulate, Amoy, RG 59, M100, Reel 14, https://catalog.archives.gov/id/210914886.

35. "The Missionaries and Their Critics," *Detroit Free Press* (Feb. 13, 1901), 4. For the mission board's defense of the missionaries, see "Looting by Missionaries," *Missionary Herald* (Feb. 1901), 46; "The Collection of Indemnities in China," *Missionary Herald* (Aug. 1901), 312.

36. Mark Twain, "To the Person Sitting in Darkness," *North American Review* 81 (Feb. 1901), 161–176.

37. Brown, *The Foreign Missionary*, 7.

38. Brown, *The Foreign Missionary*, 13–25.

39. Brown, *The Foreign Missionary*, 323–324.

40. Brown, *The Foreign Missionary*, 326–328.

41. Brown, *The Foreign Missionary*, 326. Brown argues against this point more fully in his *New Forces in Old China*, 356–357.

42. Brown, *The Foreign Missionary*, 328–332; also Brown, *New Forces in Old China*, chapter 21.

43. "The Diplomatists Concerning Missionaries in China," *Missionary Herald* (Oct. 1900), 395–398.

44. John Barrett, "Some Truths About the Missionaries," *The Outlook* (20 Oct. 1900), 462–465.

45. John Barrett, "Some Truths About the Missionaries," *The Outlook* (20 Oct. 1900), 462–465.

46. John Barrett (Late United States Minister to Siam), "Some Truths About the Missionaries," *The Outlook* (20 Oct. 1900), 462–465.

47. Rankin, "Political Values," 172.

48. Rankin, "Political Values," 165.

49. Rankin, "Political Values," 164–165.

50. Rankin, "Political Values," 151.

51. Rankin, "Political Values," 152–153.

52. Rankin, "Political Values," 167.

53. Rankin, "Political Values," 151.

54. Rankin, "Political Values," 182.

55. Rankin, "Political Values," 170–171.

10. Witnesses

1. Síocháin and O'Sullivan, eds., *The Eyes of Another Race*, 22.

2. Síocháin and O'Sullivan, eds., *The Eyes of Another Race*, 13–14.

3. Quoted in Ewans, *European Atrocity, African Catastrophe*, 195. For Casement's report, see Síocháin and O'Sullivan, eds., *The Eyes of Another Race*, 49–117.

4. On the establishment of this relationship, see Joseph Choate to John Hay, London, June 21, 1901, FRUS 1901, 205–206.

5. On the Anglo-American dimensions of the Congo Reform Movement, see Clay, "Transatlantic Dimensions," 18–28.

6. Ida B. Wells's investigations, undertaken in the same years that early reports of Congo atrocities were first appearing in US papers, identified hundreds of Black Americans lynched in the 1890s. Wells, *A Red Record*, 12–17. The NAACP estimates that nearly five thousand men and women were lynched in the United States between 1882 and 1968. NAACP, "History of Lynching in America," https://naacp.org/find-resources/history-explained/history-lynching-america.

7. Frederick Frelinghuysen to Mr. W. P. Tisdel, Washington, Sept. 8, 1884, FRUS 1885, 285–286, 295. On Stanley's work helping to establish the Congo Free State, see Newman, *Imperial Footprints*, ch. 6. On the African American efforts to evangelize the Congo and Africa in general, see Killingray, "The Black Atlantic Missionary Movement," 3–31; Jacobs, ed. *Black Americans and the Missionary Movement in Africa*.

8. Van Reybrouck, *Congo*, 59–90. On Africans serving as colonial soldiers, see Moyd, *Violent Intermediaries*.

9. On Leopold's use of religious freedom, see Kenny and Wenger, "Church, State, and 'Native Liberty' in the Belgian Congo," 161–163.

10. Jones, *In Search of Brightest Africa*, 16–21; 57–62.

11. John O. Means, "Some Reasons for Evangelizing Central Africa," Parts I and II, *Missionary Herald* (May 1880), 167–170; John O. Means, "Some Reasons for Evangelizing Central Africa," Part III, *Missionary Herald* (June 1880), 212–217; John O. Means, "Some Reasons for Evangelizing Central Africa," Part IV, *Missionary Herald* (July 1880), 251–253; John O. Means, "Some Reasons for Evangelizing Central Africa," Part V, *Missionary Herald* (Aug. 1880), 298–302; John O. Means, "Some Reasons for Evangelizing Central Africa," Part VI, *Missionary Herald* (September 1880), 335–338; John O. Means, "Some Reasons for Evangelizing Central Africa," Part VII, *Missionary Herald* (Oct. 1880), 379–383.

12. Thompson, *Light on Darkness?* 176.

13. Lambert Tree to the General Administrator of the Department of Foreign Affairs and of Justice of the Independent State of the Congo, Brussels, Dec. 23, 1887, FRUS 1888, Part I, 31.

14. Phipps, *William Sheppard*, 61.

15. Sheppard, *Presbyterian Pioneers in Congo*; Phipps, *William Sheppard*, 59–93. On Sheppard as a collector and ethnologist, see Carton, "From Hampton 'Into the Heart of Africa," 53–86; and Cureau, "William H. Sheppard," 340–352.

16. Jones, *In Search of Brightest Africa*, 63–64; Evans, *European Atrocity, African Catastrophe*, ch. 18; Dworkin, *Congo Love Song*, ch. 1.

17. Quoted in Phipps, *William Sheppard*, 140.

18. Van Reybrouck, *Congo*, 79, 86–88.

19. Thompson, *Light on Darkness*, 173–175.

20. Ewans, *European Atrocity, African Catastrophe*, 179–182.

21. On the use of cannibalism as a trope in descriptions of Africans, see Arens, *The Man-Eating Myth*.

22. William Sheppard, "Typed Transcription of William H. Sheppard Diary, 1899 13-14 September," William H. Sheppard Papers, Box 1, Folder 6, https://digital.history.pcusa.org/islandora/object/islandora%3A15919?solr_nav%5Bid%5D=1679a118308917f8e477&solr_nav%5Bpage%5D=0&solr_nav%5Boffset%5D=15#page/7/mode/1up.

23. Sheppard, "Typed Transcription of William H. Sheppard Diary, 1899 13-14 September." Dworkin, *Congo Love Song*, 53-55. On the severing of hands more generally, see Van Reybrouck, *Congo*, 90-91.

24. William Morrison, "Under What Circumstances Are We Justified in Making Public the Accounts of Atrocities and Other Forms of Injustice Done to Natives?" in Benedetto, *Presbyterian Reformers in Central Africa*, 267-274. On changing missionary perspectives on colonial violence elsewhere in Africa, see Blackler, *An Imperial Homeland*.

25. Thompson, *Light on Darkness*, 183.

26. On Leopold's attempts to control the press, see Clay, "David vs Goliath," 457-474.

27. Phipps, *William Sheppard*, 142-144.

28. Executive Committee of Foreign Missions to APCM, Jan. 9, 1900, in Benedetto, *Presbyterian Reformers in Central Africa*, 127-129.

29. Phipps, *William Sheppard*, 106-131.

30. "Belgium Has Monopoly," *Baltimore Sun* (July 2, 1903), 2.

31. *Congressional Record* (Apr. 19, 1904), 5061-5076.

32. *Congressional Record* (Apr. 19, 1904), 5061-5076. Morrison was active in getting these documents before Congress. Phipps, *William Sheppard*, 152.

33. *Congressional Record* (Apr. 19, 1904), 5061-5076.

34. Phipps, *William Sheppard*, 152-153.

35. Phipps, *William Sheppard*, 156.

36. Root quoted in Phipps, *William Sheppard*, 156.

37. Morrison address to the Boston Peace Congress, "Treatment of the Native People by the Government of the Congo Independent State" in Benedetto, *Presbyterian Reformers in Central Africa*, 206-213.

38. William H. Sheppard Papers, Box 4, 835.03.18b, https://digital.history.pcusa.org/islandora/object/islandora%3A1878?solr_nav%5Bid%5D=1679a118308917f8e477&solr_nav%5Bpage%5D=0&solr_nav%5Boffset%5D=14.

39. On missionary photography, see Ho, *Developing Mission*. On colonial uses of photography, see Foliard, *The Violence of Colonial Photography*.

40. On Congo missionary photography in the United States and Britain, see Grant, *A Civilised Savagery*, ch. 2; Hochschild, *King Leopold's Ghost*, 215-217; Thompson, *Light on Darkness*, ch. 5; Phipps, *William Sheppard*, 142.

41. See, for example, materials in FRUS (1905) from Belgium.

42. *Congressional Record* (April 12, 1906), 5112-5113.

43. Elihu Root to Edwin Denby, Washington, Feb. 20, 1906, FRUS 1906, 88-89.

44. Henry Lane Wilson to Elihu Root, Brussels, March 15, 1906, FRUS 1906, 93.

45. A. Mclean to Elihu Root, April 16, 1906, FRUS 1906, 99. On Protestant-Catholic mission relations and the relations between church and state, see for

example Au, "Medical Orders," 62–82; Kenny and Wenger, "Church, State, and 'Native Liberty," 156–185.

46. William H. Sheppard "From the Bakuba Country," printed in Benedetto, *Presbyterian Reformers in Central Africa*, 281–283.

47. Summons is in Benedetto, *Presbyterian Reformers in Central Africa*, 333–335. On the trial, Dworkin, *Congo Love Song*, 55–61.

48. Dreypondt in Benedetto, *Presbyterian Reformers in Central Africa*, 283–285.

49. Chaltin in Benedetto, *Presbyterian Reformers in Central Africa*, 290–291.

50. Morrison in Benedetto, *Presbyterian Reformers in Central Africa*, 286–289; 292–296.

51. Morrison in Benedetto, *Presbyterian Reformers in Central Africa*, 302–309.

52. Morrison in Benedetto, *Presbyterian Reformers in Central Africa*, 336–337.

53. Chester in Benedetto, *Presbyterian Reformers in Central Africa*, 347–249.

54. "Prosecution of Congo Missionaries," *Christian Observer* (Apr. 21, 1909), 2.

55. Vass in Benedetto, *Presbyterian Reformers in Central Africa*, 339–343.

56. John Daniels, "The Congo Question and the 'Belgian Solution," *North American Review* 188 (Dec. 1908): 891–902.

57. "Appeal for Missionaries," *New York Times* (May 9, 1909), 2.

58. Some of these articles cover the debates within denominational bodies over whether (or how much) to appeal to the government to help the missionary cause. Though they lost the debate, some at the General Assembly had suggested that it was inappropriate for the denomination to reach out to the State Department. The Presbyterians ultimately concluded that, while church and state were—and should be—separate, the church should apply for aid in "extraordinary cases," and this was precisely such a case. The denomination ultimately relied on the right to petition the government, finding this not inconsistent with the principle of trusting in God. "To leave all to God, and to use the means which God has placed to our hands, are not antagonistic." "Shall the Church Appeal to Caesar?" *Christian Observer* (May 26, 1909), 2.

59. "The Trial of Our Congo Missionaries," *Christian Observer* (July 28, 1909), 2.

60. "The Relation of the United States to the Congo Question," *Christian Observer* (June 16, 1909), 3.

61. The wired article appears in multiple papers under various titles. See, for example: "Two Americans Haled [sic] Before Congo Court," *Atlanta Constitution* (May 10, 1909), 3; "Trial Stirs Congo State," *Chicago Daily Tribune* (May 10, 1909), 5; "Trial Involves Congo Missions," *Detroit Free Press* (May 10, 1909), 2; "Missionaries in Suit," *Baltimore Sun* (May 10, 1909), 2; "Belgium Attempts to Silence Ministers," *Louisville Courier-Journal* (May 10, 1909), 3; "Trial of Missionaries," *New-York Tribune* (May 10, 1909), 2.

62. Felix H. Hunicke, "The Congo Question," *North American Review* 189 (April 1909): 604–614; John Daniels, "The Congo Question and the 'Belgian Solution," *North American Review* 188 (Dec. 1908): 891–902.

63. "Aid in Congo Cases," *Washington Post* (May 22, 1909), 9; "Appeal to President," *Louisville Courier-Journal* (May 22, 1909), 2; "Southern Presbyterians. Day

Set for Prayers for the Deliverance of Missionaries," *Nashville American* (May 22, 1909), 9; "Appeal to Taft Stands," *Baltimore Sun* (May 23, 1909), 2; "King Leopold Puts Americans in Congo on Trial," *St. Louis Post-Dispatch* (May 23, 1909), 4S; "Resolutions Adopted," *Nashville American* (May 23, 1909), 8; "American Consul to Aid Missionaries," *Nashville Tennessean* (May 26, 1909), 10; "Missionary Being Tried on Criminal Libel Charge in Africa," *Louisville Courier-Journal* (May 28, 1909), 8; "Congo Libel Suits Deferred," *New York Times* (June 4, 1909), 5; "Trial of Missionaries," *Nashville American* (June 4, 1909), 5; "Trial Postponed," *Boston Daily Globe* (June 8, 1909), 10; "To Appeal to Taft," *Boston Daily Globe* (July 20, 1909), 6; "Appeals to President to Protect Americans," *Indianapolis Star* (June 25, 1909), 2; "To Appeal to Taft for Missionaries," *New York Times* (June 25, 1909), 4; "Swiss League to Appeal to Taft in Case of American Missionaries in Congo," *Cincinnati Enquirer* (July 20, 1909), 3; "Socialist to Aid Americans," *Christian Science Monitor* (Aug. 2, 1909), 9; "Americans' Trials Postponed," *San Francisco Chronicle* (Aug. 7, 1909), 3; "Put Off Missionaries' Trial," *New York Times* (Aug. 7, 1909), 4; "Missionaries' Trial Begun," *Washington Post* (Sept. 21, 1909), 5; Austin Marx, "Vandervelde, Belgium's Socialist Leader, Champions American Congo Missionaries," *Detroit Free Press* (Oct. 3, 1909), D6.

64. "Letters Made Public," *Boston Daily Globe* (May 18, 1909), 9.

65. "The Trial of Morrison and Sheppard," *Christian Observer* (Sept. 29, 1909), 6.

66. "Acquittal of Congo Missionaries," *Christian Observer* (Oct. 1909), 2. The news soon spread through the secular press as well: "American Freed of Libel Charge in Belgian Congo," *Indianapolis Star* (Oct. 6, 1909), 2; "American Freed," *Los Angeles Times* (Oct. 6, 1909), I2; "American Missionary," *Cincinnati Enquirer* (Oct. 6, 1909), 3; "American Missionary Free," *Baltimore Sun* (Oct. 6, 1909), 5; "Americans Freed in Congo," *Chicago Daily Tribune* (Oct. 6, 1909), 5; "Congo Missionary Acquitted of Libel," *New York Times* (Oct. 6, 1909), 6; "Congo Missionary Cleared," *Nashville American* (Oct. 6, 1909), 12; "Missionary is Acquitted," *Boston Daily Globe* (Oct. 6, 1909), 9; "Missionary Shepherd Acquitted of Libel," *Detroit Free Press* (Oct. 6, 1909), 4.

67. William Sheppard, "From Leopoldville to Luebo," *Christian Observer* (Feb. 16, 1910), 11-12. On the ongoing work of the Presbyterian Congo mission, see Hill, *A Higher Mission*.

11. Humanitarians

1. James Barton, "Autobiographical Notes," ABC 11.4, Box 12, 249-250.

2. Barton, "Autobiographical Notes," 249-253.

3. Barton, "Autobiographical Notes," 249-253.

4. Barton, "Autobiographical Notes," 249-253.

5. Barton, "Autobiographical Notes," 249-253.

6. Barton, "Autobiographical Notes," 259.

7. On the role of religion in Wilson's political life, see Burnidge, *A Peaceful Conquest*; Hankins, *Woodrow Wilson*; Magee, *What the World Should Be*.

8. Wilson, "An Address in Nashville on Behalf of the YMCA" (February 24, 1912), Papers of Woodrow Wilson Digital Edition.

9. "The Konia American Hospital Taken," *Missionary Herald* (Dec. 1914), 572.

10. "Traveling in Eastern Turkey," *Missionary Herald* (Dec. 1914), 573.

11. "Conditions in Harpoot," *Missionary Herald* (Dec. 1914), 574–575.

12. On the information coming from American consuls, see Rouben Paul Adalian, "American Diplomatic Correspondence in the Age of Mass Murder: The Armenian Genocide in the US Archives," in Winter, *America and the Armenian Genocide*, 146–184. See also Lloyd E. Ambrosius, "Wilsonian Diplomacy and Armenia: The Limits of Power and Ideology," in Winter, *America and the Armenian Genocide*, 113–145. On missionary information, see Suzanne E. Moranian, "The Armenian Genocide and American Missionary Relief Efforts," in Winter, *America and the Armenian Genocide*, 185–213.

13. Laderman, *Sharing the Burden*, 92.

14. Morgenthau to the Secretary of State, Constantinople, Mar. 27, 1915. FRUS 1915. Supplement, The World War, Document 1347.

15. Morgenthau to the Secretary of State, Constantinople, Sept. 4, 1915, FRUS 1915, Supplement, Document 1351.

16. Yacoub, *Year of the Sword*, 38–43; 123.

17. Yacoub, *Year of the Sword*, 121.

18. Mary Schauffler Platt, quoted in Yacoub, *Year of the Sword*, 44.

19. Bryan to Morgenthau, Washington, Feb. 18, 1915, FRUS 1915 Supplement, Document 1392.

20. Morgenthau to Bryan, Constantinople, Apr. 27, 1915, FRUS 1915 Supplement, Document 1395.

21. Sharp (French Ambassador) to Bryan, Paris, May 28, 1915, FRUS 1915 Supplement, Document 1398.

22. Morgenthau to Bryan, July 10, 1915, FRUS 1915 Supplement, Document 1400; Morgenthau to Bryan, Aug. 11, 1915, FRUS 1915 Supplement, Document 1406.

23. Adalian, "American Diplomatic Correspondence," 150.

24. Knapp, *The Tragedy of Bitlis*, 15.

25. Knapp, *Tragedy of Bitlis*, 30–34. McLaren's story was briefly mentioned in "Other Stations," *Missionary Herald* (Nov. 1915), 536–537.

26. Knapp, *Tragedy of Bitlis*, 40–41.

27. Knapp, *Tragedy of Bitlis*, 44.

28. Knapp, *Tragedy of Bitlis*, 44–48.

29. Knapp, *Tragedy of Bitlis*, 51–56.

30. Knapp, *Tragedy of Bitlis*, 60–62.

31. William Chambers to Woodrow Wilson, Chatham, NJ, Dec. 10, 1915, in *Papers of Woodrow Wilson Digital Edition*.

32. Morgenthau to Bryan, July 10, 1915, FRUS 1915 Supplement, Document 1400.

33. Morgenthau to Bryan, Aug. 11, 1915, FRUS 1915 Supplement, Document 1406.

34. Barton to Bryan, July 14, 1915, FRUS 1915 Supplement, Document 1401.

35. Morgenthau to Bryan, Constantinople, Sept. 3, 1915, FRUS 1915 Supplement, Document 1410.

36. Lansing to Philip, Washington, Feb. 12, 1916, FRUS 1916 Supplement, Document 1109; Philip to Lansing, Constantinople, Feb. 15, 1916, FRUS 1916 Supplement, Document 1111; Philip to Lansing, Constantinople, Mar. 28, 1916 FRUS 1916 Supplement, Document 1112.

37. Philip to Lansing, Constantinople, July 21, 1916, FRUS 1916 Supplement, Document 1118.

38. Philip to Lansing, Constantinople, Sept. 1, 1916, FRUS 1916 Supplement, Document 1120.

39. Philip to Lansing, Constantinople, Oct. 1, 1916, FRUS 1916 Supplement, Document 1121.

40. Ambassador Elkus to Lansing, Constantinople, Oct. 17, 1916 FRUS 1916 Supplement, Document 1122.

41. Yacoub, *Year of the Sword*, 95; Moranian, "The Armenian Genocide and American Missionary Relief Efforts," 209–210; Walther, "For God and Country," 63–79. On the range of reports that reached American and European audiences, see Yacoub, *Year of the Sword*, ch. 1; and Walther, *Sacred Interests*, ch. 8.

42. Moranian, "The Armenian Genocide and American Missionary Relief Efforts," 206.

43. Moranian, "The Armenian Genocide and American Missionary Relief Efforts," 193.

44. "Social Service in Turkey," *Missionary Herald* (Apr. 1917), 176–178.

45. "A Relief Commission's View of the American Board," *Missionary Herald* (Nov. 1915), 500.

46. Laderman, *Sharing the Burden*, 999; Moranian, "The Armenian Genocide and American Missionary Relief Efforts," 194–195.

47. W. Nesbitt Chambers, "Redeeming a Battlefield," *Missionary Herald* (Dec. 1916), 549.

48. Hoffman Philip to Turkish Minister of Foreign Affairs, Constantinople, May 29, 1916, Enclosure 2 in FRUS 1916 Supplement, Document 1103.

49. Philip to Secretary of State, Constantinople, May 31, 1916, FRUS 1916 Supplement, Document 1102. This story was also told in George E. White, "The Story of the Marsovan Eviction," *Missionary Herald* (Aug. 1916), 354–358.

50. "Martyred Professors of Euphrates College, Harpoot," *Missionary Herald* (Jan. 1916), 22.

51. "American Interests in Turkey Violated," *Missionary Herald* (Nov. 1915), 498.

52. Polk to Philip, Washington, May 27, 1916, FRUS 1916 Supplement, Document 1098.

53. On Wilson's diplomacy and the eventual decision to declare war, Ambrosius, *Wilsonian Statecraft*, especially 86–87.

54. Woodrow Wilson, "An Address in Nashville on Behalf of the YMCA" (1912), in *The Papers of Woodrow Wilson Digital Edition*.

55. Woodrow Wilson to James Barton, White House, July 25, 1913, in *The Papers of Woodrow Wilson Digital Edition*.

56. William Jennings Bryan to Woodrow Wilson, Washington, June 2, 1913, in *The Papers of Woodrow Wilson Digital Edition*; Cleveland Dodge to Woodrow Wilson, New York, April 1, 1913 in *The Papers of Woodrow Wilson Digital Edition*.

57. Woodrow Wilson, "Transcript of Joint Address to Congress Leading to a Declaration of War Against Germany (1917)," https://www.ourdocuments.gov/doc.php?flash=false&doc=61; Manela, *The Wilsonian Movement*.

58. Wilson quoted in Ambrosius, *Wilsonian Statecraft*, 98.

59. "From Portland, Oregon," *Woman's Work* (Feb. 1918), 47.

60. *Woman's Work* (October 1918), 193.

61. "Bugle Calls from Mission Fields," *Missionary Herald* (Dec. 1916), 548–553.

62. Quoted in Nichols, *Promise and Peril*, 135–136.

63. "A Side Light on the War," *Missionary Herald* (Jan. 1918), 6.

64. On the financial concerns that the war brought, see, for example, Rev. William P. Schell, "Reasonable Optimism," *Woman's Work* (Jan. 1918), 5–6.

65. "The Patriotic Versus the Missionary Appeal," *Missionary Herald* (May 1917), 230.

66. "Think a Minute," *Woman's Work* (March 1918), 49; see also Mrs. B. A. Thaxter, "The Red Cross or the Missionary Society—Which?" *Woman's Work* (July 1918), 162–164.

67. "Rising to the Emergency," *Missionary Herald* (May 1917), 229.

68. James L. Barton, "Survey of the Fields, 1917–1918," *Missionary Herald* (Nov. 1918), 513–514, 522–423.

69. Mrs. Dwight H. Day, "A Chat with an Officer of the Board of Foreign Missions," *Woman's Work* (Nov. 1918), 234–235.

70. "Leave Turkey and Bulgaria Out," *Missionary Herald* (Jan. 1918), 3–4.

71. Walther, "For God and Country," 63–79.

72. Laderman, *Sharing the Burden*, 128.

73. Ambrosius, "Wilsonian Diplomacy and Armenia," 116.

74. Lansing to Stone, Washington, Dec. 6, 1917, FRUS 1917, Supplement 2, the World War, vol. 1, Document 373.

75. Robert Lansing to Woodrow Wilson, Washington, May 8, 1918, in *The Papers of Woodrow Wilson Digital Edition*. For a similar argument from Dodge, see Cleveland H. Dodge to Woodrow Wilson, Riverdale, Dec. 2, 1917, *The Papers of Woodrow Wilson Digital*. Barton expressed similar concerns in an open letter to Senator Lodge. Laderman, *Sharing the Burden*, 128.

76. *Missionary Herald* (Nov. 1918), 514–515.

77. "Why Missionary Ammunition for Pastors?" in *Missionary Ammunition for Pastors*, No. 1, 3–4.

78. J. H. Oldham, "The Challenge of the War," *Missionary Ammunition*, No. IV, 5; John R. Mott, "The Missionary Obligation in War Times," *Missionary Ammunition*, No. IV, 2.

79. *Missionary Ammunition*, No. IV, 4.

80. Woodrow Wilson, "America's Object in the War" and "A Work for All the Nations of the Earth," in *Missionary Ammunition*, No. IV, 8–10.

81. *Missionary Ammunition*, No. IV, 12.

82. James Barton, "Effect of the War upon Missionary Work," *Missionary Ammunition*, No. IV, 19–21.

83. "Our Greatest Missionary Call," *Missionary Herald* (Feb. 1918), 53.

84. Smith, *How the Battle Goes*, 5–6.

85. *Missionary Ammunition*, No. 6, 3. Similar language is present in "A Call for Volunteers," *Missionary Herald* (Jan. 1919), 25.

86. "World's Peace Conference at New Haven," *Missionary Herald* (February 1919), 48.

87. Rev. Stephen Corey, *Missionary Ammunition*, No. 6, 5.

88. Lucy Peabody, "Unparalleled Opportunities for Women," *Missionary Ammunition*, No. 6, 25.

89. "Turkey's Surrender," *Missionary Herald* (Dec. 1918), 534.

90. Walther, *Sacred Interests*, 296–313; Walther, "For God and Country," 63–79; Laderman, *Sharing the Burden*, 135–136.

91. Ambrosius, "Wilsonian Diplomacy and Armenia," 121.

92. Quotes are from Woodrow Wilson, "To the United States Congress," (May 24, 1920), *The Papers of Woodrow Wilson Digital Edition*.

93. Su, *Exporting Freedom*, ch. 2.

94. Ambrosius, *Wilsonian Statecraft*, 124. On the unmet hopes for self-determination that Wilson inspired in many colonized peoples at the end of the Great War, see Manela, *The Wilsonian Moment*.

95. Woodrow Wilson to Cleveland Dodge, The White House, Apr. 19, 1920, *The Papers of Woodrow Wilson Digital Edition*. See also Ambrosius, *Wilsonian Statecraft*, 122–124.

96. For Wilson's explanation of this strategy, see Woodrow Wilson, "Remarks to Members of the Democratic National Committee" (Feb. 28, 1919), *The Papers of Woodrow Wilson Digital Edition*.

97. Woodrow Wilson, "An Address in Boston" (Feb. 24, 1919) *The Papers of Woodrow Wilson Digital Edition*. John Milton Cooper Jr. points out that Wilson did not invoke Armenia as much as he might have done. John Milton Cooper Jr., "A Friend in Power? Woodrow Wilson and Armenia," in Winter, *America and the Armenian Genocide*, 108–109.

98. Woodrow Wilson, "An Address in Convention Hall in Kansas City" (Sept. 6, 1919), *The Papers of Woodrow Wilson Digital Edition*. See also brief mention of Armenia in Woodrow Wilson, "An Address in Reno" (Sept. 22, 1919), *The Papers of Woodrow Wilson Digital Edition*.

99. Woodrow Wilson, "Remarks to Members of the Democratic National Committee" (Feb. 28, 1919), *The Papers of Woodrow Wilson Digital Edition*.

100. Laderman, *Sharing the Burden*, 137.

101. "Flashes from the Front in Turkey," *Missionary Herald* (June 1919), 228; "Getting Busy in Constantinople," *Missionary Herald* (June 1919), 236–237.

102. "Flashes from the Front in Turkey," *Missionary Herald* (June 1919), 230.

103. "The Mission Station at Adana," *Missionary Herald* (Aug. 1919), 346.

104. "America's Duty to Armenia," *Missionary Herald* (Mar. 1919), 93–94.

105. "Today in Turkey," *Missionary Herald* (June 1919), 233.

106. "A Farewell Service," *Missionary Herald* (July 1919), 296.

107. "Editorial Notes," *Missionary Herald* (Aug. 1919), 317.

108. Emphasis in original. Wilson, "To the United States Congress" (May 24, 1920) *The Papers of Woodrow Wilson Digital Edition*.

109. Cooper, "A Friend in Power," 110.

110. Moranian, "The Armenian Genocide and American Missionary Relief Efforts," 195–196.

111. Moranian, "The Armenian Genocide and American Missionary Relief Efforts," 208.

Epilogue

1. Caitlin McGaw, quoted in "The War Stories Their Families Never Forgot," *New York Times Magazine* (Nov. 9, 2018).

2. Edward Marshall, "Yamei Kin on Japan's Hate," *Los Angeles Times* (Apr. 16, 1911), vii.

3. Mike Ives, "Overlooked No More: Yamei Kin, the Chinese Doctor Who Introduced Tofu to the West," *New York Times* (Oct. 18, 2018); Shurtleff and Aoyagi, *Biography of Yamei Kin*.

4. Theodore Roosevelt to Yamei Kin, March 4, 1904. Theodore Roosevelt Digital Library.

5. "Little Dr. Yamei Kin Answers Socialists," *New York Times* (Feb. 18, 1905), 7.

6. "Society in Washington: Interesting Lecture by Dr. Yamei Kin, of China," [*Baltimore*] *Sun* (Mar. 25, 1904).

7. "Yamei Kin's Mission," *New-York Tribune* (Oct. 25, 1904), 5; "A Woman and War: Yamei Kin Has Ideas about Conditions in the East," *New-York Tribune* (Nov. 13, 1904).

8. Edward Marshall, "Yamei Kin on Japan's Hate," *Los Angeles Times* (Apr. 16, 1911), vii.

9. The Foreign Missions Convention of the United States and Canada, "Preliminary Announcement," (Place of publication and publisher not identified, 1924), 1. For a discussion of the planning of this event, see Barton, "Autobiographical Notes," 321–324.

10. "Coolidge to Open Missions Meeting," *New York Times* (Jan. 25, 1925), 4.

11. *Ecumenical Missionary Conference, New York, 1900* (New York: American Tract Society, 1900).

12. Calvin Coolidge, "Address," in Turner and Sanders, *The Foreign Missions Convention at Washington*, 4–5.

13. Coolidge, "Address," in Turner and Sanders, *The Foreign Missions Convention at Washington*, 6.

14. Herbert Welch, "The Present World Situation" in Turner and Sanders, *The Foreign Missions Convention at Washington*, 19.

15. Brown, *Memoirs of a Centenarian*, 66–67.

16. Kennedy, *The American Consul*, 201–204.

17. Kennedy, *The American Consul*, 276.

18. Charles Hughes to Dr. Robert E. Speer, Department of State, Washington, Nov. 11, 1924, RARE DOC. H874cl, Presbyterian Historical Society.

19. See for example, Hollinger, *Protestants Abroad*, ch. 8; Sutton, *Double Crossed*.

20. McAlister, *The Kingdom of God Has No Borders*, ch. 9; Su, *Exporting Freedom*; Wenger, *Religious Freedom*; Turek, *To Bring the Good News to All Nations*.

21. McAlister, *The Kingdom of God Has No Borders,* 196.

22. J. Oliver Conroy, "The Life and Death of John Chau, the Man Who Tried to Convert His Killers," *The Guardian* (Feb. 3, 2019), https://www.theguardian. com/world/2019/feb/03/john-chau-christian-missionary-death-sentinelese; Harriet Sherwood, "Andrew Brunson: The US Pastor at the Heart of an International Crisis," *The Guardian* (Aug. 14, 2018), https://www.theguardian.com/ world/2018/aug/14/andrew-brunson-turkey-the-us-pastor-at-the-heart-of-an-international-crisis; Amanda Holpuch, "US Pastor Freed from Turkey Prays with Trump at White House," *The Guardian* (Oct. 13, 2018), https://www.theguardian.com/us-news/2018/oct/13/andrew-brunson-pastor-turkey-trump-white-house-prayer; "Remarks by President Trump in Meeting with Pastor Andrew Brunson," White House Archives, (Oct. 13, 2018), https://trumpwhitehouse. archives.gov/briefings-statements/remarks-president-trump-meeting-pastor-andrew-brunson/.

BIBLIOGRAPHY

Archival Collections

Houghton Library, Harvard University, Cambridge, MA

Papers of the American Board of Commissioners for Foreign Missions (ABC)

Library of Congress, Washington, DC

Charles H. Brent Papers
Charles Monroe Dickinson Papers
William Goodell Papers

National Archives, College Park, MD

RG 59, Dispatches from US Consular Officers, 1789–1906
RG 59, Letters to Foreign Sovereigns and Heads of State
RG 59, M17
RG 59, M179

Presbyterian Historical Society, Philadelphia, PA

American Presbyterian Congo Mission Records, 1893–1980 (APCM)
Janvier Family Papers
Mattoon Family Papers (MFP)
McCartee Family Papers (MCFP)
Presbyterian Church US China Mission Papers
Presbyterian Church US Japan Mission Records
Rankin Family Papers (RFP)
Mary E. Lewis Shedd Papers
William H. Sheppard Papers

Yale Divinity School Library, New Haven, CT

Arthur Judson Brown Papers (AJBP)
John R. Mott Papers

Periodicals

American Baptist Magazine
The [Baltimore] Sun
The Bibliotheca Sacra
Boston Daily Globe
Boston Recorder
The Charleston Mercury
Chicago Daily Tribune
The Chinese Recorder and Missionary Journal
The Chinese Repository
The Christian Advocate
Christian Observer
Christian Union
Christian Watchman
The Congressional Record
The Continental Monthly: Devoted to Literature and National Policy
Courier-Journal
The Craftsman
Daily American
Democratic Free Press
Detroit Free Press
Episcopal Recorder
Evangelical Monthly
The Evangelist
The Foreign Missionary
The Friend, a Religious and Literary Journal
Graham's Magazine of Literature and Art
Holden's Dollar Magazine of Criticisms, Biographies, Sketches, Essays, Tales,
    Reviews, Poetry, etc.
The Independent
Journal of the American Geographical Society of New York
Journal of the American Oriental Society
Los Angeles Times
The Merchants' Magazine and Commercial Review
The Missionary Herald
The Missionary Magazine
The Nashville American
The New Englander
New York Evangelist

New York Observer and Chronicle
New York Religious Chronicler
New York Times
New-York Tribune
North American Review
The North-China Herald and Supreme Court and Consular Gazette
The Outlook
The Panoplist and Missionary Herald
Proceedings of the Academy of Natural Sciences of Philadelphia
Recorder and Telegraph
Religious Intelligencer
Science
The United States Magazine and Democratic Review
The Washington Post
The Woman's Journal
Woman's Work

Published Primary Sources

Adams, Charles Francis, ed. *Memoirs of John Quincy Adams, Comprising Portions of His Diary from 1795 to 1848.* 12 vols. Philadelphia: J. B. Lippincott, 1876.

John Quincy Adams (JQA) Digital Diary. Massachusetts Historical Society, 2022. https://www.masshist.org/publications/jqadiaries/.

Aikman, Rev. J. Logan. *Cyclopedia of Christian Missions: Their Rise, Progress, and Present Position.* London: Richard Griffin and Company, 1860.

Allen, David. *India, Ancient and Modern. Geographical, Historical, Political, Social, and Religious; With a Particular Account of the State and Prospects of Christianity.* 2nd ed. Boston: John P. Jewett and Company, 1856.

American Board of Commissioners of Foreign Missions. *Annual Report.* 110 vols. Boston, 1811–1920.

American Board of Commissioners for Foreign Missions. *Manual for Missionary Candidates of the American Board of Commissioners for Foreign Missions.* Boston: Press of Crocker and Brewster, 1845.

American Board of Commissioners for Foreign Missions. *Maps of Missions of the American Board of Commissioners for Foreign Missions.* Boston: The Board, 1898.

American Board of Commissioners for Foreign Missions. *On the Use of Missionary Maps at the Monthly Concert.* Boston: Crocker and Brewster, 1842.

American College for Girls at Constantinople. *The President's Report to the Board of Trustees for the Year 1890–91.* London: Sir Joseph Causton and Sons, 1891.

American Sunday-School Union. *Missionary Manual: A Sketch of the History and Present State of Christian Missions to the Heathen. Designed to Accompany the Map of the World Published by the American Sunday-School Union.* Revised edition. Philadelphia: American Sunday-School Union, 1839.

Anderson, Rufus. *A Heathen Nation Evangelized: History of the Sandwich Islands Mission.* Boston: Congregational Publishing Society, 1870.

Anderson, Rufus. *History of the Missions of the American Board of Commissioners for Foreign Mission to the Oriental Churches, in Two Volumes.* Vol. 1. Boston: Congregational Publishing Society, 1872.

Anderson, Rufus. *Memorial Volume of the First Fifty Years of the American Board.* Boston: American Board of Commissioners for Foreign Missions, 1861.

Baptist Board of Foreign Missions. *The Second Annual Report of the Baptist Board of Foreign Missions.* Philadelphia: Anderson and Meehan, 1816.

Benedetto, Robert, ed. *Presbyterian Reformers in Central Africa: A Documentary Account of the American Presbyterian Congo Mission and the Human Rights Struggle in the Congo, 1890–1918.* New York: E. J. Brill, 1996.

Boston Athenaeum. *Catalogue of the Library of the Boston Athenaeum, 1807–1871.* 5 vols. Boston: Boston Athenaeum: 1874–1882.

Boston Public Library, *List of Books, Arranged by Authors, Titles, and Subjects.* Boston: Boston Public Library, 1872.

Brown, Arthur Judson. *The Foreign Missionary: An Incarnation of a World Movement.* New York: Fleming H. Revell Company, 1907.

Brown, Arthur Judson. *The New Era in the Philippines.* Nashville: Publishing House, Methodist Episcopal Church, South, 1903.

Brown, Arthur Judson. *New Forces in Old China: An Inevitable Awakening.* 2nd ed. New York: Fleming H. Revell Company, 1904.

Brown, Arthur Judson. *Memoirs of a Centenarian.* Edited by William N. Wysham. New York: World Horizons, 1957.

Brown, Arthur Judson. *Report of a Visitation of the Philippine Mission of the Board of Foreign Missions of the Presbyterian Church in the United States of America.* New York: Printed for the Use of the Board and the Missions, 1902.

Brown, William A. *The Why and How of Missions in the Sunday-School.* New York: Fleming H. Revell Company, 1916.

Burnet, D. S. *The Jerusalem Mission: Under the Direction of the American Christian Missionary Society.* Cincinnati: American Christian Publication Society, 1853.

Castle, Samuel Northrup. *An Account of the Visit of the French Frigate l'Artemise to the Sandwich Islands, July 1839.* Honolulu, 1839.

Dennis, James S. *Christian Missions and Social Progress: A Sociological Study of Foreign Missions.* Vol. 3. New York: Fleming H. Revell Company, 1906.

Department of State. *A Register of Officers and Agents, Civil, Military, and Naval, in the Service of the United States.* Washington, DC: Printed by Jonathon Elliot, 1816.

Department of War. *A Report of the Secretary of War, Containing the Reports of the Taft Commission, Its Several Acts of Legislation, and Other Important Information Relating to the Conditions and Immediate Wants of the Philippine Islands.* Washington, DC: Government Printing Office, 1901.

Dibble, Sheldon. *History of the Sandwich Islands.* Lahainaluna: Press of the Mission Seminary, 1843.

Domestic and Foreign Missionary Society of the Protestant Episcopal Church in the United States of America. *Missionary Record of the Domestic and Foreign Missionary Society of the Protestant Episcopal Church in the United States of America.* March 1834.

Ecumenical Missionary Conference, New York, 1900. New York: American Tract Society, 1900.

Essex Institute. *Books on China in the Library of Essex Institute: Essex Institute Special Catalogue No. 1.* Salem, MA: Printed for the Essex Institute, 1895.

Evarts, Jeremiah. *Cherokee Removal: The William Penn Essays and Other Writings,* ed. Francis Paul Prucha. Knoxville: University of Tennessee Press, 1982.

The Foreign Missions Convention of the United States and Canada. "Preliminary Announcement." N.p., 1924.

Foreign Relations of the United States (FRUS). Office of the Historian, United States Department of State. Digital Edition. https://history.state.gov/historicaldocuments.

Gammell, William. *A History of American Baptist Missions in Asia, Africa, Europe, and North America, Under the Care of the American Baptist Missionary Union.* Boston: Gould and Lincoln, 1854.

General Instructions to the Consuls and Commercial Agents of the United States. Prepared Under the Direction of the Department of State. Washington: A. O. P. Nicholson, 1855.

Goodrich, Samuel Griswold. *Peter Parley's Geography for Beginners; with Eighteen Maps and One Hundred and Fifty Engravings.* New York: Huntington and Savage, 1847.

Haines, Mrs. F.E.H. *Jonas King, Missionary to Syria and Greece.* New York: American Tract Society, 1879.

Hamlin, Alfred Dwight Foster. *In Memoriam, Rev. Cyrus Hamlin, D.D., L.L.D.* Boston: Published Privately, 1903.

Hamlin, Cyrus. *My Life and Times,* 4th ed. Boston: Pilgrim Press, 1893.

[Jones, J. C.] *Supplement* [sic] *to the Sandwich Island Mirror containing an Account of the Persecution of the Catholics at the Sandwich Islands.* Honolulu: R. J. Howard, Printer, 1840.

Knapp, Grace H. *The Tragedy of Bitlis: Being Mainly the Narratives of Gisell M. McLaren and Myrtle O. Shane.* New York: Fleming H. Revell Company, 1919.

Lansing, Gulian. *Egypt's Princes: A Narrative of Missionary Labor in the Valley of the Nile.* Philadelphia: William S. Rentoul, 1864.

Laurie, Thomas. *The Ely Volume; or, The Contributions of our Foreign Missions to Science and Human Well-Being.* Boston: American Board of Commissioners for Foreign Missions, 1881.

Liggins, John. *The Great Value and Success of Foreign Missions. Proved by Distinguished Witnesses: being the testimony of diplomatic ministers, consuls, naval officers, and scientific and other travelers in heathen and Mohammedan countries; together with that of English viceroys, governors, and military officers in India and in the British Colonies; also leading facts and late statistics of the missions.* New York: Baker and Taylor, 1888.

Mattoon, Rev. Stephen. "An Address Delivered at Bangkok on the 4th of July, 1865. The 89th Anniversary of American Independence." Bangkok: American Missionary Association, Published by request of American Residents, 1865.

McCartee, Divie Bethune. "Dr. McCartee's Reminiscences." *The Chinese Recorder and Missionary Journal.* Sept. 1, 1897: 403–409.

Memoir of Keopuolani, Late Queen of the Sandwich Islands. Boston: Crocker and Brewster, 1825.

Methodist Episcopal Church. *Fortieth Annual Report of the Society of the Methodist Episcopal Church.* New York: Printed for the Society, 1859.

Missionary Ammunition for the Exclusive Use of Pastors, No. 4: The War Test. Prepared by a Committee of the Foreign Missions Conference of North America, 1918.

Missionary Ammunition for the Exclusive Use of Pastors, No. 6: The Call to Foreign Missionary Service. Nashville: Executive Committee of Foreign Missions for the Presbyterian Church in the United States, 1919.

Missionary Ammunition for Pastors, No. 1: The Pastor as a World Leader. New York: Board of Foreign Missions of the Methodist Episcopal Church, 1916.

Mitchell, Samuel Augustus. *A System of Modern Geography: Comprising a Description of the Present State of the World, and Its Five Great Divisions: America, Europe, Asia, Africa, and Oceania, with Their Several Empires, Kingdoms, States, Territories, etc.: Embellished by Numerous Engravings: Adapted to the Capacity of Youth: Accompanied by an Atlas Containing Thirty-Two Maps, Drawn and Engraved Expressly for This Work.* Philadelphia: E. H. Butler and Co., 1860.

Morse, Jedidah. *The American Universal Geography, or, a View of the Present State of all the Kingdoms, States and Colonies I the World.* Boston: Thomas and Andrews, 1812.

Morse, Jedidiah. *Modern Atlas, Adapted to More's New School Geography, Published According to an Act of Congress, by Richardson and Lord, No. 75, Cornhill Boston.* Boston: J.H.A. Frost, 1822.

Near East College Association. *Tourist Guide to Constantinople, Robert College and Constantinople Woman's College.* New York: Near East Colleges, 1923.

Newcomb, Harvey. *A Cyclopedia of Missions: Containing a Comprehensive View of Missionary Operations Throughout the World: with Geographical Descriptions, and Accounts of the Social, Moral, and Religious Condition of the People.* New York: Charles Scribner, 1854.

Newcomb, Harvey. *The Monthly Concert; with Facts and Reflections Suited to Awaken a Zeal for the Conversion of the World.* Pittsburgh: Luke Loomis, 1836.

Perkins, Henry Martyn. *Life of Justin Perkins, DD: Pioneer Missionary to Persia.* Chicago: Woman's Presbyterian Board of Missions of the Northwest, 1887.

Perkins, Justin. *A Residence of Eight Years in Persia, among the Nestorian Christians: With Notices of the Muhammedans.* Andover, MA: Allen, Morrill and Wardwell, 1843.

Pond, Enoch. *Short Missionary Discourses, or Monthly Concert Lectures.* Worcester: Dorr and Howland, 1824.

Presbyterian Church in the USA. *The Twenty-Second Annual Report of the Board of Foreign Missions of the Presbyterian Church in the United States of America.* New York: Published for the Board at the Mission House, 1859.

Rankin, Henry William. "The Hour of China and the United States." *The Bibliotheca Sacra* 56 (July 1899): 561–578.

Rankin, William Henry. "Political Values of the American Missionary." *American Journal of Sociology* 13, no. 2 (September 1907): 145–182.

Religious Toleration in Egypt: Official Correspondence Relating to the Indemnity Obtained for the Maltreatment of Faris-el-Hakim, an Agent of the American Missionaries in Egypt: Reprinted from Published Official Documents. London: Warrington, Printer, 1862.

Rockhill, William W. *Appendix. Foreign Relations of the United States, 1901. Affairs in China.* Washington, DC: Government Printing Office, 1902.

Roosevelt, Theodore, Papers. Library of Congress Manuscript Division. Theodore Roosevelt Digital Library. Dickinson State University. https://www.theodorerooseveltcenter.org/Research/Digital-Library.

Seward, George Frederick. *The United States Consulates in China: A Letter, with Inclosures of the Consul-General in China to the Secretary of State.* Printed for Private Circulation, 1867.

Seward, Olive Risley, ed. *William H. Seward's Travels Around the World.* New York: D. Appleton and Company, 1876.

Sheppard, William H. *Presbyterian Pioneers in Congo.* Richmond, VA: Presbyterian Committee on Publication, 1917.

Shewmaker, Kenneth, ed. *The Papers of Daniel Webster, Diplomatic Papers.* 2 vols. Hanover, NH: Dartmouth College by the University Press of New England, 1983–1987.

Síocháin, Séamas Ó S, and Michael O'Sullivan, eds. *The Eyes of Another Race: Roger Casement's Congo Report and 1903 Diary.* Dublin: University College Dublin Press, 2003.

Smith, Eli, and H. G. O. Dwight. *Researches of the Rev. E. Smith and Rev. H.G.O. Dwight in Armenia.* Boston, 1833.

Smith, Egbert W. *How the Battle Goes.* Nashville: Executive Committee Foreign Missions, Presbyterian Church in the US, 1918.

Speer, Robert E., ed. A *Missionary Pioneer in the Far East: A Memorial of Divie Bethune McCartee, For More Than Fifty Years a Missionary of the Board of Foreign Missions of the Presbyterian Church in the USA.* New York: Fleming H. Revell Company, 1922.

State Department. *Diplomatic and Consular Service of US.* Proquest Congressional. 1828–1909. https://congressional-proquest-com.proxy2.cl.msu.edu/congressional/docview/t66.d71.s107a-2.4?accountid=12598.

State Department. Dispatches from U.S. Consular Officers, 1789–1906. https://catalog.archives.gov/id/302031.

Stewart, Charles S. *Private Journal of a Voyage to the Pacific Ocean, and Residence at the Sandwich Islands in the Years 1822, 1823, 1824, and 1825.* New York: John P. Haven, 1828.

Taft, William H. *The Church and Our Government in the Philippines: An Address Delivered before the Faculty and Students of the University of Notre Dame, October 5, 1904.* Notre Dame, IN: The University Press, 1904.

Taylor, Fitch W. *A Voyage Round the World, and Visits to Various Foreign Countries, in the United States Frigate* Columbia. New Haven: H. Mansfield, 1848.

Turner, Fennell P., and Frank Knight Sanders, eds. *The Foreign Missions Convention at Washington, 1925*. New York: Fleming H. Revell Company, 1925.

Underwood, Lillias. *Fifteen Years Among the Top-Knots; or, Life in Korea*. Boston: American Tract Society, 1908.

Wanless, William James. *The Medical Mission: Its Place, Power, and Appeal*. Philadelphia: Westminster Press, 1898.

Webster, Daniel. *Diplomatic and Official Papers of Daniel Webster, While Secretary of State*. New York: Harper and Brothers, 1848.

Wells, Ida B. *A Red Record: Tabulated Statistics and Alleged Causes of Lynchings in the United States, 1892–1893–1894*. Chicago: Privately Printed, 1895.

Whipple, Charles K. *Relation of the American Board of Commissioners for Foreign Missions to Slavery*. Boston: R. F. Wallcut, 1861.

Williams, Charles. *The Missionary Gazetteer, Comprising a Geographical and Statistical Account of the Various Stations of the Church, London, Moravian, Wesleyan, Baptist, and American, Missionary Societies, etc., with Their Progress in Evangelization and Civilization*. London: F. Westley and A. H. Davis, 1828.

Williams, Frederick Wells. *The Life and Letters of Samuel Wells Williams, LLD: Missionary, Diplomatist, Sinologue*. New York: G. P. Putnam's Sons, 1888.

Williams, H. F. *In Four Continents: A Sketch of the Foreign Missions of the Presbyterian Church, U.S.* Richmond, VA: Presbyterian Committee of Publication, 1910.

Williams, Samuel Wells. *Chinese Immigration*. New York: C. Scribner's Sons, 1879.

Williams, Samuel Wells. *The Middle Kingdom; A Survey of the Geography, Government, Education, Social Life, Arts, Religion, &c., of the Chinese Empire and Its Inhabitants. With a New Map of the Empire*. New York: Wiley and Putnam, 1848.

Williams, Samuel Wells. *Our Relations with the Chinese Empire*. San Francisco: 1877.

Williams, Samuel Wells, and Frederick Wells Williams. *A History of China: Being the Historical Chapters from The Middle Kingdom, with a Concluding Chapter Narrating Recent Events*. New York: Charles Scribner's Sons, 1897.

Woodrow Wilson, Papers, Digital Edition. Charlottesville: University of Virginia Press, Rotunda, 2017. https://rotunda.upress.virginia.edu/founders/WILS-01-65-02-0332.

Secondary Sources

Ahn, Katherine H. Lee. *Awakening the Hermit Kingdom: Pioneer American Women Missionaries in Korea*. Pasadena, CA: William Carey Library, 2009.

Alexander, Nathan G. "E. D. Morel (1873–1924), The Congo Reform Association, and the History of Human Rights." *Britain and the World* 9, no. 2 (2016): 213–235.

Ambrosius, Lloyd E. *Wilsonian Statecraft: Theory and Practice of Liberal Internationalism during World War I*. Wilmington, DE: Scholarly Resources, 1991.

Andrew, John. A. *From Revivals to Removal: Jeremiah Evarts, the Cherokee Nation, and the Search for the Soul of America*. Athens: University of Georgia Press, 1992.

Apilado, Mariano C. *Revolutionary Spirituality: A Study of the Protestant Role in the American Colonial Rule of the Philippines*. Quezon City, Philippines: New Day, 1999.

Arens, William. *The Man-Eating Myth: Anthropology and Anthropophagy.* New York: Oxford University Press, 1980.

Arista, Noelani. *The Kingdom and the Republic: Sovereign Hawai'i and the Early United States.* Philadelphia: University of Pennsylvania Press, 2019.

Au, Sokhieng. "Medical Orders: Catholic and Protestant Missionary Medicine in the Belgian Congo, 1880–1940." *Low Countries Historical Review* 132, no. 1 (2017): 62–82.

Batson, Benjamin A. "American Diplomats in Southeast Asia in the Nineteenth Century: The Case of Siam." *Journal of the Siam Society* 64 (July 1978): 39–112.

Bays, Daniel H., and Grant Wacker, eds. *The Foreign Missionary Enterprise at Home: Explorations in North American Cultural History.* Tuscaloosa: University of Alabama Press, 2003.

Blaakman, Michael, Emily Conroy-Krutz, and Noelani Arista, eds. *The Early Imperial Republic: From the American Revolution to the U.S.-Mexican War.* Philadelphia: University of Pennsylvania Press, 2023.

Blackler, Adam A. *An Imperial Homeland: Forging German Identity in Southwest Africa.* State College: Penn State University Press, 2022.

Blowers, Paul M. "'Living in a Land of Prophets': James Barclay and an Early Disciples of Christ Mission to Jews in the Holy Land." *Church History* 62, no. 4 (December 1993): 494–513.

Boonshoft, Mark. *Aristocratic Education and the Making of the American Republic.* Chapel Hill: University of North Carolina Press, 2020.

Borgwardt, Elizabeth, Christopher McKnight Nichols, and Andrew Preston, eds. *Rethinking American Grand Strategy.* New York: Oxford University Press, 2021.

Brückner, Martin. *The Social Life of Maps.* Chapel Hill: University of North Carolina Press, 2017.

Burnidge, Cara Lea. *A Peaceful Conquest: Woodrow Wilson, Religion, and the New World Order.* Chicago: University of Chicago Press, 2016.

Carpenter, Teresa. *The Miss Stone Affair: America's First Modern Hostage Crisis.* New York: Simon and Schuster, 2003.

Carton, Benedict. "From Hampton 'Into the Heart of Africa': How Faith in God and Folklore Turned Congo Missionary William Sheppard into a Pioneering Ethnologist." *History in Africa* 36 (2009): 53–86.

Chang, Gordon H. "Whose 'Barbarism'? Whose 'Treachery'? Race and Civilization in the Unknown United States–Korea War of 1871." *Journal of American History* 89, no. 4 (March 2003): 1331–1365.

Chidester, David. *Empire of Religion: Imperialism and Comparative Religion.* Chicago: University of Chicago Press, 2014.

Chin, Carol C. *Modernity and National Identity in the U.S. and East Asia, 1895–1919.* Kent, OH: Kent State University Press, 2010.

Chung, Mee-Hyun. "Her Name Was Lillias Horton Underwood: Revisiting Her Multidimensional Works." *International Review of Missions* 109, no. 1 (May 2020): 56–71.

Clay, Dean. "'David vs Goliath': The Congo Free State Propaganda War, 1890–1909." *International History Review* 43, no. 3 (2021): 457–474.

Clay, Dean. "Transatlantic Dimensions of the Congo Reform Movement." *English Studies in Africa* 59, no. 1 (2016): 18–28.

Clyde, Paul Hibbert. "Frederick F. Low and the Tientsin Massacre." *Pacific Historical Review* 2, no. 1 (March 1933): 100–108.

Clymer, Kenton. *Protestant Missionaries in the Philippines, 1898–1916: An Inquiry into the American Colonial Mentality.* Urbana: University of Illinois Press, 1986.

Cohen, Paul A. *History in Three Keys: The Boxers as Event, Experience, and Myth.* Rev. ed. New York: Columbia University Press, 1998.

Cohen, Warren I. *East Asia at the Center: Four Thousand Years of Engagement with the World.* New York: Columbia University Press, 2000.

Conroy-Krutz, Emily. *Christian Imperialism: Converting the World in the Early American Republic.* Ithaca, NY: Cornell University Press, 2015.

Cureau, Harold G. "William H. Sheppard: Missionary to the Congo, and Collector of African Art." *Journal of Negro History* 67, no. 4 (winter 1982): 340–352.

Curtis, Heather. *Holy Humanitarians: American Evangelicals and Global Aid.* Cambridge, MA: Harvard University Press, 2018.

Daggar, Lori. *Cultivating Empire: Capitalism, Philanthropy, and the Negotiation of American Imperialism in Indian Country.* Philadelphia: University of Pennsylvania Press, 2022.

Dogan, Mehmet Ali, and Heather J. Sharkey, eds. *American Missionaries in the Middle East: Foundational Encounters.* Salt Lake City: University of Utah Press, 2011.

Duus, Peter. *The Abacus and the Sword: The Japanese Penetration of Korea, 1895–1910.* Berkeley: University of California Press, 1998.

Dworkin, Ira. *Congo Love Song: African American Culture and the Crisis of the Colonial State.* Chapel Hill: University of North Carolina Press, 2017.

Edel, Charles. *Nation Builder: John Quincy Adams and the Grand Strategy of the Republic.* Cambridge, MA: Harvard University Press, 2014.

Elder, Earl Edgar. *Vindicating a Vision: The Story of the American Mission in Egypt, 1854–1954.* Philadelphia: Board of Foreign Missions of the United Presbyterian Church of North America, 1958.

Esherick, Joseph W. *The Origins of the Boxer Uprising.* Berkeley: University of California Press, 1987.

Ewans, Martin. *European Atrocity, African Catastrophe: Leopold II, the Congo Free State, and Its Aftermath.* New York: Routledge Curzon, 2002.

Fairbank, John K., ed. *The Missionary Enterprise in China and America.* Cambridge, MA: Harvard University Press, 1974.

Fea, John. *The Bible Cause: A History of the American Bible Society.* New York: Oxford University Press, 2016.

Fitz, Caitlin. *Our Sister Republics: The United States in an Age of American Revolutions.* New York: Liveright, 2016.

Foliard, Daniel. *The Violence of Colonial Photography.* Manchester, UK: Manchester University Press, 2023.

Georgini, Sara. *Household Gods: The Religious Lives of the Adams Family.* New York: Oxford University Press, 2019.

Ghazvinian, John. *America and Iran: A History, 1720 to the Present.* New York: Alfred A. Knopf, 2021.

Gleeson, Kristin L. "The Stethoscope and the Gospel: Presbyterian Foreign Medical Missions, 1840-1900." *American Presbyterians* 71, no. 2 (summer 1993): 127-138.

Gorman, Henry. "American Ottomans: Protestant Missionaries in an Islamic Empire's Service, 1820-1919." *Diplomatic History* 43, no. 3 (2019): 544-568.

Grabill, Joseph L. *Protestant Diplomacy and the Near East: Missionary Influence on American Policy, 1810–1927.* Minneapolis: University of Minnesota Press, 1971.

Grant, Kevin. *A Civilised Savagery: Britain and the New Slaveries in Africa, 1884–1926.* New York: Routledge, 2014.

Greenberg, Amy. *A Wicked War: Clay, Polk, and the 1846 U.S. Invasion of Mexico.* New York: Vintage, 2013.

Gulick, Edward V. *Peter Parker and the Opening of China.* Cambridge, MA: Harvard University Press, 1973.

Haddad, John R. *America's First Adventure in China: Trade, Treaties, Opium, and Salvation.* Philadelphia: Temple University Press, 2013.

Haddad, John R. *The Romance of China: Excursions to China in U.S. Culture, 1776–1876.* New York: Columbia University Press, 2008.

Hall, Catherine, and Sonya O. Rose, eds. *At Home with the Empire: Metropolitan Culture and the Imperial World.* Cambridge: Cambridge University Press, 2006.

Hankins, Barry. *Woodrow Wilson: Ruling Elder, Spiritual President.* New York: Oxford University Press, 2016.

Harris, Paul William. *Nothing but Christ: Rufus Anderson and the Ideology of Protestant Foreign Missions.* New York: Oxford University Press, 2000.

Hayford, Charles. "China by the Book: China Hands and China Stories, 1848-1949." *Journal of American-East Asian Relations* 16, no. 4 (winter 2009): 285-311.

Hershberger, Mary. "Mobilizing Women, Anticipating Abolition: The Struggle against Indian Removal in the 1830s." *Journal of American History* 86, no. 1 (June 1999): 15-40.

Herzog, Ben, and Ediberto Román. *Revoking Citizenship: Expatriation in America from the Colonial Era to the War on Terror.* New York: NYU Press, 2015.

Heyrman, Christine. *American Apostles: When Evangelicals Entered the World of Islam.* New York: Hill and Wang, 2015.

Hill, Kimberly. *A Higher Mission: The Careers of Alonzo and Althea Brown Edmiston in Central Africa.* Lexington: University Press of Kentucky, 2020.

Ho, Joseph W. *Developing Mission: Photography, Filmmaking, and American Missionaries in Modern China.* Ithaca: Cornell University Press, 2022.

Hochschild, Adam. *King Leopold's Ghost: A Story of Greed, Terror, and Heroism in Colonial Africa.* New York: Houghton Mifflin, 1998.

Hoganson, Kristin. *Fighting for American Manhood: How Gender Politics Provoked the Spanish-American and Philippine-American Wars.* New Haven: Yale University Press, 1998.

Hoganson, Kristin L., and Jay Sexton, eds. *Crossing Empires: Taking US History into Transimperial Terrain*. Durham, NC: Duke University Press, 2020.

Hollinger, David. *Protestants Abroad: How Missionaries Tried to Change the World but Changed America*. Princeton: Princeton University Press, 2017.

Hutchison, William R. *Errand to the World: American Protestant Thought and Foreign Missions*. Chicago: University of Chicago Press, 1987.

Hutchison, William R. *The Modernist Impulse in American Protestantism*. Reprint ed. Durham, NC: Duke University Press, 1992.

Hyde, Carrie. *Civic Longing: The Speculative Origins of US Citizenship*. Cambridge, MA: Harvard University Press, 2018.

Irwin, Julia F. *Making the World Safe: The American Red Cross and a Nation's Humanitarian Awakening*. New York: Oxford University Press, 2013.

Jacobs, Sylvia. *The African Nexus: Black American Perspectives on the European Partitioning of Africa, 1880–1920*. Westport, CT: Greenwood Press, 1981.

Jacobs, Sylvia, ed. *Black Americans and the Missionary Movement in Africa*. Westport, CT: Greenwood Press, 1982.

Jakobsen, Janet R., and Ann Pellegrini, eds. *Secularisms*. Durham, NC: Duke University Press, 2008.

Johnson, R. Park. "The Legacy of Arthur Judson Brown." *International Bulletin of Missionary Research* 10, no. 2 (April 1, 1986): 71–75.

Jones, Jeannette Eileen, *In Search of Brightest Africa: Reimagining the Dark Continent in American Culture, 1884–1936*. Athens: University of Georgia Pres, 2010.

Kark, Ruth. *American Consuls in the Holy Land, 1832–1914*. Detroit: Wayne State University Press, 1994.

Karp, Matthew. *This Vast Southern Empire: Slaveholders at the Helm of American Foreign Policy*. Cambridge, MA: Harvard University Pres, 2018.

Kelley, Mary. *Learning to Stand and Speak: Women, Education, and Public Life in America's Republic*. Chapel Hill: University of North Carolina Press, 2008.

Kennedy, Charles S. *The American Consul: A History of the United States Consular Service, 1776–1924*, Rev. 2nd ed. Washington, DC: New Academia Publishing, 2015.

Kenny, Gale, and Tisa Wenger. "Church, State, and 'Native Liberty' in the Belgian Congo." *Comparative Studies in Society and History* 62, no. 1 (2020): 156–185.

Killingray, David, "The Black Atlantic Missionary Movement and Africa, 1780s-1920s." *Journal of Religion in Africa* 33, no. 1 (2003): 3–31.

Kramer, Paul. *The Blood of Government: Race, Empire, the United States, and the Philippines*. Chapel Hill: University of North Carolina Press, 2006.

Kühnel, Bianca, Galit Noga-Banai, and Hanna Vorholt. *Visual Constructs of Jerusalem*. Turnhout, Belgium: Brepols, 2014.

Laderman, Charlie. *Sharing the Burden: The Armenian Question, Humanitarian Intervention, and Anglo-American Visions of Global Order*. New York: Oxford University Press, 2019.

Lagergren, David. *Mission and State in the Congo: A Study of the Relations Between Protestant Missions and the Congo Independent State Authorities with Special Reference to the Equator District, 1885–1903*. Translated by Owen N. Lee. Lund, Sweden: Gleerup, 1970.

Lazich, Michael. "American Missionaries and the Opium Trade in 19th Century China." *Journal of World History* 17, no. 2 (June 2006): 197–223.

Lazich, Michael C. *E. C. Bridgman, 1801–1861: America's First Missionary to China*. Lewiston, NY: Edwin Mellen Press, 2000.

Littell, John B. "Missionaries and Politics in China—The Taiping Rebellion." *Political Science Quarterly* 43, no. 2 (December 1928): 566–599.

Lord, Donald C. "Missionaries, Thai, and Diplomats." *Pacific Historical Review* 35, no. 4 (November 1966): 413–431.

Magee, Malcolm. *What the World Should Be: Woodrow Wilson and the Crafting of a Faith-Based Foreign Policy*. Waco, TX: Baylor University Press, 2008.

Makdisi, Ussama. *Artillery of Heaven: American Missionaries and the Failed Conversion of the Middle East*. Ithaca, NY: Cornell University Press, 2007.

Malcolm, Elizabeth L. "The *Chinese Repository* and Western Literature on China, 1800 to 1850." *Modern Asian Studies* 7, no. 2 (March 1973): 165–178.

Manela, Erez. *The Wilsonian Movement: Self Determination and the International Origins of Anticolonial Nationalism*. New York: Oxford University Press, 2009.

Mayer, Christine, and Adelina Arredondo, eds. *Women, Power Relations, and Education in a Transnational World*. Cham, Switzerland: Palgrave Macmillan, 2020.

McAlister, Melani. *The Kingdom of God Has No Borders: A Global History of American Evangelicals*. New York: Oxford University Press, 2018.

McCartney, Paul T. "Religion, the Spanish-American War, and the Idea of American Mission." *Journal of Church and State* 54, no. 2 (spring 2012): 257–278.

McCullough, Matthew. *The Cross of War: Nationalism and U.S. Expansion in the Spanish-America War*. Madison: University of Wisconsin Press, 2014.

McLoughlin, William G. *Cherokee Renascence in the New Republic*. Princeton, NJ: Princeton University Press, 1992.

McLoughlin, William G. *Cherokees and Missionaries, 1789–1839*. Norman: University of Oklahoma Press, 1995.

Meyer-Fong, Tobie. *What Remains: Coming to Terms with Civil War in 19th Century China*. Stanford: Stanford University Press, 2014.

Mills, Brandon. *The World Colonization Made: The Racial Geography of Early American Empire*. Philadelphia: University of Pennsylvania Press, 2020.

Modern, John. *Secularism in Antebellum America*. Chicago: University of Chicago Press, 2011.

Moran, Katherine D. *The Imperial Church: Catholic Founding Fathers and the United States*. Ithaca, NY: Cornell University Press, 2020.

Moreshead, Ashley E. "'Beyond All Ambitious Motives': Missionary Memoirs and the Cultivation of Early American Evangelical Heroines." *Journal of the Early Republic* 38, no. 1 (spring 2018): 37–60.

Mott, Frank Luther. *A History of American Magazines*. Vol. 2. *1850–1865*. Cambridge, MA: Harvard University Press, 1958.

Moyd, Michelle. *Violent Intermediaries: African Soldiers, Conquest, and Everyday Colonialism in German East Africa*. Athens: Ohio University Press, 2014.

Neem, Johann. *Democracy's Schools: The Rise of Public Education in America*. Baltimore: Johns Hopkins University Press, 2017.

Newman, James L. *Imperial Footprints: Henry Morton Stanley's African Journeys.* Washington, DC: Brassey's, 2004.

Nichols, Christopher McKnight. *Promise and Peril: America at the Dawn of a Global Age.* Cambridge, MA: Harvard University Press, 2015.

Nichols, Christopher McKnight, and David Milne, eds. *Ideology in U.S. Foreign Relations: New Histories.* New York: Columbia University Press, 2022.

Nishioka, Minami. "Civilizing Okinawa: Intimacies between the American and Japanese Empires, 1846–1919." PhD Diss., University of Tennessee, 2022.

Norwood, Dael. *Trading Freedom: How Trade with China Defined Early America.* Chicago: University of Chicago Press, 2022.

Papageorge, Linda Madson. "The United States Diplomats' Response to Rising Chinese Nationalism, 1900–1912." PhD Diss., Michigan State University, 1973.

Parsons, Lynn Hudsons. "'A Perpetual Harrow Upon My Feelings': John Quincy Adams and the American Indian." *New England Quarterly* 46, no. 3 (September 1973): 339–379.

Perl-Rosenthal, Nathan. *Citizen Sailors: Becoming American in the Age of Revolution.* Cambridge, MA: Harvard University Press, 2015.

Phipps, William. *William Sheppard: Congo's African American Livingstone.* Louisville, KY: Geneva Press, 2002.

Pinheiro, John C. *Missionaries of Republicanism: A Religious History of the Mexican-American War.* New York: Oxford University Press, 2014.

Porterfield, Amanda. *Mary Lyon and the Mount Holyoke Missionaries.* New York: Oxford University Press, 1997.

Portnoy, Alisse. *Their Right to Speak: Women's Activism in the Indian and Slave Debates.* Cambridge, MA: Harvard University Press, 2005.

Preston, Andrew. "The Limits of Brotherhood: Race, Religion, and World Order in American Ecumenical Protestantism." *American Historical Review* 127, no. 3 (September 2022): 1222–1251.

Preston, Andrew. *Sword of the Spirit, Shield of Faith: Religion in American War and Diplomacy.* New York: Anchor, 2012.

Preston, Diana. *Besieged in Peking: The Story of the 1900 Boxer Rising.* London: Constable, 1999.

Raffety, Matthew Taylor. *The Republic Afloat: Law, Honor, and Citizenship in Maritime America.* Chicago: University of Chicago Press, 2012.

Reeves-Ellington, Barbara, Kathryn Kish Sklar, and Connie A. Shemo. *Competing Kingdoms: Women, Mission, Nation, and the American Protestant Empire, 1812–1960.* Durham, NC: Duke University Press, 2010.

Reeves-Ellington, Barbara. *Domestic Frontiers: Gender, Reform, and American Interventions in the Ottoman Balkans and the Near East.* Amherst: University of Massachusetts Press, 2013.

Repousis, Angelo. "The Devil's Apostle: Jonas King's Trial Against the Greek Hierarchy in 1852 and the Pressure to Extend US Protection for American Missionaries Overseas." *Diplomatic History* 33, no. 5. (November 2009): 807–837.

Repousis, Angelo. *Greek-American Relations from Monroe to Truman*. Kent, OH: Kent State University Press, 2013.

Repousis, Angelo. "'The Trojan Women': Emma Hart Willard and the Troy Society for the Advancement of Female Education in Greece." *Journal of the Early Republic* 24, no. 3 (autumn 2004): 445–476.

Reuter, Frank T. "William Howard Taft and the Separation of Church and State in the Philippines." *Journal of Church and State* 24, no. 1 (winter 1982): 105–117.

Roche, John Pearson. *The Early Development of US Citizenship*. Ithaca, NY: Cornell University Press, 1949.

Rouleau, Brian. *With Sails Whitening Every Sea: Mariners and the Making of an American Maritime Empire*. Ithaca, NY: Cornell University Press, 2014.

Rubinstein, Murray A. "The Wars They Wanted: American Missionaries' Use of 'The Chinese Repository' Before the Opium War." *American Neptune* 48, no. 4 (1988): 271–82.

Ryu, Dae Young. "An Odd Relationship: The State Department, Its Representatives, and American Protestant Missionaries in Korea, 1882-1905." *Journal of American-East Asian Relations* 6, no. 4 (winter 1997): 261–287.

Ryu, Dae Young. "Religion Meets Politics: The Korean Royal Family and American Protestant Missionaries in Late Joseon Korea." *Journal of Church and State* 55, no. 1 (winter 2013): 113–133.

Ryu, Dae Young. "Treaties, Extraterritorial Rights, and American Protestant Missions in Late Joseon Korea." *Korea Journal* 43, no. 1 (spring 2003): 174–203.

Santelli, Maureen. *The Greek Fire: American-Ottoman Relations and Democratic Fervor in the Age of Revolutions*. Ithaca, NY: Cornell University Press, 2020.

Satz, Ronald N. *American Indian Policy in the Jacksonian Era*. Rev. ed. Norman: University of Oklahoma Press, 2002.

Saunt, Claudio. *West of the Revolution: An Uncommon History of 1776*. New York: W. W. Norton, 2015.

Schulten, Susan. *Mapping the Nation: History and Cartography in Nineteenth-Century America*. Chicago: University of Chicago Press, 2012.

Scott, James Brown. "The Government of the United States and American Foreign Missionaries." *American Journal of International Law* 6, no. 1 (January 1912): 70–85.

Scully, Eileen P. *Bargaining with the State from Afar: American Citizenship in Treaty Port China, 1844–1942*. New York: Columbia University Press, 2001.

Seat, Karen K. *"Providence Has Freed Our Hands": Women's Missions and the American Encounter with Japan*. Syracuse, NY: Syracuse University Press, 2008.

Sexton, Jay. "William H. Seward in the World." *Journal of the Civil War Era* 4, no. 3 (September 2014): 398–430.

Sharkey, Heather J. *American Evangelicals in Egypt: Missionary Encounters in an Age of Empire*. Princeton: Princeton University Press, 2015.

Sherman, Laura Beth. *Fires on the Mountain: The Macedonian Revolutionary Movement and the Kidnapping of Ellen Stone*. New York: Columbia University Press, 1980.

Shoemaker, Nancy. *Pursuing Respect in the Cannibal Isles: Americans in Nineteenth-Century Fiji*. Ithaca, NY: Cornell University Press, 2019.

Shurtleff, William, and Akiko Aoyagi, *Biography of Yamei Kin M.D. (Also Known as Jin Yunmei), The First Chinese Woman to Take a Medical Degree in the United States: Extensively Annotated Bio-Bibliography, with McCartee Family Genealogy and Knight Family Genealogy*. Lafayette, CA: Soyinfo Center, 2016.

Silbey, David J. *The Boxer Rebellion and the Great Game in China*. New York: Hill and Wang, 2012.

Smith, Walter Burges. *America's Diplomats and Consuls of 1776–1865: A Geographic and Biographic Directory of the Foreign Service from the Declaration of Independence to the End of the Civil War*. Arlington, VA: Center for the Study of Foreign Affairs, 1986.

Snyder, Christina. *Great Crossings: Indians, Settlers, and Slaves in the Age of Jackson*. New York: Oxford University Press, 2017.

Spann, Edward K. "New England and Early Conservationism, *North American Review*, 1830–1860." *Historical Journal of Massachusetts* 29, no. 2 (July 2001): 192–207.

Spence, Jonathan D. *God's Chinese Son: The Taiping Heavenly Kingdom of Hong Xiuquan*. New York: W. W. Norton and Co., 1996.

Stoler, Ann Laura, ed. *Haunted by Empire: Geographies of Intimacy in North American History*. Durham, NC: Duke University Press, 2006.

Su, Anna. *Exporting Freedom: Religious Liberty and American Power*. Cambridge, MA: Harvard University Press, 2016.

Suny, Ronald Grigor. *"They Can Live in the Desert but Nowhere Else": A History of the Armenian Genocide*. Princeton: Princeton University Press, 2015.

Sutton, Matthew Avery. *Double Crossed: The Missionaries Who Spied for the United States during the Second World War*. New York: Basic Books, 2019.

Taketani, Etsuko. "The '*North American Review*,' 1815–1834: The Invention of the American Past." *American Periodicals* 5 (1995): 111–127.

Thigpen, Jennifer. *Island Queens and Mission Wives: How Gender and Empire Remade Hawai'i's Pacific World*. Chapel Hill: University of North Carolina Press, 2014.

Thomas, Jolyon. *Faking Liberties: Religious Freedom in American-Occupied Japan*. Chicago: University of Chicago Press, 2019.

Thompson, Jack. *Light on Darkness? Missionary Photography of Africa in the Nineteenth and Early Twentieth Centuries*. Grand Rapids, MI: William B. Eerdman, 2012.

Thompson, John M. *Great Power Rising: Theodore Roosevelt and the Politics of U.S. Foreign Policy*. New York: Oxford University Press, 2019.

Turek, Lauren Frances. *To Bring the Good News to All Nations: Evangelical Influence on Human Rights and U.S. Foreign Relations*. Ithaca: Cornell University Press, 2020.

Tyrrell, Ian. *Reforming the World: The Creation of America's Moral Empire*. Princeton, NY: Princeton University Press, 2010.

Van Reybrouck, David. *Congo: The Epic History of a People*. Translated by Sam Garrett. New York: Ecco Books, 2014.

Walther, Karine. "For God and Country: James Barton, the Ottoman Empire, and Missionary Diplomacy during World War I." *First World War Studies* 7, no. 1 (November 2016): 63–79.

Walther, Karine. *Sacred Interests: The United States and the Islamic World, 1821–1921.* Chapel Hill: University of North Carolina Press, 2015.

Wenger, Tisa. *Religious Freedom: The Contested History of an American Ideal.* Chapel Hill: University of North Carolina Press, 2017.

Werner, James V. "Bringing Down Holy Science: The *North American Review* and Jacksonian Scientific Inquiry." *American Periodicals* 10 (2000): 27–42.

Wheatley, Jeffrey. "US Colonial Governance of Superstition and Fanaticism in the Philippines." *Method and Theory in the Study of Religion* 30 (2018): 21–36.

Winter, Jay ed. *America and the Armenian Genocide of 1915.* New York: Cambridge University Press, 2004.

Yacoub, Joseph. *Year of the Sword: The Assyrian Christian Genocide, a History.* New York: Oxford University Press, 2016.

Yokota, Kariann Akemi. *Unbecoming British: How Revolutionary America Became a Postcolonial Nation.* New York: Oxford University Press, 2011.

INDEX